WAITING FOR ELIJAH

Articulating Journeys: Festivals, Memorials, and Homecomings
General Editors:
Tom Selwyn, SOAS University of London
Nicola Frost, University of Exeter

The landscape of contemporary mobility stresses ideas of home, return, commemoration and celebration. Groups seek to mark changing elements of historical and cultural importance through architecture, narrative and festivity. Migrants and their descendants frequently travel between 'homes', reinventing and reshaping as they go. Such events can themselves attract travellers and pilgrims with their own stories to tell. Engaging with more substantive ethnographic features and linking back to classical anthropological and philosophical concerns, this series contributes to a new understanding of the Other encountered away from home but also of the Self and home.

Volume 1
Waiting for Elijah
Time and Encounter in a Bosnian Landscape
Safet HadžiMuhamedović

Volume 2
The Rite of Urban Passage
The Spatial Ritualization of Iranian Urban Transformation
Reza Masoudi

Volume 3
Travelling towards Home
Mobilities and Homemaking
Edited by Nicola Frost and Tom Selwyn

WAITING FOR ELIJAH
Time and Encounter in a Bosnian Landscape

Safet HadžiMuhamedović

Foreword by Marko Živković

berghahn
NEW YORK · OXFORD
www.berghahnbooks.com

First published in 2018 by

Berghahn Books

www.berghahnbooks.com

© 2018, 2021 Safet HadžiMuhamedović

First paperback edition published in 2021

All rights reserved. Except for the quotation of short passages for the purposes of criticism and review, no part of this book may be reproduced in any form or by any means, electronic or mechanical, including photocopying, recording, or any information storage and retrieval system now known or to be invented, without written permission of the publisher.

Library of Congress Cataloging-in-Publication Data

A C.I.P. cataloging record is available from the Library of Congress

British Library Cataloguing in Publication Data

A catalogue record for this book is available from the British Library

ISBN 978-1-78533-856-4 hardback
ISBN 978-1-80073-219-3 paperback
ISBN 978-1-78533-857-1 ebook

To Vanja Hamzić, also known as Mim't.

CONTENTS

List of Figures and Tables — viii
Preface — x
Foreword to the Paperback Edition — xiv
Acknowledgements — xviii

Introduction — 1

Part I. Time and Its Discontents

Chapter 1. Schizochronotopia, or Elijah's Pitfall — 57
Chapter 2. Time and Home — 79
Chapter 3. Time and In-Other — 113
Chapter 4. Time and Epic Residues — 153

Part II. The Many Faces of Elijah

Prelude. A River of Many Names — 168
Chapter 5. The Georgics: An Extended Poetry of the Land — 175
Conclusion. Waiting for Elijah — 234

Bibliography — 251
Index — 271

Figures and Tables

Figures

0.1	The Field, in the summer and winter, and the town of Gacko	xvi
0.2	Map of Bosnia, with indicated sites of attended rituals, the inter-entity border and my minibus itinerary from East Sarajevo to Gacko	21
PI.1	Time and Its Discontents, illustrated by Dr Vanja Hamzić	55
1.1	Fata's home in the lower Field	64
1.2	Gacko's thermal power plant	64
1.3	Church of the Holy Trinity in Gacko's town centre	72
1.4	'Ratko Mladić, Serb Hero!' Graffiti in Gacko's town centre	72
2.1	Coffee with Delva and Safeta	87
2.2	Edo and his grandmother Zahida, the storyteller	87
2.3	Elvedin and Mila under a tree	93
2.4	Eno taking a break from reconstruction of the town mosque	93
4.1	The Šolajas with their family *gusle*	164
4.2	Mount Volujak	164
PII.1	Cosmic renewal: image on a mediaeval tombstone from Visočica Mountain, illustrated by Dr Vanja Hamzić	167
PII.2	Geonyms derived from *treba*, with circles marking the hydronyms	170
PII.3	Trebišnjica, flowing through the town of Trebinje	170
5.1	George's Day in Visoko: dancing around fire on the hill of Križ	179
5.2	Meanings of Slavic derivatives from the root **yar*	179

5.3	The syncretic complex of George/Khidr in al-Ludd, Palestine	215
5.4	Prayer at the tomb of George in al-Ludd, Palestine	215
5.5	Elijah's Day service next to the church in Nadanići	229
5.6	Elijah's Day congregation next to the mosque, at the spring of Sopot in Kula	229
6.1	Extent of damage caused by the thermal power plant and the mines in the Field	244
6.2	The Field in summer	244

Tables

| 0.1 | Gacko population, census comparison | 33 |
| 0.2 | Agriculture in Gacko, census comparison | 35 |

Preface

> What are we doing here, that is the question. And we are blessed in this, that we happen to know the answer. Yes, in this immense confusion one thing alone is clear. We are waiting for Godot to come–
> —Samuel Beckett, *Waiting for Godot*

Learning *time* and *space* is like moving through a labyrinth. Paths are entangled, indirect and often misleading. Making sense of them requires some kind of anchorage – a condensed image of what is already known – a return towards *encounter*. The following pages are about concrete encounters between bodies of knowledge and beings in a southeastern Bosnian landscape known as the 'Field of Gacko', or simply the 'Field'.[1] They are also about extensions into the immeasurable fields of other encounters and encounters as a human condition. I argue that encounters can thicken into communal timespaces and, from such collective positions, encounter other timespaces.

The charting of these movements may never achieve more than an incomplete image, a silhouette.[2] The source of light, the positions of the observer and the observed, and the reflecting surfaces all change the way a silhouette is perceived. Even though I am unable to determine the reading of the following passages, it is my hope that they will not be read as historiography, and certainly not as ethnography, for I have neither the desire nor the ability to represent either history or ethnie.[3] The propositions offered in this book are situated somewhere between what my various interlocutors were trying to convey to me and what I was struggling to understand.[4] They are open to error and unfinished – fashioning a narrative out of ever-moving lives and accumulating encounters.

This book retraces a fraction of those meeting points. Relating them to the reader is not an easy task. The narratives, actions, rituals and symbols employed in the daily lives of my interlocutors are a particular kind of condensed language. I could have called it my own, as it was authorized as such, but, it was effectively different from what I knew until I encountered the Field. As with most attempts at another language, the process of listening and understanding precedes fluency of writing and speaking. Mispronunciations are inevitable. So, I start with the commonplaces, the most familiar parts of this language of encounters, and only then attempt to explore their inflections through the morphology, syntax and semantics of particular instances. I have asked myself repeatedly about the influence of my other languages, which were both upholding and hindering my analysis.

My research is dedicated primarily to the Field that has desired itself in the image of proximity, one whose lives have been encroached upon by dissociative violence.[5] Projects of ruination, grouped under the shared trope of nationalism, still ossify the discursive spaces they secured after the breakup of Yugoslavia and the subsequent war in Bosnia (1992–1995). These homogenizing narratives' incommensurability with the diversity of landscapes continues to sustain forced migration, isolation and fear. This book, however, for the most part, lacks descriptions of such atrocities. They are 'dealt with', but through a *proximity turn* (see Introduction), a decision, for lack of a better word, to delve into the Field of encounters and intimacies, many times only discernible in remnants. If you are a *Gačanin* ('person from Gacko') and, in reading this work, you find that it substantially departs from the interpretations and experiences you hold as your own, I take responsibility in demonstrating that it is based on the lives of the people who, in one way or another, share your Field.

These people, your fellows of the Field, await. After them, after this work and after me too, the Field will still be seeded with expectation. It might be oblivious to the songs of the nomadic Gurbeti arriving to the budding grasslands in springtime. It might not know the scent of rice cooked with smoked meat and nettle on George's Day. It might not echo with the titanic voices of *ganga* and *bećarac* singers or send up sparks of magic light from the graves of the Good into the evening sky. But, you might desire the Field as it turns into the colours of green after a too-long toneless cold. A nettle may well sting your leg in some coming spring. You might, perhaps, wonder what the Field, before you, has said as lightning strikes. For, you, like the rest of us who have conversed with the Field, will feel its rhythm. You will know when to hide from it and when to be embraced by it. And, you will await its *seasons.*

In Beckett's (2010) famous play, two men persistently wait for a character called Godot, who never seems to come. In the landscape made up of their conversations and a single tree, the act of waiting ultimately defines both them and Godot. The title of this book summarizes the many stories about Elijah's Day. They seldom start with the day itself, something I did not understand at first. I got used to hearing about the winter, the crops, friendships and the eagerness of waiting. *Gačani* told me how they awaited Elijah all year long and then, as soon as the day was over, the whole story was steered afresh towards next year's feast. Those who have returned to the Field since the 1990s war experienced Elijah's Day in terms of its potential for reconstruction of their communal timespace. Such friends and relatives as did come left soon after. So, the returnees resumed the planning and the waiting, in the hope that the old landscape, an altogether different kind of waiting, will return. There are many interpretations of Beckett's play. By invoking it in the title, I prefer to read it as a depiction of proximities embedded into the substance of time, and of hope.

There is another kind of waiting also laid upon the shoulders of this book's title – waiting not as expectation, but as tangled desire. It is left for generations who, like me, will not know exactly what they have not been able to meet, but will forage through traces. 'Waiting for Elijah' is a common practice during the Passover Seder – to set an additional place at the table, pour a cup of wine, leave an empty chair and open the front door – in expectation of Elijah's return. He thus becomes an absent witness. His wanting presence obliges. I have spent much of my life in Sarajevo, which had a thriving Jewish community before dissociative violence cast an ominous shadow over it in the 1940s. I have known a few Sarajevo Jews, but never a Jewish community.[6] Instead, I have walked through the city, looked through the windows of what used to be their apartments, awkwardly sat in synagogues converted into music halls and museums, desiring, without expectation, to know a bit more than I was qualified to. Listening to the recordings of Flory Jagoda, a 1940s Jewish émigré from Sarajevo, performing Ladino songs[7] she had learnt from her grandmother, I would invite dreamlike images of the topoi she intoned. This verse from one of her songs expresses the poetic and deeply social temporality of space and the affective lingering of past trajectories, day-to-day and seasonal rhythms of a shared landscape, which I want to 'translate', for myself and the Field, in this book:

Los gajos empesan a kantar	The roosters are starting to sing
Ja ez la ora de alvantar	It's already time to get up
Non asperemos il sol del dija	Let's not wait for the sun and the day
Impjez la alegra kompanija	Start up the happy gathering.
Despuez la Avdala a Šadrvan	After *Havdalah* to *Šadrvan*[8]
Kon la ćićerkas baljar i kantar	Sing and dance with the girls
A la manjana al klaro del dija	And tomorrow, at the dawn of day
Se disfazjo la kompanija	The gathering disperses.

Notes

1. The Field in this book denotes both a physical space and an analytical term (see Introduction).
2. In his life-history approach David Zeitlyn (2008: 168) employed the metaphor of 'anthropological silhouette: less complete than a biography, but demonstrably based on an individual, and honest about its limitations and incompleteness'.

3. For more on this problem see the sections 'Big History, Historicity and the Body' and 'Ethnography after Ethnic Cleansing?' in the Introduction.
4. I take 'interlocutor' to refer to more than just human beings. Latour has used 'actant' instead of 'actor' (see Latour 2005) in order to problematize the human self-entitlement to agency. In the same sense, my interlocutors are 'interlocutants' – human and nonhuman partners in conversation – never exclusive of each other.
5. This book deals with qualitatively different kinds of 'violence'. Here, it implies repression of encounter. By 'proximity', I mean spatial, temporal and affective nearness.
6. There is undoubtedly a small Jewish community in Sarajevo, so my life experience is not a qualification of its existence.
7. Ladino, Djudio or Judaeo-Spanish is the language that Sephardic Jews continued to nurture (in Bosnia, amongst other places) after their exile from Spain and Portugal in the fifteenth century.
8. *Havdalah* is the ceremonial ending of the Shabbat and holiday marked by the lighting of an interlaced candle. *Šadrvan* is a fountain in the courtyard of a mosque, but here refers to the name of a coffee house (see Papo 2008).

Foreword to the Paperback Edition

To be expelled from home and then to return, virtually or physically, occasionally, seasonally or permanently, only to discover that home has changed into something unhomely, is to be forced to reflect on what was lost and what one may hope to regain. This is the opportunity Gacko Field, the limestone valley at the southeastern corner of Bosnia, offered HadžiMuhamedović: with his interlocutors sharing with him what they, often painfully, try to figure out for themselves, he is able to glimpse and convey to us a lifeworld of intimate encounters among communities oriented to a mythological grid of landscape-attuned seasonal rhythms.

This book is then about what it takes to rebuild home when home as place and home as past get violently divorced. And when upon return to the place that was home it is no longer home. When it only lingers as memory as a phantom limb. Home and hope are inseparable, and both depend on a tissue of exchanges, a pattern of habitual encounters organized in "a system of proximities"—all undergirded by a syncretic cosmology. Syncretism is one of HadžiMuhamedović's keywords, a defining feature of the lifeworld he openly defends against the anti-syncretism of ethnonationalist imaginary.

It is only when confronted with anti-syncretic ideologies, of which the nationalistic imaginaries that destroyed Yugoslavia are only the last incarnation, that syncretism comes to the fore and becomes a strange thing in need of explanation. HadžiMuhamedović quotes Bosnian writer Abdulah Sidran's words: "I found that I have a neck only when they started strangling me." Syncretism was abruptly revealed only when strangled.

Home meant hope, hope meant revitalizing the lost past, regrowing the phantom limb, regenerating at least a part of the torn tissue of prewar sociality that hung on the traditional cycles. Thus, for home/hope to exist, it was necessary to transmit the knowledge of the "communal life, economics, intimacies and mysteries that the landscape made possible," or more vividly, the knowledge of "which hilltops are haunted, which caverns provide shelter and which plants may kill or save your life." In the absence of the young, already starting other homes elsewhere, the old were glad to transmit their mastery to the author.

Anthropologists often feel torn between their scientific and their poetic calling, between the need to explain and the need to persuasively evoke different lifeworlds. In the most memorable accounts, the two felicitously converge. The book before you is one such rare convergence.

The interested reader will find in this book important contributions to the anthropology of time and space, of ethnic nationalism and of displacement, of mobility and memory, or most profoundly, of home and hope. The rarest achievement of this book, however, is that these scholarly refinements of our understanding get transformed, by a rare alchemy, into a poetic evocation of a way of life that brings a lump to your throat.

Imperceptibly transforming himself from an ethnographer to a poet throughout the book, in his last chapter HadžiMuhamedović gathers his interlocutors from the Field into a chorus of voices that sing the progression of warm season celebrations—lightning and thunder, the willows, girls and swings, nettle and marriage, water and cornel, cattle and bonfires, flirtation and fistfights, aspens and swallows. With Virgil of Georgics acting as his poetic guide and inspired by the sinking river that begins its life in the Field and breaks forth into multiple directions, attaining a new name with each new surface, HadžiMuhamedović then interlaces this present-day ode with the "spaces and times of George and Elijah," a Frazerian journey through Classical Antiquity, Indoeuropean and pre-Christian Slavic Religion. What emerges from this long and purposefully meandering chapter is the "grand cosmological interlacement," embedded in seasonal agricultural activities and patterns of encounters across the religious divides. To talk about sociality in Gacko was to talk about visitations, flirtations and fights, mutual care and help, and of spiritual kinship, which were all organized by agricultural, ecological temporalities and rhythms. For HadžiMuhamedović, this was the shape, the mode, the flavor of sociality violently torn asunder and forced to retreat before the purifying ideologies of national imaginaries. For him as for his interlocutors, the Georgic Saints become not just codes and cyphers of lost sociality but warrior patron saints of possible revitalization.

How does the author accomplish this alchemical transformation of a scholarly anthropological account into a poetic evocation of a lifeworld shimmering as ever vanishing and ever hopeful of rejuvenation?

I suggest that the poetry of the book comes in part through what I see as the nesting chiasmi of the "articulating journeys, the festivals, memorials, and homecomings" (to invoke the title of the series of which this is the first volume), HadžiMuhamedović uncovers in Bosnia.

To start with, the landscape is another face of time, and time is another face of space. Both time and space, furthermore, are about tasks and agricultural work which are in their turn embedded in, and embedding modalities of socializing, the nearing of the Other, the proximities and intimacies that depend on distance and distinction. And the nesting of chiasmi doesn't end there.

The space (the Field) is also the space of "coffee and cigarettes" with its "long silences and sudden punctuations." It is a narrative space and HadžiMuhamedović dwells lovingly in the tension between presenting this narrative space as a single story or many diverging stories. Nor is it ultimately all about language and stories; for from another angle, it is precisely the tacit, non-discursive bodily habitus of "minute details of daily practices as evidence of landscapes rooted in the past" that is the most "resilient to contemporary political and historical discourses."

Thus, calendars are embedded in and imply stories; stories hinge on landscape and temporal cycles which are about encounters and socialites, which are in turn embedded in seasonal agricultural/pastoralist tasks. Each take turns in being both context and content, the encompassing and the encompassed, each other's figure and ground.

It is this kaleidoscopic, Rubik-cube-like shifting of chiasmi within chiasmi that is the particular power of this text. And it is often the powerful images that effect these shifts back and forth from time to space from time-space to encounters, from encounters to stories and bodies, from home to hope. It is particularly fascinating to see how, for instance, plants perform one of these perspectival shifts once the attention foregrounds them. Now, everything in the book could be seen as revolving around plants.

HadžiMuhamedović characterizes his work as "neither an ethnography nor a historiography," but rather a chronography. But why stop there? Since it is about time as space and space as time, isn't it rather a chrono-topo-graphy? Furthermore, since the Field is a site for a battle of chronotopes, thus the book is more appropriately a schizo-chrono-topo-graphy. And it is also an incipient herbarium as imaginarium (or is it imaginarium as herbarium), a study of the social and political life of karst geology, a mythological speleology....

It is this deliberate writing strategy of shimmering between opposites, of meandering like the sinking and reemerging river of many names, that makes this book so poetic, but there is a pragmatic, political reason HadžiMuhamedović chooses to write in this way. The form of the book itself is an argument against the purifying, un-mixing, de-syncretizing ideology of ethnonationalism, and a counterpoint to the tendency to analyze Bosnian religiosity through the nationalist divisions. In his own words, this way of writing, says HadžiMuhamedović, makes the book "useless for the prevalent forms of identitary violence in Bosnia."

Lingering memories as phantom limbs, shared life felt as one feels one's neck only when it is strangled, the sinking and reappearing river, Virgil's bud burgeoning from the stump of a chopped olive tree. The poetry of these images that jointly evoke the silhouette of Gacko prewar lifeworld, comes from their incongruity. This incongruity I take as an intimation of something real and alive because multidimensional and irreducible to simplifying flatlands of ethnonationalist ideology. May the reader, just as I did, resonate both painfully and hopefully with these intimations of Gacko lifeworld and leave the chair for Elijah.

Marko Živković
University of Alberta, Edmonton, AB
September 2021

Acknowledgements

There are many persons and institutions to whom my thanks are due, although my project does not necessarily reflect their perspectives.

The first amongst these is my inimitable mentor, friend, Dr Sari Wastell. She has, in many ways, made this book possible. The fieldwork for this book has been conducted under the auspices of her European Research Council-funded project, 'Bosnian Bones, Spanish Ghosts: "Transitional Justice" and the Legal Shaping of Memory after Two Modern Conflicts'. Sari, thank you for your unwavering sensitivity, theoretical vigour and intellectual generosity.

I thank Dr Frances Pine, for her trust in the potential of knowing ghosts, herbs and the moving pasts, as well as all her subtle advice and constant readiness to read and comment upon this work. I would also like to thank Professor Tom Selwyn and Dr Nicola Frost, who have recognized the value of this book and warmly guided it into their series. I thank Professor Robert Hudson, Professor Wendy Bracewell, Dr David Henig, Dr Reza Masoudi Nejad and Elitza Kotzeva for their encouragements and astute reviews. I also thank Desmond Maurer for his detailed proofreading and insightful remarks, as well as the Berghahn team for the streamlined publication process. Unfortunately, I cannot mention most of my informative conversations in academic settings. I have greatly valued the enlightening commentary of Dr Joost Fontein, conversations with Dr Magda Buchczyk, Dr Špela Drnovšek Zorko and other colleagues at Goldsmiths, SOAS, Goethe University and the University of Bristol. Invaluable financial support came from the Goldsmiths' Anthropology Department, the Open Society Foundations' Global Supplementary Grant Programme, Civil Society Scholar Awards and many other conference and research grants. I am deeply grateful for their support.

Throughout my work, certain key concepts, particularly those dealing with home and affect, have been rethought and reshaped, over the course of many conversations, academic events and teaching sessions with Marija Grujić. Her intellectual, *affective* nearness is continually important. Thank you, Marija. The same applies to Mikhail Mikhailovich Bakhtin. Through our nocturnal, 'internal' dialogues, his thoughts continue to awaken my own.

I am especially grateful to the people of Kula, Branilovići, Nadanići, Hodinići, Bahori, Križ, Kreševo and Mokro. Eno Tanović was the most wonderful host in the Field. Conversations with him, as will become apparent, are central to this book. I have only the utmost appreciation for the knowledge imparted to me by Sadet, Sabaha, Fata, Bećir, Zahida, Hamo, Milo, Edo, Elvedin, Dževad, Rusmir, Melina, Edita, Nada, Mila, Kana, Kanita, Vlado and Nina. I thank you all for making my research experience phenomenal, each in your own ways. Alma Agović, without you around, my fieldwork would have been crucially different. Travelling in your car, chasing cyclical time, lighting ritual fires, walking through caves, finding pristine lakes, getting lost in the mountain forests . . . You made it easy to find connections to the landscapes, which are now also our own.

I thank my family, great in number and every other sense, for their support and guidance. My father Fehim steered this work through his beautiful phenomenology of landscapes. My mother Amra guided it through her relentless enthusiasm for the conservation of landscapes. My uncle Rusmir was the most intimate, masterly interlocutor on Bosnian cosmologies. My wondrous Ahmed and Đula had to endure long absences on the part of their own uncle, but now have a richer storytelling to look forward to. Hatidža, Derviš and Emina, thank you for your sibling love, patience and kindness. Majka Nura, thank you for your songs, artistry and pride. Majka Kana, thank you for your stories and memory. Dues to one's family are usually repaid in short acknowledgements, but my debts reach substantially further.

Lastly and most importantly, Vanja Hamzić, your contribution to this work is immeasurable. You are an inspiring intellectual and surely my best and most fierce critic. Our intense discussions, your readings, comments and consummate designs, have made this work as much yours as it is mine, and the constant comfort of your companionship softened the 'anthropological' (and *anthropou*) loneliness. This book is, certainly, for you.

FIGURE 0.1 The Field, in the summer and winter, and the town of Gacko

Introduction

Bećir: Since times immemorial. They say: until noon – Ilija, after noon – Alija.
Zahida: That is what we used to say here. Ilija until noon, Alija in the afternoon. The fair! The Serb fair was before noon, and the Muslim one after noon.
Bećir: That was no doubt so that people could get together.
Zahida: And that's why, in history and everywhere else, it has remained: Alija and Ilija.

—Interlocutors from the Field

This book unfolds from what may seem a precise central point: noon on the second day in the month of August. Exactly then, the *silhouette* of which I write absorbs most of its layers to become vivid against the Bosnian landscapes. It is the day of Elijah, the culmination of the annual cycle, marked by festivities throughout the country. When the sun peaks above the horizon, it entangles and divides the two equal parts of the day. Of this meeting, a widely known Bosnian proverb tells:

Do podne Ilija, od podne Alija.[1]
Until noon – *Ilija*, after noon – *Alija*.

But, who are Ilija and Alija? Why do they share and divide this day? Why does their encounter, 'in history and everywhere else', define the Bosnian landscapes? What can be said of their midday proximity, well into the twenty-first century, two decades after the tectonic shifts set in motion by the 1992–1995 war in Bosnia? These vexed questions have stipulated the spatial, temporal and affective directions of this book. They pertain to the complex interformation of home, calendar, religion, landscape and community, made even more intricate by the prolonged moment of postwar uncertainty.

The following pages are about the resonance of Ilija and Alija, as respectively the Christian and Muslim faces of Elijah, in a deeply, politically polarized Bosnian landscape, the Field of Gacko (*Gatačko Polje*). Elijah of the two names was once the most significant sign of identity for this wide karst plain in the southeastern Bosnian highlands. As a harvest festival, Elijah's Day belongs to the annual cycle of the traditional calendar.[2] It was the culmination of social interaction and subsistence economy – an encounter par excellence

– a joyful mass get-together, desired and awaited all year. As a gravitational force for the entire landscape, it directed and represented the structure of social relationships. This extraordinary event is the focal point for my discussion of Gacko, because it was a framing device for life before and after the actual day. The in-between of my interlocutors' narratives was expressed by way of this pinnacle. As soon as one Elijah's Day passed, the waiting for the next one would begin.

Such community-defining waiting gained in meaning after the life of Gacko residents was violently restructured. Waiting for Elijah's return became a call for the kind of communal life that entails waiting. It was an orientation of the body and the landscape towards the rebuilding of social relations. Symbolic expressions seem to intensify when a community starts to erode and rituals are often employed as a possibility to 'reconstitute the community' (see Cohen 1985: 50–51). The postwar Field held on to the grand celebration, thus amplifying its political quality, precisely because it was nothing new. It was the best-rehearsed pronunciation of the landscape that was being systematically denied.

Ilija's and Alija's meeting is a sensitive and shifting figure of speech. Their relationship to the landscape, the calendar and each other is a metaphor for the spatial and temporal structures of life. Ilija is also shorthand for the Orthodox Christians or Serbs; Alija for the Muslims who reside or used to reside in the Field of Gacko. The ethnic engineering that climaxed in the 1990s produced a rift between these communities, locking the relationship of Ilija and Alija into the past. In its absence, the Field's memories started to coalesce into strong images of the desired structures of intimacy in the landscape. Through these desires, the past became inextricably linked to a possibility of the future.

Waiting for Elijah was also waiting for George, who inaugurated the warm season on 6 May. His day, *Đurđevdan*, was marked by the arrival of the nomadic Gurbeti ('Roma' or 'Gypsies') to the Field. George was celebrated by the 'settled' population, as well, but had become synonymous with the Gurbeti community. Although invisible to the contemporary geopolitical projects bearing on Gacko, the Gurbeti have a central place in the narratives collected during my fieldwork. For the Field, the encounter with the Gurbeti (George) is the 'beginning of time', the encounter of Alija (Muslims) and Ilija (Serbs) its culmination. With the preclusion of these encounters, time itself has been alienated from the present. It was sustained as a thing of the past and a possibility of the future. Hope was imagined in Elijah's (and George's) return, the return of the landscape as home, with which the turn of the seasons would resume.

This book is thus about time as encounter and encounter as time. The two are depicted as so inextricably linked that a crisis in one inevitably affects the other. I argue that an understanding of communal relationships and landscapes symbolized by Elijah requires prior understanding of traditional time-reckoning in the Field, in both its structural and intimate aspects. I also offer the complimentary argument, that to understand time-reckoning of the Field, we need to understand the relationship between Ilija and Alija. These temporal structures and intimacies were considered to be the substance of home (see Chapters 2 and 3). In that sense, this work is a grounded critique of the, still fresh, nationalist purifications of home(lands) in Bosnia.

Capturing the Field's phantasmagorical conversations between past and present, I ask: what happened to time, as Ilija and Alija were pulled apart? What happened to Ilija and Alija as time was fragmented and restructured? I argue that the substance of temporality and the structure of cosmological time in the Field were guided by ritualized encounters. Such encounters retained strong structural and affective dimensions, which were re-examined and given particular importance after the violent introduction of physical and discursive distances in the 1990s.

Starting from the theoretical premise that temporal systems are always expressed in terms of spatial (or relational) arrangements, this book enters into a number of conversations on time-defining intimacies and distances. The proximities analysed are not limited to 'religious' communities; they extend to various kinds of spatial, temporal and 'nonhuman' phenomena: cosmologies, seasons, discourses, fields, mountains, caverns and rivers, the world and the underworld, ruins, ghosts, dead bodies, graves and mass graves, fairies, epic heroes, animals and saints. ... In order to traverse such diverse topics, the book engages with the broad phenomenological, anthropological and historical scholarship on time, space, affect and proximity, as well as investigations into Bosnian and wider religious systems. Drawing on echoes and reformulations of the well-established folk cosmology, the book depicts a landscape with a long tradition of 'inter-religious' communication that is, nonetheless, struggling to survive under the weight of nationalist pressures. It shows the way that Bosnian landscapes and seasonal cycles, as well as persons more generally, are all formed continually by relations which shift in space and time, and in so doing both reiterate old spaces and create new ones.

The Field of Gacko was perhaps the most difficult of the many spatial frameworks that could have been adopted. At the centre of the Field lies Gacko (or Metohija), a town that was completely 'ethno-religiously homogenized' in 1992.[3] Scattered around the Field are numerous satellite villages, two of which were particularly important. The village of Kula is the site of *Aliđun* (Alija's Day), the Muslim Elijah's Day festivity. With the surrounding hamlets, it is the only part of the landscape to which Muslims have returned.

In the northeast part of the Field lies the village of Nadanići, which is central to *Ilindan* (Ilija's Day), the Orthodox Christian Elijah's Day celebrations. During my fieldwork, these loci were physically separated by a large Yugoslav thermal power plant built during the 1970s and politically separated by the town embodying the anti-syncretic nationalist discourse. As this politically and religiously intricate space is both the principal site of my fieldwork and a wide stretch of contained karst, I follow the practice of my interlocutors and refer to the Field of Gacko as simply 'the Field'.[4] Although, like any individual case, Gacko has its own historical and cosmological inflections, as the 'Field' it indicates possibilities of comparison with the many other karst flatlands of the Dinaric mountain chain, as well as with other religiously plural landscapes of 'seasonal order' affected by dissociative violence.

The cyclical calendar discussed above has been 'broken' by the war: the nomadic Gurbeti communities, once an inextricable part of the Field's rhythm, were no longer present; other important dates, rituals and forms of economy had been obscured by postwar transitions. Therefore, to understand the structure of the calendar, I needed to look into other locales. From following place through time, the investigation thus extended to following time (the annual cycle) through space: it was like piecing together a time puzzle by using a particular multi-sited approach and each time I returned to the Field, my findings allowed for more elaborate questions.

Most of the narratives, places and rituals that occupy this research relate to the warm seasons. Heralded by *Blagovijest* (Annunciation), starting with *Đurđevdan/Jurjevo* (George's Day), culminating in *Aliđun/Ilindan* (Elijah's Day) and ending with *Mitrovdan/Kasum* (Demetrius' Day), this part of the year is filled with agricultural labour and apotropaic, health and fertility rituals.[5] The fertility rituals are chiefly focused on humans, cattle and nature/crops, and these purposes often overlap in a single 'event'. As David Henig (2011: 185) has noted for central Bosnia, the days of George and Elijah 'overarch the vegetative phases of the summer period, and orchestrate agricultural activities as well as the ritual calendar'. On most occasions, the rituals are followed by an outdoor celebration or a party called *teferič*, popular fairs that usually include food, drinks, the *kolo* circle dance, community-specific songs and traditional athletic competitions. A *teferič* is always a major social event. Because of the 'broken calendar', I attended only one George's Day festivity in the town of Visoko. However, due to the differences between the Gregorian and the Julian calendars, and the alterations of traditional dates to meet the requirements of diasporic attendance, I was able to take part in four Elijah's Day celebrations in 2012 alone. Each Elijah's Day told a story of different tectonic shifts, which have affected the temporal and spatial boundaries of their respective landscapes.

This book is first a contribution to the understanding of 'shared' time and transitional temporalities in a Bosnian pastoral community, after it had experienced extensive changes brought on by the violence of the 1990s. Against its own disappearance, the past has entered into an alliance with place to render the construction of new political memory obtrusive to the Field's identity. The affective lingering of the old landscape has defined the meaning of home and hope through encounters with the intimate Others. The book also gives a reading of the sacral annual cycle heralded by the two most important 'shared' festivities – George's Day and Elijah's Day. Through a form of 'deep mapping', it provides a detailed account of the Field's traditions, as well as an analysis of the wider religious streams to which they belong.

Structure of the Book

This introduction positions my findings within the context of my methodological and ethical concerns, the main research concepts and the pertinent academic debates. As an engagement with the questions of 'evidence' and 'interpretation' in this book, the introduction is roughly divided into discussions of the problems of (1) waiting; (2) proximity, syncretism and sharing; (3) body and history; (4) ethnicity and ethnography; (5) the spatial and temporal definition of my 'field of research'; and (6) the turn towards words, remnants and affect. I first introduce the Field of Gacko through a contemporary map of 'ethno-national' Bosnia and consider the sort of discourses and practices that legitimate it. From recent geopolitical developments, which have created ruptures in my interlocutors' landscapes, I turn towards the agricultural and pastoral cosmologies in Bosnia and the structure of the annual cycle. I also discuss the methods employed, which attempt to record a variety of synchronotopic and diachronotopic encounters.

This book consists of two parts. The first part, 'Time and Its Discontents', contains four chapters dealing with questions about time and space triggered by the 1990s war.[6] Employing various personal and collective perspectives, all of these chapters problematize the uneasiness of transition from the time of one quality to the time of another. They turn towards the Field of the past lingering in the present. As these two times resist and accommodate each other and generate cross-temporal syncretic forms, their friction forms a space of debate on the possibilities and expectations of the future.

In 'Schizochronotopia, or Elijah's Pitfall' (Chapter 1), I propose that the field of anthropological inquiry in Gacko is to be found in the complex interplay between historical, mythical and intimate time and place. To make these processes intelligible and indicate the indivisibilities of temporal and spatial arrangements, I employ Bakhtin's (1981) notion of 'chronotope'. I analyse two dominant 'confronted' chronotopic formations through the collective memory of harvest festivities and a mass grave. The simultaneity of these formations and the splits they create are discussed as 'schizochronotopia', a case of opposing time–space allegiances occurring within a single body or landscape.

'Time and Home' (Chapter 2) considers the narratives and practices of home through the subtle negotiations between hope, desire and fear in the aftermath of violence in the Field. I argue that the 'possibility of return' has been seen as a problem pertaining not only to space, but also to a time of a particular quality. The lingering of bodies and landscapes, elucidated through the phenomenon of the phantom limb, appears not only as a nostalgic projection, but also as a claim over the Field's futurity. At the same time, the landscape and its humans have been migrating between different temporalities – from texture to silence – in cycles resembling the traditional division of the year into an eventful summerscape and a bleak winterscape. Between the active work on reconstruction of the prewar Field and the solitary practices of scattered elderly returnees, Chapter 2 discerns forms of collective resistance that vary in intensity and latitudes of outspokenness.

'Time and In-Other' (Chapter 3), the heart of the book, is a phenomenological consideration of the Field's time through memories and histories of encounter with the Other. The cosmologics of the Other is founded in a specific orientation of the landscape towards the nearing of the Other. This intimate Other is considered in all its spectra, not just along the lines of 'religious' difference; some encounters have 'thickened' towards the habitual more than others and are thus conveyed as part of cyclical ritual relations. This chapter introduces the concept of 'In-Other' as one of the main stipulations of the Field. The first part looks at the memories and affective remnants of the arrival of the nomadic Gurbeti, which signalled the beginning of springtime. The second part discusses the 'inter-religious' institution of *kumstvo* (sworn kinship) and the position it has been assigned in the politically polarized Field.

'Time and Epic Residues' (Chapter 4) is again about the affective remnants of one Field in another, but this time in a particularly uncanny encounter – between the 'shared' and the 'cleansed' landscape in the body of the nationalist poet. This chapter discloses nationalism as inadvertently syncretic. A textual comparison between the traditional and the modernist Gacko epics, sung to the accompaniment of the *gusle* instrument, speaks of the extensive historical and political shifts converging in the Field, but also of the affective repetition of images solidified into a 'grammar of the body'.

'The Many Faces of Elijah' is the second part of the book, but can also be read first, as one of the 'contexts' for the preceding chapters. It considers the time of the Field as it extends and talks to other calendars, mythologies and discourses. Its 'experimental' structure is markedly different from the rest of book. It shows numerous encounters, temporally and spatially distant from the Field, to be part of a wider field of Georgic rhythms. Unlike 'Time and Its Discontents', the second part may seem anthropologically 'outdated' on account of its 'Frazerian' extensions, but its content and structure are a deliberate intervention. Moving away from the focus on the Field's fractured community and how it deals with historical change, I piece together narratives related to the traditional calendar. In doing this, I offer structure and content as part of the argument: the calendar of the Field should not be confined to the outcome of ruination or dealings with postwar transitions, any more than it should be trapped in the pronounced discourse of 'ethno-religious' differences. What the Field and its cosmology have to contribute to our understanding of Indo-European, early Slavic and syncretic Balkan religions is much wider than a few decades of postwar developments can encapsulate. My interlocutors stressed the importance and diversity of the landscape before it was changed beyond their recognition. In that sense, the second part of the book is an ethical intervention as much as it is a journey through the traditional calendar.

Part II begins with a 'Prelude' and unfolds into a single lengthy chapter. The 'Prelude' probes the methodological and ethical problems of spatiotemporal extensions, through a sinking river that begins its life in the Field and breaks forth into multiple directions, attaining a new name with each new surface. This very river may be regarded as the key to unlock the proceeding discussions of a grand cosmological interlacement.

'The Georgics' (Chapter 5) are conceptualized as the syncretic poetry of the Field's warm season. They begin with George's Day, venture into multifarious connections within and beyond the Field and end with the 'long-awaited' Elijah's Day. Between the two days, chthonic creatures enter into battles with fertility deities, apotropaic rituals explain the significance of herbs and the fear of lightning, Christian saints inherit the Slavic pantheon, and Palestinian syncretic practices elucidate Bosnian Georgic conundrums. Chapter 5 establishes an 'imagined' focus group, an otherwise infeasible conversation between my interlocutors, divided as they are by predicaments of conflict and migration. As such, the Georgics are an open-ended discussion, at least partially liberated from my own interpretations. At the same time, the entire second part of the book borrows the forms of the theatrical plays and of musical compositions to accentuate the unfolding drama in the landscape, as it becomes a stage for the cosmic battles of life and death, the sequences of colours, scents and sounds, and the intensities of encounters.

Waiting to Wait

> ... we wait for the coming of what abides ...
>
> —P. Virilio, *Negative Horizon*

This book provides a temporal and spatial portrait of the Field through many different and interlaced kinds of waiting. Through narratives about the past, silence on the present and persistence of an uncertain future, waiting was the substance of bodily temporality, time in its change, passage and speed. But waiting was also part of Time. Through it, the body was situated in the landscape as the image of the cosmos. The Field's waiting was a tradition of waiting and waiting as the foremost existential imperative.

This entanglement of the Field's waiting is analytically useful, for it simultaneously provides a platform for discussion of its responses to religious, historical and political developments. Many existing texts about waiting have looked into the phenomenon as the bodily experience of time – the existential encounter of our body with the pace of the world. In the passage of waiting, Henri Bergson argued, time is lived, the world coincides with our own duration and we come to know the substance of our existence and the existence of the world (2002: 61, 176). Building on Bergson's philosophical writings, Harold Schweizer saw waiting as the 'intimacy of time' (2008: 127): 'The waiter thus feels – impatiently – his own being' (ibid: 17); 'time enters our bodies; we are the time that passes' (ibid: 128). However, focus on duration reveals but one of the qualities of waiting. It is waiting bereft of its contextual substance.

This book does discuss such intimacies with time in a suspended state of being, but it also explores conversations, dreams and fears within the context of waiting of the Field. Waiting was filled with them. Bodies were rarely 'in-between'. What happened in the duration of the postwar transition strengthened or weakened the commitment to waiting – not to resign, leave or welcome other fields – while also fostering a dialogue between the two dominant chronotopes (see Chapter 1).

Through the practices and narratives occurring in the 'time of waiting', the ensuing chapters of this book discuss a landscape 'waiting to wait the way it used to'. Speaking from the Field of protracted postwar uncertainty, my interlocutors turned towards the image that was most familiar to them, the annual cycle structured by expectation of Elijah's harvest festivity. With the other Georgic saints, Elijah encapsulates the richness of remembered sociality and the temporalities of living by the seasons. The fact that it was a 'shared' day, a literal commonplace for both Serbs and Muslims, could only be envisioned through transposition to another time. It was a possibility specifically of that time. The return of such an Elijah would inevitably entail the social outlines of the old Field and render the politics of separation unsuccessful.

The first kind of waiting was remembered. It was a waiting for 'eternal return', a supra-historical promise. The traditional cycle of the year was structured in expectation of Elijah, the fair and the affirmation of community that his day brought. The shared promise of that gathering on 2 August each year was an incentive to endure winter. Waiting for him was also to wait in dread and fear for the crops and the households. Elijah is the Thunderer and with the help of Procopius, he can bring down the wrath of lightning from the skies and set fire to painstakingly gathered livelihoods (see Chapter 5). By Elijah's Day, however, the villagers would have finished all the major work, so his fair was a relatively secure luxury. As soon as it was over, the waiting would start again. This first, cyclical kind of waiting may be said to have been for Elijah as the sign of the seasons. But, it is also historical. It spoke not only of the harvest and the fear of thunderstorms, but also of political ruptures and tectonic shifts, usually coming from elsewhere. I have given some examples of such memories at various points in the book: people remembered their descent into the Field on Elijah's Day at the beginning of the First World War, how they had to change the place of celebration because of the Yugoslav thermal power plant, or how the local branch of the Serb Democratic Party (SDS) was formed on Elijah's Day, just before the 1990s war began.... Elijah was an orientational device in the agricultural Field and so other, 'large-scale' events were experienced by reference to it.

The second kind of waiting of the Field – a fragile hope, a longing or even a dedicated investment – was a postwar temporality, which I experienced in 2011 and 2012, a waiting for the return of cosmological time, along with the communal landscape it used to entail. This other kind of waiting was again expressed by way of Elijah's Day when the Field filled up with people, music, laughter, food and dance. It was a waiting for the Field to 'resemble itself'. Reinstating the celebration, the single most important date in the Field, the few returned refugees reconstructed a piece of their home. But each time the 'diasporic' visitors said their farewells, the year was again coloured by waiting. Most 'returnees' would leave the Field and spend the winter in Mostar. Those who stayed behind were locked into piles of frost to endure until the early signs of spring with the Annunciation. They no longer had *sijela,* the winter get-togethers, to fill their cold nights with tales and songs of summer. Waiting.

Of course, there were also other kinds of temporalities, like everywhere else. Waiting for Elijah was only the most prominent conversation with postwar transitions. The changes conflated the past into one place and the present into another. Through the waiting, the two places were embroiled in a dispute over the future. This double-coded waiting – waiting to wait, and waiting in memory of waiting – was again orientational. When it was not outspokenly intentional, it was an evident bodily inclination. The second waiting was not a quality of life structured by agricultural labour, but an active negotiation of the structure and quality of social relationships in the postwar Field.

In his *Waiting: The Whites of South Africa* Crapanzano understood waiting as a kind of 'passive activity', through which the waiters lose their grip over the present and have no control over the future. He noted: 'The world in its immediacy slips away; it is derealized. It is without élan, vitality, creative force. It is numb, muted, dead. Its only meaning lies in the future – in the arrival or the non-arrival of the object of waiting' (1985: 44). For the most part, this is precisely what the waiting discussed in this book is not. In it, the world is voiced, realized, enlivened, given meaning. Rather, to give up on waiting would create the kind of disillusionment with the world that Crapanzano described. This waiting in the Field can be understood as the creative force, a strategy of dealing with an oppressive ideological formation. Waiting for Elijah may be said to have been against the odds and against the socio-political visions of the Field as to be lived according to the stipulations of national belonging.

The many proverbs and sayings about waiting charted out the logics of future waiting in the Field. When someone was in a hurry, but ran up against an unavoidable schedule, people would ironically refer to a structural inequality that required waiting: 'Cool your heels, 'till the priest's grain's milled' (1). Or, they would reference the certainty of the seasons in their advice: 'Don't die, donkey, before the mount turns green' (2). The same local knowledge recalled that waiting and subtle efforts had a particular strength: 'Silent water rolls the hills' (3).[7] Rethinking the 'agency' of waiting, Ghassan Hage (2009: 2) has proposed that we understand it not only as 'passive activity', but also as 'active passivity'. I have found it difficult to discuss 'passivity' in terms of the Field's memories and its insistence on the return of the traditional calendar as its waiting is directional, filled with content (memories and expectations). The creativity of waiting lies precisely in that it works around the impossibility of direct confrontation with the state.

Storytelling is not passive: it turns to the past, but provides an anticipation of the possible future. In fact, as I have indicated in Chapter 2, it constitutes a vital induction into the Field and its cosmology. Waiting keeps alive that which is awaited. It works towards the realization of its own goal. Reflecting on the migrants' waiting to return home, Salim Lakha (2009) has argued that their waiting is not passive, but rather an active conversation with the present, even a resistance. However, I have been careful not to qualify the overall waiting of the Field as either political resistance or political passivity, because of the diversity of individual responses. From Delva's 'probably not' through Mila's 'God willing' to Eno's investment in the 'building of foundations for future generations', Elijah was more a conversation on his own return than a qualification of any certainty. When Elijah used to be an expected certainty, the worst, jolly curse in the Field was 'May you not await [to see the] next Elijah's Day!' (*Aliđuna ne dočeko!*). Along with the discontinuation of the curse after the war, waiting has been imbued with the precariousness of the present.

The Problem of Syncretism and Proximity

> Violence in Bosnia was thus antisyncretic; aimed at
> reducing people to unalloyed ethnic identities.
> —C. Stewart, 'Syncretism and Its Synonyms'

Out of the ocean of nationalist rhetoric that developed concomitantly with this research, one right-wing politician's repetitive statement was particularly striking. It was obviously strategic. Widely reported in the news and parroted by other political figures, the claim usually boiled down to one version or another of the following:

> In Bosnia and Herzegovina, there is not a single shared holiday except for New Year and the First of May, but those are international holidays. No common holiday shared by the three peoples in Bosnia and Herzegovina is possible, because they have always been on different sides of history and marked [the holidays] in different ways; some as a victory, some as a defeat. (Buka 2015)[8]

Those who do share holidays, the same politician argued, are the Serb Republic (an 'entity' in Bosnia) and the state of Serbia. They should celebrate *Vidovdan*, St Vitus Day, 'the great Serb holiday', together.[9]

What is odd about these statements is the notion that they would make for a viable political platform: my interlocutors found it difficult to recall any popular holiday that was not 'common', 'mixed' or 'shared' by 'the three peoples' in one way or another. In the Field, where the national homogenization of space was perhaps most visible, there was a wide range of 'shared' days, not only in terms of similar and overlapping practices but also in terms of mutual visitations and joint celebrations. The above-mentioned politician did not recognize that many, if not most, people in Bosnia share the feast days of George, John, Peter, Procopius, Elijah and Demetrius, or the 1 May, or that they engage in 'boundary-crossing' rituals for Christmas, Ramadan and the two Eids, or that there is a tradition of mutual visitation for these and other holidays. The politician did not wonder whether any community other than the 'three peoples' might also have something significantly 'in common' with them. Instead, he chose the somewhat less 'syncretic' St Vitus

Day, which memorializes the Battle of Kosovo, to connect across the desired national body. The Georgic saints were left out on purpose. They were a 'shared' bomb, not to be tampered with.

Finding religious (or other) narratives and practices that are antithetical to such programmes is hardly difficult then. It is more difficult to find the right theoretical concepts with which to discuss them. The problem lies in the fact that there are a number of different, yet related, processes to be considered. Carefully looking into the histories and politics of concepts such as 'syncretism', 'hybridity', 'mixture', 'creolization' and others, Charles Stewart has demonstrated that these are 'tangled vocabularies' (2011: 48), with a 'controversial past and an uncertain present' (1999: 45). David Gellner (1997: 288–89) has, for example, advanced a typology of mixture, differentiating between bricolage, syncretism, syncretic traditions and complimentary and accretive coexistence of more than one tradition, which Stewart (2008: 7) sees as different modes of syncretism.

Since all religions (and languages, cultures, etc.) are undeniably syncretic, Shaw and Stewart (1994: 7) have argued that the problem requires a turn from syncretism towards 'processes of religious synthesis' and the 'discourses of syncretism', as well as attending to what they have termed 'anti-syncretism', or the 'antagonism to religious synthesis'. But, what are the 'discourses of syncretism'? What would be their outlines? Can these discourses be detected, if the specific term is not employed? I find it more useful to make an artificial analytical distinction between the proximities and encounters of 'different' religious communities on the one hand, and the complexly layered religious systems that present a problem to claims of exclusive ownership, on the other. This is an artificial distinction, but imagine, for a moment, encounters as synchronic and the layered religions as diachronic proximities. Encounters have a potential for the making of syncretic corpuses: the 'different' concepts, practices and communities may start to overlap, speak to each other and alter each other. Layered syncretisms bear witness to certain former encounters and continuities: as I show in Chapter 5, many 'syncretic' practices in Bosnia have discernible earlier ancestors. In the Field, the 'pre-monotheistic' cosmologies are not simply a remnant. At some point they had to be an encounter and the drama of human–nonhuman agency has allowed material and conceptual continuities across different planes of organized religion.

Diachronically 'layered' religion will often coincide with 'proximities', but not always. Syncretism might reveal a proximity that is 'of the past', which does not exist as a face-to-face encounter, but an amalgam of previous exchanges. Maria Couroucli (2012) and Dionigi Albera (2008) have argued that 'sharing' and 'mixture' should be understood as a 'common Mediterranean experience', one that has inherited the space of the plural Byzantine and Ottoman Empires. The Ottoman willingness to 'tolerate' differences and include them into the imperial system of governance did reflect on 'intercommunal' relationships, although archival research cannot capture the subtleties of everyday practices (Barkey 2008: 110–14, Bryant 2016: 5, 13–14).

The focus on the 'mixed' Mediterranean may be a logical consequence of the fact that 'unmixing' and 'anti-syncretism' are also a common experience. The 'unmixing' of religious communities, which has occurred in systematic episodes from the Western European edicts of expulsion to the cleansing of 'Islamic' territories in the twenty-first century Mediterranean, did not manufacture 'non-syncretic' thoughts and practices, but only claims to purity and authenticity. What the 'unmixing' has achieved, however, is to deprive communities of the kind of active making of 'syncretic' thoughts and practices that was possible only with proximity.

In that sense, religions in the Field of Gacko were producing their 'syncretism' before the imposition of distances during the 1990s and have remained syncretic thanks to the remnants of the Other. This phenomenon is comparable to Bakhtin's distinction between external and internal dialogue: external dialogue is spatial and occurs between oneself and another; internal dialogue is diachronic, between two layers of the one self (see Bakhtin 1981: 279–86, Holquist 1981: 427). This comparison with dialogic orientations is, of course, rendered problematic by the nonhumans, particularly the landscapes full of remnants of the Other. A syncretism that functions through such remnants is an external dialogue as the Other still may give a reply. And, the reverse is also possible: if the Other is an absent nonhuman (e.g. a landscape), as it is often the case in this book, it may still enter into 'external' dialogue through its residues in another human or nonhuman. Affective remnants complicate the matter further; they may register through a completely different material context (see Navaro-Yashin 2012; and Chapter 4).

Another problem with the analytical differentiation between 'internal' and 'external' syncretism comes with the fuzzy religious boundaries. This is the case with the Bosnian 'inter-religious' marriages (particularly since the second Yugoslavia), but also in the early modern Bosnia for those Ottoman subjects who found themselves to be 'both Muslim and Christian'. In 2012, I visited the village of Kazanci near Gacko, where two seventeenth-century endowments of Osman Pasha still remind of an early time when families in Bosnia were, albeit under different circumstances, simultaneously Muslim and Christian. Osman Pasha was a local man who 'converted' to Islam and rose through various high-ranking positions in the Ottoman Empire (see Heywood 1996: 38). He built a mosque and a church in his village. His brother served as a monk in the church (ibid). Although only the minaret of the mosque stands today, it is said to have survived the 1990s war at the insistence of the local Orthodox Christian villagers.

My attentiveness to encounters between the Gacko communities, in the observed 'Serb-Muslim-Gurbeti' occurrences, owes much to the anti-syncretic drive at odds with the 'lived religion' in the Field. These encounters stressed the similarities and intercommunal intimacy. They did not describe the borrowing from or an amalgamation of 'different' religious concepts or practices. To those who were committed to the 'shared' religion, it was a way of life pertinent, first and foremost, to the Self. No Muslim in Gacko ever told me that they celebrated the 'Christian' saint days, just as no Muslim or Christian in Gacko ever told me that they continue 'pre-Christian' rituals. Syncretism can only ever be an analytical endeavour, justified for scholarship as a tool for thinking about the trajectories of encounters.

None of my interlocutors, save for a few academics, employed the word 'syncretism' at all. Instead, they spoke of 'celebrating together', 'meeting', 'coming together', 'sharing the same day', 'traditions being the same', 'traditions being 95% the same', 'engaging in joint competitions', 'visiting each other on holidays', 'care', 'love', 'rejoicing in their holiday' etc. In all these designations, proximity and similarity rest on the possibility of differentiating between religious groups (or bodies of thought and practice). Why would these terms be conflated into units of meaning? They indicate a need to remember the reconciliation of sameness and difference at a time when difference is augmented. Such moments, as my interlocutors pointed out, have happened before. The 'unmixing' and 'anti-syncretism' in Bosnia are indeed contemporaneous with the writing of this book. Sharing has gained a particular political resonance with the advent of nationalisms, which is not unique to the region: as I show in Chapter 5, Muslim–Christian syncretism in Palestine is also voiced as a form of resistance to the State of Israel. In the Field, memories of mixture have a similar, if much less politically explicit, reverberation.

Elijah's two names are the product of difference in intimate proximity. The diagram of this relationship has been offered in the Bosnian proverb: one day with two names. As I show in Chapter 3, intimacy and Otherness were one of the main stipulations of the Field's cosmology. The question that seems to remain is the 'intensity' or 'level' of intimacy. For example, there has been an 'anthropological' discussion about whether the Serbs and the Muslims in the village of Gerzovo celebrated Elijah's Day together or separately, whether it was a case of two separate events or one (see, for example, Baskar 2012: 54). In the Field, Elijah's Day was celebrated within the religious community, but with significant interactions. This was confirmed not only by my interlocutors, but also in a 1935 interview with Đula Dizdarević, for a study of epic poetry (Vidan 2003a: 89). Asked whether Elijah's Day in Jasike was a celebration for Muslims, she replied: 'This is a celebration for the Muslims, but the Orthodox people can come as well. They come just like us'. Đula's reply relates to the particularities of 'timespace' sharing. At first, one could argue that it does not necessarily point to any kind of shared religion. Glenn Bowman (2012: 8) preferred to call such phenomena 'mixing' rather than 'sharing', so as not to presuppose either antagonism or syncretism and 'amity'. The problem addresses the need for finer methodological frameworks for the study of 'non-homogeneous' timespaces.

Azra Hromadžić (2012) argues that the everyday communication in 'mixed regions' included various sorts of intimacies, particularly through visitations, 'coffee visits, "sweet visits" (*na slatko*), visits "for joy" (*na radost*), and visits "for sorrow" (*na žalost*)' (ibid: 35). However, she holds that, since there were no 'mixed marriages' in the villages, 'practices of mixing simultaneously verified and challenged ethnic divisions' (ibid: 34). She, like other authors (for example Hayden 2002b, Kolind 2008: 207), takes 'marriages' across 'ethnic' lines as some kind of litmus test for the degrees of ethnic distance. We cannot a priori conclude that such 'mixtures' did not verify ethnic divisions. Whilst the 'mixing' in Gacko did work with the given social stipulations, verifying and challenging them, it must be noted that the relationships between the communities have grown into the tissue of everyday life and the annual cycle, to such an extent that time and space of home could not be conveyed without referencing the 'shared points'. These references are not only spatial but also temporal maps incongruous with the Dayton constellation.

Hromadžić (2012: 38–39) likewise notes that 'mixed citizens' have become a sort of 'anti-citizen' and that the 'new spatial governmentality of ethnic division' has made them unmappable.[10] Although invisible to the eyes of the state, such 'hybrid' positions can have a stronger claim over the spatial and temporal scapes unmixed by the state. Even if they did not necessarily create 'ethnically mixed' individuals (imagining for a moment that we know what that means), rural landscapes made possible the spaces of shared temporalities. So, the unmixing has created peculiar lacunas in the annual and everyday rhythms of Gacko. These absences, made vivid in memories, hopes and yearnings, reveal the significance of 'sharing'. The language of body-space-time constantly harks back to these 'mixtures'.

But, the most problematic question is the definition of what constitutes religion in the Field. Where are we to draw the boundaries in pastoral and agricultural cosmologies? Obviously, its economies cannot be discounted. Neither can landscapes and the seasonal changes. The same applies to cattle and vegetation, childbirth, weddings, medicine and food, etc. So, why should something as simple as a meeting not be part of the religious system? My claim is that it is. In a structural, discursive and affective sense, the 'inter-religious' meetings were part of the religious experience. The most important quality of the Elijah's Day celebration was the socializing as the final annual outlet. As I demonstrate in my discussion of *kumstvo* (sworn kinship) in Chapter 3, 'inter-religious' visitations were an equally important part of the same system and the encounters encapsulated a crucial part of the logics behind the cosmos.

The work of anthropologist Robert Hayden has been at the forefront of the conversation about the nature of shared religion in the Balkan Peninsula.[11] He has offered an argument pertinent to the anthropology of proximity, while managing at the same time to sideline any discussion of encounters. By his own admission, he gathered his information through 'census data, public opinion polls, voting patterns and the configurations of the contending military forces, rather than primarily [relying] on more traditional forms of ethnography' (Hayden 2007: 107). This lack of situated knowledge led him to make contentious claims regarding 'competitive sharing' that 'becomes war', which is, in Bosnia, followed by undemocratic '[a]ttempts to impose diversity after a country has been partitioned', and an implicit proposal that a 'clear recognition of this situation' may be based on 'what people are willing to accept, even if that means the injustice of partition' (Hayden 2002a: 219). It requires some 'cutting and pasting', but his support for ethnically homogenized territories has been clearly stated: this state of affairs should be accepted because violence has been more than successful. What is intriguing about Hayden's argument is that it provides a more eloquent version of the political speech from the beginning of this section and, as such, a discernible springboard for a number of academic critiques long after Huntington's (1996) thesis on the supposed 'clash of civilizations' had lost its novelty.

The shared rituals recorded in this book are competitive, only in a somewhat different sense; competition is not centred on 'ethno-religious' belonging. But the Field of shared religion is competitive, very competitive. On George's Day, children lit fires on hilltops, competing to see whose would sprout the tallest and brightest flames. In Kreševo, Catholics competed with bonfires on John's Day. When I visited the town in 2012, one of the bonfire teams drove on the back of a truck through the other team's neighbourhood. Jolly youths with nylon tights on their heads held a spray-painted rhyme 'Gornje Čelo eats shit' (*Gornje Čelo govna jelo*), which eventually burned on top of the bonfire. On George's Day, all over Bosnia, girls competed to see whose swing would fly furthest into the air. On Elijah's Day, men competed at peculiar local athletic disciplines. Groups of the same men competed in the singing of *bećarac* and *ganga* at religious feasts and fairs. Young women competed to become *namuša* (a reputable bachelorette) by garnering the most marriage proposals on Elijah's Day. On George's Day, children competed by stinging each other's legs with nettles. On Peter's Day, they competed to see who could get the most sweets from the neighbours. On Elijah's

Day, there were traditional group fistfights, but even these were commonly between men of 'the same religious group'. These and many other similar examples are the only kinds of 'competitive sharing' that I was able to record. Hayden, however, manages to elide all of them, giving nationalist spatial demarcations some kind of historical and emotional depth.

While I agree with Stewart (1999: 45) that syncretism should be salvaged as a useful theoretical tool, this book rather endeavours to discuss encounters – both the encounters affecting cosmology, and cosmological encounters – as phenomena upon which the religious system of the Field and its corresponding timespaces rest, and without which they cannot be fully expressed. Each encounter may be read as a mosaic of economies, intimacies and histories. They simultaneously take the form of synchronic and diachronic entanglements, which have influenced this book's temporal and spatial extensions (see Chapters 3 and 5).

Developing the proposal out of his research in southern Zimbabwe, Joost Fontein has called for an anthropology of proximity:

> We may do better not by emphasizing 'radical difference' but rather by cultivating an acute sensitivity to the proximities, coexistences, and continuities that derive from people's shared material and historical engagements, as a way of writing against politicized differences rather than reasserting them on ever more abstract philosophical grounds. (2011: 723)

I have tried to adopt Fontein's proposal as a particularly apt methodology for the study of Bosnian landscapes. Focusing on the 'presence of encounters' does not, as Fontein noted, avoid acknowledging difference and distance (ibid: 721). Indeed the concept of proximity depends on a certain distinction or distance and/or processes of anti-syncretism, which then need to be analytically situated. My research into proximity reveals how intimacy and distance are processed by landscapes and negotiated in spaces hidden from the main political arenas. It does not only take proximity when it is 'harmonious', but also proximity as a tension. For example, the second chapter discusses the proximity of two conflicting chronotopes and the 'frictions' (see Tsing 2004) produced in their encounters. Throughout the text, I introduce interlocutors who interpret proximities differently. Some do not want to return to the Field, others argue for varying degrees of past and/or present communication between Serbs, Muslims and Gurbeti, while yet others prefer distance. However, I also show that the annual cycle, with its traditions, included an established system of proximity (see Chapter 3); indeed, durable remnants of this system were sometimes visible even in the discourses of distance. So the question is not only how people imagined proximity, but also how proximity imagined people and their landscapes.

From Victorian Travelogues to the 'Bosnian Mosaic'

A common theme has been found for analysed Bosnian rituals in their shared and/or syncretic character and how they are narrated through encounters. Not only are they performed by contemporary Roma, Muslim, Orthodox Christian and Catholic communities in Bosnia, but they may also, without exception, be traced to early Slavic cosmology and an inheritance from wider fields, tentatively referred to as Proto-Indo-European religion. Although no systematic research has been done about this aspect of the folk Bosnian calendar, much has been published about individual elements.

It is no wonder that the early depictions of Bosnian syncretism and religious mixture came from spaces where Muslims and Christians did not live together and, thus, did not share religious landscapes. They were remarkable as a peculiarity, a mixture as seen (perhaps *only*) from the perspectives of homogeneity. Many such accounts are to be found in travelogues, particularly those of British provenance. In her detailed study *Unveiling Bosnia-Herzegovina in British Travel Literature (1844–1912)*, Neval Berber has noted that the mid-nineteenth century British interest in Bosnia was the result of new British foreign policies and interest in the Eastern Question (2010: xiii–xv). She has also noted that, up until the outbreak of the First Balkan War in 1912, such travelogues provided a mixture of Orientalist and markedly political visions. They, nonetheless, offer invaluable details of fin-de-siècle Bosnian shared landscapes.

In 1877, Georgina Muir Mackenzie and Adeline Paulina Irby, two good friends and keen travellers, published a highly political portrayal of Bosnia in their *Travels in the Slavonic Provinces of Turkey-in-Europe*. Although using the term 'nations' in quotation marks to denote the differences between the religious communities in Bosnia, they also observed certain similarities:

> The Mussulmans of Serajevo still keep St. John the Baptist's day (24th of June, O. S.), when the sun is said to dance at dawn on the top of the hill Trebovich : on that day, and on St. Elias's and St. George's days, the Mussulman population turns out of doors, and the whole side of Trebovich, especially the neighbourhood of the Moslem saint's tomb, is bright with red turbans and jackets and groups of women in white veils. (Mackenzie and Irby 1877: 8)

The Muslim nobility, the same authors further pointed out, still keep the name of their family's patron saints (ibid: 9). The anonymous author of a 'Ride through Bosnia' published by *Frasier Magazine* provided a very similar report, adding Peter to the list of shared saints (Anonymous 1875: 557). The same year, the famous archaeologist Arthur Evans travelled through Bosnia 'on foot', as he pointed out in the title of his monograph (1876). And although he considered it pathetic that 'the influence of Islam seemed to have infected' Christian rituals (ibid: 133), he described some of them in the most remarkable detail, acknowledging 'elements of grandeur and beauty' (ibid: 134). On the eve of the Assumption, he visited Komušina, a Catholic mountain pilgrimage site, where there was a large fair, an 'elegant' *kolo* circle dance, and 'cherry bonfires', 'round which the peasants clustered in social circles' (ibid). The pilgrimage survives until today, much as he described it then. Evans also recognized the transposition of early Slavic deities into Christian saints. He noted the perpetuation of the Slavic God Viddo in St Vitus. As I argue in Chapter 5, most of the main dates of the Field's sacral calendar can be traced back through significant connections to the Slavic pantheon.

Roy Trevor, in his travelogue of the Balkans, described shared apotropaic rituals at the pilgrimage Church of St John near the town of Jajce. His informant apparently witnessed

> a special throwing out of devils that took place upon St. John's day some years ago. The chapel was filled to overflowing with Moslems and Christians, men and women, who rolled upon the ground gnashing their teeth, tearing their hair and rending their clothes. (1911: 47)

On the eve of John's Day in the town of Kreševo, I myself participated in the lighting of apotropaic bonfires. Surprisingly, it was not the elderly inhabitants but the local children who told me of the fire's ability to 'ward off evil spirits'. Another, more recent, political travel diary was written by the journalist and suffragette supporter Rebecca West (2006). The latter element of her biography provides some clues as to the roots of the analysis she provided of shared fertility rituals in Macedonia. She dedicated two chapters of her bulky monograph to a very intimate portrayal of syncretic George's Day festivities, ultimately rejecting the sacrificial fertility ritual as 'shameful' and 'a conscious cheat' (ibid: 810–31).

A number of early twentieth-century researchers laid the groundwork for studies into Slavic cosmology. An 1860 treatise by Ignác Jan Hanuš was one of the first attempts to analyse the Slavic mythological calendar, its related rituals and beliefs systematically. Louis Leger (1901) tried to work out the structure of the pantheon. This method of compiling both 'trans-Slavic' and state-specific ethnological and historical data was continued by a number of later researchers.[12] In their works, the specificities of the Bosnian calendar tended to be considered as a part of the Serb and Croat traditions, if at all. As Natalie Kononenko (2007: 1) has noted, for 'Slavic peoples' folklore was often a way of defining themselves against other groups. The development of folklore studies really began with the onset of nationalisms. This is particularly true of the Balkan Peninsula and was noticeable in the 'scholarly' battle over the national definition of folklore in Bosnia.[13] Ethnologists in Bosnia contributed to the topic mainly through individual, small-scale studies published in the *Herald of the National Museum* (*Glasnik zemaljskog muzeja u Sarajevu*).[14]

In 1978–79, historian Muhamed Hadžijahić published *The Syncretic Elements in Islam in Bosnia and Herzegovina* (*Sinkretički elementi u islamu u Bosni i Hercegovini*), which looked at the different layers amalgamated by one of the religious communities. It remains a seminal work for research into shared landscapes and the folk calendar in Bosnia. However, due to its brevity, it does not point to the wealth of similar phenomena. Secondly, rapid changes to social circumstances that followed soon after the paper was published have made a significant impact on these practices: some no longer exist. Finally, the reason why Hadžijahić was able to look at 'syncretism in Islam' was because of his choice to see syncretic Islam as a diachronic composite, rather than as a matter of active engagement. In Bosnia, there are few traces of 'syncretic Islam' that are not also part of the same cosmology as 'syncretic Christianity'. His argument turns towards the layers of mediaeval Christian and early Slavic religiosities contained in the lifeworlds of the Bosnian Muslim communities. However, as this book demonstrates, in places where different religious communities live in proximity, religious mixture is a process of active 'recalibration'. It responds to historical changes and political events.

There is an ever-growing corpus of research into the Bosnian 'notion' of neighbourhood (*komšiluk*) and its meaning (or lack thereof) for inter-religious mixing and communication.[15] Based on my research within and beyond the Field, I noticed significant differences, as one would expect, in the constitution of *komšiluk,* which depend on spatial proximities of dwellings, including the proximity of dwellings inhabited by people of different religions. The many hamlets have always been scattered around the Field and the typical *komšiluk* usually consisted of a few extended family households. Some hamlets were closer together, and so the *komšiluk* included people of different religions, but this was rarely the case in the second half of the twentieth century. In fact, *komšiluk* as such did not feature prominently in the narratives of place or memories of the prewar Field. To 'mix' or 'share' in any sense, one needed either to make a journey of household visitation, or wait for the festivals. The institution of sworn kinship (*kumstvo*) in the Field, exhibited some aspects of the moral, pragmatic and affective dimensions of *komšiluk* in other parts of Bosnia (see Chapter 3). For syncretic forms of religiosity to develop, visitations and festivities had to be sustained cyclically and consistently.

In his account of shared religiosities and violence in Kosovo, Gerlachlus Duijzings has questioned the notion of stable identities: 'When we take a closer look at what happens on the ground over a prolonged period of time, we see that identity shows many ambiguities in areas like Kosovo, Macedonia and Bosnia. Contact between different groups (such as between Serbs and Albanians) has been marked by cases of reciprocal assimilation and (incomplete) conversion' (2000: 13). The need to locate well-defined boundaries around communities, as exemplified by the aforementioned Victorian travelogues, is partly a symptom of writing, of constructing a story. Ambiguities are not 'easy to think with', as Glenn Bowman noted in his editor's introduction to *Sharing the Sacra* (2012: 4), in which the essays attempt to complicate solid identitary tropes. Religious 'boundaries' in the Field were simultaneously connections and disconnections. Before writing about sharing across these 'boundaries', we need to think about the shareholders and the border patrols. For those who do research in Bosnia, ethical and ethnical pitfalls converge. Bougarel, Helms and Duijzings (2007) have suggested that we should be looking for a new kind of 'Bosnian Mosaic', a messier, more particularized one. The mosaic presented in this book, constituted around the Elijah of the Field, is a negotiation between a traditional pastoral cosmology and nationalist politics, both of which enjoy 'accomplices' and 'supporters', and both of which influence the definition of time and space (see Chapter 1).

FIGURE 0.2 Map of Bosnia, with indicated sites of attended rituals, the inter-entity border and my minibus itinerary from East Sarajevo to Gacko

Locating 'the Field': From Map to Affect and Word

The worst trait of these lands is the war, which returns every thirty years. Everyone has suffered. People do not hate each other. This is a place where it is easy to live together. Nature provides.
—Nada, interlocutor from the Field

You went into the town? Were you not afraid?
—Delva, interlocutor from the Field

This research deals with two main problems, which I have been confronting from the beginning of my fieldwork. These problems have shaped and reshaped the arguments and the topic of the book, as well as the process of cognition, that is, my paths of inquiry. The first problem is space; the second is time.

It makes some sense to open discussion of these problems with the U.S. Department of State map of Bosnia and Herzegovina. It was officially introduced in 1995 through the Dayton Peace Accords at the Wright-Patterson Air Force Base in Ohio. In the words of the Clinton family and the State Department, it brought 'an end to the devastating war in Bosnia and Herzegovina', 'transformed [the] Balkan region and remains a signal achievement in American diplomacy' (Rodham Clinton 2010). What it in fact produced was a structure of institutions through which the particular map may be enforced. The transformation started considerably before the Ohio ceremony when the Bosnian, Serbian, Croatian, U.S., EU and Russian diplomats placed their signature on the Constitution, which remains the present state of geopolitical affairs.

Bosnia and Herzegovina seceded from the Socialist Federative Republic of Yugoslavia after the Referendum on Independence in early 1992. I was six years old at the time. Shortly before, my family had moved from the small town of Brčko on river Sava in northern Bosnia to the capital of Sarajevo, so that my mother could take up a new job. My sister, who had just started her primary education in 1990, became one of 'Tito's pioneers' at a schoolyard ceremony. Brandishing her well-ironed red scarf and a blue hat with a five-pointed red star stitched to the front, she solemnly swore 'to love Yugoslavia' and 'uphold the ideas for which *our* comrade Tito fought'. I never got to be officially initiated into the Yugoslav identity; the rite of passage escaped me by a single year. There are uncountable historiographies, ethnographies, eyewitness testimonies and humanitarian reports of what happened next. I have recorded some of these accounts during my research. In Sarajevo, most of my family survived the siege. Members of my family from Brčko, Gradačac and Stolac went into exile. That 1990s war, my own, embedded into my understanding of the world, touched and destroyed different times, spaces and relations for my interlocutors in the Field of Gacko. Their lives often revealed the limits of my initial questions. It took some effort to hear and then speak again.

In a now famous essay, Renato Rosaldo (1989) described how the death of his wife produced the affective grounds needed to understand what Illongot men had been telling him about their headhunting rituals and their 'rage born in grief' at losing close relatives. The shift in his theoretical model was made possible only through the bodily impact of his new experience. Most of my findings depart from the experience I had before I was guided into certain kinds of times and spaces. My participant observation was threaded with new conversations, emotional reflections and altogether different bodies of knowledge.

After I discarded the initial 'discursive' uneasiness of closeness and distance, the Field analytically opened up to me through the affectivity of encounters. My main 'methods' became *kafa i cigara* (coffee and a cigarette). They would define the narrative space, seize the conversation and allow it to endure its extensions and rhythms. They licensed long silences and sudden punctuations. And journeys. If I were to locate 'the Field' in any particular way, I would argue towards these moments of encounters. They opened this work to the relational: entanglements which seemed to have an autonomous resonance through their lingering, residues of which abound in the Field. Yael Navaro-Yashin (2012) has described how such 'remnants and residues' produce affects, moments that we confront as a certain kind of bodily knowledge.

Throughout this book, I have made use of the affective traces in language and enjoyed recognizing that etymologies relate the words of my interlocutors to their cosmologies and ritual practices. As Bakhtin noted:

> Historically language grew up in the service of participative thinking and performed acts, and it begins to serve abstract thinking only in the present day of its history. The expression of a performed act from within and the expression of once-occurrent Being-as-event in which that act is performed require the entire fullness of the word: its content/sense aspect (the word as concept) as well as its palpable-expressive aspect (the word as image) and its emotional-volitional aspect (the intonation of the word) in their unity. (1999: 31)

I am, of course, not suggesting that 'etymology is destiny', but rather that language is layered with both defined meanings and affective residues and that it may offer extensions of analytical value at least equal to the historical contextualization. In that sense, I have made extensive use of the proverbs and sayings from the Field, discussed proximity through local idioms and spatial expressions and found clues about the calendar in the tradition of Gacko epics.

Remnants craft connections to the past, but they also interfere, trespass on the proposed present. Yugoslav communism was disrupted by remnants of earlier social forms. Banned rituals were continually practised when the state was not present and pilgrimages were made in secret. An institutionalized ideology until recently, communism now also lurks in the pile of affective materialities. Several nationalist projects from the 1990s produced further incompleteness. It remains relatively easy to name the ideology that induced destruction in any given Bosnian locale. An artificial distinction between Self and Other entered the landscapes through a process of defining the former and obliterating the latter. Sacral architecture was systematically destroyed. Houses were burned and often branded with fascist logos. Places were represented in the image of new power relations. Over two hundred thousand people were killed and two million more displaced (ICRC Report 1999: ii).

There is an uneasiness inherent to the counting of dead bodies and the mapping of identities. Political quantifications of the human suffering produced by the 1990s war in Bosnia lack the complexity of intimate narratives. I have thus decided to use only qualitative research methods. The product is a certain kind of inherently incomplete 'map from within'. It locates the various entanglements protruding in the landscapes. By entanglements, I do not imply the relationships of those groups that were officially polarized by the 1990s war, namely Serbs (Orthodox), Bosniaks (Muslims) and Croats (Catholics). To speak of those kinds of entanglements would be akin to the simple identity politics that take the Ohio map as their starting point.

Has the violence been successful? Most of this book looks at the Field of Gacko, one of the most polarized places in the world. Yet, even there, different kinds of proximity resonate in the landscape. 'Active' encounters between Muslims and Serbs have been drastically reduced, but proximities remained embodied in daily practices, places, rituals and language. Even *after* mixing, the shared character of inherited religion/landscape constitutes a certain kind of meeting, in the same way that Elijah's chair is the silent, unshakeable witness (see Preface). One example of these 'post-encounters' is given in Chapter 4: a nationalist song about the destruction of the Gacko landscape is composed through shared images and utterances. These seemingly unseverable proximities lurk behind the most unobtrusive details of everyday life, like the handling of crops, the narration of a personal memory, or the utterance of a toponym.

Big History, Historicity and the Body

> Alas, my child. Big History. But, our people did not write history. The Serbs did. The Croats did too. So much could have been written about this Kula if there were older people. But, there are none left. There are no old people here anymore. I think that I am the oldest one here, in this Kula.
> —Fata, interlocutor from the Field

Fata's lament over historiography raises a number of questions vital for this work, firstly in terms of my methodological and ethical investment and then with regards to the research methods employed. History often sources from the already objectified. Yet, as Fata said, it can also be taken from the body, the old body in particular. It can be gathered for one purpose or another, moulded into a static piece of evidence, the body as an object. What happens when we tackle the past through the body as a subject? Faced with the historicity of the old body, the oldest one left in the village, I became frightened of the power of writing, and writing over, of the larger-than-life historical fact and anthropological metaphor. At the same time, Fata offered to me, by way of her own old body, the possibility of writing as a resistance to writing. She described the chasm of being between others' histories. Bodies engage with history in different ways. Bodies also literally are history, positioned and dynamic. They can speak to other bodies, of places and landscapes with which they have an old intimacy. The young bodies extend the past of old bodies, but also open novel directions for it. As I show in Chapter 2, the problem of continuity of the Field was located in the absence of intimate proximity between the young and the old.

I was thus left with the question of how to write a portrayal of bodies and landscapes – a dynamic being of history engaged with both the past and the future – that would not become a historiography. The waiting of the Field and the storytelling about the old waiting for Elijah may also be described as 'historicity', as discussed by Eric Hirsch and Charles Stewart (2005). For them, the term

> describes a human situation in flow, where versions of the past and future (of persons, collectives or things) assume present form in relation to events, political needs, available cultural forms and emotional dispositions'. . . . Reconfiguring 'historicity' to index the fuller qualities of this social and personal relationship to the past and future makes it a complex social and performative condition, rather than an objectively determinable aspect of historical descriptions. Historicity in this sense is the manner in which persons operating under the constraints of social ideologies make sense of the past, while anticipating the future. (ibid: 262)

It is this intimacy with the past, sensing one's body that is 'of history' but also a possibility of the future, that comes across in the narratives about the Field's annual calendar interrupted in the 1990s. Responding to the fragility of the present, Elijah and George stepped out of the mytho-historical framework to assume the flesh of the Field's ('ethno'-) religious communities. As I noted, the 'Alija-Ilija' figure of speech was previously double coded to include the shorthand for the communities of the Field, but in the post-1990s, this 'second code' augmented, because it already had the possibility (and perhaps even the function) of responding to change.

One question I decided to tackle is whether this response can be affective and nonconscious (see Chapter 4). Looking at the Greek island of Naxos,

Stewart (2012) found that dreams may attain a collective agentive quality and become expressive of historical consciousness, but a consciousness that also responds to the present and anticipates, or moulds, the future. This book is about a certain kind of (day)dreaming, a rich storytelling about the past time-reckoning and encounters. Memories, then, are comparable to dreams; they absorb concerns to become the body's coping method (cf. Antze and Lambek 1996: xii).

Whilst only the Chapter 4 delves into nonconscious historicity, which I have called the 'grammar of the body', the other chapters look at the affectivity of remnants (cf. Navaro-Yashin 2009, 2012). They show how the body communicates between its own past, present and future. Stewart (2012: 196) argued that ('standard Western') historiography traditionally eschewed such forms of historicization. The value of this work is in the fact that it speaks to the past and replies to it from the perspective of positioned bodies, whilst attempting to walk around the traps of 'Big History' and ethnography.

If such a positioned project is indeed feasible, what would be its purpose? Is it justifiable to steer clear of the political implications of entering this dialogic space between the body and history? The encouragement to couple research findings with a visible 'impact' strategy has a problematic inheritance. The post-Holocaust Nuremberg Code proposed that research 'experiments' with humans ought to 'yield fruitful results for the good of the society, unprocurable by other methods or means of study and not random and unnecessary in nature' (Nuremberg Military Tribunals 1949: 182). Although addressing medical experimentation, the Code prepared the grounds for later anthropological discourses (cf. Ransome 2013: 29–32). The 'UK anthropologist' is guided towards a research ethics by which findings are communicated 'for the benefit of the widest possible community' (ASA 2012: V-1). With regard to anything written and published, there exists a possibility that it may have some 'impact', that it will 'further', 'illuminate', 'change', 'keep', 'testify to' some social process, be it an 'academic debate' or 'the state of "human rights" in Guatemala'. We often strive for those possibilities, without being able to ascertain the consequences of our work.

What kinds of effect may this book produce? Eno, one of the first returnees to the village of Kula in the Field, repeatedly told me of his trust that my work would make a difference in the geopolitical constellation that marginalizes groups of people in the Field. Such a responsibility I can neither accept nor discard. The best that can be done, I think, is to write decisively, with the multitude of narratives in mind and not infringe upon one's interlocutors' lives with further violent abstractions. Nancy Scheper-Hughes (1995) called for a politically committed anthropology. I have imagined Gačani asking me the same question she received from the inhabitants of Alto do Cruzeiro,

'What is anthropology to us, anyway?' (ibid: 411). This research, not least due to its excruciatingly slow pace, cannot answer any of the urgent needs my interlocutors continue to face. It can, however, question the various political shifts and strategies of nationalist violence in Bosnia, and point towards the discrepancies between the Field as a lived space and Gacko as an ideology in construction.

These processes are not solely pertinent to human actors of the landscapes. What might be ethical research into soil, water and trees? Environmental and heritage protection discourses are frequently poorly attuned to the complexities of landscaped relationships. The thermal power plant in the centre of the Field has been, in many ways, detrimental to both the human and the nonhuman environment. It has buried one locus of Elijah's Day festivities and polluted the dwelling areas of the nomadic Gurbeti communities. The Devon Karst Research Society (2007) described the situation as 'nothing short of a total disaster'. On the other hand, through the forty years of its existence, the plant has generated employment, new relationships and memories. These latter layers complicate the 'nature conservation' discourses. Similar questions may be raised for other landscapes, such as Djevojačka Pećina, a cave in central Bosnia, which is visited by thousands of pilgrims each August. The walls at its entrance have accumulated various etchings over centuries and in an attempt to preserve the 'outstanding value' of these etchings, the local government has put up a metal fence around them (see HadžiMuhamedović 2012). Ironically, the same human–nonhuman relationship that has been 'protected' is simultaneously being denied to contemporary pilgrims. Charlotte Joy's (2012) work on heritage conservation in Mali raised a similar question. What does conservation imply for the local community beyond a recreation of an imagined 'authentic' past? Rather than advocating for or against the fence around the walls of the Djevojačka Pećina, this book finds its ethical grounding by recognizing the variety of processes that shape its landscape and other landscapes across Bosnia.

Inextricable from the projection of purpose is the question of motivation. Why am I researching 'shared' 'Bosnian' 'landscapes'? What impelled me to ask certain questions? Pat Caplan (2003: 16) has noted that, since the fall of the Berlin Wall and the war in Bosnia, violent identity politics have moved the discussion of ethics towards the discourse of human rights. By approaching certain kinds of phenomena through my writing, I inevitably seek to amplify their presence. The fact that I was an 'eye-witness' to the violence of the 1990s did, without any doubt, inform some of my early research questions. The central one is obvious: how can we interpret the simultaneity of shared lives and exclusivist political programmes? I have relied on the methodology of hermeneutics, which, as Renato Rosaldo (1989: 7) has noted, depends on interpretive repositioning: 'Ethnographers begin with a set of questions, revise them throughout the course of inquiry, and in the end emerge with different questions than they started with'.

The methodology of hermeneutics significantly altered the 'spatial' scope of my fieldwork. The initial plan of spending one calendar year in the town of Gacko was replaced by a particular kind of multi-sited research. Firstly, because of the large-scale wartime emigration from Gacko, communication with some of my interlocutors moved to other towns or to so-called 'cyberspace'. In this space, Gacko is a place deeply related to the tangible landscape of its origins, yet one that exists in a parallel dimension. Photographs and memories are exchanged. Visitors are not 'virtual': they all know each other. Central to this exchange is a website intriguingly entitled *Gacko in my mind* (http://www.gacko.net/). It is a place that exists, not in the tangible town, but rather in spite of such Gacko. Marianne Hirsch and Leo Spitzer (2010) have written about the afterlife of Czernowitz, a place sustained in the memory of the displaced Jews, yet one that 'cannot be found in any contemporary atlas' (ibid: xiii). It was maintained through memories that amalgamated the beauty of home and the pain of persecutions. 'Gacko in my mind' similarly exists in a shared cognitive atlas. It informs the displaced Gačani (people from Gacko) about funerals, weddings, newspaper articles, political and everyday problems, as well as the major festivals. It is updated by people who now live in Mostar and the U.S.A. The antipode to *Gacko in my mind* is 'The Official Internet Presentation of Gacko Municipality' (*Opština Gacko: zvanična internet prezentacija,* gacko-rs.info). It provides thorough details on the political structure of the municipality and a 'short history' of the town. In this short, big history, all references to non-Serbs and traditions Serbs 'share' with others have been carefully omitted.

These two opposing 'virtual' landscapes assert their online authority differently. *Gacko in my mind,* like countless other web presentations and discussions of displaced Bosnian communities, pieces together an elaborate 'memoryscape' from particular intimacies with the landscape. Memoryscapes, as Nuttell (1992: 39) noted, are constructed through 'mental images of the environment', particularly through remembered places. For the displaced Gačani, this discursive process is closely related to their feelings of distance and inaccessibility. Landscapes are also memorialized as an act of resistance. Both the 'official' and the 'imagined' Gacko websites have a page dedicated to the history of the town. The former provides a short article, which selectively spans the pertinent 'historical facts'. 'Officially', Gacko is thus 'in Serb Herzegovina and the Serb Republic', and is 'the cradle of Serb spirituality and folk literacy'. The page lists census data, with particular reference to the number of Serbs, thus providing evidence that they were always the majority:

Year 1991   10,844 inhabitants (6,723 Serbs, 3,795 Muslims, others 2,179)
Year 2001   10,500 inhabitants

(gacko-rs.info)

According to the census in 1991, the website notes, there were 6,723 Serbs, 3,795 Muslims and 2,179 others. It does not note, or engage with the reasons for, the absence of the 'non-Serb' half of the population in 2001. The category 'others' here also includes both Yugoslavs and Croats, although they would have been officially recognized nationalities; in the 1991 census, the term 'others' was actually used to describe 'non-constitutive' categories, such as the Roma or the non-defined. The 'official' history of Gacko also defines major events, namely the Serb uprisings against the Ottomans and, later, the Nazis.

Gacko in my mind, in contrast, approaches the past through an assemblage. Visitors are invited to improve the website by sending 'Gacko-related documents, photographs, drawings, etc'. Snippets of books, poems and written narratives are available as a space for discussion, rather than promoting an outline for the reading of history. Photographs, stories and reports are grouped in series such as 'Forgotten Gacko' or 'The Gacko that does not exist'. This virtualized memoryscape is decidedly against ethnic divisions and wants to 'gather all those for whom Gacko was the place of their birth, who carry Gacko in their hearts, and who have any other link to Gacko, whether they have been expelled, returned or remained there'. When the authors invite contributions, they also warn against 'religious, national, racial, gender and any other kind of segregation'.

Noting the frequent status of remembered places as symbolic anchors for dispersed communities, Gupta and Ferguson (1997: 39) argue that the very denial of firm territories generates attachments to imagined communities. This tension between the 'official' and the 'imagined' Gacko websites is relevant to Fata's comment on history. The official history of Gacko, in the tradition of political histories, centres on a number of selective references to events. Fernand Braudel (1972: 21) called it *l'histoire événementielle*: 'the history of events: surface disturbances, crests of foam that the tides of history carry on their strong backs. A history of brief, rapid, nervous fluctuations'. In Fata's words, this is Big History. I capitalize the term to express the systematic, disciplinary model of such historical construction. Eventful history picks its events and interprets them. They stand as mere signifiers in need of appropriation. Paul Carter (2010: xvi) has coined the term 'imperial history' to denote the kind of history that reduces space to a stage. Its goal, he noted, is not to interpret but to legitimate, 'Orphaned from their unique spatial and temporal context, such objects, such historical facts, can be fitted-out with new paternities' (ibid). Projects pertaining to historiographize Bosnian landscapes are numerous and appear in various forms. The value of careful description drawn from the intimacy of the body is in the attempt to look beyond the 'Big History' that Fata problematized, towards more telling kinds of temporalities.

Following Time through Space

It was through *Gacko in my mind* that I first approached what I call, for lack of a better term, 'tangible' Gacko. I read about the prewar rituals shared by the Orthodox, Muslim and Gurbeti communities. Elijah's Day, I learnt, saw a large number of displaced people return to the Field; for most, however, this return was little more than a day trip. Human displacement was thus the first issue to require a widening of the spatial scope of my research. The second problem was, as I soon found, that the war had also dislodged time.

Elijah's Day cannot be understood outside of a well-structured annual cycle. George's Day, once inextricable from the calendar, is no longer celebrated, and a number of other 'common places' have become mere references. This was crucial to my methodological shift. What or who is the object/subject of my study? Instead of turning to place – the township of Gacko with its surrounding villages – or a group of spatially and temporally dislodged people who have once lived or continue to live in Gacko – I decided to approach the annual cycle and a variety of harvest-related rituals. This required a particular kind of multi-temporal and multi-sited fieldwork. I visited various pilgrimage places, festivities and smaller rituals within and outside of the state. The more places I visited, the more pieces of the 'time puzzle' that became apparent to me.

Even my research in the Field could be described as multi-sited as most of my conversations occurred in the many satellite villages around the town. Some of these villages have been polarized to the point where they can only be researched as separate loci. Branching out of a single site (however defined) allowed for productive reconfiguration of the key questions. It made sense to record conversations about food, crops, cattle, medicinal herbs and so on. The specificities of the calendar in the Field also became more noticeable. For example, the absence of the George's Day fertility rituals in the returnee's villages was understandable as young women and the Gurbeti communities were once central to this Day; in 2011/2012, there was only one Muslim girl and no Gurbeti in the Field.

This multi-sited fieldwork disrupts the geopolitical divisions of contemporary Bosnia and Herzegovina. Closely related rituals and narratives have been found on both sides of the 'inter-entity' border, as well as in Palestine and other countries. Rather than accepting the logic of recent changes, multi-sited research, as George Marcus noted (1995: 105), follows threads, conjunctions and juxtapositions bound together by the research question. As such, this book could only benefit from further spatial and temporal extensions, beyond the Bosnian contexts.

My archival and library research in London, Sarajevo, Tuzla and Kreševo has facilitated this process. Conversations with friends and colleagues who have lived or worked in other contexts have informed me of additional connections between Bosnian and other sacral geographies. The possible extensions were a reminder that careful spatial and temporal boundaries, however artificial, need to be drawn for the purpose of narrative. The scope of this inquiry was limited by my one-year fieldwork in Bosnia and stints of investigation in Palestine and Israel. Research into the annual calendar as a particular social situation depended upon a given definition of its temporal and spatial boundaries. As George Kingsley Garbett (1970: 216) noted, the extent of these boundaries as well as any increase in the events, actors and cultural forms included, all add to the complexity of a situation. My work in the Field may thus be seen as the central part of an extended case study. Synchronic and diachronic extensions into secondary sites and other parts of the calendar have informed and tested my theoretical generalizations.

Marcus (1995) considered several 'tracking categories' in multi-sited fieldwork. The one I employed – following time through space – is perhaps closest to his analysis of 'following plot, story or allegory' (109), for the folk calendar is a relatively well-structured story. It includes actors, relationships, expositions, climaxes and resolutions (see Chapters 1 and 5). Particular versions of the story will have some of their pages torn out, especially after durable political pressures. The missing pages found elsewhere are often scribbled over, adapted, printed in different colours, but the main actors and their agentive qualities will make the binding possible. The pieced collection could be understood as both a single story and many independent and diverging stories. I have come to know the Bosnian folk calendar through an inductive approach, from a web of experiences and data; my attempt here is to simultaneously present some possible unified interpretations and the more focused idiosyncrasies.

Census and Consensus: Scalar Obstacles

I have indicated that this book builds on my multi-sited explorations, well beyond the Field. However, as I have conducted the majority of my research in the Field, my arguments are primarily 'grounded' in the knowledge about the lives of its people and their Georgic traditions.[16] This, I hope, has softened my own generalizations, and made this project useless for the prevalent forms of identitary violence in Bosnia. At the same time, my research in the

Field was multi-sited itself. I worked in different locales, which experienced almost no active interchange.

Although the Field is not a large physical space, there is an intricate problem to its definition as a unit of analysis. This problem can be broken down in terms of spatial and temporal scalar obstacles. They do not allow an easy 'socio-demographic' snapshot of the Field. Firstly, I have noticed that villages beyond the actual karst field, sometimes beyond the mountain, as in the cases of Ključ and Cernica, belong to the same symbolic and social network. Only on the surface were they 'physically' separated – the steep mountain passage of Sedlo, initially invisible to me, was used to make the crossing, particularly for Elijah's Day. Secondly, Gacko as a toponym may designate either the whole municipality with the villages, or the town proper only. Thirdly, one village often serves as the gravitational point for other smaller villages and hamlets. Again, this larger village toponym may be a reference to the whole cluster or only to itself. Finally, the substantial 'migrant' communities have complicated the problem of locating the Field. It now spreads over 'diasporic' and 'virtual' networks. For all of these reasons, my work does not pertain to a municipality or a physicaly mappable landscape.

In terms of temporal scales of residence, people in the Field belonged to several distinct groups: those who did not leave the Field in the 1990s; those who left in the early 1990s and returned after 1999; those who left in the early 1990s and took temporary residence in the Field during the warm season; those who left before or in the early 1990s and visited the Field for one or a few days (mostly for Elijah's Day); and, finally, those who left before or in the early 1990s and did not return. Each of these groups dealt with different contexts of identitary, legal and economic politics.

These spatiotemporal issues are intimately related to one overtly political scalar problem encapsulated in the controversies over the 2013 'Census of Population, Households and Dwellings in Bosnia and Herzegovina'. The results of the census were eventually published but remain unrecognized by the Republika Srpska government (which published its own, entity-specific version), partly because of the disagreements over the definition of resident population. The battle revolves around the people who have claimed residence in places like Gacko, mostly as returnees, but take residence elsewhere on a part-time or permanent basis. The results of the census thus determine whether 'part-time' and 'potential' future returnees are politically visible and measurable. For this work, it raises an important question on the disclosure of anthropological data. Is it ethically justifiable to provide quantified descriptions that might risk playing into the political campaigns pertaining to define territory and belonging and thus hinder future return? In providing you with an image that the state (and its would-be state of Republika Srpska) 'sees', I thus refrain, for the most part, from verifying any of the data.

TABLE 0.1 Gacko population, census comparison

	Total	Serb	Muslim	Croat	Yugoslav	Montenegrin	Roma
1981	10,279	6,215	3,424	21	380	215	0
1991	10,788	6,661	3,858	29	84	112	4
	Total	Serb	Bosniak	Croat	Undeclared/ Others/ Unknown		
2013 prelim.	9,734	?	?	?	?		
2013 B&H	8,990	8,556	369	15	3/41/6		
2013 RS	8,710	8,316	332	13	3/40/6		

Source: Retrieved from census details published by Bureau of Statistics of the Republic of Bosnia and Herzegovina (1993), Grabeljšek et al. (1983), Agency for Statistics in Bosnia and Herzegovina (2013, 2016) and Republika Srpska Institute for Statistics (2017).

In 2013, brief preliminary results of the 2013 census had been published, noting only the number of entered or enumerated persons, households and dwellings (see Table 0.1). After some reconsideration, the Agency for Statistics in Bosnia and Herzegovina (B&H) published its final results in 2016, followed by the Republika Srpska Institute for Statistics' (RS) own results in 2017, which both included an ethnic/religious enumeration. Everyone except Serbs, Croats and Muslims ('Bosniak' in the new census) were counted as 'others', 'undeclared' or 'unknown'. The overall Gacko population, which stayed roughly the same between 1981 and 1991, decreased by 1,054 in the preliminary results of the 2013 census and by 1,798/2,078 in the final results. The difference between the preliminary and the two versions of the final results probably has to do with the political tensions over the definition of 'permanent residency'. Muslims made 35.7%, Serbs 61.6% and all 'others' 2.1% of the total population in the 1991 census (not taking 'Yugoslavs' into account). In the state-published 2013 census, Bosniaks make 4.1%, Serbs 95.1% and all 'others' 0.5% of the total population. This stark difference would suggest that only 9.5% of the prewar Muslim ('Bosniak') population and 16% of some 'others' have returned, although this percentage is actually significantly lower, as it does not take into account the seasonal residents. There is a similar problem in other Bosnian municipalities. Wagner (2008: 5) noticed that although the return to Srebrenica, as in Gacko, started in 1999 and property had largely been returned to the prewar owners by 2005, actual permanent return was 'conspicuously low'.

I have not conducted any primary statistical research as part of my fieldwork. It included around 200 interlocutors who reside or used to reside in Gacko, and many more in other areas of Bosnia. In the Field, I have focused on two villages – Kula and Nadanići – where Elijah's Day took place. Because these are clusters of hamlets, I reference a more specific toponym to clarify some statements. When my interlocutors said that they are 'the only returnees' or 'the oldest person in their village', the claim functioned within the specific spatial context. Instead of defining any 'sample' of my interlocutors at the beginning of fieldwork, I approached the villages of Kula and Nadanići and followed stories by 'branching out'. As I attempted to grasp the flow of temporary migration, visits and holidays, I often gained interlocutors unexpectedly and for a short period of time. It was relatively difficult to estimate their economic status as the well-off Gačani from the diaspora sometimes took great care not to 'show off' when they visited. I was told that there are around forty returnee families, mostly to the village of Kula and surrounding hamlets. However, the households were often inhabited by one or two elderly people. (Counting returnee and ethnic bodies is a highly controversial endeavour, even without the politicized results of the 2013 census.) Looking through the listings by age from the 1991 census, it struck me that there were 161 children bellow fourteen years of age in the village of Kula and eight of its thirteen hamlets.[17] In 2011/2012, only one child, Kanita, lived in the same space, near an empty school optimistically reconstructed after the war.

Measuring Yugoslav Time and Ethno-national Territory

My interlocutors argued that Gacko was a relatively well-off area of ex-Yugoslavia. Their subsistence relied mostly on farming and, to a lesser extent, agriculture, and they were known for the local cow breed, as well as quality meat and dairy products. However, statistical data shows a significant increase in urban population between 1981 and 1991, which roughly corresponds to the decrease in rural population over the same time, but also to the number of employees in the mines and thermal power plant in Gacko (Bureau of Statistics of the Republic of Bosnia and Herzegovina 1993, Grabeljšek et al. 1983).

The sudden modernization might be gauged from the alluringly concise propaganda documentary, *Construction of Mine and Thermal Power Plant Gacko* (*Izgradnja rudnika i termoelektrane Gacko*). It was made by Hajrudin Krvavac (1984), a Yugoslav director celebrated for the 'partisan' genre. The film begins with images of shepherds running after herds of sheep and horses through the Field in front of the power plant and a narrative on the brutality of the bare life of the peasant. The narrator states: 'Here, the human being is destined to be born, to leave and never return, or stay and battle the cold and the wolves, wretched fate and such a god, always getting worse and worse, always after the flock – one's only hope'. Through the next hour, the film describes the 'glorious' transformation of landscape in meticulous detail. These necessitous humans of the Field, it says, grew crops and buried their dead, but could not even suspect the immeasurable layers of coal lying beneath, which were about to change their destiny. To this day, however, people in Gacko remember that the plant was constructed on top of the old locus of Elijah's Day celebrations in Jasike, thus violently displacing their most important annual ritual. Knowingly or not, the film underscores this spatiotemporal intervention. The narrator notes: 'Time here will once be measured like this: there will be the time before the mine and the thermal power plant and there will be the time after them'. However, time, as encapsulated by the traditional calendar, persisted – the Muslim celebrations of Elijah's Day festivities were moved to the village of Kula. The film brings rare footage from before, during and after the violent modernization. We get to see perhaps the last traditional horse races at Jasike juxtaposed to the power plant in 1974: 'old' and 'new' time beside to each other.

A curious discussion started online http://www.gacko.net, when the editors of the portal, who live in the United States, concluded that they recognized Jasike on an old illustration from a nineteenth-century edition of the British weekly newspaper *The Graphic* (see Z.Z. and Homogeceka 2010). The 1877 illustration and the 1974 footage speak of a 'long-gone' place that still lingers in the memories of the Field. The plant, just like the more recent nationalist histories, somehow failed its purpose; it never became the sole measure of time.

The decrease in agricultural activity, according to the documentary, was the socialist dream. The plant was supposed to emancipate. Its actual effects on rural economy were staggering. Between 1971 and 1991, we see a sharp decline in the number of sheep, horses and cows owned and the percentage of actively agricultural in overall active population slides from 83.6% in 1971 to only 17% in 1991 (see Table 0.2).

TABLE 0.2 Agriculture in Gacko, census comparison

	Number of sheep	Number of horses	Number of cows	Percentage of people actively agricultural in overall active population
1971	64,166	2,414	9,719	83.6%
1981	51,887	1,225	8,953	42.2%
1991	41,829	466	7,083	17%

Source: Retrieved from census details published by the Republican Bureau of Statistics of Bosnia and Herzegovina (1991) and Federal Bureau of Statistics of Bosnia and Herzegovina (1998a).

Judging by the official reports, the company Mines and Power Plant Gacko (RiTE Gacko) employed 1,600 people in 2013 and 1,774 people in 2014 (National Assembly of Republika Srpska 2015). This is 19.7% of the overall Gacko population according to the 2013 state-published census. At the same time, the company has not employed a single returnee. So, whom did they employ? Branislav Milekić, the General Director of the Power Utility of Republika Srpska reported that special care was taken that the new employees should come from 'the lines of soldier categories, families of deceased soldiers, disabled persons and the socially endangered' (ibid). The returnees generally argued that employment was given on an 'ethno-political' basis or 'friend and party lines'. At the time of my fieldwork, the press reported that the company had employed around one hundred members of the ruling Republika Srpska party (SNSD) as well as by recommendation of the regional Orthodox bishop (Vukanović 2012).

Ethnography after Ethnic Cleansing?

The making of connections towards a larger story is often achieved by zooming out of the temporal and spatial map. The 'particular' is used to paint the picture; it is put to work for various tropes. The 'smaller scales' – the intimate, the local, the vernacular, the idiosyncratic and other literary acts, in turn, are given as the substance – such stuff as abstractions are made of. This division is understood to require constant shifts from 'synthetic' to 'analytic' methods of perception (see e.g. Vernon 1971: 202–4). The problem with fitting the detail into the larger picture, as Sari Wastell (2001) has pointed out, is that it already presumes an evaluative judgement:

> The presence or absence of scale is important because when one talks about, for example, 'global' as opposed to 'local', the scale is already in place. Nothing is particularly 'local' unless it is measured against something 'bigger', less 'local' than itself – and here so many prejudices flee from analytical view ... The scale insists that we accept each manifestation of a local context as a constituent element of a global whole, each local perspective as a subjective position in an objective reality. (ibid: 186)

The 'detail' is fixed to the 'whole', both inherently imagined in each other. However, while these scales should be problematized, they cannot be escaped; they have reified – transformed into facts of being – the knowledge and practice of relation. Ethnographies harnessing the (already positioned) 'particular' still may be able to destabilize the presumptions of their own 'particularity'. And, more importantly, they have the potential to act as a critical obstacle to easy 'synthetic' accounts.

Throughout this book, intimacy (my interlocutors' and my own) with the Field of Gacko has been useful in inquiring into the possibility of scales. It has allowed for a turn towards a bodily relation to proximity and distance, a 'thick description', as Geertz (1993) called it:

> If anthropological interpretation is *constructing a reading* of what happens, then to divorce it from what happens — from what, in this time or that place, specific people say, what they do, what is done to them, and from the whole business of the world — is to divorce it from its *applications* and render it vacant. (ibid: 18, emphasis mine)

Importantly, 'thick description' should not simply situate the arguments, but also the researcher. I sometimes wonder which 'I', I am supposed to situate, the one before or the one after this research? (The two are far apart; the latter one visits a lush, wide-limbed oak in Hampstead Heath in London – Elijah's Tree – on 2 August.) The Field situates us as well. When they told me their world; it spilled into mine.[18] I apologize, but I cannot be your native to anything clear-cut. So, instead of the more usual introductory paragraphs, I offer reflexive moments throughout the book.

To bridge the traps of abstraction and particularity, Anna L. Tsing (2004: 2) called for the study of 'friction', 'the sticky materiality of practical encounters' through which the abstract scales are enacted. My methodological choice of also turning to friction implies a necessary complication of any recognized scale, be it the national or the traditional calendric structure in Bosnia. This research points to various deficiencies of ethnography as the name for its written outcome. The 'ethnie' (or 'ethnos') in ethnography needs to be qualified or abandoned. It has abstract boundaries and dangerous consequences. It allows us to present phrases like 'ethnic conflict' (or 'ethnic hatred', 'coexistence', 'mixing' and 'cleansing') as analytical concepts. What could the 'ethnie' in ethnography possibly signify? A biological subspecies of race, a culture, or, perhaps, a group of people strung together by religious, territorial and linguistic affiliation? The analytical shift from race to culture to ethnicity has been gradual (Jenkins 1999: 87). Ethnicity became a commonplace for anthropology only in the 1960s (ibid) and the fact that it has persisted into the twenty-first century is remarkable. Ethnography is not a floating signifier: it perpetuates its object, the ethnie, and when this object is more difficult to pinpoint, we manage to find it anyway. Arjun Appadurai's concept of 'ethnoscapes' only managed to spread the 'ethnie' over a differently imagined spatial horizon: 'The landscapes of group identity – the ethnoscapes – around the world are no longer familiar anthropological objects, insofar as groups are no longer tightly territorialized, spatially bounded, historically unselfconscious, or culturally homogeneous' (1991: 48).

Perhaps we cannot afford any longer to group the findings that go against the above-mentioned boundaries under the common signifier of ethnography. Recognizing discourses and practices of ethnicity is one thing; recognizing ethnicity as an object of analysis is something else. Ethnographers have successfully problematized the kind of evidence upon which ethnographies are constructed; the remaining problem is what ethnographies are constructed to be the evidence of. Lévi-Strauss has noted this problem of representation: 'Both history and ethnography are concerned with societies *other* than the one in which we live. Whether this *otherness* is due to remoteness in time (however slight), or to remoteness in space, or even to cultural heterogeneity, is of secondary importance compared to the basic similarity of perspective' (1963: 16).

More often than not, groups with 'essences' feature in our writing and, although we are disturbing these collectivizations, the very name we ascribe to our project speaks to the contrary. We are not only critical observers of collective meanings; we are participants in their creation and perpetuation. Ethnogenesis, as it pertains to Bosnia, expands this argument; working from/towards ethnies implies a field of vision that accepts collective essence and essential boundaries. Marcus Banks (1996), in the introduction to his book on the anthropological constructions of ethnicity, sets the problem with eleven quotations pertaining to the definition of ethnicity. What becomes obvious is that there is no unified interpretation, which has probably helped the term creep into contemporary scholarship. Ethnicity, Banks notes, is nothing more than 'a collection of rather simplistic and obvious statements about boundaries, otherness, goals and achievements, being and identity, descent and classification, that has been constructed as much by the anthropologist as by the subject' (ibid: 5).

For researchers working in Bosnia, ethnicized research also implies acceptance of the nationalist modus operandi. Within the contemporary political boundaries of Bosnia and Herzegovina, ethnicity cannot be taken as the scale (or, is it scope?) of inquiry without certain levels of violence and exclusion. Officially, according to the postwar Bosnian Constitution, there are three 'constitutive peoples' and 'the others'. The constitutive peoples, namely Croats, Serbs and Bosniaks, are entities equated with the Catholic, Orthodox and Muslim communities, respectively. The designation 'others', which swallows up the identities of sizeable and historically present communities, exhibits their unimportance to the nationalist project(s). Strongly bounded ethnicities were the prerequisite for the partition of Bosnia. The Catholic Croats would merge with the state of Croatia and the Orthodox Serbs with Serbia. The logic was to homogenize territories on the 'one religion, one nation, one language, one state' model.

As Duijzings (2003: 4) has pointed out, national identities in the Western Balkans were a nineteenth-century superimposition over religious identities: 'The image of fixed, stable and permanent ethnic groups and of "ancient ethnic hatreds" in the Balkans is misleading and inaccurate from both historical and anthropological perspectives'. There was not a single religiously 'homogeneous' township in Bosnia prior to the 1990s war. From the nationalist perspective, however, the three 'ethnies' continue to be misrepresented as respectively coherent and all those who have difficulty fitting themselves into this tripartite image have been erased. 'Others' are not legitimate candidates for membership in the Presidency or the House of Peoples. Dervo Sejdić, a Roma activist, and Jakob Finci, a Jewish politician, recently successfully contested this Constitutional provision before the European Court of Human Rights. The judgement, reached in 2009, has yet to be implemented, however.

My interlocutors used a number of words, sometimes interchangeably, to identify themselves. Many were frustrated with choices on offer, especially those who had lived under Yugoslavia or who belong to 'mixed' families and 'mixed' communities. Some preferred the term 'Bosnian' for all Bosnian citizens; some found their Yugoslav identity to be a stronger mode of resistance. In the Field, however, I encountered a conflation of Serb identity with Orthodox Christianity. For the Muslims, at least those who had returned, the naming situation was somewhat 'simpler'. Muslim was both a communal and a religious designation, which is probably largely due to the ethnic provisions of the socialist Yugoslavia, which recognized a Muslim ethnicity. Some Gacko Muslims, however, employed the term 'Bosniak' as well, reflecting the development of the nationalizing vocabulary since the 1990s.[19] The meanings inferred by 'Serb' and 'Bosniak' were equally incoherent, ranging from reference to pan-national identities to just a word for a local community with certain traditions. In other parts of Bosnia, Catholics have faced the confusing processes of Croat ethnicization. The Catholic clergy in the town of Stolac adamantly preached the national unity of all Croatians during the 2012 Elijah's Day celebrations. Yet, in many other towns in central and northern Bosnia, Catholics often described themselves as Bosnians or Bosnian Croats. Duijzings (2003) has argued that the violence of the 1990s reinforced national identities within communities that previously lacked loyalties of such strength. The initially confusing tapestry of identity politics, violence, memories and self-definitions is a product of different kinds of ideological and actual proximity/distance experienced by people over a relatively short span of time.

Religious (or, 'ethnic') background as an organizing principle of life in Bosnia is arguably not a new occurrence. Yet, strong territorial boundaries of ethnic groups, as ratified through the Dayton Agreement, certainly are (Hromadžić 2012: 32). As Halilovich (2013: 10) has pointed out, although the ideology of ethnicity was crucial to both the violence of the war of the 1990s and its aftermath, 'the emphasis on ethnicity as a natural and political group identity of Bosnians has come at the expense of shared place-based local identities – defined by local geography, cultural norms, dialect, kinship, neighbourliness, a common way of life and embodied relationship with the place and social networks' (2013: 10). The group identifiers in this book cannot be true to all the different definitions encountered. I have opted for the ones used by most of my interlocutors in a given place. Thus, in looking at Gacko, I re-employ 'Serb' (instead of 'Orthodox Christian' or 'Bosnian'), 'Muslim' (instead of 'Bosniak' or 'Bosnian') and 'Gurbeti' (instead of 'Roma' or 'Cigani' or 'Bosnian'). Alternatively, I also employ the term 'Gačani' (people from Gacko), the word implying a particular notion of non-ethnic local identity.

This research is 'ethnographic' insomuch as it places emphasis on a specific style of research that, as John Brewer (2000: 11) argued, attempts to acquire 'knowledge of the social world from intimate familiarity with it'. The familiarity is achieved through the key ethnographic method of participant observation. Participant observation is primarily inclined to experiential learning that implies an understanding 'from within'. This premise relies on the idea that social situations might be better understood after a certain proximity to the humans and nonhumans who take part in them. However, it implies distance too, always being on the outside, analytical.

The ethnopolitical discourses, coming from high-level politicians and clergy, attempt to redefine the spatial and temporal qualities of landscapes. The chief ideologues, however, only occasionally visit the smaller towns and villages. They use the opening ceremonies for memorials and restored or newly built temples to give charged public speeches about ethnic boundaries, historical rights and the dangers of unstable ethnic identities. Throughout the course of the year, however, these discourses trickle down via local politicians, activists and clergy, who, to be respected and voted for, inevitably have intimate ties with their 'flock'. These local leaders position themselves as gatekeepers and my access often depended on some kind of rapport with them.

The second type of agent is the politically marginalized individual. They sustain landscapes through daily practices, a kind of embodied knowledge. For these bodily dispositions that determine enactments and their perceptions, Bourdieu (see 1990, 2002) employed the notion of 'habitus': an 'embodied history, internalized as second nature and so forgotten as history [that] is the active presence of the whole past of which it is the product' (1990: 56). Turning to habitus as the site of memory (and history) implied accepting minute details of daily practices as evidence of landscapes rooted in the past. These landscapes are acted rather than memorialized. The kind of memory they exhibit is what Henri Bergson (1911) called 'habit-memory'. It is an embodied memory, shaped by the experienced environment, which becomes apparent through the 'action itself, and in the automatic setting in motion of a mechanism adapted to the circumstances' (ibid: 87). This kind of memory is more resilient to contemporary political and historical discourses. It is a space of condensed social meaning. I frequently asked my interlocutors: Why do you engage in this ritual? What is the meaning of this festivity? The response I heard time and again was: This is how it is done. It has always been done so.

Roots of Religious Nationalism

The ethnonational terms that I have encountered in the Field have been unevenly amalgamated with religious difference; 'Muslim' and 'Serb' were often but shorthand for the religious communities. During his fieldwork in a central Bosnian Muslim village, David Henig was asked about the number of Serbs and Croats in his native Czech Republic by people who wanted to know about the Catholic and Orthodox Christians (2011: 22). Similarly, more than twenty years earlier, during her fieldwork, Cornelia Sorabji was asked if she was a Catholic or a Serb (1989: 20–21). These confused designations have much to do with the histories of nationalisms that pertained to define Bosnian (and wider) religious communities. Contemporary religious nationalisms in Bosnia may arguably be traced back to the articulation of Ottoman social pluralism. The *millet* system, which provided some self-government to the religious communities, also defined difference along religious lines. It eventually served as the basis for the imagination of national communities in the nineteenth century and the projects to create new, homogenous nation-states (Banac 1984: 64, Bryant 2016: 4, Henig 2011: 21–22). For example, the Peć patriarchate had jurisdiction over large territories inhabited by Orthodox Christians, including Bosnia (Banac 1984: 64). A similar centralized power was given to the Serbian Orthodox Church in the Yugoslav monarchy (Perica 2002: 8), one that continued in the socialist Yugoslavia. Due to the 'universalist' direction of the Muslim *millet,* Bosnian Muslims did not develop their version of religious nationalism at the same time (Todorova 1997: 172–78, Banac 1984: 66).

Vjekoslav Perica (2002) has argued that the rise of religious nationalism in the socialist Yugoslavia has its roots in the 'ethnicization' of religion that started much earlier. In the case of Serbian nationalism, based on the Kosovo myth and the cult of 'ethnic saints', the gradual fusing of ethno-national and religious identity can be traced at least to the end of the eighteenth century (ibid: 7–8). The full-scale nationalisms of the nineteenth century have been nurtured firstly on linguistic and then on religious difference (Todorova 1997: 176–77). Austria-Hungary, on the other hand, supported both the idea of *Bošnjaštvo* ('Bosniakness'), a distinct trans-religious Bosnian nationality (Banac 1984: 260) and the development of separate religious and cultural movements. Bosnian Muslims gained an autonomous religious organization and a religious leader (*Reis ul-ulema*) soon after the annexation, in 1882 (Malcolm 1995: 196). This organization was the root of what would later become *Islamska zajednica* (Islamic Community) with jurisdiction over Muslims in all the socialist Yugoslav republics. Bosnian nationality was never introduced and, although the Islamic Community was particularly co-opted by the Yugoslav state (cf. Duijzings 2000: 112), Muslims were not recognized as a nationality until 1968 (Perica 2002: xxiii).

Religious identities and institutions were co-opted into the Yugoslav nationalisms of the Second World War, not only through the equation of religion to ethnicity and the correlated crimes, but also through the fact that the 'leaders of religious organizations backed the nationalist factions directly or indirectly' (Perica 2002: 23). There were high-level endorsements from the Orthodox Church for both the Četniks and Nedić's Nazi regime in Serbia and from the Catholic Church and some Muslim clerics to the Croatian Nazi regime, although many supported the Partisans as well (ibid). After the war, much of the prior religious nationalism, now expressed as anti-Yugoslav sentiment, continued within the various diasporas (ibid: 28).

A number of events throughout the 1980s, after Tito's death, have been related to the strengthening of religious nationalism, from the Međugorje apparitions and the recentring of Kosovo and Bleiburg claims, to the trials of nationalists, many of whom would soon be at the forefront of the new ethno-national parties. In 1990, the Islamic Community commemorated five hundred years of Islam in Bosnia and 'restored' the Ajvatovica pilgrimage, whilst the Serbian Orthodox Church organized a yearlong commemoration of Serbian victims of the Second World War (see Perica 2002: 86, 120 and Henig 2012b: 756). Belaj (2012: 83–85) describes the state reaction to the Međugorje apparitions and the widespread interpretation of the phenomenon as a revival of nationalism, which included police interventions to stop pilgrim access to the site.

Teferič and the State

At the beginning of the twentieth century, four 'cultural-educational' organizations were established in the Austro-Hungarian Bosnia: Gajret for Muslims, Prosvjeta for Serbs, Napredak for Croats and La Benevolencija for Jewish people. With many local branches, they were allowed to organize public events, as well as make use of ethnonyms and national flags (Hadžibegović and Kamberović 1997). During the first Yugoslavia, *Alidun* festivities in Gacko (at Jasike), with horse races and athletic competitions, were always organized by Gajret, which would provide concessions for the sale of drinks and food. Likewise, Prosvjeta organized the *Ilindan* gatherings in Nadanići. The two organizations cooperated and even had a joint boarding school for high school students (Hasanbegović 2000). All the national/cultural societies were abolished by 1949 in the socialist Yugoslavia (Hadžibegović and Kamberović 1997: 53), although they were 'revived' in 1990. After 1949, the coordination of Elijah's Day in Gacko shifted towards the local branches of the Serbian Orthodox Church and Islamic Community. These institutions increasingly attempted to exert control over the organization of religious events (cf. Sarač-Rujanac 2014: 116, Sorabji 1989: 137–41).

It is difficult to agree on the degree and extent of the pressure that the socialist Yugoslav state applied on religious life in the Bosnian villages. My interlocutors have certainly informed me about some forms of intimidation. For example, party members were expected not to attend religious funerals, even for members of their family, and circumcizing your son risked party interrogation and excommunication. Others have noted bans of rituals and processions, police surveillance of religious practices, expulsions from the party after a child's christening and imprisonment for those who claimed to have witnessed apparitions (see, for example, Mojzes 1986: 31–33 and Henig 2011: 92, 102).

During this time, many religious practices were thus reserved for the private domain (Henig 2011: 28). Reflecting on the Yugoslav laws from the 1970s, Paul Mojzes has noted: 'No special permission is needed for activities within church buildings, but for any out-of-door activities permits must be sought, and such permits have often been denied' (1986: 29). Additionally, Bringa noticed:

> [a]n interesting parallel between the way the I.Z [Islamic Community] tended to take over and direct religious customs and rituals that had earlier been initiated by the individual household or the local community, and the way the regional branch of the communist youth organization was taking over the organization of the traditional *teferić* or fair, and, indirectly, the *sijelo* through the Saturday dance. (1995: 250)

One of my interlocutors remembered that *teferič* was banned one year by the Gacko police 'after some fight broke out'. However, this was related to the escalation of the traditional fistfights and was not understood as a suppression of religious activities. In fact, because of the 'secular' and 'folk' appearance of the *teferič* festivities, these events seem to have been able to survive in socialist Yugoslavia with little interruption. Zulfikarpašić noted that Elijah's Day *teferič* was primarily 'tolerated' as a folk rather than a religious custom (see Đilas and Gaće 1994: 54). This 'secular flavour' was preserved in the postsocialist period. The parish priest for Gacko told me how he preferred the Elijah's Day church service to the 'alcohol-fuelled' celebrations that followed. Henig's (2012b: 758) interlocutors also drew a distinction between Ajvatovica, which they saw as but a *teferič*, void of religious substance, and the prayer (*dova*) in Karići. Henig notes:

> Indeed, as some older Muslims often pointed out to me, 'Prayer for rain, it was the only place and moment where you could even meet people engaged with the [Communist] Party', as these events were usually organized with special approval under the official umbrella of traditional village parades (*teferič*) and gatherings (*tradicijonalno okupljanje*). (ibid: 760)

All of this gives us an idea about the state's allowances for *teferič*, seen as more traditional than religious, but also the imaginative strategies of circumventing the prohibitions. These strategies built on the already discussed problem of defining the boundaries of rural Bosnian religiosity.

Yugoslav socialism also appropriated the main themes of the seasonal get-togethers, so we can speak of a syncretism between the state and the traditional calendars. The 1 May (*prvomajski*) *teferič* for the International Workers' Day was, and continues to be, a widespread practice in Bosnia. It looked like any other seasonal party and occasionally incorporated ritual elements of Annunciation and George's Day, like the hilltop bonfires. The Yugoslav socialist calendar, Dunja Rihtman-Auguštin (1990: 29) has noted, did seem to follow the basics of the traditional and religious cycle of winter and spring holidays, but imposed its own rhythm 'by anticipating or postponing' the important moments. Traditional Tuesday gatherings were sometimes moved to Saturdays or Sundays to accommodate the state calendar (Henig 2015: 138). Similarly, the returnees to Gacko moved the date of *Aliđun* to accommodate the diasporic attendance (often agreed over social media). This readiness to be flexible in light of new political and social circumstances should be seen as an important element of resistance in Bosnian folk cosmology.

Despite the co-optation of religious institutions by the state, the local clergy also had day-to-day contact with the people, which diluted some of the top-down agendas. During her fieldwork in Yugoslavia in 1987–1988, Bringa witnessed a George's Day *teferič* in a central Bosnian village, which was held 'on the highest hill' (1995: 225–26). It was obviously a substantial gathering with ritual and festival elements, chiefly focused on young and unmarried girls who threw shoes over their houses to determine the direction of marriage proposals (like the nettle and bread in Gacko) and visited mills to gather water (*omaha*). On the eve of George's day, boys made flutes from the wood of young trees with which they would wake up the girls in the morning. The *teferič* included picnics and football games. Additionally, Bringa notes that Vasvija, one of her interlocutors, 'disapproved of the *hodža* for discouraging them from celebrating' (ibid: 226) and insisting on the 'Muslim new year' as a substitution for George's Day. Both the villagers and the clergy displayed certain corrective agency, basing the argumentation either in doctrine or tradition.

We can also speak of the changing circumstances and the post-1960s Yugoslav 'liberal phase' when the Serbian Orthodox Church flourished (Perica 2002: 8) and the Muslims gained recognition as a nation after the creation of the Non-Aligned Movement. The 1965 issue of the *Herald of the Islamic Community* gives a description of the celebrations marking the restoration of the Kula mosque (Bečić 1965). It reports the 'surprise visit' of Hadži Sulejman Kemura, the Head of the Islamic Community in Yugoslavia ('His Highness, the *Reis-ul-ulema*'), 'with an escort' of other dignitaries. The event was also attended by the local government officials, including the President of the Gacko Municipality Assembly and the President of the Commission for Religious Affairs. These representatives of the state are all mentioned by the title 'comrade' (*drug*). The *Reis-ul-ulema*'s speech praised Yugoslav 'democratic liberties' and appealed for the mosque to be used 'for its purpose', namely 'religious education and the performance of religious duties'. He also called for the 'brotherhood and unity' between the different religious communities, which the 'enemy' attempted to destroy in the past. Comrade Živko Lojević, President of the Municipality Assembly, expressed regrets that he did not receive a timely notification of *Reis-ul-ulema*'s visit, as they would have otherwise been able to make it more 'visible'. He further said that 'the practice of religion in our country is free' and that the cooperation (of the local government) with Islamic Community is 'good'. Other speakers also described the religious liberties enshrined in the Yugoslav Constitution. This was, according to the article, the first visit of any religious leader to Kula and the region. After the ceremony, where the people reportedly applauded in tears, a *teferič* with songs and *kolo* dance was spontaneously organized.

Although published in the official *Herald,* this snippet of life in the Field speaks volumes of the changes that occurred in the 1960s. It points to the alliance between the state and the Islamic Community, but also to their new orientation within which the village of Kula was suddenly 'mapped'. After some three hours of 'intervention', the *teferič* was something that belonged to the 'crowd' rather than the dignitaries. It was the same during my fieldwork; after the *mevlud* in the mosque and the service in the church, it was the time for the much less state-structured 'folk programme', which was often disliked and unattended by the clergy.

False Binaries and the Destruction of the Bosnian Village

Another perspective on the question of state influence on religious life has to do with the rural/urban divide. The rural settings made some allowances beyond the socialist emancipatory project. Bringa (1995: 62) argued that the village and the neighbourhood were felt as a zone where 'ethno-religious distinctiveness' was expressed much more publicly than in the cities. The villages were often difficult to supervise: the Field was on the margins of the state and most of the villages were on the margins of the Field; it took both time and effort to reach them. As this book largely speaks of a rural landscape sitting along the Dinaric mountain chain and engages with its heritage of 'heroic' epics, I will briefly outline some of the highly problematic historical and contemporary qualifications of this space, its people and its traditions. In particular, I focus on the oft-espoused idea that the Dinarides were some kind of enclave for the nationalism that erupted in the 1990s.

The 1990s wars have been repeatedly represented as the destruction of the city and the 'revenge of the countryside'. Bougarel (1999) noted how the city/village binary came to constitute a rather common discourse, variously employed by intellectuals. He traces the roots of this problem in the works of the Serbian geographer and ethnologist Jovan Cvijić, Croatian sociologist Dinko Tomašić, as well as a number of latter (particularly wartime) revivals of their arguments. Although offering principally the same schemata of social, cultural and psychological 'types', these authors prescribe different moral qualities to the (Dinaric) village: Ottoman bandits become either heroes of national liberation or criminals and plunderers; their songs are either brave yearnings or ominous aggression.

Cvijić (1922 and 1931), in his two-volume treatise of the Balkan Peninsula, established the 'Dinaric type' that is 'instantly recognizable ... with the best-expressed features of all the South Slavs'. These features are of 'deeper meaning and more national'. 'The Dinaric man burns with the desire to avenge "Kosovo"' and 'considers himself to be chosen by God to fulfil the national duty. All of these eternal thoughts he expresses in songs and stories, even in funeral lamentations' (Cvijić 1931: 15). He also notes:

> Those people are powerful and strong, generally very tall, slender, almost never obese, with face full of expression, falcon's eyes, the best breed in the Balkan Peninsula. They have almost no degenerate types. They gain with bold, highlander's morals, deep feeling for the community and a dedication that does not cease even before the most precious of sacrifices. (Cvijić 1992: 85)

In this racial constellation, he gave particular superiority to the Ottoman bandits (*hajduci*), who have prepared the grounds for national liberation (ibid: 216).

Tomašić (1993), who simply switched the moral high ground (away from the highlands), thought that the Dinaric space had produced tribal and patriarchal societies, which glorified heroism and crime, especially through the figures of the bandits (*hajduk, uskok, četnik*). He provides a list of 'original tribal and *hajduk-uskok* psychological and cultural traits ... at odds with the standards set by the Western-European civilization' (ibid: 904–5). Some of these traits are the hierarchical organization of tribes, heroism (*junaštvo*), looting and plundering. These people have, he argued, strengthened enmity through blood revenge and a quest for pride, fame and honour, which built impulsive and aggressive personalities, pushy and bullying types, who glorified their crimes in heroic songs (ibid).

Echoes of this binary were employed to qualify the viciousness of the 1990s wars, sometimes rather eloquently. Bogdan Bogdanović, perhaps the most famous Yugoslav architect and theoretician, whose scholarship dwelt on the phenomenology of the city, spoke about an 'archetypal fear of the city' (2008: 37) and the 'restless epic man' who needs to be introduced to the meaning of *pax urbana* (ibid: 128). Likewise, in one wartime interview from Geneva, Adil Zulfikarpašić, the founder of the Bosniak Institute in Sarajevo, argued that the 'natives of the city' did not cause the war, as they had a culture of moderation and tolerance (Đilas and Gaće 1994: 71). He further remarked: 'One of the tragedies of the current war is that this nonurban, I won't say semisavage, but certainly uncivilized, part of the population became the agent of warfare' (ibid). As Kolind (2008: 151–56) observed, the postwar returnees to Stolac also employed this logic to explain the violent unmaking of their town. Most of my interlocutors, however, did not have this narrative at their disposal. If anything, they sometimes reversed it, blaming those who charted out grand histories in their urban armchairs.

Beyond the ethno-racial fantasy, these arguments present other dangers. They obfuscate the traditions and cosmologies of the Dinaric villages, blurring them with the mythology of the Balkan ethno-national enterprises. They project causality between the epic and the nationalist violence. As I argue in Chapter 4, parts of the Dinaric folklore, including the *gusle* tradition, have been gradually cleansed of their original common (or, 'shared') qualities and associated with the crimes of the state(-making). Bougarel likewise argued that this '"ethnicization" of mountains' attributes is fallacious' (1999: 165). My whole book may be read as an argument on the richness of 'intercommunal' rapport in the Bosnian village, sometimes similar to, other times different from, the various other rural and urban lives across the region, but always significantly divergent from the nationalist imaginations of pure traditions.

So, what have the Field's villages contributed to warfare? Have they been the igniting loci of the 1990s violence? No, they have imaginatively endured the cascade of propaganda. Repeating the misconception of his academic colleagues, Kolind (2008: 158) notes: 'One might see these major cities as living proof against the nationalist dream of ethnic homogeneity. The cities were ethnically mixed and a cosmopolitan attitude prevailed'. Rural 'mixture', however, leaves behind less 'architectural' remains; it requires a wholly different approach, for example a move away from the spatial to the temporal structures of proximity. When it turns the highlanders into the murderers of the city, the ideology of the 'rural Dinaric type' omits the effects of the war on rural life, which often amounted to the unmaking of the village ('ruricide', if you will). I attempt to transgress this problem by also engaging with the destruction of the intangible in Gacko, a plethora of *longue durée* connections that often remains invisible to the eyes saturated by the fragmented material being of the Bosnian city.

Landscapes as Archives

Secluded upon a rock in the forest, an old man, Ajvaz Dedo, prayed to God for water to reach his village. His prayer lasted for forty days and forty nights. On the last night, he fell asleep and dreamt of two white rams colliding in the air. When he woke up, the rock beneath him had split in two and water was bursting through the crevice. So goes the legend that sustains Ajvatovica, the largest Muslim pilgrimage site in Europe, also known as 'the small *hajj*'. Each year in late June, tens of thousands pass through the crevice. I made the pilgrimage in 2012. Passage through the crevice was the dramatic culmination of a long and steep climb up the mountain. Some women took out their prayer mats to perform *namaz* (prostration, or *salat*). Others picked up pieces of the rock lying on the floor and, murmuring something indistinctly, struck it against the walls of the cliff; one girl told me it was for good luck. The rocks were taken home, as an amulet. Apparently, they also used to be milled into dust to fertilize the crops (see Hadžijahić 1981).[20] So I, too, completed the brief ritual and carried a few rocks to London in my rucksack. Later on, I gave it to friends for prosperity and fertility.

Quite a few of these thought-capturing objects have made their way into my growing collection of research-related books, documents, audio recordings, photographs and transcriptions. As they continued to inform and shape my arguments, I could not but think of them as important archival material. For, landscapes become when something distinct can be said of their selfhood; they affect, emit a tone upon us, through their (lack of) interactions, orientations and memories. They densify around the human–nonhuman fragments, revealing multiple discursive and affective layers and opening up a possibility of archival readings.

The 'historical' narratives I have collected take the form of epic poetry, folk songs and personal memories that pertain to landscapes and seasonal festivities. Most of this material has been recorded, with the permission of my interlocutors. Other collections have been added to my own. For example, Eno decided to write down all the Gacko proverbs he could remember, which amounted to ten pages of surprisingly useful analytical tools. I have received mix-tapes with traditional songs and photographs from family albums. These tangible and intangible possessions bridged the gaps in my understanding of the individual and group trajectories in the Field.

I have entered into various kinds of dialogue that informed this book. They were, for the most part, conversations, unstructured and semi-structured interviews. The annual cycle is related to almost every facet of human existence, so stories about crops, food, neighbourhoods, diaspora, wars, politics and cattle were all related to the meaning and the process of the seasonal landscapes. Overall, I ended up with some 340 hours of recorded conversations alone. Many of them turned seamlessly into kinds of life-history. After some time, when most of the obvious questions had been asked, the day-to-day, completely unmethodical, conversations seemed a more honest approach. As Antoinette Errante (2000: 20) noted, one is not confronted with a combination of 'data' and whatever surrounds it, but with something much more interesting and surprising – another person:

> I stopped listening for what I could extract from the narrative and started listening to the whole person. There is no easy way to translate this into a methodology; it is not an attitude you can feign; but it results in narrators feeling that they have an appreciative and respectful audience.

As an appreciative audience, I soon gained some rapport with the Field's villagers and was able to join in on a 'normal' day. Painting Delva's kitchen and watching telenovelas with older women was interwoven with narratives about the sacral calendar. During picnics with 'refugee' visitors, I was allowed to experience some of their encounters with the landscapes that simultaneously shaped and caused their lives to rupture. Waking up at four in the morning to join Eno and the 'reconstruction crew', feeling their insecurities in the town centre and vigorously working to piece together something that was destroyed, was crucial to my understanding of life as it is lived, rather than some ideal model of the calendar grounded in the past.

I was often able to implement the time allocation technique (cf. Gross: 1984) by closely observing and recording how individuals or groups spent their day. My presence was less intrusive as I became known to the communities. The time allocation technique was useful to understand the patterns of 'ordinary' days as well as the local celebrations. It clarified how certain actions become embodied. For example, by collecting tree branches and lighting John's Day bonfires with kids in the town of Kreševo, I understood not only the structure of the ritual, but also experienced the affective elements of gatherings which existed in the memories of my interlocutors from the Field.

I have employed the 'life-hi/story' method, mostly in the villages of Kula and Nadanići. The syntagm 'life-hi/story', as opposed to 'life-history', suggests that important dimensions may also be found in fiction. As Jeff Titon (1980: 278) noted, '[a] story is made, but history is found out. Story is language at play; history is language at work'. Stories about fairies, magical sparks and supernatural caves have often been more informative than a mere chronology of events. Some of my interlocutors were extraordinarily gifted storytellers. My translations cannot do justice to their narratives, although I have included them throughout this book. People able to skilfully tell a story are 'perceptually attuned' to gathering information about the environment, as Ingold (1993: 153) noted, but also to guiding others through the landscape with that knowledge.

While knowing the language proved an extremely important asset, I soon understood that knowing the language and knowing how to communicate are not necessarily the same (see Agar 2007). The language of my interlocutors was not only much richer than my own, but also reflected an intimate knowledge of the Field. I made an attempt to understand the symbols, dispositions, histories, and then listen to the stories again, after attaining some feeling for those contexts. Similarly, Evans-Pritchard (1951: 79) argued that being able to think in the symbols employed by the community is a prerequisite for understanding how they think and what they are talking about. This knowledge comes mainly from experience. Joining the *kolo* (traditional circle dance) during the seasonal festivities, feeling the kind of *communitas* it creates, gives a different perspective on all those depictions of *kolo* on mediaeval Bosnian tombstones and its centrality at popular fairs. Having to learn this language within language made me uneasy about assuming the role of 'native ethnographer'. I kept repeating the question raised by Coleman and Collins (2006: 9): 'How close to home is "home" . . . ?'

Cognitive Mapping

> Every story is a travel story – a spatial practice.
> . . .
> . . . the map has slowly disengaged itself from the itineraries that were the condition of its possibility.
>
> —Michel De Certeau, *The Practice of Everyday Life*

Fieldwork is a specific kind of spatial practice. It always begins with some type of map into which the researcher descends. Upon deciding to go to

Gacko, a place I had never visited before, I was not equipped with much more than a discursive geographical package. I employed my knowledge of the correspondingly discursive economies and, instead of opting for the central Sarajevo bus station, I chose the cheaper ticket from the eastern suburbs of Sarajevo. My travel itinerary was already indicative of the kind of geography-in-the-making to which Gacko had been subscribed in the 1990s. After its departure from Eastern Sarajevo, or 'Serb Sarajevo' as it was officially known for a decade, the minibus stopped to let off and receive passengers at homogenized villages and towns along its route. In other words, we had been carefully driven through the jurisdiction of the Republika Srpska, the 'Serb Republic', one of the entities forged in the war of 1990s and confirmed through the Dayton Peace Agreement.

Like pages from a political science publication on postwar Yugoslavia, dark masterpieces of nationalist masonry along the road rendered memory from their strategic public positions. However systematically arranged, these monuments were far from monumentality in their mismatch of the belated modernist impetus and a postmodern language. Passing through this 'new history' seemed to be a rather common experience for my fellow passengers. They kept mostly to themselves while the popular music on the radio ornamented their silence.

Heads noticeably turned towards the outside only once we had reached the picturesque village of Tjentište. Opening beneath the mountains, stood a monument par excellence, a battle site of the Second World War marked quite literally by the 'life and times of Tito'. The battle was portrayed in the celebrated Yugoslav film *Sutjeska,* starring Richard Burton in the role of Tito. Known as the 'Valley of Heroes', the memorial was a much more eloquent 'truth' on this path of various victors. Its irrefutable simplicity, designed to echo the horrors of battle, instead awakened nostalgia for a time that seemed equally simple. This was a monument to itself, to the kind of Zeitgeist that gave birth to it, not to the bloody event that happened exactly seventy years before my fieldwork. As such, it stretched from an interval into an altogether different kind of time.

On another trip to Gacko, two young men sitting in front of me started a passionate refutation of the current political rhetoric. One of them said something that I typed into my mobile phone: 'If it weren't for the daily news, I wouldn't know where I live. They are constantly inciting people; the RS [Serb Republic] will secede – the RS will not secede. And they themselves are lounging and taking coffee'.

The minibus soon passed some 'SNSD Dodik' graffiti and road signs on which any words in the Roman alphabet had been sprayed over. Milorad Dodik, the president of the SNSD party (the Alliance of Independent Social Democrats) and President of the Serb Republic, has built his career upon the idea of the Serb Republic's autonomy from Bosnia and Herzegovina. The discursively (re)mapped space, as I learnt from my eavesdropping, has shifted landscapes and its people into an identity crisis.

The method of cognitive mapping, which I used in different locations, attempts to look at space beyond the official map, from the perspective of embodied spatial and temporal practices. Although the method traditionally turns to the spatial elements of landscapes, the calendar-related places discussed in this research and the trajectories of rituals and everyday practices combine to make it an equally legitimate endeavour into the temporal. Building on Bourdieu's arguments, Gell (1985) preferred to differentiate between mental mapping and what he called 'practical way-finding', as the latter centres on the agent. The kind of 'practical space' he describes – embodied and activity-based – corresponds to what I have encountered in this research.

I employed this method in a number of ways. I often asked my interlocutors to draw a personal constellation of their landscapes. The maps were usually part of a story, and so depictions of specific itineraries or relational spaces. Eno's memories of nomadic Gurbeti ('Roma') communities and their camping sites in the Field were substantiated by his map of almost military precision. In the town of Visoko, Melina charted for me the movement of Roma people on George's Day celebrations. The central points on these maps were not the squares or main roads; they were determined by the specific story. To invoke De Certeau (1984: 129) once again, '[w]hat the map cuts up, the story cuts across'. The folk, sacral calendar cuts across all kinds of boundaries. I made many of the cognitive maps myself, either as I was charting them in front of my interlocutors, while listening to their stories, or when I amalgamated the different narratives with my own movements through the landscapes. Kimberley Powell (2010: 553) has argued that cognitive mapping methods foreground the mutually constitutive aspects of place and social relationships. To varying degrees, the maps that inform this research also contain my own presence within the web of spatial and temporal engagements.

The third type of cognitive mapping method that I have employed was experimental. It produced a discussion between the archival maps and the cognitive maps as archives. The 'Dayton' map of Bosnia was well known to all of my interlocutors. My research in two private archives in the towns of Tuzla and Sarajevo led me to copies of fin-de-siècle Austro-Hungarian and Yugoslav military maps of the Gacko region. The Austro-Hungarian Empire made the first detailed maps of Bosnia in general. They contain many older topographic details. The Yugoslav military maps, however, contained enough topographic information to be considered 'classified' during the 1990s war. I carried a printed copy of these maps with me. Many stories developed from the recorded toponyms, terrain and infrastructures. Some places did not exist or were no longer accessible. Others unearthed memories. The reverse process was also useful. My interlocutors analysed the maps after specific conversations, reflecting upon the similarities and discrepancies between the maps and their experiences.

Starting from Tilley's (1994: 19) argument that 'names create landscapes', I have implemented an auxiliary method of toponomastics, a study of place names and place naming, in order to understand the memory, history, emotions and practices associated with specific sites. The vast scholarship on Proto-Slavic mythology was central to this endeavour. Through the semantic and etymological analyses of place names, I established countless links between contemporary practices and the Old Slavic pantheon. Similar ethnographic analogies, possibilities of correlating landscapes of the past with those of the living communities, were made through other objects, narratives and practices.

The methods used in this research have attempted to overcome the gap between the large-scale abstractions, most often violently encroaching upon Bosnian seasonal landscapes, and the embodied knowledge of the Field's inhabitants – 'the world as it is known to those who dwell therein' (Ingold 1993: 156). The book, as I have argued, is neither an ethnography nor a historiography. Following my attempts to understand the multiple facets of time-reckoning in the Field, I would rather describe it as a chronography.

Notes

1. Ilija is pronounced as 'Ill-ee-uh' and Alija as 'Ah-lee-uh'.
2. As a general rule, I write 'Elijah' and 'George', not 'Saint Elijah' and 'Saint George' as the designation of sainthood does not occur in common Bosnian names for their feasts (*Ilindan/Aliđun* and *Jurjevo/Đurđevdan*). Exceptions to this translation may be found in quotations, references to hagiographies or when my interoluctors themselves refer to sainthood.
3. Despite the apparent success of the homogenizing conflict, this book speaks to the tangible and intangible remnants of shared life as obstacles to religious 'purification' in the Field.
4. This research began in October of 2010 and ended in October of 2015. From September of 2011 until September of 2012, I was based in and around the Field of Gacko, but also conducted investigations in numerous other locations in Bosnia (Ajvatovica, Foča, Kladanj, Kreševo, Međugorje, Mokro, Prusac, Ratiš, Sarajevo, Stolac, Tuzla, Visoko). I have conducted some research in Palestine and Israel in December of 2013 and January 2014. I prefer to understand 'fieldwork' as inclusive of my writing and conversations in other spaces as well.
5. In many parts of Bosnia, the warm season also includes Muslim *dove* (prayers, particularly for rain), some of which have grown into occasions of pilgrimage. The prayer meetings were usually organized in relation to George's Day (on subsequent Mondays and Tuesdays) and usually ended before Elijah's Day (cf. Henig 2011: 187).

6. With other authors, you will encounter different phrases for the 1990s conflict in Bosnia (e.g. 'civil war', 'war on Bosnia', 'Bosnian war', etc.). I use the phrase '1990s war', not to avoid this discussion, but to indicate that the systematic, nationalist orgy of violence in the ex-Yugoslav countries was, and continues to be, co-orchestrated. Precisely because of that, the phrase 'civil war' (as applied to Bosnia) needs to be discarded. Was it, however, a war 'on Bosnia'? Due to its perceived religious (or 'ethno-national') 'mixtures' and 'diversity', Bosnia suffered a purification similar to parts of Serbia, Kosovo and Croatia. The 1990s war was thus primarily a series of systematic, militarized, territorial nationalist campaigns, which were expressed most vehemently in spaces where the perceived diversity positioned strategies of Othering. A general term, 'the 1990s war', could then be applicable to the violence in Bosnia, Croatia and Kosovo, which all had the same nationalist foundation (regardless of 'who' the perpetrators or the victims are).
7. In Bosnian: (1) *Polahko dok se hodžino samelje*; (2) *Ne crkni kenjče dok gora ne ozeleni*; (3) *Tiha voda bregove valja*.
8. All translations are mine, unless indicated otherwise.
9. See 'Vučić i Dodik: Da zajedno slavimo Vidovdan!' published in the *Telegraf* on 13 June 2014. (Retrieved 12 June 2014 at http://www.telegraf.rs/vesti/politika/1112114-vucic-i-dodik-da-zajedno-slavimo-vidovdan on 13 June 2014.) This strategic discourse was conceptualized by Nenad Kecmanović, a scholar closely allied with the Serb hard-line nationalist politicians, in his book *The Impossible State: Bosnia and Herzegovina* (2007: 7, published in Bosnian).
10. See also Hromadžić (2011 and 2015).
11. See, for example, Hayden (2002a, 2002b, 2007), Bowman (2012) and the responses following Hayden's (2002a) article in *Current Anthropology*.
12. For the Slavs in general, see Ovsec (1991), Gimbutas (1971, 2004), Kulušić (1979), Mikhailov (2002), Kononenko (2007); for Serbs and Croats, see Nodilo (1981), Gavazzi (1939), Čajkanović and Cajić (1995), Belaj (1998).
13. Hadžijahić and Purivatra (1990: 186–87) compiled a bibliography on these tensions.
14. See Lilek (e.g. 1893, 1894) and Truhelka (e.g. 1894, 1941) amongst many others.
15. For a discussion of the more prominent scholarship on *komšiluk* see Sorabji (2008) and Henig (2011: 116–36, 2012a).
16. Throughout the book, I have adopted the adjective 'Georgic' to describe the ecological aspect of the pastoral and agricultural calendar. As a noun, from the Greek *geō-* ('earth') and *ergon* ('work'), 'Georgic' indicates the focus of both my interlocutors' narratives about the calendar and this book (see Haddad 1969 and Chapter 5 of this book). I capitalize it, because the folk annual cycle in Bosnia (and elsewhere) begins with George's Day.
17. These figures were reported for Kula proper, as well as Bašići, Branilovići, Drugovići, Hodinići, Međuljići, Mekavci, Muhovići and Stolac (Federal Bureau of Statistics of Bosnia and Herzegovina 1998b).
18. Katherine P. Ewing (1994) has nicely described the 'epistemological abyss' often created between anthropologists and their interlocutors, one that I have tried to transgress by leaving both the book and myself open to the Field's ontologies.
19. 'Bosniak', it should be noted, has largely been synonymous with 'Bosnian' in historical records since the Middle Ages.
20. Henig (2012b) and Sarač-Rujanac (2013 and 2014) have written about Ajvatovica in terms of its political contexts.

PART I

TIME AND ITS DISCONTENTS

CHAPTER 1

Schizochronotopia, or Elijah's Pitfall

Epoch is time; literal time is the representation of time through its own alienation.
—R. Wagner, *Symbols that Stand for Themselves*

Epochs make, epochs break.
—Proverb from the Field

Facing time in the Field prompted me to ask again Roy Wagner's questions: 'Are there different *kinds* of time, or merely different ways of *counting* time? Does time have a structure, as a clock does, or does it merely seem to have a structure, *because* a clock has one?' (1986: 82). I approached this as an ontological problem, shifting to understand how time is conceptualized in a specific context, rather than assuming a priori that I know its measure. This chapter posits that, in the Field, there are indeed distinct, even conflicting times, seldom primarily structured by the clock. Understanding their discrete qualities is a matter of looking into the spatialities – their proximities, distances and trajectories – as well as the discursive and affective contents they facilitate.

One local proverb, from the long list that Eno, my host in the Field, kindly prepared for me, read: *Vakat gradi, vakat razgrađiva*. Now that I need to translate it, I benefit greatly from the context in which I came to know it. The Bosnian word *vakat* comes from the Arabic *waqt,* meaning 'time, period, moment or instant' (Wehr 1976). A highly literal translation of the proverb could be 'Time constructs, time deconstructs', or 'Time makes, time breaks'. *Vakat* is not abstract time, however. It is qualitative and critical, like the Greek *kairos,* rather than quantitative and linear, like *kronos* (cf. Crowley and Hawhee 2004: 45). It is the time of something or for something. *Vrijeme* is another Bosnian word for time, but, unlike *vakat,* it can also denote the weather or the passage of time – time as some invisible substance – an infinitely long tunnel. *Vrijeme* can pass, but *vakat* is always fixed, whether in the past, present or future. Thus, the *vakat* in the proverb might better be translated as 'epoch', a determinate period with a particular, overwhelming quality that becomes apparent only in retrospect. Roy Wagner (1986: 85, 86) has traced the idea of epoch through its Greek meaning of 'stoppage' or 'cessation'. It is a self-defined 'piece' of time, 'impervious to the direction, movement, and subdivision of literal time'.

In narratives about the Field of the past, my interlocutors would nostalgically conclude: 'Such was the *vakat* . . .', or, referring to the strangeness of the present day, lament: 'What can you do, such *vakat* has come!' For them, it expressed an understanding of historical episodes with both desirable and undesirable qualities, but only insofar as they occur within a predestined existence. I do not wish simply to locate *vakat* within the religiosity of my interlocutors, but rather to recognize its intangible force as a condensation of life's episodes into an ethos that is both time- and space-specific. It references a body of discursive practices that produce the dominant time–space relationship. These epochs, as the proverb reminds, are doomed to be swallowed by their own temporality. *Vakat* is time with a mortal face. It determines what can and what must be done, whether it is the cyclical harvesting of crops, fleeing into exile or the reconstruction of evermore-cyclically destroyed places.

Mikhail Bakhtin (1981) coined the term 'chronotope' to indicate the indivisibility of spatial and temporal categories, admittedly only with regards to its function in literature.[1] Time, he noted, 'thickens, takes on flesh' and 'space becomes charged and responsive to the movements of time, plot and history' (ibid: 84). I employ 'chronotope' as a heuristic device to think of the divergent social currents in the Field. Chronotope is a discernible alliance of time and space, a time 'thickened' in a landscape and a set of practices and relationships, a space articulated through a time of specific quality. Each chronotope has its own story.

Lives of the Field tell many stories. Their actors can (or have to) function within more than one and even in apparently contrasting chronotopes. Unlike Bakhtin's literary image of 'man who is always intrinsically chronotopic' (ibid: 85), I argue that people and landscapes are sometimes trapped between discursive timespaces and thus 'schizochronotopic' (from the Greek Σχίζειν – *skhizein* – 'to split').[2] I have encountered two salient overarching chronotopes as 'collective themes' in the Field. They both relied on certain kinds of past and laid claims to the Field's future. One is told through proximities, the other through distances between religious communities. The first theme, which I call the 'Gacko sacroscape', embodies the cycle of life. The second one, or the 'Gacko ethnoscape', propels itself through the cycle of death. I will turn to the problem of their convergence later in this chapter.

For now, I want to make a brief separate visit to each of these chronotopes in order to outline some of their main performative elements and locate the nodes in the landscape through which they claim authority. This will allow me then to compare the qualities of the time–space relationships that pervade them.

Gilbert et al. (2008) have already argued for what they called 'temporal multiplicities' in Bosnia:

> Indeed, many with whom we work seem to experience and occupy multiple temporalities, often simultaneously. As people mobilize latent chronotopes in interactions, they draw on the moral valence, authority or identity embedded in different temporal horizons.... Anthropology in the region presents evidence for how people live within and in terms of temporal multiplicities, and how these overlapping temporalities nonetheless cohere in a sense of self. (ibid: 11)

Jansen's continued engagement with the temporalities of postwar Bosnian landscapes, particularly his *Yearnings in the Meantime* (2015), reveal both the possibilities and the limits of comparison across the various Bosnian contexts. The constitution of desires for and discourses regarding 'normal lives' in his case study of Dobrinja, a suburban apartment complex in the capital, is different from the transitions occurring in a (post)pastoral karst field located on the margins of the state and in the interstices of several intrastate borders. Yet, the temporal 'fractures' and 'entrapments' are evident in both landscapes (see HadžiMuhamedović 2016).

The grid desires that Jansen (2015) aptly described for Dobrinja are, in the Field, much less a matter of lives ordered by the workings of the state and much more a concern for lost 'normality' of the annual cycle 'gridded' by the traditional calendar. As if describing the situation in the Field, he noted: 'The "ought" was thus opposed to the "is" but intimately related to the "was" (Jansen 2015: 39). People in Dobrinja performed their desires for 'normal' lives by waiting for the bus (and the visibility of the state's order); people in the Field waited for Elijah (and the visibility of the community thus structured).

Sacroscape: Ilija and Alija Share the Sun

The first collective chronotopic theme rests upon the images of life in the Field as structured by the traditional calendar, but swallows into itself everything that was disturbed by the 1990s war. It signals a pastoral landscape, where even the difficulties of the day-to-day have an enchanted inflection. Thomas Tweed introduced the term 'sacroscape' to argue for certain types of spatial and temporal religious flows that transform 'peoples and places, the social arena and the natural terrain' (Tweed 2006: 62). They are not to be conflated with sacred or religious space, because they are not exactly manifestations of any particular doctrine or form of piety, but rather traces, as Tweed notes (ibid). They are amalgamated traces of immeasurable lengths of time and widths of space. They presented to me a constant ethical problem in thinking about the temporal and spatial scales of research (see Prelude to Part II). Was it appropriate to relate my findings to the name of a nation-state? If not, which other designations might be better suited?

My recognition of the Field's sacroscape as Bosnian does not preclude a wider or narrower designation, but rather highlights some common traces in a constant flux of existence. The Field's sacroscape is thus a bundle of intimacies collectivized by the proximity of humans (and nonhumans) to each other as well as their relationship with the cosmos as the supralandscape. As such, it does not follow the boundaries of ethno-national religious exclusion. The Orthodox Christian, Muslim or Gurbeti defined their identities in the Field through more or less the same body of practice and belief, whilst maintaining certain modes of differentiation.

When I first descended into the Field, it was winter. We drove in through Čemerno, filmic mountain peaks whose name evokes sadness and distress, perhaps because of the difficult nature of the pass. I was breathless at the sight. As the bus rolled down, a capacious karst field opened suddenly before us. It was my first encounter with the Field. It seemed endless. The snow-covered land had lost the strong outlines of the horizon, melting it into the sky.

I experienced this descent many times afterwards, but the first one has lingered through the memories of its excitement. I thought, this is what one imagines when uttering the word 'landscape'. It seemed stated, uninterrupted, almost paradigmatic, and I lost focus on the detail. It took me a substantial while to notice the image of Draža Mihailović, the infamous Second World War general of the Serb royalist guerrillas (Četniks), on the wall of the bus stop, the ruined houses or the nationalist graffiti around the town. It still seems possible to me to arrive at one bus stop, but two different places.

The snowy Field may present the visitor with a picturesque image, but it is nonetheless a formidable obstacle for those who know what it yields. One of my interlocutors had to use improvised skis to reach his house and, the year I was there, a helicopter bringing supplies to cut-off villages crashed and broke up. The few, mostly elderly, postwar 'returnees', used their homes only during the summer. They had to leave each autumn, fully aware that life over the long winter really depended on a well-prepared household. There had to be plenty of food and herbal medicine for the humans and the cattle, as well as wood for heating. Half of these supplies needed to be preserved by Tryphon Day (*Tripundan*), on 14 February, which was considered to be the middle of winter. Even getting to school was difficult, as Osman, one of my interlocutors, recalled from his childhood; mothers would give children newspapers and matches to ward off hungry wolves coming down from the forests. Most social interaction would cease and the livestock were confined to the stables.

Imagine this landscape starting to change, to wake up from the frost. There is a complete transformation of both the land and of social activity. In the sacral calendar of the Field, 7 April saw the first important shared ritual. It is called *Blagovijest,* literally 'Glad Tidings'. This is the Feast of the Annunciation, according to the Julian calendar. The uncertain horizon begins to melt and the earth reveals its humane form. To mark this change, children from the villages would seek out the highest hilltops and light tall bonfires around the Field in the evening. Their flames, breaking into the dark, abstract space and communicating with each other, signalled a shared approach to the landscape. These panoramic gestures have faded into the darkness of time unravelled by the war.

The meaning of the *Blagovijest* fires may be drawn from another local proverb: 'The Annunciation – and the cattle into gluttony!'[3] Or, in Bećir's version, 'The Annunciation, glad tidings – the cattle into gluttony and the herdsmen into coma!'[4] Children herding the animals to pasture would sing this rhyme. Their mothers would knit them woollen bags and load them with food to last the entire day. Nezir remembered this well:

> When I was little – and my mother had seven of us – we would all look forward to *Blagovijest.* We were excited at the prospect of lighting the biggest bonfire. And by the fact that the following day we would be taking the cows and sheep out to their first pasture after the harsh winter days. And, because our mother would bake *pogača* [a type of rich, leavened bread], with a boiled egg in the middle on top. It was our tradition. On the eve of *Blagovijest* we would run around and gather large piles of wood to compete with the surrounding villages, both Serb and Muslim. Whose fire would stand out best in the evening light, whose flames would grow tallest?

The Annunciation, as the point of entry to the ecological cycle, already exhibited the multiple layers of the Field's time-reckoning. Evans-Pritchard's (1939, 1940) discussions of the Nuer people's concepts of time bear great resemblance to the Bosnian sacroscape (and, I imagine, the annual cycle of many other pastoral communities). He likely made the mistake of arguing for a significant difference between Nuer and European time-reckoning. His famous distinction between 'oecological time', as a reflection of the human relationship with the environment, and 'structural time', as human beings' relationship to each other (1939: 189), cannot be easily recognized in the Field, as its social relations are part of the overall rhythm of the environment. A dark Field lit up in the same colours of fire expresses its ontology; neither simply syncretic nor anti-syncretic, it reconciled difference and sameness in its own way.

The annual cycle shaped human activities and various sorts of economies, which in turn structured relationships. Sacrospace was, first and foremost, connected to function and proximity, but was more fluid than 'sacrotime'. Time was an indispensable organizing element of subsistence and, as such, had a much more defined structure. As Alfred Gell (1996: 17) noted, such time is 'concrete, immanent and process-linked, rather than being abstract, homogeneous and transcendent'; each part of the year was elucidated through the tasks required. Such time does not have the same value throughout the annual cycle. A rough sketch might divide the year into a long, arduous and uneventful winter (for Nuer, this is the dry season) and a warmer part, when all important human and nonhuman activity occurs (see Evans-Pritchard 1940: 102).

Spring's entry into full swing, on 6 May according to the Julian calendar, is marked by Đurđevdan/Jurjevo, George's Day. This is a pan-Bosnian festival, but also exists in various forms throughout the world of springtimes. It focuses on movement, rejuvenation, birth, children, potency and, especially, female sexuality. In the wake of dawn, before the daylight is set, young women go either to the water slopes or the watermills and disrobe.[5] Then they proceed to wash their faces with *omaha*, the magical water that brings health and prosperity. Young men wake up early to watch the ritual from a safe distance, while the girls attempt to hide. In some places, on the eve of George's Day, they decorate their house doors with *miloduh* (literally 'kindspirit'), the hyssop blossom. As evening falls, the young men sneak up to the houses to steal or scatter the *miloduh* of the girls they like. The girls who know, or at least hope, this will happen, then pretend to be angry and complain about the loss of their 'virginal' flowers. The young women are pushed high into the air on swings attached to large trees. The married women lash themselves with withies (*vrba*), hoping to get pregnant. Children run around, stinging each other with nettles, and the cattle are fed a mixture of herbs for health. This celebration, however, only marks the entry into the season of hard labour. It reflects the advent of the annual phase, but ultimately functions to align each task with its appropriate timing. Utilitarian elements of the calendar are inseparable from their sacral character, as numerous apotropaic and fertility rituals testify. An attempt at deciphering this springtime communication is given in Chapter 5.

Procopius' Day, 21 July, was another shared ritual in the Field, but this time one of passivity. Neither Serbs nor Muslims would ever do any work in the fields, with the cattle or the haystacks on that day. Why? Lightning would strike a haystack or a shed. Hail would destroy the crops. Procopius thus stands next to Elijah as heir to the Proto-Slavic God of Thunder. Even after the 1990s war, those who had no fields to plough and no cattle to take care of told me they would never consider breaking the rule. This seemingly unreasonable adherence demonstrated their chronotopic commitment. Home was a matter of landscaped temporality carried on by the body.

Seasonal change brought the nomadic Gurbeti ('Roma', 'Gypsy') communities to the Field. They used to settle in the same places each spring; during my fieldwork, all those places were uninhabited. Post-Yugoslav boundaries have been drawn across what used to be Gurbeti nomadic paths. Prior to the 1990s war, they worked at tinning copperware for the 'settled' communities, generally receiving in return fresh farm produce or cooked food. As their livelihood depended on the 'settled folk', the Gurbeti migrated into the towns, where their primary modes of earning a living often became junk collection and begging. The Gurbeti function, and place and time in the Field are perfect examples of how the season-shaped economies produced desires and familiarities (see Chapter 3). Agencies, collective and personal, human and nonhuman, all played a role in maintaining and changing such intimacies.

The events of 2 August are unequivocally central to the Gacko sacroscape. Muslims call it *Aliđun,* Serbs *Ilindan.* It is the day of Elijah under the Julian calendar, a turning point of the summer, and marks the end of the harvest and the heavy workload. Between them, George and Elijah merge the faces of Jarilo, the Proto-Slavic deity of spring, Perun, the Proto-Slavic deity of thunder, and Khidr, the 'Green One' of the Mediterranean traditions, along with various other mythological characters (see Chapter 5). Investigating Levantine religiosities, Haddad (1969: 27) grouped George, Khidr and Elijah under the common denominator of 'georgic saints', noting that their three main features are fertility, power and the continuity of life. I adopt this adjective throughout the book, not just to indicate a group of characters endowed with seasonal potency but also to describe the kinds of landscape and syncretic system to which they belong.

All Muslims and some Roma refer to Elijah's Day as *Aliđun,* which Kerima Filan (2011a: 18) has interpreted in terms of the Turkish words *Ali güni,* or 'Ali's Day'.[6] There is a possibility that the name may be a reference to Ali ibn Abu Talib, the son-in-law of the Prophet Muhammad, although my interlocutors have not proposed such an interpretation. Miroslav Niškanović recorded *Aliđun/Ilindan* festivities in the village of Gerzovo in Western Bosnia that are closely related to another Alija, the epic hero Alija Đerzelez, as the toponym Gerzovo itself suggests (Niškanović 1978: 163–68).

My own data does not reveal links to any particular 'historical' character. The Day of Ilija and the Day of Alija are one and the same. The distinction really lies in just one letter and I would argue that the original intention of the proverb (Until noon – *Ilija,* after noon – *Alija*) was to underscore the

Figure 1.1 Fata's home in the lower Field

Figure 1.2 Gacko's thermal power plant

simultaneity of sameness and difference. Ilija, a very common traditional Serb name, and Alija, a very common traditional Muslim name in Bosnia, epitomize the common person. The root of both names is the same: Ali and Eli both mean 'high', or 'ascension' (Smith 1884, Wehr 1976). Ilija and Alija share their most important day equally, each getting precisely half. The bond between them, to which they 'ascend', is noon, the sun at its peak.

The reasons for this division are unknown. I abandoned my first thought, namely that Ilija took the earlier part of the day and Alija the later as a comment on religious conversion.[7] I discarded these notions because they never showed up in any of my many conversations from the Field or elsewhere, but also because the central Christian and Muslim festivities on 2 August really did have different timings. The reasoning again seems to be spatiotemporal. For Serbs, the day started with the Morning Prayer in the Church of St Elijah in the village of Nadanići; Muslims gathered near the mosque in the village of Kula after the Noon Prayer. Some of my interlocutors suggested that the division might have been pragmatic, so that people could attend both festivities and visit each other, while still managing to celebrate at their own temple. There are, of course, lives of sayings, which go beyond any imagined 'original' meaning. It is important, however, to note that my interlocutors only ever interpreted this saying in terms of similarity and sharing.

At the time when I wrote this book, the Muslim and Serb villages seemed worlds apart. Between them stood the thermal power plant (with its lignite mines) built during Tito's time, its white slagheap the size of a small mountain. Of the few mostly elderly Muslim returnees to Kula, only the younger ones did not remember that the festivities used to be held elsewhere, much closer to where the Serbs still hold theirs. Eno had childhood memories of it:

> I remember it. I was quite young when I went there with my late grandmother. *Aliđun* was celebrated at a place called Jasike [The Aspens], with huge aspen trees giving comfortable shade. This is a place that, unfortunately, no longer exists today. It has been buried. It is where the waste from the thermal plant is dumped. It was seized during construction of the plant. It [expropriation of the land] was done legally; there's nothing special about that story. But, this is where the first *Aliđun* festivities took place: horse races, marathons, various athletic disciplines, long jump, shot put . . . Many loves started there, marriages were forged . . .

However, just as the thermal power plant increased the distance between the two loci of festivities, it also generated proximities. This gigantic monument to communist vigour propelled women to seek jobs outside of their households and their newly acquired social mobility was a chance to exchange experiences. Nada from Nadanići remembered that 2 August was a nonworking day for Muslims and Christians alike: 'So, my [Muslim] girlfriends would tell me about what they do; I would talk about *Ilindan*. It was all very similar. We would give each other our good wishes'.

In 1935, almost a century before Eno told me about the change in the location of the Elijah's Day festivities and half a century before the thermal power plant was built, Đula Dizdarević gave a description of the festivities as they used to take place:

> We have a celebration on *Aliđun* Day here in the field by Jasike in the summer. All the girls from the villages usually come. The whole world is there.... They come from Stolac, from Mostar... People dance, sing, and at the end there is a race.... A horse race, and then men race. And there is an award, whoever comes first gets the award. (Vidan 2003a: 89)

Elijah's Day is the culmination of the social calendar, the warm part of the year suitable for various types of communication, mainly through group work (*mobe*) and gatherings at home that last deep into the night (*sijela*). As Eno told me, everyone knows that winter is approaching and that this feast is their final outlet. There is an abundance of food and drink. Some enjoy group singing and dancing, while others enter athletic tournaments. Younger people flirt with each other; the elderly sit in the shade and talk. Expatriate relatives and refugees come back. Fistfights between groups of men were not uncommon either, although I did not witness any; they come as a sort of ritual cleansing of the emotions. All communication is condensed into this one day, which commemorates the social life of the community. Eno was not sure how best to describe to me what Elijah's day is. He struggled with it as if suddenly required to describe something universally understandable, like walking or being born. He said:

> No matter whom you ask, no one will be able to give you a definition. It has always been celebrated. They will all mention some traditions or other. I have not been able to find it any books. It's not in the Qur'an. It comes as an unwritten rule. It is a day that depicts one place of people (*jedno mjesto ljudi*).

This 'place of people' was thus summarized in the cycles of Elijah. I have called it 'sacroscape', the image of the prevailing, landscape-bidden way of life in the Field before the 1990s. Today, however, neither its time-reckoning nor its space-reckoning can be considered apart from the nationalist 'theme'. The image of their sacroscaped relationships thus needs to be contextualized within the other chronotope.

The spatial boundaries of sacroscape are fluid. They are outlined by the proximity of people, both 'oecological' and 'structural'. Households are the basic units of neighbourhoods, which in turn gravitate towards a larger village with a church or mosque and a water spring (the two are usually close to each other). Beyond this setting, however, there is the elusive spatial concept of *kraj,* which literally translates as both 'end'/'periphery' and 'area' (related to *kroj*: 'cut', 'shape'). Like *vakat,* the notion of determined time introduced earlier, *kraj* has a certain condensed quality. It is relational, subject to reference, a space with an identity of a place. To say that something is *kraj* means that it is a space with some combined condition. This identity may take into account the topographic particularities of landscape. The Bosnian word for landscape is *krajolik,* meaning 'the image of the *kraj*'.[8] This image shows that landscapes are indeed social processes (or 'cultural', see Hirsch 1995), because the Field as *kraj* is impossible to 'map' without knowledge of the relations that constitute it.

I found it confusing, at first, that *kraj* could signify the Field of Gacko in one sentence and the much wider area of southeastern Herzegovina and Montenegro in the next. Its identity may be stretched depending on the context of the narrative. *Kraj*'s main constructive element, however, is exchange, in the form of work, trade, marriage, sworn kinship, household visitations and socializing during festivities. The Field as a shared space is thus always rendered through the temporal. Halilovich (2013 xvi, 10–11) has looked at another similar term, *zavičaj,* employed by displaced Bosnians, which may translate as a place, a region and a community of home and encompasses 'the wholeness of person-in-place and place-in-person'. Focused on shared patterns of local lives, it transgresses (national, ethnic, religious, etc.) differentiations. *Zavičaj* is etymologically related to Proto-Slavic *vyknoti* – 'to get used to something'. Although it has elasticity similar to *kraj,* the term *zavičaj* always unmistakeably implies a home that can be longed for. Not every *kraj* can be *zavičaj.*

Ethnoscape: Ilija and Alija Share a Mass Grave

No evil times without snow.
...
Snow falls, not to cover the hill but to reveal
the footprints of every beast.

—Proverbs from the Field[9]

The 1990s war distorted the relational space of the *kraj*. There is now much more than a power plant standing between Muslims and Serbs in the Field. This barrier is epitomized by a town homogenized and imbued with the ethos of nationalism. For the returnees to the village of Kula, the town is a hostile crossing. They live in their village enclave, outside of which lies uncertainty. The 'closest' place to them is the city of Mostar, physically much more distant before the war. Delva, a widow who comes back to Kula alone, but only during the warm season, returning to Mostar during the winter, could not believe that I had walked around Gacko taking photos of a Serb festival. 'Weren't you afraid?' she asked.[10]

Amongst my Serb interlocutors, I noticed that discomfort about nationalism was more readily expressed (to me) by the elderly. Like the Muslim returnees, they would hark back to the essential values of the sacroscape, to what they saw as an inimitable consonance of landscape and its humans. Delva's question highlighted the peculiar schizochronotopia in the Field. She was faced with the task of reconciling the visibility of discursive distance and her own experiences of proximity. At the outbreak of war, before they were put onto buses and exiled, the women and children hid in the mountain caverns for a month. Delva's first thought was to go and find her Serb neighbour, who helped her get supplies and eventually save everyone. Her friend Fata recounted this event:

> The man who saved us is still here in Cernica. His name is Spasoje Šarović. He is from Cernica just like Delva Zekić. When we were all here in this mountain, she maintained contact with him. She would head down over the mountains at night to find him at home, so he could go to Gacko and try to arrange something for us. Old people, women and children stayed in the mountain. She managed to get the buses to come to a nearby field and take us.

The lack of trust between communities that once commonly feasted together, maintained neighbourly relations and entered into sworn kinship (see Chapter 3) is reproduced through the systematic reiteration of the second chronotope I want to introduce, the 'Gacko ethnoscape'. It does not relate to Arjun Appadurai's (1990) concept of ethnoscape, as he was primarily concerned with the globalization and deterritorialization of 'ethnicity'. I use it to argue for quite the opposite – the production of homogenous spaces through the ever-violent politics of ethnicity (an 'ethnocidalscape', as one colleague suggested).

My own definition, pertinent to the Field, is thus closer to Anthony Smith's concept of ethnoscapes. He understood them as 'landscapes endowed with poetic ethnic meaning through the historization of nature and the territorialization of ethnic memories' (Smith 1999: 16). However, his attempt to locate the premodern sparks of nationalism is fraught with a problematic understanding of 'ethnicity'. He imagined 'ethnies' or 'ethnic communities' as the relatively tangible identities of groups with their own 'ethno-histories', shared memories, beliefs and distinct cultures (ibid: 127, 141). By distancing the ethnic from the national scale, he invited a common misinterpretation, describing the 1990s war in Bosnia as 'a complex and protracted antagonism', and 'the most bitter and intractable ethnic conflict' (ibid: 152). The conflict in Bosnia, and here I presume that Smith, like many others, has primarily in mind the war of the 1990s, was not itself ethnic, but rather about the definition of ethnicity and, as such, its violence was no more complex than any other similar modernist endeavours. In fact, the logic of the violence was rather simple. Ethnicity, as I understand it, is a presumption of conflating biological, cultural and emotional resemblances. Coming up against the Field, all such presumptions fail.

The chronotope I recognize as the Gacko ethnoscape refers to the life swept away by the currents of the ethno-nationalist projects of ruination. This chronotope became vivid through the definition of territory and the reappropriation of time and place. It seeks to reposition its characters. In the ethnoscape, places exist for the sake of the nation-space. They are taken on as a unique, palpable presence that can testify to an abstraction. Time is likewise structured through a reiteration of symbolic places and events (as precise historical truths and warnings for the future). Such time is primarily homogenized by a politically carved protraction of antagonism and anguish.

In the 1990s, violence entered both the public and the private spatial configurations of the Field, with strong notions of territory, borders, defence and martyrdom. Geographer Robert Sack (1983, 1986: 27) has noted that human territoriality is always an attempt to define and enforce control over social relationships. One such project was succinctly worded by Vojislav Šešelj, a nationalist ideologue tried for war crimes before the International Criminal Tribunal for the former Yugoslavia (ICTY): 'The borders of the Serbian people are marked by our graves, destroyed churches, burnt villages, Serbian pits, slaughterhouses, concentration camps, Jasenovac. The Serbian borders are the most remarkable borders in the whole world' (Bojić 1992). These borders, which may be understood as 'the very substance of nationhood' (Sidaway 2007: 166), are imagined and actualized through landscapes of pain and fear. The space they delineate is recentralized through the politics of schooling, healthcare, and law, as well as through the production of constant threats to social legitimacy. Hegemonic space always functions through the acquisition, claim and redefinition of places. Its symbolic narrative continues to be, sometimes literally, inscribed upon places in such a way that they are linked together into an abstract imaginary. The life of this narrative depends on its ability to embed itself into emotional geographies.

The central square of Gacko was adorned by bronze statues of 'notable local Serbs' such as 'Count' Sava Vladislavić and the 'outlaw' Stojan Kovačević. Near a site where a mosque was razed to the ground in 1992, on the main intersection, a new Church of the Holy Trinity has been erected. In appearance and size, it resembles none of the other, older churches in Gacko. Like many other postwar churches in the region (and throughout the 'diasporic worlds'), in fact, it is a 'replanted image' of Serb nationhood.[11] It echoes the style of the beautiful mediaeval monastery of Gračanica in Kosovo. Now a semi-independent country, Kosovo continues to function as a 'place' of great symbolic importance for Serb nationalism, primarily centred through the myths about the battle that took place on the Field of Kosovo in 1389, between the Ottoman army and the Serb mediaeval crown (aided by Bosnians and Croats). The introduction of this symbolic language into Gacko thus projected a unified identity. A distinct nation was being forged through designated 'authentic materials' from the past (see Smith 1999: 12). In 2013, as part of a municipal project to 'beautify Gacko', a wall next to the church was 'adorned' with graffiti saying: 'Kosovo and Metohija, the soul of the Serb man!' The traditions of local Orthodoxy were thus systematically subjected to pan-ethno-national unification, and the style of the new church was part of that discursive formation.

On his visit to Gacko in May 2012, Patriarch Irinej of the Serbian Orthodox Church stood in front of the new church to announce: 'To the joy of all Serbdom, my soul is peaceful when I say: "This is the Piedmont of Serbdom"'. By making this reference to the role of the Piedmont region in the Italian national unification, he assigned Gacko a vital role in the maintenance of the ethnoscape. A month later, using a slightly different wording, he offered the same emotional centrality to Kosovo, which 'was, is and will be the Serb holy land – the Serb Jerusalem' (V.N. 2012). Such 'myths of ethnic election' imply responsibilities to honour the designated ethno-ethical principles and sacro-political rituals (Smith 1999: 130). Territory and religion are conflated into a single identitary trope. During Trinity Day, which has been instituted as the official day of the Gacko Municipality, the politicians and the clergy paraded banners with images of saints and Serbian national flags around the town centre. This 'sacralized' stroll is politically performative. Its function is to legitimize the new chronotope by drawing on the affective registers of the old one. As Massey (1994: 169) has pointed out:

> When black-robed patriarchs organize ceremonies to celebrate a true national identity they are laying claim to the freezing of that identity at a particular moment and in a particular form – a moment and a form where they had a power which they can thereby justify themselves in retaking.

Gacko's ethnoscape worked through a proven formula of alliance between political and religious authorities. The problem, as I demonstrate later, is that religion in the Field does not conform to institutional frameworks. Gacko was cleansed of its deemed 'non-Serbs' and decorated with a nationalist assortment. Everywhere I looked, on the walls of the hotel, houses and cafés, there was graffiti glorifying men indicted for war crimes by the ICTY. I walked and read these marks on space: 'Šešelj is coming', 'Ratko is our hero' ... They all seemed to have been written in the same ominous hand. When I spoke to a Serb family in the village of Nadanići, they mentioned that the prominent nationalist Vojislav Šešelj is from the area: 'You know that he's from the Popovo Field? But, we don't like him. Why did he need to meddle with politics? He didn't do any good'. Nation was far from being the main topic of conversation for my Serb interlocutors in Gacko, yet the graffiti seemed to indicate a massive outpouring of shared sentiment. Dževad later told me that they had all appeared the same night in both Gacko and the neighbouring town of Nevesinje. Even a small sample reveals that these literal inscriptions of the ethnoscape bear too many similarities to be spontaneous. As Nettelfield and Wagner (2014: 70) noted regarding a monument to dead Serb soldiers in Srebrenica, such interventions are 'part of the same political imperative – to "hegemonize" public memory, through selective remembering and forgetting, that has been promoted by officials throughout the entity of Republika Srpska'.

The construction of a Bosniak (Muslim) ethnoscape was also in progress. In August of 2013, a year after my fieldwork, a large central *šehid* memorial was constructed next to the graveyard in the village of Kula. *Šehid* is a word of Arabic origins, meaning 'victim' or 'martyr'. The memorial was designed as a *turbe,* an open-sided domed mausoleum of the sort traditionally built for notable Muslims in Bosnia. The inaugural ceremony was attended by representatives of various veteran associations and included saluting soldiers, flags and folksongs about battles. In his speech, the representative of the Islamic Community said that 'Bosniaks should be proud to have preserved their honour'. Bosniaks, according to him are those 'whose religion is Islam and who speak the Bosnian language'.[12]

As already mentioned, my oldest interlocutors expressed the most uneasiness about nationalism. For them, shared life was just life. It was neither 'the idea of Bosnia' nor a love of tolerance. Proximity and communication were simply a matter of their life histories. They did not speak of coexistence (*suživot*), but of existence (*život*). Bosnian poet Abdulah Sidran has somehow perfectly captured this distinction:

> Those who ask me what I think about coexistence, I dispatch to go co-fuck themselves. People exist, they don't coexist. Coexistence is the assassination of existence, the denial of existence, something that came with the nationalist parties, one step to apartheid, one step to racism. . . . I found out that I have a neck only when they started strangling me. (2011, my translation)

To me, this is a perfect depiction of syncretism, one abruptly revealed when strangled. To say that something is somewhat the same and somewhat different does not imply that any purity-claiming entities engage in mixture. The syncretism of the Field is ex post facto.

For some of the people I met, the ethnoscape was the dominant theme. On one of my many taxi rides between the town and the villages, I slipped

Figure 1.3 Church of the Holy Trinity in Gacko's town centre

Figure 1.4 'Ratko Mladić, Serb Hero!' Graffiti in Gacko's town centre

into an uneasy conversation with the young driver. I reflected on the abundance of graffiti celebrating Šešelj, and asked if he had noticed that they were all written in the same hand. He first responded with deathly silence, one of the few times I was actually worried for my safety because of other humans. Then, he turned to me with the most serious face and said: 'I don't know where you're from. Here, he's a hero'. It just so happens that he was driving me to the house of a Serb man who passionately criticized the same nationalist interventions. Nevertheless, I could see why being silent was inevitable in certain contexts, leaving the audibility of nationalism to portray its paths as well trodden.

The Paradigmatic Abyss

A major punctuation in the Gacko ethnoscape is the Korićka Jama, or Jama Dizdaruša, a natural pit in karst rock, used as a convenient dumping ground for the corpses of murdered Gacko residents on at least two occasions during the first half of the twentieth century. It served as a mass grave, first for Muslims, mostly from the Dizdarevići family at the beginning of the First World War, and then for Serbs from the village of Korita at the beginning of Second World War. Ivo Lučić (2012b: 325) has described how these pits, a common feature of the Dinaric karst, considered the dwellings of mythological creatures like witches and fairies, became symbols of the painful political history of the area, as many of them were turned into mass graves by the Ustaše, the Croatian Nazis.

The local word for such pits or crevices is *jama*. As its etymology is not entirely clear (see Skok 1971: 752), it may be noted that the word *jama* is pronounced 'yama'; Yama was the early Vedic deity of death and the underworld (Bodewitz 2002). Early Slavic cosmology incorporated a reverence for chthonic beings. The association of chthonic dragons and serpents as well as of semi-chthonic fairies, with caves and the gullies of disappearing rivers, is well documented later in this book (see Chapter 5). As the cosmology of the Field reveals significant links to Proto-Indo-European beliefs, one might hypothesize that these pits were symbolic places of death long before they became mass graves in the twentieth century. These would then be two qualitatively different kinds of death, the former taken up by the Field's sacroscape and the latter by its ethnoscape.

The style of my interlocutors' narratives about this particular place differed markedly from that of the public ceremonies dedicated to it after the 1990s war. It was Fata, an elderly Muslim 'returnee' to the village of Branilovići, who first told me about this pit:

> It is known as the Korita or Dizdarevići pit. In that war [Second World War] Serbs were thrown into the pit over Muslims. It was in 1942. The Dizdarevići [a Muslim family] had been thrown in there sometime before. I am not sure when. It was the Ustaše [the Croatian Nazis] who threw in the Serbs. But when the Serbs had thrown those Dizdarevići, an old Serb man had come up and told them: You have started to fill it up with Muslims, but it is yourselves will fill it up. And that's where the Ustaše threw them. But there were some of our people, too. There were some of our people [Muslims] with the Ustaše, as well. But, mostly it was Ustaše from the town of Široki Brijeg who came here, wearing those fez hats, as though they were Muslims. And there was a woman, Rahima, who had a house there, and next to her there was a Serb house, where a woman with a small child lived. So when they [the Nazis] came, Rahima pleaded with them: Please don't hurt my neighbour. Please don't hurt the child. They killed the child with a sabre. And they slaughtered her. And where did they take her, to that pit, somewhere... With a sabre! A sabre! Well, that is just, that is... it's... They had fez hats, as if they were Muslim. My God! And then there was a pogrom and some of our people were with them [with the Nazis] as well, there were some of us, some of us...
>
> I haven't gone through there. They say a cross has been put up, a Serb memorial. And underneath them, Muslims were tossed! There you go.

Fata's house was destroyed in the 1990s war. After a decade of exile, she returned to her village, where she was recently a victim of a hate crime committed by a group of drunken men. Her attempt to narrate the killing of Serbs, which happened some seventy years ago, had left her speechless at times. Many of the Serb intimate memories were equally distant from the ethno-nationalist master narratives. They never spoke to me about their 'martyrdom' in the Korita pit.

In Milija Bjelica's gruesome testimony of being thrown into the pit in 1941, there is a moment when the two chronotopes meet (in Dedijer 1992: 155–164). Facing the moment of death, he looked up at the mountain named after the principal Proto-Slavic deity, Triglav, whose three heads symbolized power over the heavens, the earth and the underworld (Loma 2001: 539): 'The bright moonlight lying on the rocky peaks of the Bjelasnica and Troglav mountains sank into darkness and was lost in the horror of what was expected' (ibid: 159).

The date of 4 July, when most of these killings occurred, has now been turned into a public ritual. The massacre became a crucial event, one which outlined the official Serb identity and its territorial claims. The seventy-year commemoration in 2011 was organized by the Orthodox Church and local government officials. Families of the victims were spoken of as 'descendants of the martyrs' and academics were brought over to give lectures about the event. One of them gave a 'module in history', reminding the audience that their Muslim neighbours had a 'criminal and sadistic urge to destroy everything Serb' (Nezavisne Novine 2011). The regional bishop noted that the pit is 'a symbol of all Serb wars, massacres and martyrdoms as well as the paradigm of Serb suffering and salvation', as per the established dictum.[13]

The sacralization of the ethnoscapes is a 'shared' practice too. As Michaela Schäuble noted, the Croatian post-1990s war memorialization of 'communist atrocities' at the sites of similar karst *jamas* works to dehistoricize the historical event and install memories into the realm of the sacred (2011: 48, 51). These events, she has argued, commemorate 'sacrifice' as the foundation of the nation and construct emotional bonds between the living and the dead, but they are highly selective endeavours (ibid: 46). Not all suffering is equally 'commemorable'. Schäuble sees this as a 'politics of (self-)victimization' (ibid: 29).

By way of this discursively selective suffering, the Field was seeded with the very essence of the national abstraction. It was occupied with ordained dead bodies, which naturalize power, and symbolize its loss and the need for it to be regained (Donnan and Wilson 1999: 149, Musabegović 2008). The human body was equated with the national body and the abyss was reappropriated into a warning that 'salvation' from death may only be achieved through a well-defined national identity.

Conclusion

Since the 1990s war, the Field has existed in-between two overarching chronotopes, or two dominant time–space themes: an ethnoscape and a sacroscape. They were intertwined. The sacroscape became discursively apparent in juxtaposition to the ethnoscape; the ethnoscape strengthened its position through selective alliances with the sacroscape. The creation and maintenance of strong borders required a particular kind of emotional geography. Nationalism reinforced its grip over the landscape and its human beings, by way of religion and through a territorializing discourse of dead bodies. It omitted the shared character of life, religious practices, economies and death in the Field.

The sacroscape has survived in the silent memories of the elderly and in the functional heritage of the cyclical calendar. Humans and nonhumans were stuck in the middle of the two grand chronotopes, two muscular, mutually exclusive, temporally specific stories about the same place. The simultaneous life of opposing alliances within the same body/landscape calls to mind W.E.B. Dubois' (2007) concept of 'double consciousness', which he used to describe the racialized context of the fin-de-siècle U.S.A.: 'two souls, two thoughts, two unreconciled strivings; two warring ideals in one dark body, whose dogged strength alone keeps it from being torn asunder' (ibid: 8). In the Field, there is a peculiar feeling of both proximity and distance embodied in the most noticeable notions of time and space, which I call 'schizochronotopia'. It is not that the human personalities are split, but rather that their paths are interchangeably leading towards different exists in the maze of overlapping timespaces. The noon sun is both the meeting and the parting point for Alija and Ilija, the two faces of Elijah. Landscapes, like a semantic field, are a process of construction, deconstruction and reconstruction (cf. Bender 1993: 3). The faces of Elijah are still being negotiated in the Field. As I demonstrate later on, the sacroscape has also informed certain creative strategies of political resistance.

In one cross-examination during the trial of Slobodan Milošević before the ICTY, the very defendant, interrogating a witness from the Field (Witness B-1122 2003), asked them to recall the days when the nationalist SDS party was establishing its Gacko branch:

> Q: ... but as in point 10 you say that the first large scale rally of the SDS was held on the 2nd of August, 1990, in the village of Nadanici?
> A: Nadanici.
> Q: Right, Nadanici. I don't know the names of those places in that region. Anyway, it was organized by the church and it was held in front of the church, and it was held on the date of an Orthodox holiday?
> A: Yes, that's right.
> Q: Now, do you have an explanation as to what was happening there? Now, if the church organizes for an Orthodox religious holiday, a rally of citizens, Serbs who are of the Orthodox faith, to have them meet in front of the church for an Orthodox holiday, what about it?
> A: Well, the Orthodox holiday of the 2nd of August is well known as Ilindan, St. Ilija's Day.
> Q: Yes, everybody knows that.
> A: And on that day, on St. Elijah's Day, there was a traditional festival that was held, but that particular day, St. Elijah's Day was used to set up the Serbian Democratic Party ...

Witness B-1122 thus gave a description of a moment when the two chronotopes met. My argument is in some ways contained in this testimony: the sacroscape 'was used to set up' the ethnoscape. The chronotopic distinction I have underlined in this chapter may be seen in the light of Benedict Anderson's argument about imagination and space (1991: 6). All time and space may be understood as imagined. It is rather the style in which they are imagined that distinguishes them. The sacroscape is a timespace imagined around the Field's seasonal rhythms and bodily proximities. The ethnoscape purports to be the sacroscape, yet delineates its own distances first. It is the plasticity of violence that takes on the form of the local cosmology, while being essentially opposite to it. Ethnoscape is about abstraction. It works to replicate the same master narrative in all the 'pixels' of the nation-state image. Commemoration of select places and events is the basic flesh it must have, if it is to be collectively imagined at all. Elijah's Day in Nadanići was strategically used for its emotional centrality, and, in Milošević's words, 'everybody knows that'.

The pits of the Dinaric karst were incorporated into many nationalist projects, each of them constructed in opposition to the others. In her research of the commemoration at the mass graves of the Dalmatian-Bosnian borderlands, Michaela Schäuble (2011) has described these pits as the sites of historic revisions. She noted the changed direction of communication between the dead and the living: 'Whereas in the immediate post-World War II years the dead haunted the (forcibly repressed) memories of the living, since the late 1980s the living seem to haunt the dead in an attempt to secure them as allies for their changing political endeavors' (ibid: 53).

The speaking dead of the Field have also become silent, I was told. *Utvare*, the ghostly apparitions and the *nur* magic sparks from the graves of the Good (*Dobri*), are abstaining from the present. Like their living beings, they too exist on the other side of the chronotopic rift. Their hauntings have become a journey into a different world. In the pastness of place, the once uncanny took up a residence more homely than the punishing everyday.

By situating this chapter in the Field's chronotopically complex positionality, I have also attempted to offer a 'grounded' comment on the ethics of anthropology of the fictitious 'post-conflict' space. Geopolitical narratives must not be taken at face value. For *Gačani*, there can still be no 'Balkans' or 'Bosnia' without the sacral folk calendar. Motifs of violence and pain must be approached from within, or else we risk perpetuating the ideas that created them. Researchers need to seek out and elucidate the finer points of social phenomena trapped between discourses and practices, abstractions and palpable life. This is especially true of the Field, where memory and commemoration are complexly intertwined with the historical/national, the folk/mythical and intimate time and space and where political resistance may not be understood without the knowledge of pastoral life and its grand cosmology. These encounters are traced here through a journey between intimate narratives and public discourses of life and death. Ironically, as the loci of Ilija's and Alija's celebrations grew further apart, the bodies of Ilija and Alija entered a new morbid intimacy within a mass grave.

Notes

1. For a wide-ranging application of this concept to social phenomena, see Jon May and Nigel Thrift (eds.) *TimeSpace: Geographies of Temporality* (2001).
2. One esteemed colleague reproached me for 'pathologizing' the Field through the apparent similarity of the terms 'schizochronotopia' and 'schizophrenia'. This is cer-

tainly not my intention, although my interlocutors have understood the timespace rupture as a certain kind of affliction. Related to this, see Jansen's (2015) conversation on what he calls the affliction of 'Daytonitis' and Torsten Kolind's (2008: 69) description of the incongruous postwar mixture of despair and optimism in the town of Stolac, which 'sometimes also existed almost schizophrenically'.

3. In Bosnian: *Blagovijest a goveda u obijest!* The word *obijest* could also be translated as 'hubristic luxuriance'.
4. In Bosnian: *Blagovijest, radovijest, goveda u obijest a čobani u nesvijest!*
5. It was never made clear whether the girls removed all their garments and veils or their nudity was just partial, but strongly narrated due to the excitement of the ritual. My interlocutors would say: '*Djevojke se skidaju*', which literally translates as 'the girls undress'.
6. In Bosnian, this would be 'Alija's Day', as per the mentioned saying.
7. For example, there is another seemingly similar saying: 'Lay down as Kata [Christian], got up as Fata [Muslim]' (*Legla Kata, ustala Fata*), which I have heard elsewhere, but never in Gacko or in any kind of connection with Ilija or Alija. I must note that I have no 'ethnographic' information as to the actual meaning of this saying.
8. The word *krajolik* is most probably a nineteenth-century coinage, reflecting the use of *landschaft*/landscape (see Bilušić Dumbović 2014). My interlocutors seldom used it.
9. From the Bosnian original: '*Zla vremena bez snijega nema*' and '*Ne padne snijeg da pokrije brijeg već da svaka zvijer otkrije svoj trag*'.
10. The festival was Trinity Day (*Trojčindan*).
11. See for example the New Gračanica Monastery in Illinois, U.S.A., or the Cathedral of Christ the Saviour in Banja Luka, Bosnia.
12. See Rijaset.ba, 2013: 'Gacko: Otvoreno centralno šehidsko obilježje za gatačke šehide', 9 August. Retrieved 13 July 2015 from www.rijaset.ba/index.php?option =com_content&view=article&id=17372:gacko-otvoreno-centralno-sehidsko-obilj ezje-za-gatacke-sehide&catid=201&Itemid=457.
13. See *Glas Srpske*, 2011: 'Korićka jama simbol stradanja'. Retrieved 25 May 2013 from http://www.glassrpske.com/drustvo/panorama/Koricka-jama-simbol-stradanja/ lat/58881.html.

CHAPTER 2

Time and Home

> If, as history, the past lies behind us, as memory it remains very much *with* us: in our bodies, in our dispositions and sensibilities, and in our skills of perception and action.
> —T. Ingold, 'Introduction' in *Key Debates in Anthropology*

'I do not measure time by the clocks anymore, nor by the scorching walk of the sun', wrote Desanka Maksimović, a Yugoslav poet, in a short love note that my mother recited to me as a child. 'My day is when his eyes return, and night when again from me they depart'.[1] Desanka was waiting for 'his eyes', and, as Levinas would argue, we all wait for the face of the Other to make sense of our Self (see, for example, 1969, 1989). The fabric of our own temporality is always made visible through relationships with that which lies outside of us. 'Even Eternity', Bakhtin wrote, 'possesses a valuative meaning only in correlation with a determined life' (1999: 65). We were born and are dying not through the knowledge of ourselves, but through others and the Other at large.

In the Field, there was a time for the cockerels' song, a time for prayer, a time for coffee, a time to begin and to break the fast, a time to light a three-pointed candle, a time to watch attentively for lightning in the sky, a time when the Gurbeti caravans appeared on the horizons, a time for winter get-togethers, a time to plough and then to harvest the earth ... The whole landscape seemed invested in timemaking and timekeeping.

When Zahida married Bećir in 1955, she was sixteen. They lived with Bećir's family for a while and then decided it was time to separate (*da se odvoje*). They did not separate from each other, but from their family home – the households separated.[2] Everyone wept, but knew it was time for the couple 'to go their own way'. Zahida's embarrassment was so great that, for weeks, she would only pass by the old house at night, sneaking past to fetch water from the Sopot fountain. Their sorrow was not eased by the fact that the two houses were no more than ten metres apart from each other.

People of the Field could tell time by the sun and the mountain, Eno told me. They knew it by how 'the shadow spans its length twice' and by the cockcrow. The first cockcrow announces the dawn, the second comes with the break of light and the third when the sun has already risen. However, I heard no roosters crowing in Eno's hamlet when I lived there. Eno's time seemed to have been entirely structured by work on reconstruction of the mosque in the town centre. He would get up around four in the morning to perform *sabah*, the dawn prayer. It would already be time to leave the hamlet when he woke me up. We would put on rubber boots and head through the dew-covered slopes of grass, towards the neighbour who would already be waiting for us by his car. As we tumbled down the rocky village road, the Field opened before us, bathing its expanses in early sunlight. This was Eno's remuneration for the day of strenuous masonry ahead of him. I never once heard him complain about the uncertainty of the future, or even of fatigue. His tireless work to 'restore life in Gacko' was important for the other returnees, though they seldom expressly shared his investment in that future. 'Eno is a good man', they would tell me. 'God knows what we would do without him'.

People of the Field could tell that a *kijamet* (end of the world, disaster, bad weather) was 'in preparation' when birds flocked to the stables and the cattle became unsettled. When the villagers sensed another kind of *kijamet* in 1992, it signalled the time to hide. Like the birds, they flocked to find shelter in their landscape. They hid in mountain caves for two months. The spatial and the temporal conditions of their exile were woven into each other.

They knew the hiding places. The mountains were etched into their bodily memory. The alliance of landscape with qualitatively different kinds of time was inherited as almost a reflex, rather than a thought. Đula Dizdarević, interviewed in 1935 as part of a study on epic poetry, recalled the beginning of war in 1914:

> I listened to the cannons at Plana as they shot at Bileća, and we listened, and in the morning we ran.... We didn't lock our houses, close the doors, or bring anything..., just ran barefoot and naked to Ključ, then to Zagradci, and spent the night on Baba Mountain. There, that big mountain is called Baba [Grandmother].... We spent the night there and then came down here from Baba in the morning on the very day of Elijah. (Vidan 2003b)

Her movement from the mountains into the Field was a shift from one extraordinary kind of time to another. Between George's Day (which signalled fertility) and Demetrius' Day (the beginning of winter), it was the time for work in the fields. Right in the middle of the two, on 2 August, was Elijah's Day, the culmination of the year and the most expressive affirmation of community. In its condensed sociality, it was the binary opposite of hiding. The locus and the time again forged an alliance. In the open Field, it was impossible to hide.

Time is social. It exists between my body and the body of another and, in most social spaces, this trajectory cumulates in shared notions of time. The landscape of the Field, a social network of humans and nonhumans, lingered, ingrained into the structure of the local calendar. Stories of 'before the war', their characters and their settings were always depicted as deeply implicated in their timing. People seldom told me about their experiences of living in exile during the 1990s war; instead, I heard stories of how they left their homes and stories of their return. In-between, away from the Field, was non-time. Their 'toolbox' for time-reckoning was primarily equipped with the spatial elements of the old landscape.

Their main reference points were 'before the war' and 'after the war', the former rich in detail and the latter usually expressed in sober contrasts and unfinished sentences. I would spend hours hearing about the male choirs causing the village lamps to burst with their *bećarac* tenors during the Elijah's Day festivities, the village boys lined up in makeshift dresses for their circumcision rite of passage, the seasonal succession of medicinal herbs in the Field, the intricate workings of fairies (*vile*) and ghostly apparitions (*utvare*).

A sigh meant that my interlocutors had been shaken up into sudden lucidity. Something had broken through their temporal transposition and we were back in the now, the 'after the war', the absence summed up by a short lamentation, a sip of coffee, a deep pull on the cigarette and the heaviest of silences.[3]

The past had been filtered into an unquestionable image of home. In that past, there are no significant ruptures, conflicts or fears. The 'current' landscape of Gacko was seen as a shadow of its poetically homely predecessor. It no longer performed the once-basic economic and social functions, and, most of all, it was far from any feeling of safety. Yet, it elicited the old landscape, like a fading photograph of a dead ancestor that invites a life narrative. It came alive through the past; it withered away through the 'present'. The present was thus broken up into an elicited 'present-past', felt as stable and homely; a recurring and unwanted 'present-present', felt as uncertain and unhomely. Stef Jansen and Staffan Löfving (2008: 15) have highlighted this temporal scale of home:

> Home itself, then, needs to be problematized, and particularly the self-evidence with which it is territorialised. If we fail to do so, as we indicated above, home is all too easily represented unwittingly as a timeless entity in an unchanging context of origin, something that is particularly inappropriate if we take into account that that context is often one of dramatic transformation, such as war or socioeconomic restructuring. There is, then, an important temporal dimension to experiences of home.

Looking at forced/involuntary movements of people, they further noted: 'However, the home that has been lost has not simply been left behind in another place. Rather, we would argue, it has also been left behind *in another time*' (ibid, emphasis mine). Halilovich has likewise argued that, for displaced Bosnians, 'the original place is not located in space anymore, but in time which has passed' (2013: 10). Employing the emic term *zavičaj*, he described the distinct scapes of home that continue their lives despite the fact that they have been destroyed or are spatially distant (ibid: 11).

These findings of other anthropologists working in Bosnia bear great resemblance to the temporal fissures I have encountered in the Field. Halilovich, Jansen and Löfving were concerned with refugees, people who have left home behind in another place. However, I would like to extend the argument by acknowledging the temporal loss of home experienced the returnees, people who occupy what is, only nominally, 'the same place'. The place, however, really is not the same. Another one, felt as home, is in the past. It only breaks into the present as a lively memory. It guides and affects. The body speaks and sees through it. Such home 'of the past' is real. The present is not real. The present is not home.

The kind of past that the Gacko returnees narrated, solid and almost epic, corresponds to their traditional forms of oral history (see Chapter 4). The turn away from the recent painful past, however, also seems to be related to the lack of interaction. There was little opportunity to negotiate memory, make the past less bounded. As Nettelfield and Wagner (2014: 79) have argued, the process of return opened up these conversations in Srebrenica. At the same time, the particular positionality of the Field was also a project of conservation; it propelled the past into the future. As Halilovich found, '[t]he loss of place as an important "anchor" of social identity gets compensated for – or "kept alive" – by the memories and stories of the place lost' (2011: 43).

Looking at a photograph of his house in Bombay, Salman Rushdie wrote in his *Imaginary Homelands*:

> 'The past is a foreign country', goes the famous opening sentence of L.P. Hartley's novel *The Go-Between*, 'they do things differently there'. But the photograph reminds me that it's my present that is foreign, and that the past is home, albeit a lost home in a lost city in the mists of lost time. (1992: 9)

Home is, then, a locus allied with a time of specific quality. The question of hope, of whether the lost can be imagined as somehow regained, asks whether the return of time is possible. This is what Hirokazu Miyazaki called the 'method of hope', which requires a 'radical temporal reorientation of knowledge and its resulting replication of past hope in the present' (2004: 130). The postwar reproduction of the Field's traditional waiting is also methodical. In its cosmology, life only ever goes into hiding and resurfaces with George's fertile potency. Nothing is ever really lost. Everything belongs to cycles. Even the flickering remnants of this knowledge were understood as a sign that home will once more align its spatial and temporal presence.

The Limits of Hope: The Refugees, the Displaced, the Returnees

Based on his research with Bosnian 'displaced' persons, Jansen noticed a simultaneous yearning for home and a reluctance to return to a place that no longer provided decent living (2009: 55). In the Field, these yearnings are most strongly voiced around *Aliđun*, the Muslim Elijah's Day festivities, when people come to the village of Kula from all over the world, for one or more days. They have different perspectives on the possibility of hope for home. Firstly, there are those known collectively as 'the diaspora', who live in a variety of other countries, mostly in Western Europe, North America and Croatia. They fall under the legal category of *izbjeglice* (refugees). Secondly, there are those who live in Bosnia, particularly in the cities of Mostar and Sarajevo, who are legally defined as *raseljena lica* (displaced persons). Lastly, there are those who have, in one way or another, come back, and are colloquially (and legally) referred to as *povratnici* (returnees). Their 'identity' is thus imbued with migration, even if they are understood as spatially 're-anchored'.[4]

The Elijah's Day reunion of individuals from these three 'groups' highlights the variety of their 'migrant trajectories'. It brings to the surface their context-contingent formation of desires, attachments, distances and expectations from home. If we consider not just the spatiality but also the temporality of home, the analytical framework of 'migration' needs to include a wider range of situations where 'home' may not be readily attainable or definable.[5] The Field is a case in point. 'Return' is seldom resolved by the re-inhabitation of place. What follows is rather a process of returning, a precarious investment in the transplantation of the past into the Field of the future.

Nicholas de Genova (2002: 424), in his paper on undocumented migrants, has called for a shift towards research into distinct migrations rather than insistence on some kind of generic migrant experience. For, 'there simply is no such animal', he has noted (ibid). He was primarily concerned with the fallacy of the conceptual framework of the (im)migrant as such, but the Gacko case extends his argument to more spatially and temporally specific migrations. In Bosnia, these distinctions started to form on group levels, triggered by the nationalist warfare of the 1990s. The war was a catalyst for different trajectories of migration, shaped by the levels and forms of violence, foreign refugee laws and various other constraints of resettlement. The extent of the continued visibility and audibility of nationalist propaganda, coupled with the availability of aid programmes at the local and regional levels, gave further shape to group migrant identities. There was also significant variance within the local populations in terms of the economic circumstances affecting exile and return and with regard to the personal life trajectories. Many families from the Field already had an established presence in other countries before the war. Their migration was eased by expatriate family and friendship networks or the knowledge of a foreign language. For example, the history of seasonal Yugoslav workers in Germany, the so-called *gastarbajteri* (from the German *Gastarbeiter* – 'guest worker'), together with the relaxed German refugee settlement programmes, produced a large Bosnian 'diaspora' in that country (see Ramet and Valenta 2011).

In places like Gacko, which were institutionally hostile to the process of return, age was an unavoidable factor. Only *đuturumi* (the frail and elderly) returned, I was told. The problem of hope was tied to the absence of the next generation. In the village of Kula, right next to the house of Kanita, the first and only child of returnees, the large, reconstructed school stood empty. Its windows had been broken and the chairs were primarily used during Elijah's Day celebrations, to accommodate the diasporic visitors. Restored in 2000, under a Spanish grant entitled 'Support to Sustainable Return', it was a hollow reminder of hope and its discontents.[6]

The legal document that regulated migration in the entity of the Republika Srpska forced migrants to 'migrate' swiftly between legal categories.[7] They ceased to be 'displaced' as soon as they entered upon the status of returnees (Article 9). Article 10 of the same legal act noted: 'The status of returnee shall cease by the expiration of the 6-month deadline, counting from the day when the competent body issued the certificate of returnee status'. The idea that people in Gacko could have regained their lives (spatially and otherwise) within just six months is divorced from any kind of reality. Their distimeplacement lasts for almost three decades now. Eno has described the circumstances when they 'returned' to Kula thus:

> When we had just returned, we would clear [the rubbles of] our houses. We would come at night, only to find mines beneath the boards and scaffoldings. You've heard of that one returnee woman who died in [the village of] Jugovići. I was a soldier, but what we endured in those days was far beyond even the frontline. The fifth day of return and, just imagine, they were shelling us with six-millimetre mortar shells! But, it is what it is, all part of that game, you know. It is all a struggle. That struggle is constant. Intimidation of returnees is a part of it all.

For the duration of that six-month period, returnees were entitled to social welfare 'provided they are unemployed' (Article 14). Up to the time of my fieldwork in 2012, no returnee had found employment in any public office or business in the town of Gacko. What they did receive were bits of notorious 'pre-election' attention and promises. They often expressed apprehension when the town was mentioned. Even the group that worked on the reconstruction of the mosque in its centre decided to halt their works during an Orthodox procession.

Of course, no general, common experience of home can be postulated for either the Gacko returnees or refugees. For Dževad, who started a small-scale business producing milk in his hamlet of Bahori, 'sustainable return' seemed more than a likely possibility. My first Gacko-related interview was with him in Hotel Bristol in Mostar, and although those notes and recordings were later stolen on the London Underground, I vividly recalled his words. He exhaled, in a manner that I often observed with others later, a dreamlike, 'syncretic' scape I wanted to understand, and one that certainly shaped my initial sighting of the Field. Dževad was also adamant about the attainability of return and he had rekindled relationships with his Serb neighbours in the Field. Yet, out of a population of forty-two people in Bahori before the war (see Federal Bureau of Statistics of Bosnia and Herzegovina 1998b), only he and his wife lived there twenty years later. Their children went to the U.S.A. and Sweden, where they led their own 'new' lives, without the prospect of return.

Delva, on the other hand, was silent on such hopes. She lived in another part of the Field, in the village of Kula. Returning only during the warm months, she stayed with her children in the city of Mostar during the winter. Her hope of return was only ever short-term – to come back the next spring. I came to know this most affectively when I helped her paint the walls of her kitchen. Next to her dwelling room, it looked exposed, unhomely. She gave me her son's old shirt, so that I did not soil mine. When we were done, she cooked a beautiful chicken dish for us and we watched television together. Much later, I noticed on one of the photographs the apron that she was wearing that day. Adorned with red apples and white flowers, it said: 'Home sweet home', in English. I still wonder how ontologically removed from the Field this image was and whether we can ever allow ourselves to speak of home, as such.

When Safeta, Delva's neighbour, saw me taking on this limited recuperative project, I offered her the same favour, which she very happily accepted. I never got to paint Safeta's kitchen, however, as I was leaving for another fieldwork location the morning after. Looking back at these moments, they seem to have gained in importance. Safeta's and Delva's restored kitchens, the warming hearts of their homes, stood for their hope of return. In the Field, these spaces can also be said to be an emblem of relatedness (and women's role therein), so the intervention also seemed to make a political point about the community (cf. Carsten 2004 on the 'heat of the hearth'). This was not a bold, uttered hope like Dževad's, but a reserved and solemn one, which was performed through a small restorative task.

As we spoke about the cyclical calendar, Delva reminded me of a saying about *hajduci,* the epic outlaw heroes: 'George's Day – the outlaws' assembly. Demetrius' Day – the outlaws' parting'. The spring allowed the outlaws to congregate out in the woodlands and the mountains, away from their usual homes. But, they would find shelter at the warm hearths of home with the first sign of approaching winter. Like other cosmological characters, *hajduci* are primarily used for spatiotemporal orientation. Home is thus where you want, and need, to be in the winter. Contrary to the old proverb, Demetrius' Day saw Delva and the other returnees pack up and make their way to the unhomely. She and others could hang tough through the summer with their small gardens, but winter required a well-organized household and a community (including sworn kin; see Chapter 3) to get you through hard times.

In the introduction to his *Principle of Hope,* Ernst Bloch wrote: 'Hope, superior to fear, is neither passive like the latter, nor locked into nothingness' (1996: 3). However, I am not sure I understand this particular formulation. The fear and the hope of the Field's returnees were not mutually exclusive. Rather, they challenged each other's persistence and channelled each other's expressions in everyday life. The delicate hope produced by this dialectic seldom acquired the manifest superiority of Bloch's utopian hope. It was understood that 'what had been' and 'what is now' are embroiled in a mortal combat over some future plateaux. As Frances Pine noted, through the fear that lies in uncertainty, '[h]ope is also always mirrored or shadowed by its opposite, despair' (2014: 96). Hope in the Field is a dialectical process. It expresses a need by navigating between obstacles and desires.

Waiting for a temporally distant home was expressed in emotional and discursive shifts. Kolind (2008: 77) noted that the tensions between the need to remember and forget the war in Stolac have often been conveyed in contradictory statements. Wagner observed a similar phenomenon with people in Srebrenica who waited for some news on the bodily remains of their family members: 'For surviving family members, conceptualizing the missing person's absence involves mediating memories, imagination, hope, and resignation' (2008: 7).

The tensions between the yearning for home and the fear of return were often resolved by death. Bodies (were) returned to be buried 'where they belong', close to their destroyed homes and dead ancestors. I spent one summer afternoon on an outing with the Čustović family in the village of Cernica. We camped between the graveyard and the stone rubble that used to be their home or, in fact, which is their home. One of their sons was working as an expert for an oil company in Texas and the other as a DJ in Croatia. No-

FIGURE 2.1 Coffee with Delva and Safeta

FIGURE 2.2 Edo and his grandmother Zahida, the storyteller

body had immediate plans to live in the village. Their outings were becoming a recurrent practice, a peculiar ritual of 'being at home'. Elvedin, the older of the two sons, explained this attachment:

> It is too deep a feeling to be contracted into a definition. You are pulled in by certain energies. Some people talk about roots. I am drawn by something... As if something has remained here that waves and summons, longs to be paid a visit, or as if a part of me is here, waiting to be reunited, as if a man is incomplete if he departs from it.

Elvedin's grandmother, Fata, went into exile shortly before the war and had been one of the first returnees. I was puzzled by this fact, as there was not a single habitable house on their land. 'Her *mejt* (corpse) returned amongst the first', Elvedin explained. 'She asked to be buried here next to her husband'. Others have told me that a Gurbeti (Roma) family, who, as part of a nomadic community used to inhabit Gacko only during the warm seasons, came back from Belgium to bury someone in a local cemetery.

Rather than exhibiting the 'symbolic capital' that is the quality of 'the fallen' and 'the martyrs', and so supporting the territorializing politics of the mass graves, which is actively employed in the Field (see Chapter 1), these returnee bodies were an intimate strategy of dealing with the loss of home, which could not otherwise be regained. Once the struggles of the present had ceased, the grave was a way of anchoring the body into the desired past. The body, as Elvedin said, is then reunited with a part of itself. In this union, the bones join the 'summoning' landscape – they turn towards the living. Within the tapestry of affective remains, these bones/bodies/ancestors act upon the exiled. To return dead is, for many, a hope.

The dead insist on reoccupying the space (see Nettelfield and Wagner 2014: 32). Similarly, as Halilovich notes:

> For many of the displaced survivors, returning to their destroyed villages to bury their dead is seen as an act of reaffirming the continuity of their local identities as well as an act of resistance and defiance. For survivors, these are crucial steps in regaining control over their memories in place, even if they now live thousands of kilometers away. The return of the dead becomes a symbolic return of those who survived. By re-burying the dead, survivors are re-grounding themselves – their identities, life-stories and communities – in the place that was taken away from them. (2011: 44)

If politics are more or less systematic and defined streams of action, these repatriated bodies are not political symbols, although they are symbolic and attest to political changes. As Elvedin suggested, they make up emotions too complex to be defined. In her *The Political Lives of Dead Bodies,* Katherine Verdery (1999: 29), admittedly arguing only for postsocialist 'political' corpses, noted: 'Dead bodies have another great advantage as symbols: they don't talk much on their own (though they did once)'. Gacko's dead bodies do talk, however. They even have a tradition of talking; the graves of the Good (*Dobri*) used to emit *nur* (light), seen as sparks shooting into the evening skies.[8] They talk through the landscape and, within them, through the living humans.

On a short walk past the graveyard, Elvedin took me through the ruins of his grandmother's home. Blocks of stones had plummeted down the hill and into interiors long ago conquered by the resilient shrubbery. Someone's cow was grazing in the courtyard. Muslim returnees to the village of Kula thought it a sign of their dispossession when Serb herdsmen used their pastures without permission. This cow in the ruins of Fata's home, I thought at first, was the same kind of violent demonstration, an act of demarcation.

Elvedin went up to certain flowering shrubs. 'These are flowers and medicinal herbs planted by my grandmother', he said. 'She tended to them. There's *nana* (mint) if you're upset; *sporiš* (vervain) if you have a stomach ache; *majčina dušica* (wild thyme) for this and that...' The names of the herbs resonated by some strange twist of fate. *Nana* means grandmother in Bosnian. *Majčina dušica* means, literally, '(grand)mother's little soul'. They grew there, amongst the ruins, traversing at least two worlds, infused with the timespace of these people's home. Neither Elvedin nor I could find the rights words to explain the beautiful, frightful feeling of standing in front of them.

A bit beyond the ruins, we approached an elderly woman who sat in the shade under a tree. She was the 'Serb herdsman' I had imagined earlier. It was her cow that roamed through Fata's house. We greeted her and I stood beside Elvedin as he spoke to her. Her name was Mila Šuković. She had been, it turned out, Fata's neighbour and friend. They had 'cared for each other' (*pazile se*) and taken coffee together, as good neighbours do. She deplored the demolishers. 'May God grant life together again', she said. Her exact phrase was: *Dabogda da ponovo bude zajedno života*. It is not easy to translate. She used *dabogda,* a common Western Balkan composite adverb with an optative grammatical mood, which literally translates as 'may-God-grant'. It expresses hope and desire, but may simultaneously introduce the understanding that the wish is far-fetched and improbable. 'It [destruction] has happened before and passed', she added. I was not sure how to understand her words – as hope, desire, loss, pessimism – or their uncanny coexistence.

Vincent Crapanzano (2004: 100), building on the work of Walter Pater, distinguished between hope and desire, for hope depends on 'some other agency – a god, fate, chance, an other – for its fulfilment'. Both, he noted, are based on the ethics that depends 'on one notion or another of the real – of a realism that limits fantasy and its enactment' (ibid). Mila's *dabogda* was perhaps situated somewhere between the reality of a landscape in ruins, a desire for the past and her life through and beyond previous ruinations. It was divorced from hope as described by Minkowski, in which 'I see the future come toward me', which 'penetrates further into the future than expectation' (1970: 100, see also Crapanzano 2004: 104). The *dabogda* was neither expectation nor simply a prayer-like solicitation of some futurity. It was, at once, hope, desire and its own refutation.

Mila's intimacy with Fata's home dispelled my earlier thoughts of intrusion. It was, after all, a home of her own. I scorned myself before this mighty herdsman. As I watched her conversation with Elvedin, two people whose lives had taken such different trajectories and met in some timespace – both alive and dead – of the past, but also of the present and the future, I got a glimpse of the workings of the landscape they called home. We all stood there in our moments of 'ordinary affects', as Kathleen Stewart (2007) beautifully described them, affected and affecting. Our pasts and paths, our sudden encounter, the ruins of Fata's (Mila's) home, our own homes, for each of us made intimate connections within a shared fleeting moment under the shade of Mila's tree. For, ordinary affects, Stewart (2007: 3) pointed out, 'work not through "meanings" per se, but rather in the way that they pick up density and texture as they move through bodies, dreams, dramas and social worldlings of all kinds. Their significance lies in the intensities they build and what thoughts and feelings they make possible'. This text is possible insofar as such *touch* and the strength drawn therein make it.

In those ordinary affects of ours, the 'exiled' Muslim, the 'non-exiled' Serb and I, the 'young researcher' confused by whether or not he was researching 'his own home', knew nothing for certain about the workings of the future, except that home, as a trope of chronotopic being-belonging, was unquestionably there to linger, in that dead house, with the dead body, both sprouting summer flowers.

Reimagining Hope/Home

> Memory is part and parcel of survival and return.
> *Pamćenje je u sklopu opstanka i povratka.*
> —Eno, interlocutor from the Field

In his work on the temporality of home in Bosnia, Jansen (2009) argues that refugees were reluctant to return once confronted with a place that offered no prospects for a sustainable life. He noted: 'For a place to become home (again), then, required a sense of hope' (ibid: 57). Starting from my research in the Field, which was largely with returnees, I would propose rearranging this statement: For hope to become a place (again) requires a sense of home. Hope, as a commonplace, needs at least a glimmer of the homely. Movements, however slow, towards the restoration of the 'Gacko in my mind' (the telling title of a website for Gacko's exiled community) have started to create a platform for a similarly slow emergence of hope.

For Eno and his crew, this became apparent through their commitment to reconstructing Gacko's mosques and graveyards. Eno found guidance in the local proverb, 'Traditions are more important than the village'. He elucidated this conundrum by drawing a necessary link between the restoration of time and the restoration of place, the possibility of regaining a life, and not just 'living'. Hope has been dependant on their capacity to reimagine home, a place in the past tense, and the attempt to re-inscribe it into the future continuous.

Sarah Wagner (2008: 5–6) noted how 'familiar objects', holidays, celebrations and other occasions that once gave rhythm to the life of the community and the household, accentuated the absences in Srebrenica. They had a hold over the returnees' lives. Elijah's Day was the condensed image of the Field as home, the most familiar spatiotemporal sight. The returnees' re-establishment of this gathering brought back the well-known faces, images, sounds and scents, but also accentuated the emptiness of the landscape after the visitors left.

Many of my interlocutors who did not live in Gacko anymore thought the Field had already become a 'lost cause', that the returnees' attempts to reinstall their lives there were futile. Mujo was one of them. 'There is nobody in the town', he said. 'You might find ten families or so [in the villages] after the snow, twenty at most. These places are lost for the Bosniak people'. Yet, much of the 'diaspora' was inclined to attend the Elijah's Day festivities, a possibility which had opened up only as a consequence of the returnees' presence and their 'restorative' efforts.

Other members of Eno's family lived and worked in the city of Mostar. Sabaha, his wife, came to stay with him in Branilovići whenever she could. Her job provided the financial security otherwise unattainable in the Field. Previously, the only major source of income available to the population, besides farming, had been the thermal power plant, whose workforce was 'ethnically purified' in the 1990s. One evening Sabaha and I were sitting on the porch watching Eno trowelling on his knees in the garden. He had just returned from reconstruction work that had started before dawn. With both sadness and admiration for his intense assiduity, she whispered to me: 'He couldn't stay away from home'. Was he fighting windmills or creating the grounds for life in this place? Others have asked the same question, but never Eno himself. If nothing else, his projects seem to have reinforced the resolve of others to return each following spring.

Eno argued that restoring the Elijah's Day gatherings was immensely important for return. 'All that is revitalized contributes to return', he told me. The restoration of traditions makes people feel safer, as he explained:

It's not only that they feel safer, but it's also important to have a group of people – one generation – because that historic task has befallen us, our generation. If we fall to our knees, generations after us have automatically succumbed. Had we not achieved something and borne these hardships, if we hadn't rebuilt . . . For example, how could you forfeit a mosque that people had worked on under much more difficult conditions? How could you give up your house, your property? That task lies with our generation. We have to lift all onto its feet in this worldly mission, so that our children and generations to come can take over. And, what can be taken over? You can take over only that which has foundations. A child cannot take over a house if weeds and nettles are sprouting from it. Who is going to want to live in such an environment? So, the first step, a strong foundation needs to be built, so that generations after us can take over and perhaps even thrive.

He juxtaposed weeds (*korov*) to the homely. Energetically rupturing through stone and overflowing gardens, weeds feed on absence. Their removal is full of meaning, as my friend Marija and I spent some nights considering.[9] In her poem 'Scenic Route', Lisel Mueller (1996: 179) described the dearth of pruning gaining ground: the houses along her road are waiting, abandoned, collapsing into themselves, the fruit in the trees is growing smaller each year, the fields are taking over. . . . In this landscape changing beyond recognition, she asks, what remnants will be there upon return, to voice some previous lives?

> . . .
> What we will recognize
> is the wind, the same fierce wind,
> which has no history.

The wind, however, may be packed with history, one that emerges in the same way as any history does, on the basis of situated inference. If nowhere else, it may initiate the past in one's own bodily presence, always amalgamating different kinds of trace, just as I reconstructed the Field in every post-'Katrina' home overgrown with ivy in New Orleans.

By making sense of his efforts as a historic time, a 'mission', a 'struggle', a 'battle', Eno seemed to have accepted the burden others felt unable to carry themselves. His hands-on work towards hope and that towards home were synonymous, simultaneous. The drive was projected into the future beyond his own life, just as he felt it projected by his ancestors into his present. The effects of these 'makings of home' were not confined to Eno and the reconstruction crew. Their interventions in the landscape – the slow but visible return of the mosques, the houses and Elijah himself – have been embryos of something that people need, before any potential discourse of hope, to move increasingly through space like they used to, with less fear and a stronger entitlement to yearn for a temporally distant place.

FIGURE 2.3 Elvedin and Mila under a tree

FIGURE 2.4 Eno taking a break from reconstruction of the town mosque

Phantom Landscape: Home as a Lucid Dream

> The phenomenon of tradition – the people's desire not to be lost in time and space.
> *Fenomen tradicije – želja naroda da se ne izgubi u vremenu i prostoru.*
> —Eno, interlocutor from the Field, 2012

Maurice Halbwachs (1992: 43–60) argued that memory only exists within certain collective frameworks that are built up, brushed up and reworked. They appear as 'reconstructed pictures', summarized and deposited, as if in a collective 'memory bank', formed by the pressures of society and the needs of the individuals who remember. Such memories are adjusted realities. They densify around dialogical and affective webs between the various actants.[10] In the Field, the discrete and intimate desire for the home of the past contained signs of collective attunement. Within the small community of returnees, such desire was abundant. It was negotiated through, and always contrasted to, the present.

Drawing attention to a gap in Halbwachs' treatise, Connerton (1989: 39) has pointed out that, in order to propose the concept of and engage with collective memory, we must first look at specific acts of memory transfer. This implies a turn towards the processes, spaces, places, times, events, actors and relationships that facilitate these 'collective frameworks'. Connerton located the perdurance of memory particularly in commemorative ceremonies and bodily practices, which make this transfer by way of '(more or less) ritual performances' (ibid: 40).

The Field's turn to the cyclical rhythms of bodies and landscapes has produced a collective positioning – a kind of pre-discursive consensus. Given the absence of a younger generation, however, the transfer of memory has shifted from public performance to a kind of intimate chronicle. The narrative was energetically searching for its place. Unstationed, this bodily immersion in the past landscape lingered like a phantom limb; its sensations were (re)lived with the excitement and texture of immediacy, before regressing into the acknowledgement of loss.

I was offered, in their daydreaming, a landscape that had long appeared to me the sole topic of this research. It was only when I started transcribing my recorded conversations that I noticed the endings, the 'regressions':

That's how it was . . . But, today, there's all sorts of troubles . . .

—

What can you do? . . . Where there used to be seven hundred households, now there are thirty souls, all cripples like me . . .

—

There, that's how it was. There was beauty, there really was . . . There were many things, but there you go . . .

—

But now, by God, none of that exists. The villages have died out, almost completely. Died out...

—

Ah, these were beautiful traditions... Now, it has all dissipated; nobody practices them anymore.

—

It really was *rahatluk* [a blissful time]. Joyful folk. People didn't have much, but they were content with little. And now...

—

We didn't have a lot, but we all lived in beautiful harmony. And now, everyone has [wealth], but nobody is content.

—

There is no life, not here... It won't... There is no... There is no... There is no... There is no life...

—

By God, there was lots of stuff before, my son, and today it cannot be. They've taken all of this. Today, nothing can be as it was before.

—

They are no more... There are no more fairies, no Good ones. There is nobody to see *utvare* [ghosts, apparitions], nor to experience *nur* [supernatural light from the graves of the Good]...

These and hundreds of similar 'temporal adjustments' were how long narratives of 'how it used to be' often ended. The 'present' committed repetitive acts of violence upon the affectively returning landscape. All the epilogues were moments of disenchantment. In them, the Field of magic beings and 'Goodness' had dissipated. The general tenor of narration would take a sharp turn, from rich and vibrant descriptions, visceral and tactile reconstructions, and often laughter, towards brief, fractured and sober realizations of an explicit loss and the usual moment of silence.

Elaine Scarry (1985: 172) argued that physical pain might resist language, but also simultaneously 'shatter' it by 'deconstructing it into the pre-language of cries and groans'. The awakening silence following narratives is a shattered language, or a 'post-language', a bodily arrest at the overwhelmingly un-narratable – echoing Adorno's (1981) words about the possibility of post-Holocaust poetry – an inexpressibility marking the point where the two chronotopes face each other. Language seems to bear sounding aestheticization and is rendered coarse-grained by the body.

Silence in the Field is a response to the 'present', an inability and a bodily refusal to protract the 'unwanted' horizons. In his study of the instances when the Western Apache 'gave up on words', Keith Basso (1970) has argued that silence, like speech, required a knowledge of channels and codes of communication, that silence also responded to specific situations and individuals. Sometimes, he noted, silence was an appropriate response to intense grief, because speech was unnecessary – it augmented sadness and became a physically strenuous endeavour. The silences of the Field were affectively instructive. My body too recognized when to let go of words, to allow the non-linguistic realization to wash over. I also became proficient in warding off the heaviness of one chronotope with a welcome question about the other.

Halbwachs, perhaps by way of his own dealings with a war, described a route of 'dreamlike states', or 'contemplative memory', a passage encountered by the Gacko returnees as well. Such a past may offer a way out of the 'present' and is thus never free of it:

> Yet, if we flee in this way from the society of the people of today, this is in order to find ourselves among other human beings and in another human milieu, since our past in [sic] inhabited by the figures of those we used to know. In this sense, one can escape from a society only by opposing to it another society. . . . (1992: 49)

These 'escapes' to the past, Halbwachs argued with regard to the elderly, are dreamlike states, even yearnings. Formed by societal pressures, in contrast to the present, they appear as moments of relaxation (ibid: 47, 51). Episodes of the Field's 'temporal retreat' may then be understood as a coping mechanism and a longing for home. Such home is the residual past of the body that resonates through another timespace. It is a lingering protrusion into the scapes of its own loss. Its phantom existence demands something through the body and from the body.

Phantom limbs, Maurice Merleau-Ponty noted, often preserve and perpetuate the exact position they occupied at the time of injury. They are not lost, because the (remnant of) the body does not cease to allow for them (2005: 88–84). Landscapes of home, the fusion of human–nonhuman interventions upon the body, are as much an interiority as they are an exteriority. They make possible the inter-penetrative forms of the World and the Self. They are both the growth of the body within and as part of the World and the growth of the World within and as part of the body. When some part of this biotic attachment is severed, and particularly if the split is sudden and unwanted, what remains carries in itself the presence of what is lost. The lost 'limb' is not a desire only – it acts, it feels, it lives. Through its endurance, it insists that the body be extended into the world as it always was. What Merleau-Ponty noted about the phantom arm is true of the lingering Field as well, namely that, '[t]o have a phantom [landscape] is to remain open to all the actions of which the [landscape] alone is capable' (ibid: 94). To have a phantom Field of home, then, is to maintain a bodily projection towards the communal life, economies, intimacies and mysteries that the landscape made possible.

Heonik Kwon's elaboration of Merleau-Ponty's analysis evokes the schizochronotopic state of the Field: 'Extending this phenomenology of the human body, we may say that the amputated part of a social body maintains two contradictory realities at once; namely, the historical reality of a living whole and the given reality of missing parts' (2008: 79). Bodies and landscapes can (and sometimes need to) accommodate contradictory realities. It is no wonder that this problem is prominently illustrated through the wounded body, for such a body simultaneously belongs to history and projects a future; it is *gone,* but also has the possibility of continuity. Landscape can be the body's ally. It is part of the social and 'individual' body. As much as we hold it, it holds us too. Sometimes, the memories of landscape may be effectively invisible, like the places of Gurbeti dwellings in the Field, but attain a resounding voice in liaison with its situated humans.

Kolind (2008: 245–47) observed that older people in the town of Stolac tended to idealize the past as 'a trouble-free, harmonious and pleasant time, from which all problems and sorrows had been weeded out'. He saw it as an escape from the 'dominant present' and 'overwhelming memories', but, simultaneously, as a political comment on the present and the construction of hope for a different kind of future. This past has some qualities of the Gacko mythical narrative in which details are smoothed out until they blend in with the basic cosmological pattern. Kolind notes:

> Instead they tried to forget or develop mechanisms for handling the violent memories. The creation of an undamaged and uncontaminated past was such a mechanism. It became an ocean to dive into, a place where the nightmarish present was sealed, set apart from the war and its tragic consequences. Sometimes people also projected the past into the present, and lived for a moment in the belief that soon everything would be as before. In this way memories of the past offered an alternative to the depressing future and the sad memories from the war. (ibid: 245–46)

Likewise, the idealized past of the Field was more than a coping mechanism: it was a resource with political qualities. It claimed a space otherwise occupied by a qualitatively different time.

Marianne Hirsch and Leo Spitzer (2010) have written an evocative account of Czernowitz, as 'a place that cannot be found in any contemporary atlas' (ibid: xiii), but which nonetheless exists, calcified in its past, in the memories of its Jewish inhabitants and their children. Even after multiple name changes, annexation of the city to the Kingdom of Romania, Soviet occupation and pogroms following the Romanian Nazi programmes, Czernowitz remained an image of home, frozen in a time when it was multicultural and tolerant. Hirsch and Spitzer argued that this projection should be understood as a 'resistant nostalgia' and a strategy against Romanianization (ibid: xv).

Is 'escape home' a form of resistance in the Field? Should we read (micro)political acts into the intimacies of such extensions into the past? If so, what constitutes resistance? Obviously, the past is deployed in opposition to the present; it rejects the lay of the land. As such, it delegitimizes, if only informally, the nationalist politics institutionalized in the Field. The past landscape, narrated as the once dominant model of social life, has shifted into a counter-discursive mode. While modes of outright resistance do exist, for example through the restoration of events and buildings, narratives of Gacko's past seldom acquire the exposition of a conventional political act. In the sense of James Scott's 'weapons of the weak' (1985), the Field's reluctance to cooperate with newly prescribed time may be understood as form of everyday, bodily defiance. To understand these demands, a scaled-down notion of resistance needs to be proposed, one which includes both the will to remember against the politics of forgetting and affective differentiation. They sustain counter-landscapes, albeit ones older than their hegemonic amalgams. As a source of contrast to domination, affect is located in between the many elements of the landscape; it thickens through numerous juxtapositions. Rather than resistance, this form of difference might be better termed 'affective (op)positioning'.

Resistance, Maria Hynes has argued, does have this affective dimension, 'a more-than-reactive, barely recognizable, less-than-conscious mobilization of bodily potentials, which is an exploitation of the margins of openness in every situation, an activation of new capacities of bodies and an interruption of our more determinant modes of sociality' (2013: 573). These 'lurking' capacities, I would suggest, are not confined to isolated bodies, or human bodies for that matter. They are always relational. The flowers sprouting in the garden of the late Fata, the rubbles of her home, and Mila, her Serb friend who curses the destruction, may all figure in one's affective calibration, an allegiance to the 'old' landscape and implicit refusal of the 'new' one.

There are other instances, however, which span both landscapes and which should not be glossed over. These include an array of emotional attachments implicated on 'both sides', which obscure the face of exclusive discourses. Nationalism, as a particular form of our failed modernisms, always seeks to legitimize its modernity through essentialized discourses about the past. In the Western Balkans, like so many other spaces, it has latched onto 'tradition', subjecting it to extensive homogenization. Take for example the shared tradition of epic songs and their accompanying *gusle* instrument, which were nationally purified within and beyond the Field (see Chapter 4). Simply accepting that they nowadays often reek of violence, glosses over the restorative claims of a community that remembers them as a shared institution of oral history. It is up to those in the Field, and other fields, to somehow reconcile, or more precisely, live with, these opposing strivings – to be in possession of two narratives at once.

Many of my interlocutors who kept abiding by the shared Field had kinship (and sworn kinship) ties to individuals who continue to be involved in the politics of separation. They constrain contrasting narratives. There are also economic dependencies on government or political institutions and public factories, particularly the 'ethnically clean polluter', the gigantic thermal power plant and its associated lignite mines, both of which continue to transfigure the Field into an industrial wasteland. And, most importantly, there are the institutions of religious authority – the Serbian Orthodox Church and the Islamic Community, which seek to sanction sacroscapes. These institutions, although both centralized, work with different effects on different scales. By the time their various pamphlets and programmes trickle down to local religious figures, they are a messy commitment. The priests and the imam contribute to the definition of the 'true' Serb/Bosniak; they are implicated in political ceremonies and networks. But, they also work against divisions. One of the Orthodox parish priests and the imam occasionally meet for coffee in the local café. I was invited to one such meeting, which was strangely 'normal', considering the structural inequalities it had to overcome. The same priest had condemned an attack on the imam, from whom he received a copy of the Qur'an as a gift.

It is now indisputable fact that religious institutions collaborated with the political elites throughout the turmoil of the 1990s. For the ideologues, they continue to be the major points of access to the community. When I showed them the photographs I took at the Orthodox Elijah's Day, the Muslims in Kula pointed to the prominent presence of individuals who have formed the political elite since the atrocities of the 1990s. In spite of this, in smaller places like Gacko, how the priests work is informally regulated by their parishioners. In her ethnography of a 'mixed' village in central Bosnia, Tone Bringa has described some of these mediating engagements of religious figures, who acted as intercessors between the political/religious authorities and the villagers (1995: 208).

The town of Gacko is, in many ways, more strongly committed to the ethnoscape. Those whose economies are sustained by the new chronotope have claimed the town as their own. The villages, physically and discursively on the margins of this new Field, have an investment in the futurity of the old Field. Survival in the village is not a matter of knowing the 'right person' and finding employment, but of knowing the land and its seasons, or, in other words, knowing the Field's cosmological prescription. The resuscitation of the past can therefore also be 'strategic'. Silences on the margins, the silences of afflicted bodies, may be understood as 'productive anxiety', as they do not allow the ethnoscape to take root.[11]

Silence obscuring the ethnoscape is part of the same perlocutionary act as rich narrative revealing the sacroscape: it qualitatively positions the body and the landscape as antithetical to the refashioning of the Field. This book attempts to follow these unsettling tensions between the two chronotopes. It makes brief and scattered excursions into the ethnoscape, but remains committed to the sacroscape, thus joining the Field's bodily resistance to the recent, violent reorientations of time and space.

Fields of the Old: Memory and Education

> Well, it's not easy. You see how beautiful this Gacko is?
> *Pa, nije lahko. Vidiš ti kakvo je ovo Gacko lijepo?*
> —Zahida, interlocutor from the Field

The past tense of home is one of the common themes running through my conversations with the people of the Field. However, the age of my interlocutors and their children, their prewar, wartime and postwar trajectories, family narratives and memories of home have all shaped their different relationships with the Gacko landscape. Most of the people with whom I developed significant conversations were elderly, partly due to the age of returnees. The younger displaced generations had often conceived new lives in other places. The older people welcomed opening up their (past) landscape to me, as did I. I was inviting them to transfer their no-longer-valued knowledge to me. They enjoyed it. They laughed. In the all-too-common absence of younger family members to inherit and keep the local traditions, I was the recipient of mastery meant for someone else. Asking them about George and Elijah, I, a stranger to their calendar, seemed to have been able to conjure up a feeling of home.

There was a steady drain of young people from the Serb communities. The younger people whom I met in the town already had defined plans for education and work elsewhere. Their departure meant that they would likely never come back to live in the Field again. Marija said that she would study fine arts in Belgrade or Banja Luka. I offered to introduce her to my father, who teaches at the Academy of Fine Arts in Sarajevo, but she politely refused, explaining that she had already investigated the art programmes in the other two cities and was ready to make her choice. Such young people as do stay in the region, gravitate towards the new centres, which respect the fault lines of ethno-nationalist formations. While Marija and other young Serbs chose Belgrade in Serbia and Banja Luka in the 'Serb Republic', Edo, the only semi-permanent Muslim resident of their age, studied in Mostar, in the 'Federation of Bosnia and Herzegovina'. Many times, the prospects of education and jobs have led younger generations to depart for (and remain in) the European Union or North America.

Nobody likes to live in a village, the Šolaja family told me. There were four of them, with an average age of eighty, living together in the Serb village of

Nadanići. They lamented the fact that the villages were dying out. Even if they did stay, people would feel abandoned in a deserted landscape without schools or doctors. There were new requirements of life, they told me, which had rejected the benefits of the village. Through the summer, they were sure to stock up on basics, to last until next George's Day. Nada thought the village provided security, even now:

> There is still abundance in the village. We smoke meat, for example. We slaughter pigs in the autumn. We have cheese and *kajmak* [clotted cream]. If for some strange reason a whole bus load of people were to visit a village house now, they would have enough to eat. In the town, they buy what they need personally and . . . What will they do [if food is scarce]? Village households always had enough during the wars; even during this war we didn't feel hunger. We kept cows. There wasn't any fighting here. They [men] went to war, God knows, but we looked after the gardens. We had fruit, cows, cheese, pigs, chicken and all of the stuff you do on your own land. You provide for yourself. You have your own wood. Everything you have is your own, so long as there's someone to work for it. But in the town, God, if you didn't have electricity, water and communications for two days, you'd die. Here, begging your pardon, but even if the water does run out, we can still go to the toilet in the fields and bring water from the spring. The town is not like that. Still, regardless, nobody wants to live in the village.

In the Muslim villages, the specific security of making and having something 'of their own' also used to be the foundation of survival. It was in the first detachment from the land that their agony began. Fata's worst memory of exile was her grandson Edo's hunger while they were hiding in the mountain caves: 'I'd no milk for him. His mother's milk had dried up in the breast and he was just seven months old'. When she and the others surrendered, a Serbian soldier in the detention centre brought her some milk: 'But the weather was crazy – the sun, the rain, the ordeal – and the milk went sour'.

Even though Edo had only just been born when he went into exile, he had vivid memories of what the landscape was like before the war. He was a babe in her arms when his grandmother ran for shelter in the caves of the nearby Baba Mountain – a mountain whose very name means 'grandmother'. These two grandmothers held his life in their embrace, even before he could fully open his eyes to see them.

When I met Edo, he was living and studying in Mostar. He went back to the village every summer to stay with his grandparents and help out with reconstruction work on the mosque. When he spoke, he knew every toponym, local narrative and medicinal herb. After meeting Zahida, his grandmother, I understood why. She was a storyteller, like the Athapaskan and Tlingit storytellers in the work of Julie Cruikshank (see Cruikshank et al. 1990, Cruikshank 2005). Like theirs, Zahida's stories were simultaneously individual and communal, mythic and historical. She would weave the 'how it used to be' into a past that was of her own body and of the whole landscape.

I took many walks with Edo across his family's land. Behind the remnants of their houses in the hamlet of Hodinići, we would enter a wide area of hilly meadows packed with Illyrian burial mounds (*gomile*) and mediaeval Slavic tombstones (*stećci*). We did not just walk; he steered me through it. He said that he often wandered down these same paths alone, sometimes at night.

There was little to suggest that, apart from the first seven months of his life, he has always been 'displaced' from that landscape. I asked repeatedly how he knew the things he was telling me. He would reply: 'I learnt it from my grandfather and grandmother. I grew up with them', or 'I heard it from my grandmother and she heard it from someone older'. Place and time, their subjects, allegiances and destinies, are then a form of inheritance – in Edo's case, one steadily acquainted with his body.

In my conversations with his grandparents, Edo would habitually interject to give a more detailed explanation of a harvest custom or the ghost-like apparitions (*utvare*) that could be seen on hilltops and in graveyards. He also introduced me to the world of local shrubbery:

> I know about *gavez* [comfrey], it is a very medicinal herb. There is also *sporiš* [vervain]. *Sporiš* is also known as the outlaw's herb [*hajdučka trava*]. That tells you everything. It heals wounds, the stomach. There are some species of *kamilica* [chamomile] here. Then, there is *maslačak* [dandelion]. *Zova* [elderflower] can be found now – it is used for tea. Then, in autumn, there is *trnjine* [blackthorn]. It is like some sort of wild cherry. Then, there is *šipurike* [rosehip], *džanarike šljive* [wild plum]. I don't think that kind of plum is to be found anywhere else but here. Then, there are wild pears and wild apples. There is lots of stuff.
>
> *Žara* [nettle] is one of the first plants to grow in the spring. You know it's, I won't say a harbinger, but one of the first plants. For George's Day, as the spring festival, it is cooked in a *pirjan* [a ragout] with beans, potatoes and meat.
>
> That's it. Nettle tea is drunk as well. It's good for cholesterol and, they say, the circulation too. It boosts the heart's functions. It's used for cholesterol because people ate food with a lot of fat here. Gacko cheese and Gacko *kajmak* [clotted cream] are famous. Smoked meat ... With smoked meat, you cook nettle. So, it's a medicine for cholesterol. We have walnut, pear, cherry, plum, but also wild strawberries and mulberries.

It is important to note that Edo's narratives about Gacko do not distinguish qualitatively between what might be 'his own' experience and that of his grandparents. I do not know if he has picked the herbs he mentioned. I am certain that he has never witnessed a George's Day festivity in the Field. Neither did he see the snow he mentioned, the one that 'fell in the seventh month of 1976', but he knows what snow before Elijah's Day implies for the crops in the fields. His grandmother demonstrated the same kind of connection to the stories she had heard. She dramatized, with vivid gesticulation, the 'mythical' stories that used to be recounted at winter get-togethers.

Marianne Hirsch developed the concept of 'postmemory' to argue for the transgenerational transfer of experiences, particularly after traumatic events, when children live their parents' memories as their own (1999: 8). Although the displacement of Zahida's family certainly was a traumatic experience, it was not the main topic of her stories. She provided Edo with an induction into the overall landscape. It was strategic. To know which hilltops are haunted, which caverns provide shelter and which plants may kill you or save your life, was deemed a necessary part of an in-depth education, one she had received in much the same way.

Building on Henri Bergson's distinction between memory as representation of something learnt by heart and the memory of a lived act, Sarah Wagner argued that the Srebrenica families' 'lived' memories of their missing relatives become fragmented and less specific over time (2008: 130). What becomes obvious in the narratives of my interlocutors is that the Field and its rhythms were firstly recounted as a memory of representation, a sort of lesson on landscape, learnt by heart. Bodies may then travel to the early moments when these lessons were internalized, to reveal the 'processes of incorporation'. These memories populate the permeating images of the landscape with more specific fragments and textures.

Lejla, whom I met on the plane to Sarajevo, had also left the Field as a child. With Sara, her baby girl, playfully bouncing on her lap, she told me about her doctoral research and her book, newly published in German. Like many others, she led a life only marginally related to Gacko. She had been highly educated into other kinds of knowledge. The landscape Edo was being 'pulled towards' elicited almost nothing from her. She spoke of it as somewhat sad and dangerous, with little hope of prosperity for the returnees.

As most of the younger generations had either left or were preparing to leave, I wondered whether Edo, who seemed 'equipped' and willing to live in the Field, would return after his studies. His grandparents, Bećir and Zahida, had mixed feelings. Through their own 'return', they knew that life in the Field was unlikely without a community.

Me: Would you prefer that he returns to live here?

Bećir: We would.

Zahida: No, by God, not until the conditions are there for it. And they are not.

Me: And if the conditions were there?

Zahida: Well, if the conditions were right, if he were with people, if he had you, if there were twenty of you ... What would he do here alone? What would he do on his own? But, it's not easy; do you see how beautiful this Gacko is? I would like, more than life, for my grandchildren to live here.... But young people are not returning.

Bećir: They will. They will. They will.

The Little Bride: On Time and Solitude

> I was sitting in the house one evening, alone. What to do? I can't watch the TV anymore. I pick up the phone and dial a number. A woman answers. Hello. – Hello. What are you doing? – Nothing, watching TV. So, we start talking – she is alone too – and we agree to meet. She was here the other day for lunch.

This story is not from the Field. A woman who 'returned' to her home, another small town in Bosnia, recounted it to me the last time I saw her, shortly before she passed away. Her words replayed, so many times, in my head, as I was getting to know the elderly men and women who had returned to live in the deserted landscapes of their Gacko hamlets. I listened to the normalcy of relationships as constituted in their memories, which they considered the basis of a good, or at least a better, life. I watched their strategies of dealing with solitude and against loneliness.[12] Such situations were not exclusive to the returnees, although they were more pronounced. Many of my Serb interlocutors argued that the long process of young people's migration to the cities had left the villages on the brink of disappearance. Others have been faced with solitude much more suddenly, through exile and return.

If there were to be an anthropology of solitude and loneliness, it would have to be an anthropology of communication. We would have to dive into the worlds of connections, longed for or rejected. We would have to look into what people are struggling to regain or discard. We would have to trace the spatial and the temporal qualities of solitude and loneliness and the techniques of coping with them. Even when to be alone is a matter of choice, it is one predicated on the condition of relationships. Of course, the lines between voluntary and involuntary solitude, much like those of displacement, are blurry. Many solitary people did not have to return to the Field. They could have lived in exile with their children or within diasporic communities. Yet, the condition of being alone is not about the lack of social networks only, as discussions of urban solitude inform us (see for example Coleman 2009).

One is always in the midst of others, thrown into the consequences of their presence and absence. But these are not just any others whom we want or do not want to be with. These others are constituted in us, filtered through our being in the world with or without them. If disconnection from others is solitude, loneliness is a disconnection within a desire for connection. In Gacko, loneliness appears as a form of displacement and distimement shaped by the small scale of Muslim and Gurbeti return, the shrinking population of the Serb villages, and the 'inter-ethnic' distance produced since the 1990s. Loneliness depends upon an image of some integrated whole – a family, a neighbourhood, a friendship, a home. Loneliness as nostalgia for home is a need for a former sociality, for those others who constituted our landscape and for the intimacy and security that such relationships provided.

This is what Perlman and Peplau (1981) called the 'discrepancy perspective' to the social psychology of loneliness. Loneliness, they argued, is 'a discrepancy between one's desired and achieved levels of social relations' (ibid: 32). It is not constituted simply through the absence of social contact, but through the desires, expectations and needs of what social contact ought to be (ibid). Loneliness in the Field is a discrepancy between the present and the past of the landscape. It is loneliness on a large scale – a need, a desire – for social networks that have been systematically unravelled.

The land itself is perceived as lonely. It is unattended, desocialized, confined and withdrawn. 'There was a path towards the old tombstones on the mountain', people would tell me, 'but it was overgrown by brambles'. Or, they would say, 'Gurbeti used to camp there each spring, where those brambles are now'. If the weeds I mentioned earlier signified an unhomely house, these shrubs, called 'thorns' (*trnje*), were the image of an unhomely landscape. This land was also silent – it ceased to communicate through miraculous phenomena. It no longer yielded fairies, ghosts or other figures with a divine connection to it.

People lived lonely lives in Gacko and had their own strategies of coping with it. On two opposite sides of the Field, a group of elderly women, Orthodox Christian and Muslim, found similar ways for solitary existence. Each evening, with rhythmical punctuality, they would rush towards the television set and, for an hour, dive into the dramatic world of Indian cinematography. The next afternoon, they would watch reruns with the same degree of attention. The show was a soap opera called *Mlada nejvesta* in Bosnian, literally *The Little Bride,* though a more 'correct' translation would apparently be *The Child Bride – Strong Relationships of Tender Age.*[13]

I watched a bit of it with them to see what all the fuss was about. To make a long story short, a very young low-caste girl, the protagonist, is married off to a high-caste equally young boy. She is smart, smarter than the husband at least, but is repeatedly taught not to reveal this fact publicly. She goes to live with the boy's family, where a dominant, wise and somewhat cruel matriarch, the boy's grandmother, makes her life difficult. She is not the only bride in the household, but is the youngest. The family is large, tight-knit and full of controversies arising from 'traditional' social hierarchies.

There was a comforting certainty in the characters' daily return. The women would wait eagerly for them, planning household chores so as not to coincide with the episodes. There was also a sense of familiarity, as the show constructs (very) long psychological portraits. The camera is achingly slow. Each shift in the storyline is followed by minutes of dramatic and scrutinizing glances, performed by all the characters in each scene. The Bosnian subtitles of the entirely Hindi conversations were barely necessary. The gesticulations and the gazes were enough to grasp the development of the narrative.

I am not merely stating the obvious, that television shows are a symptom of modernity, often comforting us in our times of solitude and loneliness, or that we immerse ourselves in a world of known virtual characters in order to experience the social communication we otherwise lack. No, *The Little Bride* is more telling. It resonated with the personal experiences of these women. With certain noticeable differences, it spoke to their loss of an intensely social landscape, as projected through their memories. None of them was eager to dedicate the same amount of time or attention to *Süleyman the Magnificent*, a Turkish soap opera running concomitantly with *The Little Bride*, with much greater success in the region. One of the women explained: 'I don't like to watch Süleyman. There is too much blood and violence. I watch the *Bride*'. The Indian show rekindled pieces of the Field known only to their bodies.

Nura's 'Little Bride' Story

There were not many proposals in those days.[14] Brides used to be 'stolen' (*krale se*). I was sixteen, going on seventeen, and he was twenty-six. So I went, on the devil's business, to a place where there was singing, you know, to a *kolo* (circle dance). And I sang: 'Oh, village of mine – in the midst of you a boundary – shortly will I turn my back on thee'.[15] And Sakib's aunt yelled: 'By God, you won't leave this village so long as I'm alive!' And, by God, that's how he double-crossed me (she laughs). But, we lived well; we had a fine marriage. I was famed for beauty (*bila na namu*). There were seven or eight lads here; which of them was going to grab me (*ujagmiti*)? And so, by God, it was Sakib that did. I was the tenth (bride) to come to the house! Imagine, so young! He was a player (*vrtež*). He sang, danced, did lots of stuff ... We lived well, without quarrelling. He never once slapped my face, not that I ever really deserved it, either. Never. But, he was a player. Everyone asked how come the best girl went for him. Oh, how people mourned over me! When I got married, my poor late mother smoked three or four packs of cigarettes before the dawn; that's how much she wept over me.

And, let me tell you, I wasn't allowed to get married – too young. So, they said, we should go to court to get permission and your parents have to come. I won't go to court, ever, I said. I won't, I just won't! So I waited 'til I was eighteen and then got married. They brought me in and he wasn't allowed to sleep in his own house for seven days, so that he wouldn't try to get to me or anything. That was the tradition. There were *đerdeci* (nuptial chambers) then. A *đerdek* is when they shut you into a room. After the wedding, on the first night, the *hodža* (Muslim priest) comes and recites the *dova* (prayer).

There were no marriages with Serbs here (in the villages) and few even in the town, maybe a couple of kids ... Though, there were some that we know of. Everybody married into places close by. Lads would come here for

Elijah's Day (*Aliđun*) from all around to court the girls. And in the same way, the local lads went to other places.

Should I tell you? We got married in the second month. And, in the spring, as there wasn't any work in Gacko, just peasant life, Sakib and some twenty lads went to the town of Prozor. And there they found those Bosnian girls and that. And these (girls) knew the Gacko lads from here were hardworking. And so, by God, my Sakib becomes involved with one Senija. And well, forgive me, I became pregnant with a child. So, they said, Sakib found a girl. Sakib found a girl. And, there was this neighbour Mujo, his wife ran away. But I said, by God, I don't care. One bites the dust, another come must.[16] And all the village (was asking): how are you managing it, Nura? Fine, by God. Let him go, if he must. And, by God, that Senija tried to make an alliance with me – she didn't have anybody either. She had some sheep and whatever. So, by God, she sells it all to come to Gacko with him. God help us. And he somehow came to his senses and ran away from that Senija and came back here. And when he did, everyone said: Look, Sakib's come back! People listened, thinking we will get into a fight. God forbid, I never did anything of the sorts.

Behold, one day, the postman was going the round of the villages: Nura. – What? – Here, he says, Sakib's got a letter. So, I took it nicely and, when he came home in the evening, I gave it to him. I said: 'Here. There's a letter for you'. And, he just looked at me like this . . . – and tore it into a thousand pieces (she smiles). By God, that's how it was. Youth, youth! Youth, by God. By God, that's how it was back then. And today, by God, I don't know. Today, it seems to me, people just go wherever they want. There's all sorts today. Ha! All sorts.

Mejra's 'Little Bride' Story

There were sieves (*rešeta*), because the grain had to be sifted (*redilo se žito*). The bride takes the sieve and throws the grain over her head. *Pogače* (traditional festive round bread) were baked then. The bread is also put into the sieve. It is taken out and broken up over the bride's head. And in that sieve there is also an apple. She throws that apple over the house. And the bride breaks up that bread and then divides it up amongst everyone around her. Then the sieve itself is hurled over the house. On the way to her new home, the bride throws a *dinar* (a coin) into the first waters she comes across. Her arms and legs would be tattooed with henna for the day.

Every bride used to kiss the threshold of the house. I also kissed it when I arrived. She puts a *musaf* (Qur'an) under her arm. Your father-in-law and mother-in-law or your brother-in-law welcome you and then you take that sieve and that grain and do all these things and put the *musaf* under your armpit. You kiss the *musaf* and bow down and kiss the threshold, and then they take you into the house. Nowadays they carry the bride into the house. Now it's different. I kissed the doorstep and still kiss it today. Whenever I leave, I say, 'Stay with God (*alahimanet*) my little house; stay well and alive for me. And when I come back, I say, hello (*mehraba*) my little house, I see that you are well for me'.

After the bride arrived, it used to be that she had to sit alone in a dark corner (*dubi u buđaku*). Her head is covered and she sits there – they said that the 'bride serves' (*dvori mlada*). The bride stays there, until her mother-in-law gives her the word. Once she does, the bride immediately cooks coffee and starts tidying up. I made pie with filo pastry that same afternoon.[17] They were arguing about how skilled I would be. Father (in-law) took the pie to show the others how good it was.

Then, there's the *nakonče*. The *nakonče* is the child put on the bride's lap. A male child. If there are no male children in the house, one is brought from the neighbourhood. It is always male. No females. If there are no male children in the neighbourhood it doesn't matter where they are from, as long as it's male. And the bride, when she is taken from her parents' house, prepares a present for that child. The money and the *boščaluk* (gifts wrapped in cloth), it is all prepared in advance. When they put that child into her lap, she gives him the presents, turning him around three times, saying *bismilah* ('in the name of God') and kissing him.

Those were the traditions. And today, there's nothing. . . . Today, when an elderly person enters the house, the bride (the young woman married into the house) remains seated. Whoever enters, the bride just sits there, dumb . . . But me, as old as I am, believe me, believe me, I never ever welcomed even the tiniest male child seated. As soon as a male child would peek around the door, I'd stand up for him. It was all respect. For an elderly woman too . . . That's how it was. And today, they disrespect the old and everyone else. 'What do you know?', they say. 'I am not a slave. You toiled like slaves'. They say, 'You didn't live, you slaved'. I used to tell them, 'You hens, have you no shame, just sitting there? When an older man enters, why won't you rise?'

A woman's life in the village was non-existent. She did every possible kind of work. She ploughed, milked the cattle, cleaned (*kidala*) the stables, took care of and cleaned the cattle. She did all of that. I did all of that. My husband always respected me for it. He was always scolding me. He would say: 'Stop running about! You'll wear out those legs and we'll have to carry you around'. But, I couldn't take it slowly. That was my trouble.

There were no buses then; people used to go to work on foot. So, I would wake up at three in the morning. I prepare everything the night before, so I only needed to boil the coffee. I had it prepared in the pot (*ibrik*). I had set out the clothes for him (the husband) to wear. If it rains, I have an umbrella or a raincoat . . . If it snows, if it's a blizzard, you wrap him in cloth. There were no cars, no buses. But, it was important to me that he worked, that he had a government job, so that I can today enjoy the pension he left me, God rest his soul, and am not dependent on anyone.

So, I would wake up at three in the morning, make coffee, wake him up, get him ready, and he would go to work. I would then check up on the cattle. If it was dirty under the cows, I would clean that up nicely. Back in the house, I would light the fire, boil the water for coffee, drink the coffee and then mix the bread. The bread rises; I knead it and put it into the oven. Then, what will I prepare for the children? I make them breakfast. And, in summertime, who will take the cattle to pasture? The children round up the cattle. I then prepare lunch and take it to them. It wasn't carried in a bag. I bake a pie, some meat, prepare everything, put it on my head and carry it up to them. In the evening, the cattle come back and their dinner waits for them. The children are washed. They eat dinner. Then, the children go straight to bed, tired from jumping and playing all day long. That's how it was then ...

In the Absence of the Everyday

> People don't communicate like they used to. Now they have the television. It's nothing like it was.
> —Anđelka, interlocutor from the Field

I have recorded several other bridal stories. The patterns that emerge from them all reveal a rite of passage filled with symbolic actions, but also the structured relationships within and without the family. In the narrating act, grammatical tenses shift between past and present. Events were thick with detail, emotions and gestures, constituting another kind of present – a reanimated past. Outside of it was the 'real' present, waiting like an intruder to break up and end the story.

Outside was a stark absence of the relationships as narrated – loneliness, if you will. The dense rhythm of their bygone everyday life, along with the difficult responsibilities it contained, grew quiet upon return to the same houses, now empty of their own purpose and latching on to the regularity of structured familial life in an Indian soap opera. The representation of the Indian household with its extended family, a strong-willed matriarch and mother-in-law, and the obstacles faced by the girl occupying the very bottom rung in the succession of many brides, all reminded them of a landscape to which they themselves had belonged.

Loneliness seems to homogenize time. It begs a return to the point before a significant rupture in the social fabric had occurred. After such a wounding, Merleau-Ponty noted: 'Impersonal time continues its course, but personal time is arrested' (2005: 83). To endure the passage of impersonal time, it is embedded with images of the familiar. From within their longed-for habitat, people carry those episodes when social communication was at its strongest – rites of passage, neighbourhood get-togethers, village festivities, family narratives and so on.

Anthony Cohen (1985: 98–99) argued that past social relationships, as 'repositories of meaning', may become a kind of resource for the present: 'The manner in which the past is invoked is strongly indicative of the kinds of circumstance which makes such a "past-reference" salient. It is a selective construction of the past which resonates with contemporary influences'. If there are pasts that resonate with loneliness, which are selected to be kept and nurtured, other pasts seem not to be as invited by the Field's returnees. The fact that the other soap opera was avoided because of excessive blood and violence might have some connection to the general silence about the content of the 1990s war.

In his analysis of the different 'types of forgetting', Paul Connerton (2008) failed to note the possibility of such a process as 'forgetting in order to remember'. Of course, it is difficult to distinguish between forgetting, inability to recall and refusal to recall, much like it may be impossible to locate the differences between memory, ability to recall and intention to recall. Perhaps, to reverse Connerton's (1989: 39) argument about collective memory, in order to talk about collective forgetting, we need to look into the specific voids in the acts of memory transfer and ask what is excluded from inter-generational communication.

There are probably many different kinds of loneliness, too, in the Field like anywhere else. Although it sounds like a paradox at first, some loneliness does appear to be collective. Such chronic, collective loneliness is formed through similar absences infringing upon collective webs of meaning. People can thus deal with solitude in strikingly similar ways, finding their day-to-day paths through the collective everyday of the past. They wait for *The Little Bride* on the TV. Like Mejra, when she leaves each autumn, they kiss their doorsteps and ask their houses to wait for them. And, they wait for Elijah to return.

Against the Unhomely

> Without the cradle, there is no return.
> *Bez bešike nema povratka.*
> —Sejo, interlocutor from the Field

> A home is made a home by the kids.
> *Kuću kućom čeljad čine.*
> —Proverb from the Field

What is displacement, then? Legal forms after the 1990s war in Bosnia have, I would argue, intentionally misunderstood it. Like Jansen and Löfving

(2008), I propose that temporality must be taken as a viable variable. I could call it 'distimeplacement', but time and place are really only the frames of what has been lost – the complex system of relationships and sensations which the timeplace allowed for. The Field's bodies, strung between historicity and futurity, have generated their own desired map of transition. Phantom voices of the old Field – textured, lively and abundant – were actively negotiating the unwanted present. Through affective temporal transpositions, they seemed unwilling to forfeit their claim over the land and the body. Carefully threading through the uncertainties of the present, fear and hope have been created into a hybrid way of being. Home, which meant many things, all of them different from the 'present', was performed daily, almost as a prayer and any sign of home's restoration, from the reconstructed buildings, the birth of the only returnee child, the Elijah's Day diasporic arrivals, or the resolve of the dead bodies to come back, was taken as a limited indication of the future. Home was the prerequisite for hope.

Phantom extensions of home are not simply a remnant; they are an affective opposition, a counter-discursive modality. The practices of loneliness also make a collective claim upon the landscape. They attempt to situate the body away from the 'present'. The unhomely Field of the 'present' was incomprehensible, almost unutterable. If uttered, made fully conscious, it risked ossifying into inescapable permanence. Its phantasmagorical impositions thus had to be endured, like a recurring nightmare.

'Home is made home by the kids.' 'Without the cradle, there is no return.' The former is a proverb much older than the latter, postwar statement, yet both embody the sense of continuity vital to the understanding of home. Home is thus a sense of being with a before and an after. To have hope (an after), the past must be a part of it. Otherwise, as Eno said, people get lost in time and space. The reader should keep in mind, throughout the book, this deeply existential meaning of memory.

The Field of the old – 'the colourful carpet echoing in festive songs' – found numerous paths to the body. It had no hesitation about the kind of reply that should be given to the hegemonic fields. It could do but one thing: unimagine the absence of youth who would inherit its cyclical time – inherit home – and give their limbs to the phantom. The old returnees knew the first cosmological truth to be acquired in the Field: when George kills the dragon, he does it through the rebirth of all, the laughter of children perched on swings and the fertility of the Maiden's womb (see Chapter 5).

Notes

1. This is my translation; for the entire poem in the original language, see Maksimović's (2012: 120) selected works.

2. See Tone Bringa's (1995: 47–50) discussion of the separation of communal households in central Bosnia and the shame involved.
3. Halilovich also noticed that Bosnian memories of displacement were 'most often made up of fragments, where gaps, silences, sighs and body language tell as much as spoken words' (2013: 13).
4. As Professor Robert Hudson kindly pointed out in his review, there is a ghostly meaning to the word *povratnik* (returnee), of something, or someone, that comes back to haunt.
5. Marija Grujić and I have given this argument further attention through our panel 'Post-Home(land): Being and Belonging after Spatial and Temporal Alienation', organized as part of the 2015 IUAES Inter-congress in Bangkok.
6. Nettelfield and Wagner (2014: 89) similarly argued that the humanitarian efforts aiming at 'quick impact' in Srebrenica were frequently unattuned to the circumstances of returnee lives. For information on this and other Spanish grant programmes in Bosnia, see *Open Aid Data,* retrieved 12 January 2014 from http://www.openaiddata.org/purpose/64/111/50/.
7. 'The Law on Displaced Persons, Returnees and Refugees in the Republika Srpska', *RS Official Gazette,* no. 42/05 of 26 April 2005.
8. *Dobri,* literally translated as 'the Good', were people considered particularly pious, wise and endowed with supernatural abilities. Sometimes, they were local healers.
9. See Yael Navaro's descriptions of her Northern Cypriot 'ethnographic field of prickly bushes, thorns, and thistles growing over an appropriated and unkempt plain' (2009: 13).
10. For the conceptual distinction between 'actors' and 'actants' and Actor–Network Theory, see Latour (2005).
11. 'Productive anxieties', Vanja Hamzić (2015) argued in his study of home-reckoning in the *khwajasara* communities of Lahore, are 'a set of one's collectively and individually acquired life skills that unsettle the affective and cognitive "truths" and "commonplaces" about one's Self and the Other as well as the spatialities and temporalities habituated by such knowledge'.
12. There is an uneasiness inherent in the observation and analysis of loneliness, from the perspective of my own body. In discussing such fragile moments of intimacy, where unfulfilled desires are laid bare, I have chosen not to identify my interlocutors by their real names.
13. See the *Wikipedia* entry for *Balika Vadhu,* http://en.wikipedia.org/wiki/Balika_Vadhu, retrieved 10 October 2014.
14. Names have been changed in these bridal stories, given the sensitivity of some of the information.
15. *Selo moje, nasred tebe međa, brzo ću ti okrenuti leđa.*
16. She used the proverb *Jedan se otego, drugi se protego,* which I give here in my own clumsy translation.
17. She said *sukala pitu,* which means that she had to demonstrate the elaborate process of making and rolling out filo dough, the layers of which are supposed to be thin enough to see through and without any punctures. Such pies are then filled with a choice of stuffing, most popularly a type of spinach (*zelje*), ground meat, cheese, potato or pumpkin.

CHAPTER 3

TIME AND IN-OTHER

> . . . we are disposed because we are exposed.
> —P. Bourdieu, *Pascalian Meditations*

> When man truly approaches the Other he is uprooted from history.
> —E. Levinas, *Totality and Infinity*

> How can a being enter into relation with the other without allowing its very self to be crushed by the other?
> —E. Levinas, 'Time and the Other'

I descended into the Field on a grey, piercingly cold early afternoon. The road leading from the town to the village of Nadanići gloomed vacantly. Not a car, not a human being, no movement but the wind. My eyes vigilant, surveying the snowy hills for the hungry wolves from Osman's childhood memories. I wished I had taken some newspapers and a lighter to ward off their imminent attack.

As the road bent, three silhouettes entered my horizon: a man and two cows. We continued walking towards each other for some time, growing closer, larger and more discernible to each other's eyes. I walked in some sort of expectation. Did he?

Finally, we met. I clumsily greeted him by invoking God's help. *'Pomoz-Bog!'*, 'God's help!' I said, in the Orthodox fashion, guided by the relative proximity of St Elijah's Church. *'Bog ti pomogo!'*, 'And God help you!' he countered. 'Would you happen to know anything about Elijah's Day near the Church?' I asked, randomly interjecting the celebration of the summer's climax into that dead of winter. 'How could I not?' he said (the village was basically synonymous with it). I was now walking in what was opposite from my initial direction, with him. He couldn't really go anywhere. The unrushed pace of his cows and the inescapable presence of my face started off our conversation. Settled in his company, I completely forgot about the wolves.

He stopped, pointed to a house and instructed me: 'Here, just go inside.' His house? I was not completely sure. I walked through the front yard and, as I was about to open the front door, two women appeared behind it. *'Pomoz Bog!'* I rehearsed. *'Bog ti pomogo!* – 'Come in, come in. It's cold.' Smitten, I said I didn't want to bother them ... but the man had said ... – 'It's cold. Come in. Are you hungry?' I turned to look for the man whose name I had not caught, but he had already continued on his way.

∙ ∙ ∙

This chapter looks at encounters between the I and the Other as the very substance and structure of time. I consider two collective memories of 'fractured' encounters, in order to locate in them the underlying logic of the Field's calendar and the affectivity of proximity that the time-specific Field allowed for. Its cyclical concept of time accommodated the continuous 'novelty' of traditional encounters. Such time was situated in friction, in the world continuously produced by the *touch* of different bodies. Their movements in relation to each other endowed the landscape with its qualitatively distinguishable time. Levinas (see 1991: 159, 1989: 43) looked on the face of the Other as the becoming of ethics, the first philosophy, a face that is always exterior to us due to the 'inevitable *orientation* of being "starting from oneself" toward "the Other"' (1969: 215). Yet, the World, in its novelty for my body, approaches me before the Self does, so any eventual 'I' is always already disposed by way of my exposure to the 'outside', one that I collect and internalize in a particular way. The Other inducts me into ontological positions, becomes inseparable from my selfhood, even when I seek to alter or reject it.

I do not presume that the sacral, political, ethnic and national identities of the Field were a priori seen as some Other writ large. Rather, I argue that encounters with Others determined the forms and contents of the Field's cosmology. These are *any and all* Others that form part of the simultaneously revealed and concealed exteriority of the World. They do include Gurbeti, Muslims and Serbs, but also the mountains, the nymphs, the wolves, the dead, the epic heroes and the saints who guard the seasons and the weather, as I argue later in this chapter. This Other is constantly on my horizon, the Other which looks at me and whose presence gives specific shape to an otherwise abstract worldly container. I can only presume that it would be abstract, for I am never and nowhere without the Other, not even when the Other is expelled from my immediate territorial reach.

Meaning, Bakhtin (1981) argued, comes about precisely as a consequence of dialogue with the Other, a position different from the I. It is dialogic. '[Each] word in language is half someone else's', he wrote, 'it exists in other people's mouths' (ibid: 293–94). The utterance as a repetitive meaning-making act is oriented towards the Other; it is addressed and anticipates a response (see Bakhtin 1986: 60–102). The Others considered in this chapter are those without whom the word, which is an entire scene enacted in the landscape, would not fully be capable (see Chapter 4).

The term 'Other' is inextricable from a sense of difference as distance. The Other and the Self become simultaneously through a process of Othering and Selfing, which, although many times understood as such, never are mutually exclusive. Given that I want to primarily focus on difference that is not positioned as antithetical, but inclusive of proximity, difference reiterated by my interlocutors as integral to the meaning making of the Self, I invent here another handy term, 'In-Other', which should be read interchangeably as a noun, a verb and an adjective.[1] In-Other is: Internal and Other, Integral and Other, Intimate and Other. Between the imagined polarities of alterity and sameness, In-Other is a very real hybrid, not an oxymoron as some might surmise.

Intimacy is a relationship which affectively and cognitively acknowledges that someone or something has a hold over ourselves from a position of proximity, that they have been significantly included within us. Essentialist political ideologies cannot cope with In-Other, which, though very close to the notion of intimacy, adds the recognition that the intimate one is also an other. The common word for intimacy in the Field is *bliskost,* meaning closeness (from the Proto-Slavic *blizъ,* 'near'). Two other words used were *intimnost* and *prisnost. Intimnost* comes, through the Latin *intimus* (inmost, closest), from the Proto-Indo-European noun for entrails (De Vaan 2008: 306). It suggests an inclusion of another body into one's own. *Prisnost* also expresses the spatial relation (by way of encounter), but etymologically contains the temporal dimension of 'always, forever' (Skok 1972: 44). It posits that encounter is a bodily promise; it does not efface the Other, but confirms it, provides for its fullness inasmuch as the Self can embrace it.

In-Other is also a habitual process of investment and reiteration, as my interlocutors reminded me. In the following pages, you will notice that they described intimacy through the concept of care. They would say: 'we cared for each other/looked after each other' (*pazili se*), which entailed a relationship with affective, moral and ritual dimensions. For Levinas (1998: 166), this care, the 'I-for-the-Other', is a 'responsibility that commands' in the proximity of the neighbour. Bakhtin (1999: 51) noted that '[a]ll spatial-temporal values and all sense-content values are drawn towards and concentrated around these central emotional-volitional moments: I, the other, and I-for-the-other'. Listening for proximities (and distances) requires proximity. The anthropological advantage of spatial and temporal closeness and in-depth inductive analysis helps researchers avoid the abyss of ideological projects. For example, Hayden's (2002a, 2002b, 2007) previously mentioned arguments about 'antagonistic tolerance' and 'competitive sharing' in

Bosnia are clearly challenged by the shared Field, where people have 'cared for each other'. That they cannot make sense of the political antagonisms in light of that care is a significant critique of the nationalist undertakings. I show how this care had more than affective qualities, that it was also a temporally, spatially, ritually and ethically structured phenomenon.

Levinas' question: 'How, in the alterity of a you, can I remain I, without being absorbed or losing myself in that you?' (1989: 52) finds an answer in the Field. If In-Other transposes into no more than I, then I can no longer consciously be, for the temporal and the spatial dimensions constituting me are dissolved without In-Other. If my world were but a blank, without In-Other passing through, there would be no measure for it, no time and no space. In-Other is not just any other, it is the syntax and semantics of my Self. Its externality-in-proximity demands its internalization. I tell my Self and grasp the flux of my Self by way of In-Other, which includes all the 'human' and 'nonhuman' outsideness by which my body is anchored into the World. So, it is ontological through and through.

Time is In-Other in shifting proximities – a landscape moving through the body – approaching and engaging the world of the I. It is constituted by movements, shifts and changes of different kinds. Some changes belong to the experience of the everyday – prayer, coffee, news, gardening, weather; others are cyclical and enduring – day, night, seasons, crops, birth, death, rites of passage and so on. Then, there are those rupturing turns – wars, environmental disasters, often followed by the destruction of habitat, floods, pollution, exiles and the extinction of various life forms. Most of them are interwoven and they all seep through the human body and the landscape, as they themselves change form.

For those of my interlocutors whose bodily memory of the Field included much of the twentieth century, wars had a cyclical quality too. In Nada's words, they 'return every thirty years'. They 'have come before and passed', as Mila assured me. Their bodies-landscapes 'switched' to 'survival mode' in the 1990s: Muslims fled to the well-known caves in the mountains for safety; Serbs prepared for a 'long winter'; the nomadic Gurbeti did not return in the springtime of 1992 or in those that followed. Face-to-face encounter with In-Other continues to be an integral part of the Field's rhythm, whether in practice or in memories of practice. The relational quality of time is revealed particularly in the absence of and desire for relations – in solitude – as I argue in Chapter 2.

In the following pages, I consider two streams of relationships that made the Field's time, both of which reveal the process of In-Other. Firstly, I look at the absent Gurbeti (sometimes also 'Roma' or 'Gypsy') communities through the memories of Serbs and Muslims in the Field. Secondly, I discuss *kumstvo* (sworn kinship) relationships between Serbs and Muslims. Finally,

I consider the role of the In-Other as time was being restructured by the political projects of essentialized Otherness. In all of these examples, I argue, Otherness is the main driving force of a particular intensity of intimacy. And, in all of these examples, In-Other is the way to *tell time*.

The Falling Gurbeti of Spring: In-Other and the Habitual Strange

> According to some unwritten rule, they were like an integral part of nature and the life of this place.
> —Eno, interlocutor from the Field

How does your body move from spring to spring? How does your spring move from body to body? How do you wait? For whom do you await? With whom do you greet the changing colours of the season? Do you predict the future by the temper of the Georgic skies? What is the face of your spring? Is it forever moored in the echoes of a fleeting world?

In the Field, the spring advances against the restraints of the winter horizon. The green widths rupture and fires are lit on the peaks at their edges. The pale buds of *zdravac* (rock cranesbill) blossom before your eyes. Your mother takes you to the space in front of the shed, places your head upon a tree stump and swings towards it with an axe. She trims your hair. It will grow better. You watch boys thrusting, high up in the air, girls perched on swings tied to old trees. Brides-to-be attentively crouch over the leaves of nettle they planted in front of their houses the night before, unriddling the direction of their marriage proposals. And you always see Gurbeti, as they begin to fall. You see them falling. You see them, as if they were still falling ... Laughter seeps warmly from your chest towards your interlocutor, affectively transforming the Field he sees around him. He looks at the curious images you've placed on a translucent tracing paper against the background of an empty landscape. Gurbeti start to fall, in the intensity of your memories, with you, with your body. As if they were still falling ... For, if they did not fall, how would you ever know it was spring?[2]

Eno described the landscape's longing:

> The families arrive ... How many? – Around ten *čerge* [mobile households]. Children come here to the villages. Gypsy women tell fortunes with cards. Girls wait for them to find out how they will get married. There were so many of them. We knew everything about them, their every step. After a long winter, believe me, people longed for them just like they longed for spring. Just like when you wait for your exam dates, or the way a feast is expected, so people waited for the Gypsies. And we prepare some tools for them to fix, they throw those beans, so many things ...

The cyclical, vernal arrival of the Gurbeti to the Field depicts the dynamic existence of a landscape formed between human bodies on the move. It is a vicarious arrival, for the Gurbeti have not returned since the 1990s war began. They came back, but only in the visceral memories of Muslims and Serbs with whom they once existed at spatial and temporal intersections. They came back to outline an uncanny form of belonging – to anchor bodies and landscapes through their very absence.

Rather than offering a historical account of a community or 'intercommunal' life to which no historiography has ever pertained, my goal here is to portray time as a perspective on the Self through In-Other. Such a perspective implies first a certain established, habitual, encountered Otherness, as integral to the definition of time. Repeatedly expressed by my interlocutors as an 'unwritten rule' or a 'tacit agreement', the position of the Gurbeti in the Field was tied to the local expression of the layered pastoral calendar. As the most durable foundation of cosmological thought, this 'calendric life' was also rendered into the desired chronotopic identity of the Field after the 1990s war.

This request for the Self, not as it is, but as it was and ought again be, then also entailed In-Other, indispensable to spatiotemporal and affective anchors. There was a plea for the return not merely of body to place but of the Self through In-Other – the return of a positioned body to a web of relationships that continued to define it in an eviscerated landscape. In-Other, embedded into both the experience and structure of time, was revealed as other but intimate, different but the same, strange but common, an unalienable alien, a habituated novelty. I remembered this *problem of being* every time I went to London's Golders Green and simultaneously existed with and beside the Haredim who walked through the park in distinct attires, lit menorahs during Hanukkah and sold kosher meat in their butcheries. They were, perhaps only in my field of vision, ontologically within and without me. As a frequent visitor to the area, I was simultaneously habituated to and surprised by their participation in my own space and my participation in theirs. I started to define myself and my temporal-spatial map of London by way of including their difference into it. I maintained this landscaped intimacy alongside, or through alterity. It was stimulated by boundaries and crossings. The loss of the self in the other, the loss of the other, Bakhtin called 'an impoverishment of Being' (1999: 16). Racisms and nationalisms are such impoverished endeavours; difference is only ever approached through its denial, the renouncement of the possibility to be In-Other.

Despite the proximity, village life in the Field had designated distinct spaces from which Gurbeti, Muslims and Serbs approached each other. Introverted in terms of marriage possibilities, they necessarily perpetuated a certain kind of social differentiation. The habitual daily and ritual exchange functioned within such frameworks. For those who lived in the town of Gacko, as in other relatively urbanized areas, communal differences partly transformed into new shared identities. Postwar narratives of resistance to nationalist divisions were often expressed from this position of urban identity, as 'We are not Serbs or Muslims, we are simply *Brčaci* [people from Brčko]', for example. This kind of resistance was not particularly common in the town of Gacko, perhaps because it has seen a zero rate of postwar return. Dževad, a returnee to the village of Bahori spoke about get-togethers with his *Gačani* friends in the *Gradska kafana*, the central town café, as evidence of a certain 'stabilization'. Such recuperated meetings were a different kind of habitual strange – an uncommon day-to-day – a chronotopic pile-up.

The habitual, Sara Ahmed noted, is not readily perceived, yet, through its enactment, things become part of the Self, so that:

> Habits, in other words, do not just involve the repetition of 'tending toward', but also involve the incorporation of that which is 'tended toward' into the body. These objects extend the body by extending what it can reach. Reachability is hence an effect of the habitual, in the sense that what is reachable depends on what bodies 'take in' as objects that extend their bodily motility, becoming like a second skin. (2006: 131)

One's *skin* attains 'presence' when it dramatically changes, when it is alienated, when another kind of *skin* is contrasted against it, when it suffers or enjoys ... Its taken-for-grantedness is disturbed in unusually intemperate climates. A chronotopic shift, likewise, awakes the recognition of body's reachability, sometimes turning it into desire: exile and return may beckon the intimacy of home, a dead body may evoke *kafenisanje* (socializing over coffee), and a seasonal feast might emphasize communal bonds. Intensely socialized and desocialized timeplaces have a particular potential for awakening the *skin* as the Self in its worldly extensions.

Ahmed called these turning points of various intensity 'moments of disorientation' – 'they are bodily experiences that throw the world up, or throw the body from its ground' (2006: 157). It is too strong a phrase to be used for the vernal return of the Gurbeti, which had been simultaneously habitual and new. It was an expected occurrence, yet a noticeable change accentuated by the co-orchestrated performance of humans and nonhumans – a moment of reorientation, rather. The rejoicing cattle, children and plants, the births, the Gurbeti music and dance, the scents and the colours of the Field shook the dormant winter bodies into an exciting and new, if familiar and old, state of consciousness.

Kolind (2008) described how his interlocutors in Stolac experienced the 'unmaking of the world' with the onset of the 1990s war. They had to 're-question previously taken-for-granted social relations, values and moral categories' including the 'non-conscious routine practices and categories' which can be made conscious (ibid: 49–50). He noted:

> the everyday world possesses a taken-for-granted-ness that is fundamental to processes of identification of oneself and the Other, and to avoid feeling bewilderment and confusion. And it is the damage to such everyday worlds with their predictable social routines and identities that constitutes a core element in many people's war experiences. (ibid)

The concept of disorientation as a sort of pre-reorientation might be rather more applicable to the fragmented survival of the Gacko landscape after the 1990s war. Immense changes to the Field – the ruination of its social through the elimination and disconnection of the humans and nonhumans who dwelled therein – produced not only a state of crisis and uncertainty, but also of reflexivity. The Field was alerted to its ontology. So, my second question is: What perspective comes after imposed distance and the interruption of habitual time and place? I am particularly interested to see whether the new positionalities in the Field reveal something crucial about the structural and affective qualities of time. It is an open-ended conversation with Yi-Fu Tuan's proposal that '[i]t is only when we reflect on the commonplace activities that their original intentional structures reemerge' (2011: 127). I should begin the first part of this conversation by noting two phenomena widely noticeable during my research in Gacko: the Gurbeti were depicted as a temporal and spatial 'commonplace' of the prewar Field; and the postwar Field accentuated their importance in the identity of the calendar.

Although they actually used to arrive earlier than 6 May, all narratives relate them strongly to George's Day. Typical descriptions of their arrival ('they brought warmth, the fair, rejoicing, the new year …') were interchangeable with descriptions of George's arrival. Memories of the Gurbeti follow the calendric model of relationships, or, rather, a relational model of the calendar. The same can be said about memories of communication between Serbs and Muslims. They show how the In-Other positions not only the Self in ontologically specific Time, but also how it establishes the substance and structure of time as such. This proximity with the In-Other is ritually confirmed, for, without In-Other one is timeless and placeless. The removal of the In-Other from the Self – its relegation to the Other – was systematic and violent, but ultimately unsuccessful. Unwittingly, it left myriad traces, clues known only to those who have also known the In-Other. The physically disentangled communities of the Field have resorted to residues of such intimacies to locate themselves temporally and spatially.

In their narrative reconstructions of life with Gurbeti, the 'settled' Serbs and Muslims simultaneously reshaped their own perceptions of Gurbeti chronotopic residency. Previously described as 'falling' (*padali*) onto the

Field, rather than 'arriving' or 'returning' to it, the vernal comings of the Gurbeti were construed as random, temporary and sudden. In postwar recollections, however, they were endowed with a fixed, cyclical identity without which the time and the space of home could not be spoken. Paradoxically, it is in their absence that the Gurbeti have been acknowledged as permanent residents of the Field. The new desire was not for the Gurbeti to fall, but to return to fall, to *return to return*.

'Gurbeti' was a word I came to know shortly upon asking about the spring. It was how the local 'settled' population primarily referred to the nomadic people, who are also known as *Romi* (Roma) or *Cigani* (Gypsies). Gurbeti might have been a 'self-referential ethnonym'. I cannot know, as there were none in the Field during my fieldwork in 2011 and 2012. Almost everything I have learnt about the Gurbeti was recounted to me by Gacko 'settled folk', some of whom were living in exile. This narrative orientation is part of my argument about the knowledge of time through the In-Other, which would require extension had I actually met a Gurbeti person in the Field. During a conversation at a conference in Oxford, as I was telling her about research, one colleague from Serbia told me that she was Gurbeti. My excitement, justifiably, seemed to confuse her – I began to assign to her my affective retention of the Field. This text is then not about the Gurbeti per se, but reflections on the Gurbeti of the Field imparted by my non-Gurbeti interlocutors – the Gurbeti as In-Other. Such perceptions, of course, were not all the same intensity or detail. They revealed different kinds of interaction, where intimacy and distance were not exclusive of each other.

Whilst attending the Roma community's celebration of George's Day in the central Bosnian town of Visoko, a local woman described to me the discomfort she had felt at hearing a 'Hayat TV' presenter use the word *Cigani* (Gypsies). Indeed, it is often understood as derogatory in Bosnia and elsewhere, so I decided to discard it as a general rule, even though, when 'non-Roma' people from Gacko used the word *Cigani,* it almost never translated as an insult within their narratives. But, to be precise, neither *Cigani* nor *Roma* was fully correct in the Muslim-Serb comments on the Field; 'They were *Gurbeti* and that's how they were referred to', I was told. The places where they 'fell' were thus called *Gurbetišta* ('Gurbeti places').

Gurbeti is also a language, or a distinct dialect of the Roma language, spoken by groups across the Balkan Peninsula (see Tahirović Sijerčić 2011). Etymologically, the word comes through Turkish *gurbet,* from Arabic *garaba,* which means 'absence from home'.[3] The Arabic *garib* (plural *guraba*) is used for 'strange' and 'foreign', but also 'remarkable', 'astonishing', 'wondrous', and 'baffling'. The otherness of the human bodies and landscapes on the move grew into basic lexical units of time-reckoning. While uttering the word 'Gurbeti' in Gacko evoked a feeling of springtime, the Arabic *gurub* denoted the setting of the sun.⁴ In the postwar constellation of the Field, the words, the bodies and the land engaged in an uncanny play of intimacy and distance. The Serbs and Muslims away from home, even if presently living where home used to be, could not speak home without inviting vivid memories of the Gurbeti, whose very name implied that their home was somewhere else.

My friend Yılmaz, born in Turkey and now living and working in London, explained the meaning of the word through migration:

> I am in *gurbet* in the UK. *Gurbet* is the foreign land, far from your motherland. It applies to work migrants, like the *Gastarbaiter* in Germany. It can also describe exile for refugees. *Gurbetçi* are people who are in *gurbet*. In Turkey, I could be called *gurbetçi*. There are many songs about gurbet.

However, unlike Yilmaz, nobody in the Field could explain why this particular ethnonym was related to the people who used to return each spring. The same problem occurred with other ethnonyms in the Field. Rather than the religious designation *pravoslavci* (Orthodox Christians), they used the national/ethnic *Srbi* (Serbs). *Muslimani* (Muslims) were, however, ethnicized in religious terms, although the postwar ethnic/national *Bošnjaci* (Bosniaks) did make an occasional appearance (mostly in the narratives of the few politically engaged individuals). While the genealogy of these ethnonyms may allow for historical and political contextualization (see Introduction), it does not account for the local and personal semantics, which translate 'Gurbeti', first and foremost, as those who arrived to the Field in springtime and marked the new season with extensive celebrations.

The second image of the Gurbeti is formed through a particular kind of economy; they tinned copper dishes and repaired other household items in exchange for farm produce and cooked food. Bećir and Zahida, the elderly Muslim couple who had returned to their hamlet of Hodinići, remembered that George's Day was particularly significant for the Gurbeti and in respect to them:

Bećir: Wheee, they would party [*teferičili*] ... Par-ty!!! It was music, anything you can imagine ... food, drink, spectacles ... Eeeeh ...

Zahida: They would come to [our households] throughout the summer. They tinned kitchenware [*kalajisali posuđe*].

Bećir: By God, they did! We looked after each other [*pazili se*]. By God, we did. Oooh, ooh! A lot!

Zahida: By God, we did. In the valley, just after this first village, there would be fifty *čerge* [tents/mobile households], maybe more ... I was a girl then. [Bećir laughs as if experiencing it anew.] The valley is called Pečuriš, like the mushroom *pečurka*. They had an accordion, and ... [Bećir laughs heartily again.]

> The Gypsy man would play and we flocked, both men and women. We would all come to sing and dance with them.
>
> Bećir: They bothered nobody...

Zahida's and Bećir's interjections of excitement resounded in my body as I walked through the vacant Pečuriš valley where the Gurbeti used to 'fall'.[5] It was guarded by a scattering of mediaeval tombstones (*stećci*), Illyrian burial mounds (*gomile*) and a corroded barrel inscribed with the blue letters 'USA' used to trench-up a postwar check point.

Late winter gave way to spring, then rolled into grassy summer, without song, as if time were fathomable beyond one's body, detached. The muteness stood violently over the valley. It was no longer an empty, but an eviscerated space. The inaudibility was different from the one I had heard before Bećir's laughter re-inhabited the karst with his memoryscapes.

The *teferič*, as organized by the Gurbeti upon their arrival, was not just any kind of party.[6] It was an outdoors fête or fair of the sort that follows most religious feasts and rituals in Bosnia. Such fairs usually include food (particularly spit-roasted meats), drinks, the *kolo* circle dance and various types of folk music. It is an opportunity for youthful flirtation, matchmaking, idle entertainment before and after the labours of the warm season and the kind of condensed communication unavailable during the winter months. *Teferič*, even the word, carries an ethos of happiness, intimacy and engagement beyond social (or class, cultural, religious or ethnic, if you will) differences, and is, as such, particularly suited for communion with In-Other. It is, conveniently, a time extracted from the daily labour that would otherwise constrain bodies to their closest and most familiar community, whether the house, the extended family household or the village. When the festival does include some of the more formalized religious rituals, they are performed before the *teferič* starts, thus remaining open for visitors from beyond the immediate religious community.

Certain spaces in the Field belonged to the Gurbeti, I was told, 'as if given by the state'. Although never legalized, their inheritance of specific seasonal residencies was, according to my interlocutors, acknowledged and respected by the 'settled folk'. The cognitive maps I collected generally included four to six *Gurbetišta* (Gurbeti places). Located close to the roads and the water springs, but sheltered from the wind, these were places where the Gurbeti lived and worked during the warm seasons, where they held their 'big weddings', where their children were born and where they buried their dead. Despite their steady history of habitation, the Gurbeti did not feature in the nationalist programmes that swept through the Field in the 1990s. They 'simply' did not return with the coming spring. Without the resonant orientation of intimate narratives, the embeddedness of Gurbeti presence in the spatial and temporal identity of the Field could easily have been obscured. Apart from some graves and unofficial toponyms, the only traces of their bodies still to be found in the Field are the memories of the seasons. In these memories, however precarious, the Gurbeti had both a historical and a suprahistorical importance for the Field. As Eno told me: 'According to some unwritten rule, they were like an integral part of nature and the life of this place. . . . They are somehow – in their history, and in our history – they are somehow related to us'.

The importance of Gurbeti rested upon an integral otherness, one that functioned in the cosmological and everyday constellation of the Field and added to its overall rhythm. Yet, to deem this integration purely functional would be to deny it the amplitude of the face-to-face encounter. The schedule of seasonal labour was attended by literal Gurbeti rhythms. The melodies of their instruments were the sound of the Gacko spring. Many of my interlocutors danced to it. During the month of Ramadan, the Gurbeti made sure that Muslims woke up on time to begin their fast. They walked through the villages, door to door, before dawn, beating their drums and shouting: 'Wake up boss! Wash the pots, cook the *halva*!'[7] When the elderly Safura described this Gurbeti call, she did so to correct her son, who had claimed that the only alarm clock they had were their cockerels. Their time was made possible for them by Gurbeti – 'an integral part of nature'.

Intimate knowledge does not preclude Otherness as a form of association. Indeed, intimacy is a process that simultaneously retains and surmounts separation. It does not depend only on human (and nonhuman) lives led in dialogic proximity; it relies on the difference of In-Other growing into the tissue of the Self. Only through In-Other do space and time become one's own, and only through it can they be spoken. In-Other began with the contents of the wide Field – the 'natural clocks' – the morning cockcrow and the hungry winter wolf, the migrating shadow on the mountain, one's own shadow cast upon the soil, the burgeoning soil, its deciduous and evergreen flora as well as the human beings suspended into the landscape and towards one's body from various directions.

Springtime, as 'Gurbeti time', was thus equally, if not more, the time of the 'non-Gurbeti settled folk'. The Gurbeti's arrival lay within the wider traditional calendar. They were awaited and yearned for in winter, as they are yearned for in their postwar absence. The 'Gurbeti places' also lay within the wider Field of Gacko, which were, like springtime, defined by their namesakes. Established in functional proximity to Serb and Muslim villages, for which they repaired tools and tinned copper dishes (*kalajisanje*), these places were inherited into 'non-Gurbeti' cognitive maps with the first memories of childhood. The chronotope of the Gurbeti may then be summarized through George's Day, which initiated the wider chronotope of the warm season. After the war, both emerged as the encompassing chronotope of the Field's desired past.

Kajmak and *Slatko*: The Home-Made and Bitter-Sweet Affect

> 'Things – even people – have a way of leaking into each other,' I explain, 'like flavours when you cook...'
> —Salman Rushdie, *Midnight's Children*

When the Gurbeti talked business with the Muslim and Serb 'settled folk', they would rarely ask for money, preferring to engage in so-called 'natural economy', receiving chickens, eggs, cheese, *kajmak* (a type of clotted cream), cooked foods or other home-made produce. For example, Avdija would tin Fatima's copper baking pan (*tepsija*) and, in return, Fatima would bake a pie (*pita*) for him in that same pan. If Avdija delivered a quality service, Fatima was able to reciprocate with a quality product. That *tepsija–pita* economy, like the landscape and the communal relationships it drew into itself, was predicated upon Avdija's and Fatima's face-to-face.

Nezir, a local botanist, told me about the process of tinning in more detail. The Gurbeti used a plant called *preslica* or *rastavić* (*Equisetum arvense*, or field horsetail), which contains a lot of oxalic acid. It was used to rub the copper dish clean. The second stage involved pouring a layer of molten tin (*kositar* or *kalaj*) over the dish to protect it from verdigris and give it a radiant finish, so that it 'shines like a mirror'. This business was a personal transaction. The 'parties' forged long-lasting friendships. Eno remembered Avdija, a Gurbeti man, from his childhood:

> Avdija was a good friend of my late grandfather. He visited each year. I was little. As time passed, I followed these events. My late grandmother would always cook lunch for his visit. Avdija would always bring presents – something for me, a dish for my late grandmother ... He would spend the entire day here, and even the *slatko* [a sweet chutney] was prepared for him, as it would for [the visit of] the dearest family member.

Slatko is a condensed product – a preserve bursting with affect. Its name literally translates as 'sweet'. Various kinds of garden fruit or, often, the petals of spring roses are cooked into a rich compote and stored for special occasions. Upon entering a home, guests may be welcomed with a small serving of *slatko* and, always, a glass of water to tame its sweetness. The relationship between host and guest is compressed into this dish. It is both a catalyst for and a consequence of certain affections. *Slatko* is rarely intended for household or daily use. It is usually kept for the guest. In fact, what I discovered in the Gacko narratives is that the intimacy of home and life with In-Other were often expressed through the homemade. Bryant (2016: 21) similarly noted that Turkish and Greek Cypriots remembered their lives together through the process of making halloumi.

Much of the information I gathered could not be included in this book: hundreds of hours of recorded conversations, detailed descriptions and erratic scratch-notes, scanned archival material, photographs and reminders I can no longer decipher. Amongst all of them, I kept going back to one still-life image: Zahida's meeting with Hajrija in a refugee shelter. They met in the city of Mostar, shortly after their expulsion in 1992; Gacko had already been 'freed' of their Otherness. The paths of Zahida, a 'Muslim, Bosniak, Bosnian, settled Gacko woman returnee' and Hajrija, a 'Gurbeti, Roma, Gypsy, nomadic Gacko woman who died in exile', intersected in home, and its absence. Through these various designations, their bodies and their landscape simultaneously enacted or attracted distinction, distance, Otherness and sameness, proximity and intimacy. 'Their' identities were employed to carve out the treacherous gorges for lives required to be quantifiable. Their meeting kept coming back to me, asserting its centrality in my writing, precisely as means to deconstruct the hegemony that latched onto their bodies and their landscape in the 1990s.

They had befriended each other through the usual kind of economy. Zahida gave Hajrija cheese and *kajmak* in exchange for restoring her copper cookware. Gacko *kajmak* is a rich dairy cream that ripens for months in a *mijeh,* an animal-skin sack. Regionally, the best quality *kajmak* was widely synonymous with Gacko. It was produced from the milk of the equally famous local cow breed. *Kajmak* was thus a 'condensed' marker of the Gacko landscapes, its daily life, subsistence and broader economy. Indeed, *kajmak* was for the 'settled folk' what *kalajisanje,* the tinning of copper dishes, was for the Gurbeti – an existential mastery – an indispensable knowledge of survival. Whilst Zahida and Hajrija exchanged their identities, they also produced the face of the Field as such.

War swept through the Field in 1992. Zahida's houses were turned to rubble and the Gurbeti lands fell vacant. Zahida was living in someone else's home in Mostar when Hajrija found her. They had coffee. Hajrija was now a beggar, displaced from much more than simply a form of economy. Zahida recounted the meeting-in-exile:

> She had heard about me and came to see me. Three times she came to the neighbourhood (*mahala*), came and sat with me: 'Eh, my Zahida, will there ever again come a time when you give me some of your *kajmak*?' 'By God, my Hajrija, no, never again. No, my Hajrija, never again will our eyes look upon Gacko. Never.'

The connection she crafted through her recollection was one that escapes language and our usual modes of research. I eat *kajmak* differently after the Field. It somehow captures a series of (sometimes incommensurable) scales.

Malinowski (2002: 18) called these moments 'imponderabilia', 'spun [with] the innumerable threads which keep together a [community]', yet which cannot simply be recorded, as they require some grasp of 'their full actuality'. My interlocutors' affective registers, the visual and the aural gaps between their narratives and their landscape, their *kajmak,* coffee and *slatko* set out on the table to welcome me, the memories of my own grandmothers' glistening jars of rose petal *slatko,* recorded something in my body not too difficult to estimate – a sweetness – and the bitterness of its absence. These non-historiographic moments were touched upon before me, as a token of a chronotopic Self that could not be without its In-Other, and that, perhaps, could no longer be.

Time in the Field was defined by the Gurbeti in at least two ways: their pre-war presence and their postwar absence. Both were orientational and disorientational, in that they constituted a fixed place of desire and a sudden change in the landscape. The vernal arrival of the Gurbeti was a temporal compass, a heuristic device for the yearly orientation of love and rituals, labour, subsistence and communal life. It was an indispensable, habitual surprise. Their abrupt 'falling' was also disorienting – an ever-new, remarkable and perplexing occurrence. The ethnonym 'Gurbeti' indeed contains etymological links to the thrill of difference. The seeming paradox of habitual strangeness reveals something about the Field's time: the heterogeneity of its (human and nonhuman) dwellers is mapped onto seasonal change. The temporal and the spatial-relational thus invariably indicate and anchor each other.

In the introduction to his *Time: The Familiar Stranger,* Julius Thomas Fraser, a noted 'chronographer', observed: 'The passage of time is intimately familiar; the idea of time is strangely elusive' (1987: 3). Closer to the body than anything else, speaking in the turns of the landscape, marking the tides on the *skin,* yet never fully certain and palpable, time itself appears as the familiar stranger. In the Field, In-Other was attuned with temporal rhythms, producing an itinerary of relations within and beyond a single year. The stranger also needs to be made one's own. Weather and time share the same word in most South-Slavic languages – *vrijeme.* This study of seasonal rituals indicates that the wanton weather, in need of apprehension and pacification, was at the conceptual (and etymological) base of time-reckoning. The weather–time stranger, unpredictable and thus dangerous, was approached through rituals to secure basic life (often expressed in the literal and symbolic image of the crops);[8] this is the figure of the summer Elijah, who may at any time choose to strike or spare the haystacks. The next part of this chapter discusses the temporal qualities of the Field's inter-religious sworn kinship, which provides an even clearer link with weather–time habitual strangeness.

I based the second of my questions about the Gurbeti and the Field's time on Ahmed's (2006) notion of moments of disorientation and Tuan's (2011) claim that the 'original intentional structures' of commonplace activities might be revealed in the personal and communal reflections following such moments. While the prewar 'falling' of the Gurbeti contributed to annual (dis)orientation, it was their postwar absence that constituted the most significant change in my interlocutors' lives. The temporal and spatial identity of the Field was so invested in its Gurbeti components that George's Day emerged as one of the most prominent signs of the past, second only to Elijah's Day.

Intimacy with Others retained its significance in the narration of time, even after the process of filtering through the many other images towards a stable place of memory. Not having been suffocated by nationalist discourses, an acknowledgement of deep relations with the Gurbeti flourished. It was a part of the 'old' landscape that could freely be desired. It revealed the In-Other as a strategy of claiming chronotopic belonging. In his *Time and the Other* (1983), Johannes Fabian critiqued the oppressive use of time in anthropological discourse, which (re)creates the traditional disciplinary object of the Other. Through various techniques of temporal distancing, he argued, such discourse effectively 'denies coevalness' of anthropologists and their interlocutors. Fabian and I are approaching the questions of time and otherness from different methodological angles. I am primarily attempting to describe the habitual spatiotemporal proximities in the Field. It is, rather, my interlocutors who have denied the coevalness of the 'old' and the 'new' Field, whilst often participating in the maintenance of both. Implicitly, there is a danger of reading my descriptions of the Field's time as an ideal, impervious structure. On the contrary, the cosmic, mundane, political, intersubjective, and so on, times of the Field were interlaced and changing. When persons and institutions stabilized them, they effectively projected a particular political argument about relationality.

Through the temporal anchoring of the In-Other, the Field petitioned against the nationalist Othering. Even without the Gurbeti themselves, time still *was* by way of reference to them. From signs of the warming landscape, they were transformed into markers of that landscape as a whole. The 'new' temporal position they occupied was still desired, albeit through contained hope rather than the past expectation of a certainty.

Kumstvo: On Time and Trust

Kum is closer than a brother.
Kum is sacred.

—Saying in the Field[9]

Otherness in the Field is an unpredictable and therefore dangerous exteriority. If not familiarized, it looms over one's existential bases – the crops, cattle, body and community. Pacifying the Otherness of the Cosmos required the establishment of a habituated, rhythmical rapport – a ritual bond. To thoroughly ensure their benevolence, all Others needed to be ritually included into the Self. These Others, with powers to aid and harm, were the agentive entities guiding the sun, the lightning, the rain, human and nonhuman fertility, social life and death. The Field's cosmology worked to remove their dangers by offering *formulae of rapport*.

One such traditional answer was the institution of *kumstvo*, an 'additional' kinship formed through several different kinds of allegiance. Maintained through the cyclical calendar, it is best described as a contract of intimacy with the Other. This section unfolds through three concomitant goals. Firstly, I offer a hermeneutic of Otherness in need of ritual appropriation through *kumstvo*. Secondly, I look into the temporal (calendric) arrangements of this type of bond. Lastly, I analyse the meaning of *kumstvo* as an 'intercommunal' (or, 'inter-religious') institution through the narratives of the Field's inhabitants.

What is *Kumstvo*?

Kumstvo has been variously translated as 'godparenthood', 'ritual/spiritual sponsorship' or 'spiritual/ritual/fictive/sworn/extended kinship',[10] yet it is a concept that resists its English translation, as it carries certain idiosyncrasies in Bosnian contexts. It is understood as one of the most important social relationships, usually in the form of an old bond between two families. Proverbially, one's *kum* is closer than a brother. And if you ask, as I did, what *kumstvo* is, the reply you are likely to receive will be a description of how it is. Sometimes, though, I was offered a more 'precise' definition. So, in the words of my interlocutors, let's begin by noting that, in the Field, 'it was a common approach' and 'the greatest bond of friendship between Serbs and Muslims'.

Kumstvo entails a plethora of specific relationships. Most attempts at systematization mention three to four types.[11] The first one, known as 'wet *kumstvo*', is enacted as part of the child's baptism. The second two are known as 'dry'. The first dry *kumstvo* may be forged at weddings, when the *kum* is witness to the union of the couple and subsequently an intimate household friend. The second 'dry' bond is the shorn-hair *kumstvo* (*šišano/striženo*), confirmed by the ceremony of cutting the newborn's hair. The fourth type of *kumstvo* is forged for protection from trouble (*po nevolji*). Hörman (1889) and Hangi (1906: 115–16) additionally mentioned circumcision *kumstvo* (*sunetsko*) in Muslim families. Another closely related form of alternative kinship is activated by the exchange of milk, through nonmaternal (or wet) nursing, and the ritual exchange of blood, whereby the actors become spiritual or sworn kin.[12]

Despite the different designations, all forms of *kumstvo* exhibit a certain apotropaic and initiatory quality. The confirmation of the bond involves the hair, milk, blood, skin and bodily proximity of those initiated. Its corporeal promise yields an affective capacity. Čajkanović (1973: 164) thought that the differentiation between baptismal and shorn-hair *kumstvo* should be understood as purely formal, since both imply the initiation of a child into the community, although he considered the latter an older 'pre-Christian remnant'. Of course, circumcision and wedding *kumstvo*, as well as milk kinship, are also forms of initiation into the community. The exchange of milk and blood suggest that the other person is incorporated within the Self's body.

Further evidence that it is a form of kinship contract is the fact that marriage and sexual relationships were not allowed between *kumovi*, a ban that transferred down the generations.[13] As inter-religious marriages in the Field were not common, according to my interlocutors, this prohibition made more sense within certain forms of *kumstvo*. Muslim women in the Field would not cover their faces before Orthodox Christian men, Osman told me, as 'with a *kum*, it was as if a brother or another member of the family were there. There was no hiding'.

In the inherited forms of *kumstvo*, where the original bonding act (*kumovanje*) is obscured by time, *kum* is understood to be the male, *kuma* the female, head of the households on either side of the relationship. However, when my interlocutors spoke about *kumstvo*, they mostly employed the plural *kumovi*, which was a reciprocal designation for the whole family line with whom the pact of intimacy had been made. In this sense, time usually only increased the number of individuals who could directly be included in the relationship. Čajkanović (1973: 164) noted that the institution must be old and 'certainly pre-Christian', as the word for *kum* is 'more or less' common to the Slavs, Lithuanians and Latvians.[14]

Its etymology has been linked to the Latin *commater/compater*, literally co-mother/co-father (Skok 1972: 231–32, see also Mitterauer 2010: 71). Skok (ibid) notes that *kum* should be understood as a hypocorism of the words for co-parenthood, which would imply that *kumstvo* might have primarily been defined through one's relationship with a child. It does not have to be an abbreviation. Zaliznjak and Shmelev (2007) have argued that the prefix *com* has two predominant meanings: 'joint action' (including 'reciprocity') and 'bringing/coming together'. Similarly, the Latin preposition *cum* stands for 'with' or 'together with'; so, 'companion' is *cum panis*, one who partakes in the sharing of bread. The Bosnian suffix *-stvo*, in this case, signifies the quality or state of the word *kum*. This is exactly how my interlocutors described *kumstvo*, as *communitas*, a state or quality of being with, together. It is manifested as a reciprocal bonding act and the resulting relationship of intimacy, affinity, care and trust, reaffirmed through bodily presence in times of joy and sadness.

Kumstvo: To Make the Other Intimate

'It was never really Muslim with Muslim or Serb with Serb, but exclusively Serb–Muslim', Osman told me about *kumstvo* in the Field. The same exclusive arrangement was to be found throughout the wider Herzegovina region, particularly around the neighbouring towns of Nevesinje and Bileća, which similarly had largely Serb and Muslim pre-1992 populations and experienced the same levels of polarizing violence after the beginning of war. Because of this peculiarity, my primary concern is the 'inter-religious' (or 'inter-ethnic', if you will) form of *kumstvo* as narrated in the Gacko Field. How was it structured? What kind of actions did the relationship imply? And, finally, what happened to these bonds after the advent of nationalist violence?

Bogišić, in his 1874 'socio-legal' treatise, noted that shorn-hair *kumstvo* 'emerged between Christians and Turks, since the Turk cannot enact *kumstvo* in the first two [categories]' (ibid: 176).[15] This 'inter-religious' shorn-hair *kumstvo* was considered more significant than marital or circumcision *kumstvo* in some parts of Bosnia (Hangi 1906: 116). Bogišić wanted to describe the qualitative differences between *kumstvo* relationships in the various South-Slavic regions. For Bosnia, he briefly noted that it meant 'trust, care, love, aid, etc.' (ibid: 388). Other fin-de-siècle researchers have noted the 'inter-religious' specificity of shorn-hair *kumstvo*. Kosta Hörman (1889) provided an account of this ritual between 'Muhamedans and Christians' in Herzegovina, noting reciprocal gift-giving. It reveals the ritual centrality and magical property of the *kum*:

> *Kumovanje* [the instituting act of *kumstvo*] occurs before the scissors have touched the child's hair, and has to be performed in the morning, while the day is advancing. The child's father invites friends and relatives to his house, and they have to arrive in the morning, to welcome the *kum* with great ceremony. The child is dressed in the finest garments. The *kum* takes the child on his lap, and one of the child's relatives brings in some bowl, usually glass or ceramic, with clean water and holds it under the child's neck. The *kum* takes the scissors and cuts some of the child's hair, firstly above the right ear, then from the top of the head, and, finally, above the left ear. The cut hair falls into the water in the dish. When he has completed this, *kum* throws some coins into the water – according to his wealth – five or ten *plete* of zwanzig, a ducat, and even more, as much as he wants or wills.[16] The gathered company will also throw coins into the water. All that money will be divided amongst the *hizmećari* [the servants/help]. (Hörman 1889)

More than a century and two polarizing wars later, Emin gave me a remarkably similar, if less detailed, description of the shorn-hair *kumstvo* traditions in the Field:

> *Kumstvo,* you see, since there were no Croats in our area . . . *Kumstvo* was the greatest bond of friendship between Serbs and Muslims. People observed each other, discovered each other and offered *kumstvo* to each other. And that *kumstvo* was based . . . Let's say a male child is born, and a Serb man, chosen by you, is invited. With his family, he comes to visit his host and cuts the child's hair and then the visits continue between those *kumovi.* They visit each other all the time. Then their children inherit the *kumstvo*; they all call each other *kumovi,* and so on.

Emin's emphasis on the absence of Croats in Gacko is important. Croat is the common 'ethnonym' for Catholics, the third most numerous 'ethno-religious' identity, which was formerly present in most Bosnian urban areas. In the Gacko municipality, however, the total population of 10,788 in 1991 included only 29 declared Croats, all but one living in the town itself.[17] Under Emin's logic, had there been a Croat community in Gacko, their inclusion into the bond of *kumstvo* would have been appropriate. 'But, what about the Gurbeti? I asked him. 'Were the Gurbeti Roma families ever considered for this role?' 'There were no Roma in Gacko', he replied, but then ventured into the usual description of their spring residency in the Field.

Why were the Gurbeti generally incompatible with *kumstvo* – in contrast to Muslims, Serbs and Croats? The answer, I believe, reveals something crucial about the nature of the institution. It was the difference in their relationship to place. They were described as 'falling' (*padali*) onto the Field, not arriving or living there. The local attitude towards Gurbeti presence was obvious from Osman's paradox: there were no Roma in Gacko – they returned each spring. They were predictable, but not constant. Their departure at the end of the fertile season, when the hardships of winter were just about to commence, made them unreliable candidates for *kumstvo.*

The *kumstvo* bond exhibited its full significance in times of need. The Gurbeti presence in Gacko was unstable, if cyclically predictable, unreliable enough not to fulfil the requirements for the contract. Croats elsewhere, as 'settled', did forge shorn-hair *kumstvo* with Muslims and Serbs. Ivo Sivrić (1982: 75) argued that it was 'rude to refuse' such a bond. Filipović (1969: 39) noted that Catholic Christians and Muslims entered into *kumstvo* in central Bosnia, much like Orthodox Christians and Muslims in Herzegovina. According to him, a man and a woman could also form the bond between themselves and it often happened even without the hair cutting, prompted by a certain amount of *rakija* (brandy).

Accounts of *kumstvo* mostly predate the dissolution of Yugoslavia.[18] Eugene Hammel's (1968) *Alternative Social Structures and Ritual Relations in the Balkans* is the most systematic investigation of *kumstvo* to date. Although a work of admirable detail, it dedicates only one paragraph to '*kumstvo* and inter-ethnic relationships' (ibid: 88). Whilst haircutting was the most popular mode of establishing such alliances, he noted, Christians also enacted circumcision *kumstvo* for a Muslim child and Muslims enacted baptismal *kumstvo* for a Christian child (with some creative ways of circumventing the Church prohibitions of such alliances). More recently, however, David Henig's (2011: 96) ethnography on Muslim cosmology in central Bosnia has revealed that it is either a waning, regionally absent or transformed custom. He notes that he did not find *kumstvo* to be deemed particularly important and that it was usually forged within the extended family. From my limited information on central Bosnia, the institution has been transformed while still retaining some of the logic of In-Other. For example, Amra, from the central Bosnian village of Čevljanovići, made sure to choose *kumovi* for her children, explaining that the candidates needed to be 'someone good, but initially not too close'.

One tradition recorded in Bosnia was to leave a child at the crossroads so that the first person to pass by throws a coin at them, gives them a name and cuts their hair, thus becoming their *kum* (see Kabakova 2001: 318). This custom seems to have been particularly important for sickly newborns, who were taken in front of the house on the morning of the new moon, so that the first passer-by was made the shorn-hair *kum*, 'be they man or woman, Muslim or Christian, or even a black Gypsy' (Hangi 1906: 115–16).[19] Filipović (1969: 105) described how one mother from the town of Modriča observed the ritual in silence, even though the passer-by gave the child a name different from the one previously chosen. These instances confirm the sacrosanct position of the *kum* and the powers of the destined In-Other. Intimacy with a stranger can even be lifesaving.

In-Other at Large

One clue to the logic of *kumstvo* as intimacy with the otherwise unpredictable Other is the recorded tradition of similar alliances with animals or supernatural beings. In one Herzegovinian folksong, the first child is promised in *kumstvo* to a (were)wolf in order to deter an imminent attack (Nodilo 1981, Part 4: 34). Others mention apotropaic *kumstvo* with fairies or nymphs (*vile*) and evil spirits (Kretzenbacher: 1971) as well as with snakes, wolves, weasels and mice (Čajkanović 1973: 164).

The Other, approached through the Georgic tradition of the Field, is then the landscape, mysterious at large. It is offered the essence of the body, drawn into a spiritual contract through the sharing of the Self. The harmful uncertainty of being with the Other is managed through the taboo of blood, the principle that 'one's own' is inviolable. So, the 'religious' Other-made-intimate is not to be excised from the overall logic of the landscape. My exploration of 'inter-religious' *kumstvo* comes with this important caveat, not to think of the Field's cosmological In-Other in the simple terms of contemporary sacro-political identities. The Other is firstly the landscape beyond the border of the body, a web of actants settled into a symbolic order.

Interwoven into mysterious Otherness are the mytho-poetic heroes of the Western-Balkan epics. Although of different religious or political backgrounds, these heroes often form alliances of *kumstvo* or sworn brotherhood/sisterhood (*pobratimstvo/posestrimstvo*). Rather than attempting a survey of this immense topic, I offer a few illustrative examples.

One song recorded in the Field in the nineteenth century tells the story of Husein the outlaw.[20] After some high-profile, and so particularly dangerous, adultery, he takes refuge with a nobleman, Vuk Jajčanin, who welcomes him with 'coffee and *rakija*', hugs him, kisses him and makes him a sworn brother. Kinship 'in trouble' (*po nevolji*) is here confirmed by the very act of protection. Protection can also come from supernatural beings, as in the song about Mitar, the mason of the Višegrad bridge, who finds a fairy (*vila*) in the river.[21] In exchange for her own life, the fairy offers him 'sworn brotherhood by God' (*pobratimstvo Bogom*), so that he is able to ask for her help with the bridge when he needs it. Kinship binds the parties into a promise of care; no harm can come after such intimacy is attained. This is expressed in the song about the frail, twelve-year-old, 'pre-heroic' Omer, who, venturing across a dark mountain, encourages his horse by telling him of the safety of the sworn intimacy with 'the dark wolves, our sworn brothers', 'the ravens – our interlocutors', and 'the fairies – our sworn sisters'.[22]

While all the epic heroes exhibit Georgic qualities, two stand out: Alija Đerzelez and Prince Marko. Always followed by their trusty horses, they fight dragon-like creatures, while also exhibiting dragon-like properties.[23] The supernatural strength of both characters comes from them having suckled at a fairy's breast in childhood (see Lord 1991: 214, Hörman 1996: 761), which is, of course, the already mentioned milk kinship. For now, let me turn to the spiritual alliance between Prince Marko and Alija Đerzelez.[24]

In one narrative recorded by Hörman (1996: 761–65) Alija and Marko have the same uncanny dream. Their fairy sworn sisters instruct them separately to find each other and become sworn brothers, for, in the course of their quest, each would find a hero better than himself. They embark on their respective worldwide searches until they find each other and become sworn brothers rather than sworn enemies (which they also are in the rich Bosnian and Serbian epic opus). Their emotional meeting is recorded in one epic song.[25] The last poetic image, reproduced here, is of Prince Marko recounting to his mother how he found Alija:

Ja potekoh Đerzelez Aliji;	I ran to Đerzelez Alija;
pa zagrlih Đerzelez Aliju.	and I hugged Đerzelez Alija.
Udariše mi suze od očiju,	Tears leapt from my eyes,
udariše mi niz bijelo lice,	leapt down my white face,
pa ja grlom junačkijem viknuh:	and I shouted with a hero's throat:
'Hvala Bogu i današnjem danu,	'Thank God and the day that's in it,
kad ja nađoh svoga pobratima!	for I've found my sworn brother!
Ja sam, pobro, Kraljeviću Marko!'	My sworn brother, I am Prince Marko!'
Kad to čuo Đerzelez Alija,	When Đerzelez Alija heard this,
ruke širi, u čelo me ljubi.	he spread his arms, kissed my forehead.
Tude smo se, majko, upoznali,	There, my mother, we met,
i tude smo s', majko, pobratili.	and there, my mother, we became sworn brothers.

There is no insinuation of protection or alliance in the song, but rather a sense of a preordained spiritual unity. It suggests that a rethinking of the 'ethnographic' data is required. The epics continue to be an important mode of articulation for the Field; sworn brotherhood and *kumstvo* have nuances of meaning 'outside' of the song. In the following pages, I explore some of the affective, temporal and protective qualities of this institution.

Time to Meet

The dedication and intimacy produced by *kumstvo* take precedence over any utilitarian functions in the accounts from the Field. The logic of the institution was based, at least partially, on proximity and affection. Intimacy might have been useful for economic security or as a pacifying method, but it also became the objective. It was confirmed through encounters, usually in the form of visitations between households. Meetings were arranged along the festivities of the traditional calendar, but included all the critical moments in the participants' lives, such as marriages, births, deaths and times of need. The functionalist disregard for the emotional and affective dimensions of *kumstvo* has been repeated by Hammel, who concluded that *kumstvo* was utilitarian 'despite the explicit folk theory that the relationship is one of mutual love, friendship and respect' (1968: 43).

As a heritable form of extended kinship, *kumstvo* played an important role in broadening the social network (see Hammel 1968, Devrnja Zimmerman 1986: 115). It was created between households rather than individuals and implied a reciprocity of investment. Karadžić (1852: 314) had already argued that all the family members were considered *kumovi*; as the bond was not exclusive to individuals, it could be preserved through many generations. So, the usual response to the questions 'Who is your *kum*?' and 'To whom are you *kum*?' is a family name in the plural, Hammel noticed (1968: 9). This type of kinship created unbreakable bonds between the households involved (see also Kabakova 2001).

Osman's narrative indicated that, rather than simply a contract, it became an intimate and moral imperative:

> For example, in my personal case, my grandfather, my father's father, was *kum* to a girl from the Šuković family. She was greatly devoted to our family, as we were to hers. For example, I had eight sisters, three brothers – there were thirteen of us altogether, including my uncle's two children, and she knew all our names, where each of us married – she paid close attention to it until she died. She died a year or two before the war [1992]. We used to visit her house. She was married into the Avdalović family. With that house too, we were friends, *kumovi*, eternally. We called her aunt Mara. It simply created a moral obligation to take care of each other. So, for example, a Serb from Bileća and a Muslim from Gacko, or a Serb from Nevesinje and a Muslim from Gacko, or vice versa, would become *kumovi*, and they were most faithful to each other, in all aspects.

Because the relationship seems to have been inherited in perpetuity, some families did not know exactly when the originating act took place. The mutual dedication to care and affection was confirmed through the rhythmical sharing of joy and hardship. They visited each other for holidays, weddings, birthdays and funerals, exchanged gifts, provided accommodation and protected each other in times of need. 'Your *kumovi*', Hasiba exclaimed, 'are closer to you than some parts of your own family!'

The *kum* was supposed to give the biggest gift in the original ritual, but also to receive an equally substantial return. The households then continued to exchange gifts throughout the long-lasting relationships. Nada told me how women used to comb and knit sheep's wool for traditional clothing, which was later given in dowry, but also as gifts to *kumovi*. Things that are said to be 'as if to bring out when *kum* visits' (*kao za pred kuma*) are exceptionally nice (see Karadžić 1852: 314). The reciprocity was important enough to produce the saying 'If *kuma* gave her *kum* no gift, she give him no cause for worry, either'.[26] So, the gift certainly wasn't 'free', but then, to quote Mary Douglas' foreword to Marcel Mauss' famous treatise, '[a] gift that does nothing to enhance solidarity is a contradiction' (2002: x). *Kumstvo* gift-giving entailed a promise to care and be near, through the 'times of need' and in spite of day-to-day distances. It cuts across the lines of distinction thanks to the obligation of reciprocity in love, care and protection, because, while the intimacy of a kinship may be taken for granted, intimacy beyond 'sameness' requires some kind of reiteration.

So, when would *kumovi* visit? According to Hörman (1889): 'The *kum* is considered the foremost friend; the *kum* may visit the house at any time, the girls of the household do not cover before him. . . . when a [child] needs help or advice, it will always look to its *kum,* and he will do whatever he can'. Vucinich (1976: 176) similarly noted that '*kums* were present at one another's homes in times of crisis, death, weddings, and on the patron saint day'. In the Field, they also paid visits at the start of spring. Osman said: 'I remember as a child, that Serb families came to Muslim villages on George's Day. Although they didn't live there, they would visit their friends, their *kumovi*, on George's Day'.

One must remember that, in the Field, George's Day, unlike Elijah's, used to be a rather intimate affair, confined to the villages.[27] Even visits between villagers were not very common. So, for *kumovi* to visit, and on a day of importance for their own household too, must have exhibited a particular kind of intimacy. Some celebrations, even if 'exclusive' to one or the other of the religious communities, were also shared. Thus, Serb *kumovi* would visit Muslims for the two *Bajram* (Eid) festivities, while Muslims would reciprocate for Christmas and Easter.

'Intercommunal' visits also occurred on the biggest of the Field's occasions – Elijah's Day (*Ilindan/Aliđun*) – which was celebrated by Serbs and Muslims during different parts of the day, in increasingly separate locations. The visits might themselves have been the reason for the temporal allocations, so that Ilija, the Christian face of Elijah got the morning, and Alija, the Muslim face of Elijah, got the afternoon. Christians went to church in the morning, before their *teferič*, while Muslims attended noon prayers in the mosque, before theirs.

While most of my interlocutors confirmed the strength of *kumstvo* communication across 'religious/ethnic' lines, different generational perspectives, or chronotopic dissonances, emerged as salient examples of the 'friction' (after Tsing 2004) between the Field and political changes on the larger scales. I spoke to Šemsa and her daughter Meliha (both pseudonyms), who argued spiritedly about the intensity of 'inter-religious' communication. Fifty-year-old Meliha's position was that 'the two nations were never affectionate to each other'. She saw friendships as having started only in late socialist Yugoslavia, with the establishment of the thermal power plant in the 1970s, and had never seen 'a Serb and a Muslim joining hands in the festive *kolo* (circle) dance'. While her mother agreed that for the younger generations friendships had indeed expanded thanks to the new, 'mixed' workplace, she explained the exact circumstances of 'inter-religious' visitation, through the 'intersection' of gender and religion:

> Well, you didn't. Girls didn't go. . . . But when Elijah's Day (*Aliđun*) came round, when it took place here, then everyone would gather (*zbubali se*). There were more of them than of us. That's how it was. That's how it was. And then our lot would do the same and go to Nadanići [the village of the Serb celebration] – the lads, that is – gals didn't go, but lads did.

While women from one community may not have gone to the other community's gathering, they were certainly present at their own Elijah's Day celebration. With so many people arriving from other places, it would surely have been difficult for anyone, let alone a child, to distinguish between Serb and Muslim visitors. Would they recognize their own *kumovi*, at least? Šemsa's and Meliha's family, for some reason, didn't have any, which is possibly why the daughter's memories excluded Serb–Muslim visitations. Of course, the bridges a researcher builds between contradictory stories are always somewhat arbitrary. A Field populated by older people suggests that an in-depth examination of this question should venture further than I have, into the diasporic communities. Overwhelmingly, though, my interlocutors narrated a chronotope of *kumstvo*-bonding. Looking at the prewar phone book for Gacko, which gives no residential details, Homogeceka (2011) exclaimed: 'No wonder. Gacko people did not need it at the time. A neighbour knew where his neighbour, *kum* and friend lived'.

The intimacy I describe here has a temporal note. It is not determined solely by the 'important occasions', but they provided rhythmical reciprocity to the relationship. As mentioned, births, deaths, marriages and festivities, particularly the days of George and Elijah, were the major impetus for *kumstvo* visitations.

Asim Bašić appeared as a witness during the trial of Stanšić and Župljanin before the ICTY (IT-08-91). The accused were later sentenced to twenty-two years each for their crimes, inter alia, in Gacko. Pidwell, the Lead Prosecutor, asked Bašić to describe the relations 'between Bosniaks and Serbs' before the war. His reply included festive visitations as a sign of intercommunal bonds:

> Before the war, the relationships were excellent until the moment some paramilitary formations came from Serbia about a couple of months before the war. Before that, everything was excellent, we socialized, we celebrated our religious holidays together. It was good.

Times of Need and Protection

Let us venture into the function of *kumstvo*. While looking into the utilitarian aspects of the institution, I want to keep in mind that it is regarded as a relationship of love. For my interlocutors, the bond was far from a simple cost–benefit analysis. In fact, rather than taking intimacy as the means to a reciprocal promise of safety and resource sharing, it is equally justifiable to understand intimacy as the goal, and the contract to aid and protect as the instrument.

Unlike the town centre, the villages scattered around the Field have rarely been mixed in terms of religious denomination. This is not surprising considering that each of them had sprung from not more than a few families gathered around a shared place of worship. In such circumstances, *kumstvo* was also an alliance with another village community. It provided an extended web of support. Lockwood (1974: 258) noted that both Muslims and Christians had a preference for *kumstvo* with people 'from afar', arguing that the 'institution is considered too important a relationship to endanger by day-to-day interaction'.[28] Filipović (1969: 141) likewise mentioned avoidance of *kumovi* from one's immediate environment – so as to circumvent any arguments. The proximity of *kumovi*, 'closer than family', is less a spatial measure and more an affective one.

The types of assistance and protection that one could expect were not predefined and usually adjusted to chronotopic circumstances. Spiritual kin households would often share resources and agricultural equipment or form a united workforce at harvest (known as *moba*). You turn to your *kumovi* in any kind of need, for example to rebuild a home, as Zorica recalled:

> Let me just add one crucial point. If the house or business of one *kum*, whether Muslim or Serb, were to burn down, the first to jump to help would be the *kumovi* from the other side. They would either provide material support or join in the rebuilding. It was the greatest bond of friendship.

Assistance was inscribed into the relationship, as a crucial ethical imperative of intimacy shared beyond times of need, in 'good times' (or, 'in sickness as in health'). The two kinds of times sustained each other. Marriage, at least in the Field, seems comparable to *kumstvo*. It was an expanded kinship, one that required a contract (of love, care and sharing), a promise and bodily 'immersion' as well.

Who do you turn to in bad times? The response is a matter of emotion, as much as (or more than) one of function. Lockwood (1974: 258) argued for the practicality of an extra-local *kumstvo* bond, as it provides a 'home-away-from-home and is used for overnight lodging whenever convenient' and may be an important source of material and nonmaterial aid. Rade, from the village of Zalom near the town of Nevesinje, told me about the days of tobacco smuggling in the Kingdom of Yugoslavia. The gendarmerie would patrol the area and all the smuggling activity had to take place in the dead of night. He said:

> Serbs and Muslims would enter into *kumstvo*. *Kumstvo* lasted for a hundred years. People would take up to thirty kilos of tobacco. It was dangerous. They would come [into a village] at night and whisper: 'Where is our *kuma*? Where is our *kuma*?'

The *kuma*, or the female head of the bonded household, would shelter them for as long as they needed protection. She would provide food and a place to sleep. Such protection was crucial, because life was difficult in the Kingdom of Yugoslavia and got much more difficult during the Second World War. Rade told me: 'You were always on the run, from the *Ustaše*, from the Partisans, from the *Četnici*, from the Italians'.²⁹ The narrated strength of *kumstvo* raises the question of the fate of whispers for protection during the 1990s war. Was it not a time when shelters would be activated and one's *kumovi* would jump to help?

In the Darkest Hour

The sentiment in the Field was that *kumstvo* had become a rarity, mainly because of the small scale of return. More systematic research on diasporic communities would have certainly revealed the extent of preserved relationships. Many of my interlocutors noted that even during the 1990s war the traditions held good in certain forms. Hasan found the survival of these bonds to be a proof of their strength:

> For example, even during this war, I maintained contact with the Brenje family. The relationship was that good. There are other such stories. So strong were those *kumstvo* relationships, you should write it down, that [they persevered] even under the shock of war, in 1992, when Gacko was attacked and [the village of] Fazlagića Kula was burnt to the ground on the eve of 18 June. There were cases of Muslims hauling their tractors to their *kum*'s house, to be kept safe through the war and later returned. Or, for example, my cousin buried some gold [before being expelled], and his Serb *kum* knew the lay of every stone [on his land]. When the war ended, they met near Mostar and Ahmo [the cousin] told him: 'Braco, I buried some gold there, you know, in the corner beneath that one board, so bring it to me if you find it. The next Saturday, he went and dug up the gold and the (Deutsch) marks, fifty thousand marks, and brought it all to him. There are still good relationships. There is a good number of Serbs in Gacko who disagreed with what happened between 1992 and 1995. They took a critical stance towards those who burnt, destroyed, looted and killed, but they don't dare report them. They snub them on the street, or in the café, but those criminals have never been brought to justice.³⁰

The war of the 1990s was filtered through sworn kinship as 'yet another' time of need. Hasan's narrative reveals the interplay of three qualities of *kumstvo*: trust, moral obligation and intimacy. Such bonds imply not only visitations and assistance, but also an intimacy with your sworn kin's everyday existence – knowledge of their land, of 'every stone'. As a durable ingredient of your life, *kumovi* know what matters to you. After Dževad and his family fled their village of Bahori, their *kumovi*, the Vukovići family, managed to salvage some of their family photographs. Dževad saw such instances as a sign that *life together* may be, slowly but surely, reassembled.

Betraying *kumstvo* was always one of the worst transgressions any human being in the Field could perpetrate. It grew into the *genius linguae*, as a parable for children. When 85-year-old Fatima was a young girl, her father asked her to help him fetch in cows that had spent the night in a remote part of the Field. On the way, they had to pass three Muslim graves (*mezari*), and Fatima heard an *ezan* (Muslim call for prayer) coming from them. She remembered: 'My father said that these were children who had been killed by their *kum*, a Serb'. Experiences of *ezan* and supernatural light coming from graves were usually considered to imply the goodness of both the 'spirit' and the 'recipient'. The full horror of the tale that Fatima's father imparted is not in the murder itself, but rather in the fact that the *kum* – the very person trusted for love, care and protection – could betray a promise. Some *kumstvo* relationships were apparently betrayed in a similar way at the beginning of 1992, when the war in Gacko started. Hasan (pseudonym) mentioned that people were killed *na vjeru* (through trust), when soldiers would call out the names of their *kumovi* and promise them safety if they come down the mountain, only to kill them when they did. A witness in the case against Kunarac et al. before the ICTY (IT-96-23 & 23/1) also pointed out that the perpetrators who set fire to a barn full of people in the Gacko area included *kumovi* of the victims. In this account, too, *kumstvo* is mentioned to heighten the incomprehensibility of the act – harm coming from one's sworn kin.

Many have argued that sworn kinship historically had a significant sociopolitical impact in hindering or damping down 'ethno-religious' conflicts and blood feuds between families and increasing security through loyalty, trust, friendship and assistance.[31] Enemies often made peace through the very ritual of *kumstvo*.[32] Wendy Bracewell (2000) analysed the records on sworn brotherhood in the borderlands between the Venetian Republic, the Habsburg Monarchy and the Ottoman Empire in the seventeenth century. She argued that it reveals both the presence of cohesion, tolerance, common interests and shared values across religious/political lines (ibid: 30) and the enduring conflicts that entailed a need for such alliances. In her view, such studies might have more 'pertinent' applications: 'The topic of frontier blood-brotherhood has obvious contemporary relevance given the tendency to interpret current conflicts in the region in terms of ancient and irreconcilable religious and ethnic enmities, and also given the hope of finding ways in which enmities have been (and can be) overcome' (ibid: 31).

Sworn kinship and other forms of inter-religious intimacy in the Balkan Peninsula have been much deeper than the 'frontiers'. While they seem to have occasionally functioned as a form of conflict control, their meanings and bearings transcend the contexts of 'enmity'. Positioning such relationships in terms of violence (and its resolution) *only* may be problematized through anthropological research. Historiography has yet to develop methodologies for approaching the fullness of historicity in bodily encounters. It has the possibility to see social relationships as activated in a certain way and to a specific effect, but the affective webs usually escape it. The contemporary relevance, the hope to be found in sworn kinship, was highlighted by some of my interlocutors as well, not as a strategy of reconditioning the political polarization, but rather as a way to separate chronotopic allegiances, as evidence of intimacy and morality across 'ethno-religious' boundaries.

Bloch (1973) warned against functionalist analyses of kinship that disregard accounts of morality in the links they assert between motive and effect. Sworn kinship did play a role in securing safety, protection and easing conflicts, but such effects were rarely, if ever, identified by my interlocutors as the motives for entering the relationship; however, safety and protection are, certainly, possible extended qualities of sworn kinship. Bloch also noted that moral delineations should be understood as related to the adaptability of such social ties:

> I have tried to show that it is only because of the fact that to the actors kinship is moral, that is non-specific and long-term, that it produces an adaptability potential to long term social change. If more rational ties were used, i.e. ties which are the fruit of a process of maximization, they would be more efficient in the short term but more costly in the middle and long term. (ibid: 86)

Kumstvo does seem to be a highly adaptable and resilient relationship. The morality of spiritual kinship has been confirmed through many narratives of trust and protection in times of need. Paradoxically, both the legendary and the witness accounts of betrayal reinforce the morality of *kumstvo,* as they are seen to be incongruous with the basic tenets of the relationship.

Like and Unlike? Some Historical Data on Kumstvo

Pobratimstvo or ritual brotherhood, Bracewell (2016: 3) argued, was usually, but not exclusively, forged between 'like and like', individuals of the same gender and religion. *Kumstvo,* however, functioned in quite a different way; it was about transforming difference into intimacy, for various intents and purposes. Firstly, it was often (and in Gacko, as a rule) a bond across religious difference. Secondly, men could be *kumovi* for girls, and women *kume* for boys. Thirdly, gender really did not present a significant boundary, as the bond was ultimately created between households, not individuals. *Kumstvo* between 'like and like' was perhaps usual in terms of wealth due to the expectation of reciprocal gift-giving. To contextualize the Field's narratives, let me briefly present some historical data on the practice in Herzegovina and the region.

One of the earliest detailed accounts of Bosnian shorn-hair *kumstvo* was published in a fin-de-siecle edition of *Zora,* signed simply *Mostarac* ('man from Mostar'). Arguing that such customs are well preserved in Bosnia and especially in Herzegovina, he noted:

Shorn-hair *kumstvo* is forged by the Orthodox and the Muhamedans between each other, whilst the Muhamedans also do it amongst themselves. Shorn-hair *kumstvo* is performed mostly in the following circumstances:

1. When one cannot have children because they keep dying;
2. When a child falls ill and can neither die nor get better;
3. When mutual arguments and blood feuds are pacified;
4. When affection occurs (*kad se neko zamiluje*); and
5. When the child's first hair is cut.

(Mostarac 1896: 158)

He added several important explanations (ibid: 158–59). In all the above cases, the child's hair must not have been cut since birth. In families whose children had been dying, the midwife would take their newborn to a crossroads, lift it towards the first passer-by and say: '*Kum,* take the *kumstvo* – God and Saint John'. The passer-by would be obliged to accept. If the child and the passer-by were both Orthodox, then the passer-by would be a baptismal *kum*. If the child is Orthodox and the passer-by Muslim, or vice versa, then the shorn-hair *kumstvo* would be performed. He gave us one important caveat, which points to the magical apotropaic qualities of the hair-cutting ritual. If the child was very sick, the shorn-hair *kumstvo* would be performed regardless of religion. In cases of feuds, inter-religious *kumstvo* would be shorn-hair, but the Orthodox would be baptismal. In cases of affection, one person would invite another to cut their child's hair. In these cases, *kumstvo* would be performed before noon, while the day is advancing, followed by a ceremonial lunch to which the closest friends, other sworn kin and the family of the new *kum* would be invited. Gifts would be exchanged. These visits would continue rhythmically later on. Depending on *kum*'s religion, there were slightly different incantations during the hair-cutting ceremony. Muslim women would not cover their heads in front of the *kum* and his brothers.

Mostarac's forth category, literally expressed as 'when some begin to caress/touch each other', implies that the affection of encounter (besides magical or other benefits) could be the basis for *kumstvo*. Unlike much of existing research on Bosnia, I focus exactly on this gentle touch (*milovanje*), full of history and transgressing history. This is a departure from the functional analyses like Hammel's (1968), as well as Bogišić's understanding of shorn-hair *kumstvo* through 'Turkish patronage' (1874: 176). Hannes Grandits (2014: 17–18) noted that *kumstvo* was generally an instrument in the building of bridges intended to overcome social segmentation and oppositions. While the pacification certainly was an important aspect, it stood alongside the apotropaic and affective dimensions.

Petar Ivančević (1897) informed us that sworn brotherhood (*pobratimstvo*) in Bosnia was widely practiced both within the Orthodox and Muslim communities and amongst their members. According to him, it was very rare for Catholics to enter into this bond with either Muslims or Orthodox Christians and the practice was generally less frequent in the interior and more visible along the various Bosnian borderlands (see Filipović 1969 on Catholics entering into inter-religious *kumstvo*). He mentions one instance from the town of Brčko, of a Muslim man approaching an Orthodox man to ask for *pobratimstvo* because his wife had dreamt of it three times. After accepting, the said woman did not cover in front of him anymore, because he was considered kin. Ivančević also noted that, in cases of inter-religious *pobratimstvo,* the priest would not be consulted. The bond was confirmed through ceremonial hugs, kisses and continual care and exchange of gifts between the families.

There are many other accounts of inter-religious sworn kinship. At the end of the nineteenth century, Marko Miljanov observed the abundance of *kumstvo* and *pobratimstvo* between the Orthodox Montenegrins and Muslim Albanians, 'with more love than between full brothers' (1967: 70–71). Similarly, Šijanec (1917: 301) described shorn-hair *kumstvo* as both an intra- and inter-religious tradition of the Catholics, Orthodox and Mohamedans in Bosnia. In his *Muslims of our Blood in South Serbia,* Jovan Hadži Vasiljević (1924: 44) argued that there are abundant examples of *poturčenjaci* (convert Turks) forming shorn-hair *kumstvo* with Christians and that it implied relations of closest kinship. He noted examples in the Prizren area when *kumovi* transformed the bond from baptismal into shorn-hair after converting to Islam. Likewise, Nametak (1962) argued that, in Podgorica in Montenegro, Muslims entered into (shorn-hair) *kumstvo* with the Orthodox and, rarely, with other Muslims.

In some places, even the people from different families who shared a *kum* could not get married (see Filipović 1969: 104, Bajraktarović 1961: 100). This transformation of difference into the closest form of kinship was underscored in Gacko. Unlike consanguine marriage, which was permissible after some degree of distance, with sworn kin it was always prohibited. Most of my interlocutors spoke about the longevity of these bonds, inherited through many generations, which highlights the care invested into *kumstvo* as a form of property. As Nikola Pavković noted:

> *Kumstvo* is a par excellence transferable and heritable property. In stable socio-cultural systems, *kumstvo* is a very durable and inheritable inter-family connection. It imposes *kumovi* with the strictest exogamy, which is stronger and more consistent than kinship exogamy. Without great peril, *kumstvo* was not changed or broken. (1982: 32)

There are noticeably different reports about *kumstvo* in Bosnia. Perhaps the discrepancy between the *pobratimstvo* in 'interior' and 'borderland' Bosnia, as noted by Ivančević (1987: 415), may also be hypothesized for inter-religious *kumstvo* to some extent. Sorabji, who conducted her fieldwork in Sarajevo in the 1980s, did detect instances of shorn-hair *kumstvo*, but noted that 'the bond formed by this type of *kumstvo* was weak; there was no expectation that it would engender lasting friendship or obligate mutual aid and it was not believed to create a spiritual tie between the parties involved' (1989: 34). She was herself offered the bond by a friend/interlocutor (ibid: 61), which likely expressed some of that *kumstvo*-related 'proximity with distance'.

Some authors have reported the changing patterns of *kumstvo* since the second half of the twentieth century, particularly a move from the durable household bonds towards the 'like and like' model. Earlier practice of looking towards somewhat spatially distant villages to maintain peace amongst *kumovi* was waning (Trifunovski 1957: 163). Filipović (1969: 104) noted that many people have instead started to pick their friends from school, army or workplace. This individualization and acceleration of ritual kinship relations was simultaneous with the rapid Yugoslav modernization, the transformation of dwellings and different flows of migration. When the war broke out in the 1990s, both the politics of ethnicity and forced migration further reflected on these networks. Nadje Al-Ali (2002: 253) argued that the disruption of extended family structures was one of the most evident changes in the lives of Bosnian refugees. Halilovich (2013: 78) noted that many inter-religious *kumstvo* bonds were destroyed. My research shows that some were certainly preserved, 'in the dark times', just as the relationship stipulates, but further anthropological ventures are required.

Kumstvo *and* Komšiluk

Anthropological contributions since the 1990s war did not substantially engage with the Bosnian institution of *kumstvo*. However, another form of social organization received much more attention. *Komšiluk*, the Bosnian word for 'neighbourhood', transformed into a category with considerable and disputed analytical baggage. I compare and contrast some of the arguments made about *komšiluk* to the ones I propose about *kumstvo*. In particular, I return to the moral, pragmatic and intimate aspects of *kumstvo* and its role in structuring the relationships between individuals and groups.

Both *kumstvo* and *komšiluk* reveal significant differences across the various Bosnian terrains. Whereas *kumstvo* in south and southeastern Bosnia seems to have been largely 'inter-religious', it was not always the case in other areas. Likewise, *komšiluk* does not entail the same structure of relationships in different places. The differences cannot be simply attributed to the rural–urban divide; the dwellings in Bosnian villages are diversely organized. As already noted, *komšiluk* did not seem to have primacy in the social/spatial constitution of the Field.

Occasionally, *komšiluk* has been interpreted with reference to 'inter-religious/ethnic' proximities and distances. Bougarel (2004: 123) discussed it as a fragile institution, whose peaceful relations exist only when guaranteed by the state; otherwise 'diverting into crime'. The reason why *komšiluk* was so fragile and ominous, Bougarel (ibid) further argued, is to be found in the kinds of ethnic/religious/national separations it maintained, as evidenced by the infrequency of mixed marriages. Bringa's (1995: 66–84) more nuanced contribution depicted *komšiluk* as but one of the many intersecting contexts through which the differences and similarities are simultaneously played out. Illustrating his argument through Bougarel's and Bringa's work, Hayden (2002b: 161) proposed that *komšiluk* was a relationship 'antithetical to one based on intimacy: marriage'. In his words: 'Essentially, then, the practices of *komšiluk* happened relations between individuals as representatives of groups who chanced to live in close proximity, while the groups themselves remained in structural opposition, unmixable' (ibid). Hayden's mixtures seem to require marriage.

Kumstvo was neither primarily a condition of spatial proximity, nor was it usually a bond between individuals. One's sworn kin, more often than not, lived in another town or village. The pragmatic spatial distance was a possibility of intimacy between communities that would otherwise not get many chances to meet. *Kumstvo* indeed reveals the fallacy of understanding *komšiluk* as 'antithetical to the intimacy of marriage'. *Kumstvo* bonds were considered stronger and more important than the 'blood' family relations. Interestingly, Bryant (2016: 23) noted a similar qualification of the neighbour in Cyprus, who 'may be more important than family' (2016: 23). Sworn kin occupied the central place in the image of prewar home. So, the prohibition of marriage between sworn kin does not indicate a 'structural opposition', but rather structured relations and increased intimacy. The logic of these group relationships has been misunderstood by Bougarel and Hayden. The problem possibly lies in the application of the researchers' own conceptions of intimacy and kinship to the research context. It strikes me as a kind of emancipatory project.

Sorabji (2008) and Henig (2012a) criticized the fallacy of employing *komšiluk* to interpret the relationships between the Bosnian 'ethno-religious' groups. Such discussions confused the metaphorical and the primary meaning of the term (Sorabji 2008: 97) and depicted 'ethnoreligious groups (i.e. Bosniaks, Croats and Serbs) as the basic constituents of everyday life in Bosnian society' (Henig 2012a: 4). The neighbourhood in the Field, likewise, did not structure any kind of relationships between groups, although it was occasionally employed to counter the political projects of the 1990s. Delva, a Muslim woman, negotiated the safe passage of women and children from the mountains with the help of Spasoje, her Serb neighbour and

Dževad predicted the possibility of the Field's restoration through the rekindled relationships with his Serb neighbours. Such moments never implied that *komšiluk* was somehow defined by ethnic and religious difference, but rather that the intimacies it produced were sometimes a welcome contradiction to the ideology of the 'unmixable'.

Kumstvo in the Field, on the other hand, was primarily a relationship between groups, firstly between Orthodox Christian and Muslim families, but also between their villages (which were often not much more than extended families) and implicitly between Christians and Muslims of their horizons. It was ritually confirmed and intentionally perpetuated through the intimacy and utility of care. Although we cannot speak of postwar transformations as if the 1990s war had been the only polarizing conflict, there is a sense of *kumstvo* reflecting upon the qualification of the more abstract Muslim–Serb relationships. As evidenced by other 'intra-communal' examples, marriage with sworn kin was not prohibited due to the difference in religion, but because of the powers accorded to the sworn kin; the intersection of marriage and *kumstvo* risked the contraction of one's social network. And, though it did work through difference, it was an institution antithetical to distance, which is why recognizing the possibility of In-Other is so important.

Kumstvo, like *komšiluk*, had moral, intimate and pragmatic qualities. Sorabji (2008: 107) argued that neighbourly relations in Sarajevo entailed a moral duty, that they could be enjoyed, benefited from or be a source of frustration. In rural central Bosnia, Henig noted, they entail 'both moral imagination and social pragmatics of the everyday rhythms of life' (2012a: 13). This temporal quality of social structures is important because the ordinary and the extraordinary exist in a symbiotic relationship. *Komšiluk* belongs to the day-to-day; *kumstvo* does not. *Komšiluk* is primarily a spatial proximity, a common space guides its temporal rhythm; Kumstvo is primarily a temporal proximity, where the time (of something and for something) gathers people into the same place. The bond is maintained through seasonal visitations and meetings, but also through the moments of celebration and adversity. It is a contract to synchronize the being of I with the being of Other, to fashion a common 'rhythm of life'.

Rekindled Time: Where Is My **Kuma***?*

In one Serbian epic, the Earth blames the Sky for tormenting it with snow and ice, 'from Michael's Day to George's Day'. The Sky is quick to turn the blame on the Earth, for it deserves no better treatment. It is filled with lawlessness, including disrespect for the bond of *kumstvo*.[33] Folk sayings warn: a *kum* is sacred; a *kum* is closer than a brother; be careful not to stand even on your *kum*'s shadow; a *kum* is respected on Earth and God in Heaven.[34] These are just a few of many, many more.

One exonerating reply, I imagine, the Earth could have given would have pointed out the considerable strains under which *kumstvo* exists. In particular, anti-syncretic institutional pressures have a long history. Bracewell (2000: 34) described how seventeenth- and eighteenth-century Catholic hierarchs and Franciscans worked to suppress practices of 'inter-religious' sworn brotherhood and shorn-hair *kumstvo* for fear such alliances might erode religious distinctions and lead to apostasy. A certain disciplining of inter-religious *kumstvo* was noticeable through the twentieth century. Hangi (1906: 116) mentioned that the Orthodox and Catholic Church were exerting pressure on the communities not to take Muslims as shorn-hair *kumovi*, while Muslims were more 'liberal' in that sense. Filipović (1969: 52) similarly argued that priests wouldn't condone *kumstvo* between Catholics and Orthodox Christians, though many were eager to enter such arrangements. Add to this melting pot of pressure on the Field the three polarizing wars of the twentieth century.

As my research clearly demonstrates, all the weight of these bans on inter-religious *kumstvo* did not hinder the continuity of such relationships: they continued after the crimes against Serbs in Gacko during the Second World War and they have continued since the crimes against Muslims in Gacko during the 1990s war. As noted, research that includes wider diasporic communities, as well as their internet social platforms, would no doubt produce a better idea of the fate of inter-religious *kumstvo* since the last conflict. Judging by the resilience to the previous wars, we could expect the institution to continue well into the future. It is still an active contract in many parts of Bosnia. But, the Field has experienced poor birth rates and a very small scale of Muslim return. Having a variety of *kumstvo* bonds at hand, the Orthodox communities of the Field could transform it into a religiously introvert practice only. These processes are yet to unfold and it will be interesting to see whether *kumstvo* dissipates, changes its structure or experiences a revival of its old forms.

To recapitulate: *kumstvo* is an old institution of intimacy in the Field. It was understood as a moral imperative to love, care, aid and protect. Its maintenance was ensured in good times through meetings and visits arranged in line with the traditional calendric festivities and other causes for celebration, and in times of need, which ranged from a place to stay overnight to the saving of lives. Such relationships survived the 1990s, but it remains to be discovered to what extent.

This type of kinship followed chronotopic changes in the Field. The qualitative measures of time defined the way *kumstvo* could be 'activated', but *kumstvo* also redefined time – through the affectivity of its perseverance, it resisted the political appropriation of time and place. On a hopeful note, a conclusion to this discussion might look like what Nezir said to me about *kumstvo* encounters:

> And particularly now [after the 1990s war], the delights of imparting these good wishes are being rekindled. There is something *within* that drives human beings to rejoice in one another's religious celebrations. It is practiced today, as well. Even today, such festivities fulfil the function of connecting and reconciling people.

Conditio Humana?

The relationship expressed in this chapter through the concept of In-Other is not posited for all Bosnian landscapes, or no more than it is for landscapes in general. As the examples of the Gurbeti arrival and of *kumstvo* relationships in the Field demonstrate, In-Other was approached in many different modes, but always in strong correlation to the cyclical calendar, through which the meaning of home was defined after the Field had been cleansed of its intimacies and Others. The implication of such encounters for the cosmological framework of the Field is, however, part of a wider inherited system. Meeting an outsider had a particular cosmic and apotropaic meaning in almost all Slavic traditions (see Plotnikova 2001: 525). There were signs of these traditions in the narratives of my interlocutors but, of course, nothing is fully generalizable across time or space. The cases of the 'falling Gurbeti' and *kumstvo* demonstrate that the unravelling of affect, magic, landscape, the past and the future may only ever be a forced analytical endeavour. For those who live 'by them', they are part of the same condition of being in the world. We gather glimpses, write up silhouettes, but 'being' is always much wider, complex and more specific.

In his chapter on taking care of neighbours' shrines in Bosnia, Bojan Baskar (2012: 51) argued that this 'attitude toward "familiar other" [is] characteristic of a number of Bosnian contexts'. But, it is not just familiarity; it is also an 'alternative' or 'sworn' familiality and intimacy. The intimate Other was the content and form of cosmic Time in the Field, but my concern with intimacy has shifted the chapter's focus from the structure of time to its experiences and the affectivity of encounter. The resonances of food, for example, spoke to the bodily, the communal, the spatial and the temporal, but also to the historical changes and the futurities of the Field.

Cvetana Georgieva (1999) has argued that Bulgarian Muslims and Christians have developed a 'system of living together', maintaining trust and peace through ritualized actions, like the participation in each other's holidays and gift exchange. She noted: 'The "other person and the others" are transformed from "foreign" into "familiar different" individuals, hence they are perceived not as a menace, but rather as an inseparable part of the complex world of everyday life' (ibid: 68). Kolind (2008: 213) believed that a similar approach to differences is applicable to Bosnia, that they were nurtured and familiarized rather than understated or exaggerated. This process of familiarization is often ritualized. As Anja Peleikis notes for a religiously 'mixed' village in Lebanon:

> Yet shared local identity was not a given simply because of the fact that Christians and Muslims used to live in one place. On the contrary, social relations across confessional borders had to be confirmed, and reproduced again and again through the diverse everyday practice of neighborhood relations, mutual assistance in agriculture, and attendance at religious rituals of the confessional "Other". (2006: 134)

In the Field, this confirmation rhythmically punctuated the annual cycle through visitations, gift-giving, shared economy and celebrations, as well as the individual's lifespan, through the ritual bonds, joy, sorrow and moments of need.

What is the difference between intimacy with one's Self and intimacy with the Other? What is the difference between intimacy with those for whom we enact an idea of sameness and those who are positioned as different? One can indeed become a stranger in one's own home and in one's own body, whether ethnic, racial, religious, political, gendered, sexual, or otherwise. Some bodies can be cast aside, exchanged for others or transformed. These new alliances and alienations imply that we are always already anchored in sets of bodies, often ones which are naturalized through each other. *Our own* bodies are thus never really our own; they are an inheritance accepted or refused. These bodies stake a claim over us before we get to stake any claims through them. All of *our own* bodies are set with and against *others' own* bodies. But if intimacy with *our own* is construed as inevitable and often eschews a responsibility for ritually maintaining its own position, intimacy with the *other's* body requires some kind of structure. This structure is to be found in the old Field, a manual for the condition of a human being set against, within and through the being of the World.

Notes

1. My Bosnian translation of In-Other is *U-Drugost*. The prefix *u* signifies 'in, within' and *drugost* is 'otherness', related to *drugi/a* (second, other), *drug/a* (friend), *društvo, družina* (company, society), *držati* (to hold) and *drugačije* (different). *Drugost* etymologically entails the meaning of In-Other as embraced difference; it comes from the Indo-European root *dher-* 'to hold' (see Skok 1971: 445–49).
2. Discussed later in this chapter, the nomadic Gurbeti were described as 'falling' (*padali*), rather than arriving to the Field.

3. See Hony and Fahir's (1957) *Turkish–English Dictionary* and Wehr's (1976) *A Dictionary of Modern Written Arabic*.
4. Thus, Maghreb is the place where the sun sets, as opposed to Mashriq, where it rises.
5. Other than Pečuriš, there were 'Gurbeti places' in at least four locations near the village of Kula: (1) before the village of Međuljići, towards Zborna Gomila, on the left; (2) at Pusto Polje, right after Stepen – a place called Bajdine; (3) near the village of Habuli, before the village of Kula, just off the road; and (4) in the town, behind Klaonica ('the slaughterhouse'), on the left.
6. Etymologically, *teferič* (pronounced 'teferich') is related to the Turkish *teferrüc*, meaning 'pleasure trip, a stroll for pleasure, diversion, excursion' (see Hony and Fahir 1957). Bosnian *teferič* is often the central, or the only, part of festivities (particularly George's and Elijah's Day), as well as of certain kinds of pilgrimage (as in the cases of Ajvatovica and Djevojačka Pećina). Any picnic-like gathering, especially if it entails a larger group of people, may be colloquially described as a *teferič*.
7. In Safura's words: '*Ustaj aga! Peri tavu, kuhaj halvu!*' Halva is a sweet dish, of which a particular variety is traditionally made for the break of the Ramadan fast in Bosnia.
8. Recorded across Bosnia, the phenomenon of 'rain prayers' fits into this orientation, which is, of course, related to the potency of the Biblical Elijah (see Chapter 5). Such is the curious fifteenth-century text, so-called 'Kunovo inscription', which was inserted into the trunk of a pine tree (see Dizdar 1969: 296–98, 423; Hadžijahić 1974). Discovered at the beginning of the twentieth century in the village of Ječmišta, relatively close to Gacko, this magic inscription sought to dismay the devil (by his many names) and the diabolical, crop-destroying weather he causes. Commissioned by twenty-nine named Muslims, the text invokes 'God, the four evangelists, and the three hundred and ten holy fathers and sixty martyrs, and Christ and Holy John', amongst others. A similar fifteenth-century 'prayer for wheat and wine', found near Mostar, adds another interesting obstacle for the devil, intimidating him with 'the four rivers encompassing the whole of earth' (see Dizdar 1969: 243).
9. In Bosnian: '*Kum je bliži od brata.*'; '*Kum je svetinja.*'
10. See, for example, Lockwood (1974: 256), Hammel (1968), Henig (2011: 96) and Devrnja Zimmerman (1986: 115)
11. See, for example, Bogišić (1874: 176), Kabakova (2001: 317) and Low (1922: 184).
12. The participants thus become spiritual/sworn brothers (*pobratimi*), sisters (*posestrime*) and mothers (*pomajke*). For the examination of milk kinship in the Balkans, see Bringa (1995: 146–49) and Parkes (2004). For sworn blood kinship, see Čajkanović (1973).
13. See, for example, Kabakova (2002), Low (1922: 184) and Mijatovich (1917: 160).
14. I would add the Suomi *kummi*, although the Finns have borrowed it from Slavic languages.
15. Bogišić's Turk was, of course, the Slavic Balkan Muslim.
16. Writing this just over a decade after the annexation of Bosnia and Herzegovina by Austria-Hungary, Hörman noted that the gifts were in Habsburg coins. *Pleta cvanciga* means a set of coins each worth twenty *kreuzer* (or possibly *gulden* or *forints*), while *ducat* was a silver or, more commonly, a golden coin. I thank Desmond Maurer for this clarification.
17. See, Federal Bureau of Statistics in Bosnia and Herzegovina (1998b).

18. Peter Parkes' (2004) article, an interesting comparative analysis of 'milk kinship' in the Balkans and northern Pakistan, does include a discussion of *kumstvo*, but without contemporary ethnographic data from the Balkans.
19. However, Hangi (1906: 116) noted that, if the child was not sick, people might arrange for a specific person to pass along the road.
20. See 'Đerzelez Alija i Vuk Jajčanin' in Buturović (1995: 110–20)
21. See 'Zidanje Ćuprije u Višegradu' in Buturović (1995: 145–49)
22. See 'Hrnjičić Omerica' in Buturović (1995: 325–64).
23. See the interesting essay on the 'Georgic' properties of Alija Đerzelez and Kraljević Marko by Alija Džogović (2013).
24. Čajkanović (1973: 163) noted that epic sworn kinship was also established between Prince Marko and Alil-aga, 'by God and St John'.
25. See the song 'Đerzelez Alija i Kraljević Marko' in Buturović (1995: 491–93).
26. See in Čajkanović (1973: 67): '*Kuma kuma ako nije darovala, nije mu ni brige zadavala*'.
27. George's Day was more prominent in other places. In the town of Stolac, it involved a merry inter-religious gathering, with a progress up to the ruins of the old fort, where people would feast and socialize. In the town of Visoko, the same inter-religious crowd still joins the Roma community for celebrations next to the Carica water spring.
28. Lockwood (1974: 256, 268) presented several arguments which I find erroneous, namely that, for the Bosnian Muslims, *kumstvo* does not forge group, but individualistic relationships and that it is not heritable. This might have possibly been the case in central Bosnia around the town of Bugojno where Lockwood conducted his fieldwork in the 1960s (ibid: 258), but was certainly not true for the wide area of south and southeastern Bosnia and Herzegovina.
29. Rade said: '*Bježiš vazda, od ustaša, od partizana, od četnika, od Talijana*'. Partisans, according to him, committed violence, just like the Croatian Nazis, Italian fascists and Četnik Nazi collaborators did. He recalled one man being killed by the Partisans for taking a shoulder (*plećka*) of meat.
30. All names in this narrative are pseudonyms.
31. See, for example, Hörman (1889: 36–38), Tomašić (1948: 79–80), Čajkanović (1973: 164) and Filipović (1982: 144).
32. See Foley (1990: 203) and Fine (2007: 71, 91, 203).
33. See Nodilo (1981, Part I: 32). In another version of the song, recorded by Karadžić (1823: 4–7), the complaint is made by 'Elijah the Thunderer' (*Gromovnik Ilija*) to 'Fiery Mary' (*Ognjena Marija*). God distributes powers to saints and they attack the lawless Earth.
34. I recorded the first two sayings in Gacko. The third is mentioned by Filipović (1969: 39), and the fourth by Kabakova (2002).

CHAPTER 4

Time and Epic Residues

Davno bilo sad se spominjalo,
ko no Gjurgjev danak na godini,
ko no dobar junak u družini.

Scenes of yore, nowadays recounted,
Like the day of George upon the year,
Like a good hero in a fellowship.

—A *gusle* epic from Bosnia[1]

What happens when I try to articulate an order of things, but keep being failed by my lexicon? Could some unintended residues of socialities, deeply mapped in my language–landscape–body, project onto my world their own reckoning? Am I complicit in the perpetuation of the worlds in which these remnants reside? This chapter considers the perdurance of memory and the affects made possible in traces, which further complicate the idea of social agent. Such forms of knowledge have the potential to surprise us, to turn back on our conscious discursive practices, reach beyond the territories mapped out by our intentional and directed recollections. In the artificial distinction between the knowledge of the mind and the knowledge of the body, this nondiscursive, nonconscious baggage may seem as if it belongs to the body. This is because it often resembles and thus may be confused with, bodily reflexes. It is knowledge, but of the kind that seems like a knee-jerk. It communicates to us and from us, but we might not explicitly qualify it.

I have already discussed the kind of sharing and encounters that resist political divisions in the Field through desired memories of the past. Here, I locate shared landscapes in the nonvolitional, nonconscious bodily dispositions whose repression would require an unreachable onto-linguistic exile. Massumi argued for a distinction between nonconscious and the Freudian unconscious, as 'repression does not apply to nonconscious perception; ... nonconscious perception may, with a certain amount of ingenuity, be argued to apply to nonorganic matter' (2002: 16). Its affective capacities attach to mountains and crops, things, songs and everyday vocabularies, economies and modes of movement through space. In the transition from the shared Field to the ethno-nationally homogenized one, former socialities protruded as innumerable traces. Looking at Turkish-Cypriot landscapes, Navaro-Yashin has asked about the affectivity of remnants after exile and destruction:

> What is left of social relations with the other community is the other community's objects. What remains, as well, is the memory of a sociality which included the other community in the recent past. Relations with the other community persist in the imagination through interactions and dealings with their abandoned properties, spaces, and belongings. (2009: 2)

Belonging to the same affective formations, the landscape and the (human) body in the Field had the potential to activate each other in a certain way. One such common disposition was the always lurking possibility to communicate the syncretic cosmology and the Gurbeti–Muslim–Serb proximities.

Bowman (2012: 6) used the notion of 'practical nostalgia' to argue that certain sites and practices of shared religion are 'neither conscious nor ideological', but could instead be seen to involve a 'habitus' of sharing. Whilst there was evident nostalgia in the Field, the affective dispositions of bodies and landscapes that I wish to discuss are not necessarily nostalgic. Nostalgia, as I see it, is a directed feeling, enunciated and different from affect. Massumi (2002: 27) argued that, while both involve certain kinds of intensity, emotion should not be confused with affect. Emotion, he noted, is a 'recognized affect', an 'identified intensity' (ibid: 61). Affective traces occur to the body and landscape, but the possibilities of their activation (for example, into feelings of desire, nostalgia or repulsion) are open.

This chapter describes an 'unidentified intensity', an uncanny encounter in the Field. It looks into the affective remains of the Field's shared sacral geography, located in the abyss between two discourses of communal life. Gacko entered the twenty-first century as a town awash with an aura of ethno-national violence in the aftermath of systematic destruction. Within the apparent coherence of socio-political intention, I found numerous ways in which the Field's postwar existence was 'double-coded', with its bodies and landscapes simultaneously occupying two grand chronotopes. Here, I locate some of the social reflexes of a plural and syncretic landscape in the least likely of places – a nationalist epic song about 'ethnic cleansing'.

Epics of the Field were traditionally oral arrangements, memorized rather than written on paper or recorded by other technologies. They were, however, recorded in landscapes. New songs relied on established formulae (see Parry 1971, Lord 2000). Their specific mode of enactment required a repetitive usage of strong and consolidated 'phraseology' of landscapes. As a particular form of text, traditional epic echoed the images of such landscapes and channelled them into the time of 'nationalist' epics. Such songs became the sites of an uncanny syncretism between the 'pre-nationalist' and the 'nationalist' Field. The resulting discourse, which was primarily expressed through the modes of the discourse it systematically denied, may be described as 'schizodiscursive'. Bakhtin's definition of linguistic hybridization is useful here:

> What is hybridization? It is a mixture of two *social languages* within the limits of a single utterance, *an encounter, within the arena of an utterance,* between two different linguistic consciousnesses, separated from one another by an epoch, by social differentiation or by some other factor. (1981: 358, emphases mine)

In recognizing that differentiations of many kinds can be a starting point for syncretism, mixture and encounter, he provided a useful tool for discussing the Field beyond the mere opposition of syncretism and anti-syncretism. He furthermore distinguished between intentional or conscious and organic or obscure language hybrids (ibid: 359). The obscure hybrids are nonintentional, or at least not intentional in the same manner as the conscious ones. These obscure hybrids, I argue, may be affective, forming along the lines of encounter between the nonintentional remnants and discourse.

The following pages turn to one obscure, unintentionally hybrid textual formation, a strange 'encounter within the arena of an utterance' from the Field. I refer to it as 'uncanny' because of the inter-chronotopic proximity it reveals. Freud's (1955) discussion of *unheimlich* (unhomely), translated to English language as 'uncanny', did not simply equate it to the strange and the unfamiliar. He saw it as inextricable from *heimlich* (homely), arguing that 'the "uncanny" is that class of the terrifying which leads back to something long known to us, once very familiar' (ibid: 220). I take one of these encounters between the known and the frightening to argue that the shared Field affectively protrudes through sedimented traces and that it can be ascribed with some uncanny methods of survival.

The *Gusle*: From Outlaws to War Criminals

If there were two parts of the year for the peasant in the Field, the warm half was when the social life blossomed, and the cold winter was the time to draw close around the hearth and tell stories. Small gatherings known as *sijela* (literally, 'sessions') extended into the night and the absent landscape was recapitulated in all its mytho-poetic glory. One tradition of this storytelling was the epic song commonly known by the name of the instrument accompanying it – *gusle*.

I have already mentioned the Field's proverb: 'George's Day – *hajduk* assembly, Demetrius' Day – *hajduk* parting'. Hajduks were the Balkan outlaws of the Ottoman Empire.[2] Wendy Bracewell (1992: 11–12) noted that these were 'short-lived bands with little formal organization or support'. They were also mythic figures of folk stories and songs, somewhat like the English Robin Hood – they too resided in nature and embodied its qualities. According to the epic tradition, hajduks appear in direct communication with the many magical beings, otherwise hidden from mortals. These epic heroes would gather with the advent of spring on George's Day and embark upon exciting and dangerous adventures until the onset of winter.

These outlaws were also the main protagonists of the *gusle* songs. Their position 'outside of society' is of crucial importance, and their 'return to society' just before the winter is a testament to this point. With warm seasons, they ritually re-entered what Victor Turner (2008) called 'liminality', a timespace of detachment from the social structure. Outside of the ordinary social positions (and law), they would come closer to the magical essence of nature and express the comradeship of *communitas,* which Turner associated with liminality – the moment when a generalized social bond is possible, a 'natural' universal equality that is not possible and attainable 'back in the society'. He noted: 'Folk literature abounds in symbolic figures, such as "holy beggars", "third sons", "little tailors", and "simpletons," who strip off the pretensions of holders of high rank and office and reduce them to the level of common humanity and mortality' (ibid: 110). As nature withdrew, so the hajduks also withdrew from the woodlands and mountains to occupy their structural roles. The other traditional name for hajduks was *četniks* (or *četnici*; see Malcolm 1995: 238), related to the Turkish word *çete,* meaning 'gang', crew', 'band of rebels' and again implying the sense of liminality and *communitas.*

It is from these real and symbolic outlaws that the First and Second World War guerrillas took their name. Bracewell (2003: 24) argued that the multiplicity of meanings ascribed to 'bandits' in the Balkans coalesced into a nineteenth-century nationalist symbol of resistance to the oppressors.[3] She described how the hajduks were gradually modelled into 'quintessential representatives of the Serb state-building tradition, with their military virtues, their heroism, and their ardent sense of national mission' (ibid: 28). The Serbian state at the beginning of the twentieth century promoted the constitution of armed rebel groups modelled in the image of the insurrectionary hajduk bands (*čete*) (see Bougarel 1999: 167, Bracewell 2003: 30). The participation of such groups in the Balkan Wars (1912 and 1913) and First World War gave new, malicious meaning to the word *četnik* (Bougarel 1999: 167), one that continued into the 1990s war as well.

The crimes of the *Četniks,* as Nazi and Fascist collaborators in Second World War, were not open to debate in the socialist Yugoslavia following the swift execution of their leader Mihailović and others in 1946.[4] While they did indeed represent Serbian royalist nationalism, their full self-ascribed name was: The Yugoslav Army in the Fatherland. In 1941, they produced a memorandum entitled 'Homogenous Serbia', which called for the cleansing of non-Serb elements from Serb lands and the creation of a Serbia which would include Bosnia and Herzegovina, Dalmatia and Montenegro, as well as chunks of Croatia, Slavonia and Albania (Malcolm 1995: 241). The *Četniks* also provided a prominent ideological image for the ethnic and religious cleansing that swept through the Field in the 1990s. Those designated as incompatible with this image were killed, held in concentration camps or expelled, and their temples and houses were systematically destroyed. Bracewell (2003: 33) noted some academic attempts to explain these crimes as logical developments of the epic poetry, as 'myth enacted'.

In 2008, a few months before the mosque in the village of Kula was burnt to the ground for the second time, Lutvo Fazlagić received a handwritten letter from two self-styled *Četnik* 'dukes' (see Hodžić 2008). It contained a very explicit threat to the few Muslim villagers who had returned, inciting revenge for the killing of Serb villagers in Korita by the Croatian Nazis and their Bosnian Muslim collaborators from Gacko in the Second World War (see Chapter 1). The letter, handwritten in an almost academic manner, with headings and indentations, gave two quotations. They are broken passages from modern songs styled upon the *gusle* epics. One of them reads:

> No more *balije* [pejorative for Muslim men],
> nor *bule* [veiled Muslim women, sometimes used pejoratively],
> Fazlagića Kula [the largest Muslim village in the Field] has fallen.

The distant echo of the heroic epic tradition in these ominous lines is more complex than it seems. The *gusle* is a type of object with much to say about Balkan history. This one-string, lute-like instrument could, at first, invite images of Balkan 'heroic' nationalisms in practice. Such images are not at all far-fetched: a wide repertoire of nationalist messages continues to be sung to the sounds of this instrument. Many *gusle* songs reminisce about the Second World War *Četnik* general, Dragoljub 'Draža' Mihailović, whose name and image were rehabilitated by the Serbian nationalists during the 1990s wars in the Balkans, including a framed portrait inside the central Gacko bus stop. The Četnik repertoire of *gusle* songs is fraught with a genocidal ethos;[5] from an epic tradition sung by Dinaric Christians and Muslims alike, *gusle* were gradually reconstructed into a marker of pan-Serb ethno-national identity. However, this process started much earlier than the Second World War, as Albert Lord noted:

> The fever of nationalism in the nineteenth century led to the use of oral epics for nationalist propaganda. The poems glorified the heroes of the nation's past; they depicted

the struggles of the nation against outside foes. Hence the hero emerged as a 'national' hero, and the poems themselves were labelled 'national' epics. (Lord 2000: 7)[6]

In the 1990s, *gusle* were amalgamated with a new heroic discourse. The instrument was instrumentalized to lend legitimacy to war criminals. One of them, Radovan Karadžić, found guilty for genocide, war crimes and crimes against humanity before the ICTY, appeared in *Serbian Epics,* a documentary filmed by Pawel Pawlikowski in 1992. Radovan Karadžić went to the house of Vuk Karadžić, the nineteenth-century Serbian folklorist and language reformer, where he performed with *gusle* and pointed out the physical and patronymic similarities between himself and the 'father of the modern Serb nation' (Živković 2011: 91).

What once used to be a shared tradition came to be regarded as the exclusive domain of one identified *ethnie.* Eno, a returnee villager from Branilovići, told me of this gradual cleansing:

> So, even if they don't ascribe *gusle* to us [Muslims] a lot, it isn't the case. I know that each village had two to three *gusle* singers. I can name some for you, if you like.... In this village, I know of two *gusle* singers, the late Fehim Džubur and Muharem Džubur. Then there is Smajo Zekić ... Ekrem Čampara, I have heard him with the *gusle.* He is a few years older than me.

When I asked Eno if there were any *gusle* singers there now, he replied:

> Well, very few. You won't find many here to sing for you. Right now, there is nobody. But, people used to come to evening sessions (*sijela*); long winter nights, lots of folk would gather, you know, and attentively listen to these songs.

The nationalizing of the *gusle* also had implications for Serb households. Although there was a *gusle* festival in the town, the instrument was no longer a common feature of the village life. The Šolaja family from the village of Nadanići showed me a maple *gusle* made by their late neighbour Stanko Radmilović in 1956. Nada Šolaja told me: 'You see, everything has gone to pieces. This is something every Serb household had before. Perhaps that is true now as well, but, by God, I don't know'.

When this 'before' had ceased was not exactly clear to my Serb or Muslim interlocutors. The roots of the gradual loss are most probably to be located in the twentieth century as a whole, which began by turning *gusle* into a *Četnik* and nationalist emblem, to be followed by almost half a century of socialist aversion to both the *Četniks* and their nationalism, and so implicitly to 'their' traditions, followed by the resurgent nationalism of the 1990s, which propagated violence through the *gusle,* but also mainstreamed the tradition through 'cultural events'. In May 2015, Mihailović, the Second World War *Četnik* commander was politically 'rehabilitated' through a judicial process in Serbia (see B92: 2015).

The Lofty Mountain of the Fairies: An Affective Grammar

Instead of attempting to situate the instrument further historically or politically, I would now like to establish the uncanny relationship between two epic songs which share certain constructive elements. The first, which pertains to the Gacko Field itself, is widely disseminated through *YouTube*.[7] It feeds on local cosmologies and important *topoi*, as well as traditional verse arrangements:

Gleda vila s Volujaka,	The *vila* [fairy] looks down from Volujak [mountain],
čisto Gacko od Turaka.	Gacko is clean of the Turks.
Ne vidi se niđe bule,	There's nary a *bula* [veiled Muslim woman] in sight,
Fazlagića nema Kule.	Fazlagića Kula [Muslim village] is no more.
Nema fesa, ni dimija,	No more *fez* [Muslim men's hats], no more *dimije*
niti hodže da zavija.	[Muslim women's pantaloons],
Čast ti svaka Gacko ravno,	no more *hodžas* [Muslim priests] to howl.
kad si čisto pravoslavno.	Praise be to the plain of Gacko,
	so pure and so Orthodox.

Gusle melodies seem to have been composed simply to follow and accentuate the stages of the epic storyline, rather than to be heard autonomously. The *gusle* player (*guslar*) is always the singer as well. It was habitually the male domain, to be sung at sessions (*sijela*), even though women did participate in the tradition as well.[8] The sound of the instrument provides rhythmic punctuation and the performative ambiance. It sets the stage.

Many *gusle* songs were recorded in the Field and the surrounding regions during the 1930s by Harvard professors Milman Parry and Albert Lord, forming the basis for their famous *Oral-Formulaic Theory* (see Foley 2005), which looked into the different conventions employed to construct epic narrative discourse (Edwards 1983: 151). They argued that, in their performance of *gusle* songs, some of which were four times the length of this chapter, Yugoslav singers had to resort to received formulae and themes. They repeated certain metric set pieces, groups of words and themes to construct a successful narrative (see Lord 2000: 4). These narrative units (themes, rhythms and arrangements), they argued, come to be repeated as the unconsciously habituated 'grammar of poetry' (see Parry 1971, Lord 2000). The discursive elements are stored in the singer's 'toolbox' to allow for quick performative assemblage.

The heroic epic that has been reappropriated into nationalist narratives, lent its compositions, images and themes as signifiers of authenticity – an unbroken connection to the cultural and historical authority of the traditional poetic heritage. In the above cited 'genocidal' epic, the composition, images and landscapes protrude through the intended semantics. Indeed, these formulae are the pillars of authenticity supporting the song's claims. They provide the necessary mytho-historical legitimacy.

The introductory image, where the Slavic fairy observes Gacko from Mount Volujak, is a composition whose necessity can be argued on the grounds of either a call to authenticity or the embodied conventions of singing or, most probably, both. Milman Parry died too young to know the full extent of the nationalist turn that his Yugoslav epics would have revealed and Albert Lord's passing coincided with the dissolution of the Socialist Federative Republic. In *Singer of Tales* (2000: 65), however, Lord did note how a singer perpetuates meanings older than his memory through adopted epic conventions: 'His oft-used phrases and lines lose something in sharpness, yet many of them must resound with overtones of the dim past whence they came'.

Such examples of nationalist currents in epics allow several readings beyond their own striking exclusivism. In the first reading, like other ideological art forms, *gusle* songs may simultaneously represent a discourse, work towards its reification and offer the most useful ways of its deconstruction. The singer instrumentalizes the instrument, its authoritative and mythic voice, its embodied images and verses, to produce a sense of continuity. This is a proper neoclassical trick. The epic conventions are akin to the ionic columns and the tympanum incorporated into the facade of the British Museum, which propose a connection between the Greco-Roman cultural spaces and modern Europe. They are a historicizing tool, an inheritance claim. In the second reading, the nationalist *gusle* songs reveal mythic landscapes to which the singer and his audiences were habituated. These spaces are so familiar that they grow into the constructive tissue of any storytelling; they become part and parcel of the syntax. The singer, in his slippage, reveals more than was intended. He sings about ethnic cleansing but, paradoxically, the only way for him to do so it is through the intimate knowledge of the Other and traditions shared within the Field.

The poet provides an entire list of 'things Muslim', citing the largest Muslim village of Kula and noting the *fez* worn my Muslim men, the *dimije* pantaloons worn by Muslim women, *bula* as the name for veiled and religiously educated Muslim women and *hodža* as the title of the Muslim priest. In referring to the *hodža*'s 'howls', he is mocking the sounds of *ezan*, the call for prayer from the minarets that echoed through the Field. The nationalist *guslar* thus exhibits an intimate knowledge of his landscape, the one whose destruction he is celebrating. Such knowledge somehow fails to legitimize the essential difference between Serbs and Muslims, rather underscoring the interwoven identities through which the singer has learnt to compose.

These moments in the singer's narrative contain some of the interpretative potential of the remnants, analysed by Navaro-Yashin (2009, 2012), who employed the concept of 'ruination' to 'refer to the material remains or artefacts of destruction and violation, but also to the subjectivities and residual affects that linger, like a hangover, in the aftermath of violence' (2012: 162). The resulting affective possibilities are both projected onto and emanating from the remnants (ibid: 171). The ruination I analyse here is of a Field calcified in mytho-cosmological epic representations. These residues, I argue, are affectively present in the style and vocabularies of the new *gusle* performances. They are consolidated scenes of a shared landscape, an unavoidable protrusion into a song which adheres to the politics of essential distance. Remnants thus have something of their own affective agency. Suddenly, through the horrors of 'purged Gacko', one is offered an image of veiled women and men with *fezzes* walking through the Field, sounds of prayer from the minarets and the wonders of fairies residing on top of Mount Volujak.

Consider again this nationalist epic in comparison to a much older one, recorded in Bosnia by the Austrian fin-de-siècle ethnographer Friedrich Salomon Krauss (1908: 376–80). Two mythical Georgic characters, Prince Marko and his sworn brother, the winged Reljica, are pondering how best to survive the winter. Their winter, as for the epic outlaws, is marked by two shared festivities; it begins with Demetrius' Day and ends with George's Day. Prince Marko asks winged Reljica if he knows of any wealth to be looted:

Su čim ćemo prezimiti zimu	What shall keep us through the winter
od Mitrovog dana jesenjega	from Demetrius' day autumnal
do proljeća dana Gjurgjevoga?	till the day of George's spring?

Winged Reljica's reply is reminiscent of the nationalist epic:

Pobratime kraljeviću Marko,	Sworn brother Prince Marko,
jesam čuo a kažu mi ljudi,	I have heard what people have told me,
tamo ima polje Gacko ravno,	there's a flat field of Gacko,
a viš njega Čemerna planina,	and above it Čemerno, the mountain,
a na više Volujak planina,	and above that Volujak, the mountain,
a u planini zeleno jezero,	in the mountain a green lake,
u jezeru sedam vila,	in the lake seven fairies,
sedam vila sedam drugarica	seven fairies seven companions
kod jezera na rosnoj livadi.	on a dewy meadow near the lake.

This old epic thus locates the sacred fairy-inhabited landscape of Mount Volujak, which the nationalist singer used in his opening verse. The *vile* (fairies) are the main protagonists of this song and Volujak, above the 'flat field of Gacko', their natural habitat. In the nationalist epic, however, the fairies appear as mere reference, without any obvious connection to the plot. Krauss (1908: 376–77) noted that the fairies who dwell on Volujak and all the other high mountains of the region were held so sacred that they were honoured by pilgrimages to their caves and praised in many *gusle* songs. Indeed, I too have heard many stories about fairies: I visited *Vilina Pećina* (Fairy's Cave) in the village of Ključ, one of their many residences around the Field; they also used to bathe at the spring of Sopot in the village of Kula.

Another song recorded in Gacko focuses on the same magical *topos* (see Vidan 2003a: 175). This time, a local lord, the Bey Ljubović is ordered by the sultan to capture the fairy and bring her to Istanbul:

> *Jesam čuo, jesam razumio*   I have heard, I have understood
> *da imade Gacku ravnome*   that in the plain of Gacko
> *na visokoj Volujak planini*   on the lofty mountain of Volujak,
> *a nekakvo zeleno jezeru,*   in some green lake
> *u jezeru b'jelu vilu kažu.*   there is a white *vila*, people say.

The fairies thus linger, affectively, through the continuation of a particular kind of grammar. In order to understand this grammar, it is important to note that in epic poetry what constitutes a word is the entire scene. 'A fairy looks down from Mount Volujak' cannot be fragmented. It is an internalized formula of sacral landscape and mytho-poetic language embodied as such, thick with affect. John Foley noted:

> What quickly becomes apparent is that within the oral tradition a 'word' is a speech-act, a unit of utterance, an atom of composition and expression. As such, it is never what we literate users of texts mean by words. For a South Slavic *guslar*, a single 'word' is never smaller than a phrase, and it can be a whole poetic line, a scene or speech, and even the whole epic story. (2004: 21)

My use of 'affective remnants' is not discourse free. I argue that the remnants of one discourse can affectively protrude into a new 'space'. They lose discursive positions they once held, but continue to exist through their conveyors – the instrument, the landscape and the body (never entirely separate from each other). They continue, almost like an involuntary reflex, beyond the new discursive positions they are relegated to. As such, they disturb, or have the potential to disturb, the ideas of a cohesive, pure ethno-national Field from within the very body of the Field's ethno-nationalist.

As for the fairies in the times of new epic heroes, Zahida, an elderly returnee to the village of Hodinići, told me that they are no longer to be seen. Wise creatures as they are, they must have a good reason. I listened to Zahida:

> There were *vile* [fairies] before. Let me tell you about one Hiđuša Mujovica [a woman from the neighbourhood]. Women used to wake up early and take the bulls to plough the earth. So, the bulls would be given hay to eat at three in the morning. Well, this woman had no water. People woke up: no water. So, she went to Sopot, this spring. And she got to Sopot – the *vila* didn't sense her.

When, lo, there at Sopot: a *vila* washing her face. Hair down to her feet: golden. Hands: golden. She: golden. 'Oh,' she says, 'woman, you've startled me. Listen, she says, woman, go home but tell no one, she says, don't tell even your family. I will fill your lap.' They wore *dimije* [baggy women's trousers] in those days, God bless you. So, she scooped like this and folded like this [hand gestures]. And the woman spread out her *dimije,* and lo, the *vila* filled them with gold.

And she met her first neighbour, there at Hida's house. This is the living truth. 'Why did you wake up so early?' 'Oh my dear, I had no water, but you should know what I saw.' 'And what, you poor thing?' 'A *vila.*' 'Sit down,' she said, 'you fool.' 'I did, by God.' She came into the house and took a bucket and lo, her lap was full of coal. Everything had turned into coal. 'Eh,' she said, 'you crazy woman, you shouldn't have told even me, much less anyone else.'

Old people used to tell this story. Bećir's grandmother is from the Hide family. It is the living truth, the living truth. I don't know when it happened; it was a long time ago, at the beginning of the twentieth century.

The Living Truth

Are certain affectivities projected onto the ruins by the subjects who make them or who live in their midst? Or do the ruins exude their own affect? Once again, I would argue that both are evident.
—Y. Navaro-Yashin, 'Affective Spaces, Melancholic Objects'

The long twentieth century took the heaviest of its modernizing tolls on the Field. The once pronounced cosmological composition was steadily evicted from its epic expanses into remnants. The landscape hid, chronotopically, keeping in reserve its fairies and songs. When surfacing, it appeared in strange situations, always to some extent affecting what can be said about it.

From Hiđuša's uncanny encounter with a fairy to the uncanny encounter of the magical Field with the nationalist Field in the epics, this chapter offers a glimpse into the formation of a body-grammar. This grammar is not how people talk about the world, but how they talk the world, or rather sing the world. It erodes the projects of 'ethno-religious' cleansing, making sure that *singing the world otherwise* would be difficult at least. It hands over deeply embodied traces of a shared landscape, ingrained, clinging to movements and utterances, rejecting deportation, finding new syncretic forms. By looking at the sacral geography as located in epics and the narratives of my interlocutors, I argue that the nationalist discourses promulgated in the area destabilize themselves through the affectivity of these particular remnants – embodied themes, images and compositions.

These affects are *epic,* defining of a landscape and its grand cosmology, yet they are also ordinary, messy with the variety of historical and personal

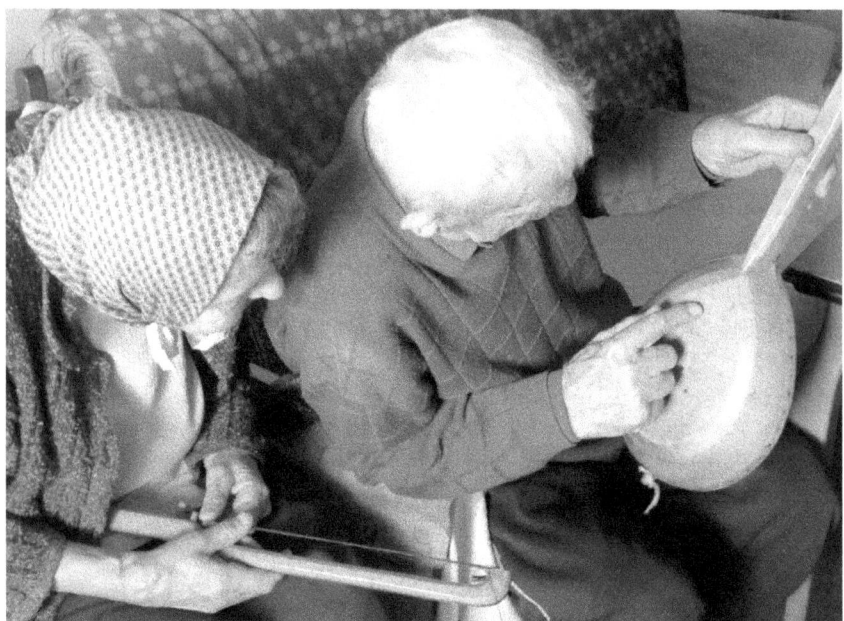

FIGURE 4.1 The Šolajas with their family *gusle*

FIGURE 4.2 Mount Volujak

trajectories in the Field and the possibilities in the everyday. Ordinary affects, Stewart said, are 'about bodies literally affecting one another and generating intensities: human bodies, discursive bodies, bodies of thought, bodies of water' (2007: 128). These bodies leave different kinds of more or less perceptible impression upon each other. One body is never fully effaced from its webs of relations; it acquires an extension, or an afterlife, in another, making itself impossible to circumnavigate.

Only through the embodiment of landscape is it feasible that the *guslar* sings about ethnic cleansing, yet, paradoxically, his intended positionality ruptures with traces of shared traditions. Thus, in a poetic twist of faith, the nationalist *guslar* cannot do away with the Other, without doing away with himself.

Notes

1. This is an extract of a *gusle* heroic song performed by Hasan Šašić in the Bosnian town of Jablanica, recorded at the beginning of the twentieth century by the Austrian ethnographer Friedrich Salomon Krauss (1908: 394–405).
2. 'Hajduks' is the common English pluralization of the singular 'hajduk', whereas the Bosnian plural is *hajduci*.
3. See Bracewell's (1992: 11) discussion of the historiographic arguments on what she called the 'hajduk ideology', or the question of religious and national consciousness of the hajduks.
4. I capitalize the word *Četnik* when referring to the Serbian nationalist formations rather than outlaws. For a summary of *Četnik* politics and activities of the Second World War, see Noel Malcolm's work (1995: 233–58).
5. What I mean by genocide here is its legal definition, namely the 'intent to destroy, in whole or in part, a national, ethnical, racial or religious group' (Convention on the Prevention and Punishment of the Crime of Genocide, Article 2).
6. Lord (2000: 7) further noted: 'In some Slavic countries the word *narodni* has a useful ambiguity, since it means both "folk" and "national." As a term to designate oral epic "national" is woefully inadequate and an insidious imposter'.
7. Versions of this *gusle* song seem to appear only on *YouTube,* where they are described as 'authentic'. One was published by skituljko039 as 'Gacko ravno-izvorne pjesme uz gusle (izvorna grupa Stara Hercegovina)', (see https://www.youtube.com/watch?v=_FtJNMziEoQ, retrieved 20 October 2017) and the other was published by StefanKVSRS as 'Gusle – Fazlagića gori kula' (see https://www.youtube.com/watch?v=nS0le2glYYU, retrieved 20 October 2017).
8. There was a distinct and rich genre of 'women's songs' in the Field (see Vidan 2003a), but women also carried on the traditions of heroic 'male' songs.

PART II

THE MANY FACES OF ELIJAH

Prelude

A River of Many Names

One of the longest sinking rivers in the world begins its life in the Field of Gacko.[1] Its waters emerge as two streams beneath the mountains of Čemerno and Lebršnik, their life-sustaining force briefly erupting onto the wide plateau and then tumbling back into the Dinaric karst, carving out thousands of secret chambers on their journey. Those places where the river surges back down towards depths unknown are called *ponor*. The name comes from the Proto-Slavic feminine noun *norà*, meaning 'den', 'lair', 'abyss' or 'chasm' and the verb *nerti* (Church Slavonic *ponrěti*), meaning 'to enter', 'go deep into' or 'hide oneself' (Derksen 2008: 349, 355). The wealth of such phenomena in the Western Balkan Peninsula propelled the word *ponor* into the international karstological dictionary (Monroe 1970: 14). Sinking rivers in Bosnia are called *ponornice* – streams hidden in deep lairs.

There is some difficulty in finding the right word for our secretive river. Each time this *ponornica* resurfaces, it takes on a new name. At least nineteen current names can be traced for its outward presences to *anthropoi*, but none for its inward-looking streams. Those names include: Jasenički Potok or Jasenička Rijeka, Gračanica, Dobra Voda or Platički Potok, Vrba or Vrbska Rijeka, Mušnica, Ključka Rijeka, Klinje Jezero, Obod or Fatnička Rijeka, Miruša or Bilećko Jezero, Trebišnjica, Ombla or Dubrovačka Rijeka, and Krupa (cf. Kazazić 2006, Lučić 2012a: 14). In each of these names, the water and the overground human–nonhuman networks have flooded into each other. Hydronyms have created toponyms and oronyms and vice versa. However, the rivers may take some precedence in these relationships.[2]

Amongst the many sections of this river, the Trebišnjica is one of the longest and most outspoken. It flows through the old town of Trebinje (see Figure PII.3). The river and the settlement share the root of their names, which is to be found in the Proto-Slavic word *treba* for 'sacrifice' or 'sacrificial altar' and comes ultimately from the Proto-Slavic *terb*, 'to clean, extract, or purge',[3] but is also related to 'need, necessity' (Skok 1971: 501, Lučić 2012a: 17), as in the Bosnian verb *trebati*, 'to need, to want'. Thus, the 'longest' and 'most easily discernible' name for the river that 'hides itself' in 'chasms' refers us back to the sacrificial cleansing of necessity, revealing an etymological link to certain old European apotropaic purification rituals.

Many surviving geonyms in Bosnia are derivatives of *treba*. The map compiled here, while not exhaustive (Figure PII.2), indicates some characteristics of early Slavic cosmology. The 'cleansing, sacrificial potential' is attached mostly to hydronyms (particularly sinking rivers) and oronyms (particularly mountain peaks).[4] This vertical relationship reveals a sacred geometry located between the deepest depths and the highest heights.

The metaphor of the sinking river expresses something of the relationship daily lives and walked landscapes have with symbols and, ultimately, what lies beyond/beneath. Some sources and some streams of such knowledge may be attainable through ascertainable spatiality and temporality. They are imagined as being fully graspable through encounters and discourses. When such knowledge emerges across human paths, eroding bits of the overground into its rush, sections of the stream take on new names and possibilities, yet the subtext of an older connection remains. It is a deeper current that relates the many outward faces of the stream to each other by way of those secret chambers where the water returns to itself, crushing the many washed-away stories and events, merging what seems unlikely or faraway. The hiddenness of its depths is always an affective possibility of intimate relation with other-selves, physically or symbolically distanced from our-selves.

The life of this sinking river is also an ethnographer's cautionary tale. Hydrologists and speleologists have not been able to survey most of its features. We humans remain puzzled by its strength, speed, length and direction. It flows northwest, while overground, but completely changes direction underground (Lučić 2012a: 16). In fact, about all we can say for sure about the complex system of the sinking-and-rising Gacko river is that some of its singled-out qualities are at best capable of generating incomplete remarks about what is an inherently imagined system. To make a complete survey of its chambers and paths, we would have to destroy it.

The second caveat this river makes is related to our responsibility towards an important, albeit unattainable connection by ways of the unseen. The underground course of the Trebišnjica was systematically excavated for its hydropotential under the second Yugoslavia (Lučić 2012a: 22): the water was redirected for the use of several power plants that provided electrical energy for the Yugoslav republics; new cement waterbeds were constructed; underground tunnels guided the river towards a number of completely new catchment areas; and the damming seriously altered the native flora and fauna (ibid: 23). According to karst hydrologist Petar Milanović (2002), the overall project for power generation on the Trebišnjica includes seven dams, six artificial reservoirs, six tunnels and four channels. He noted that '[u]pon full completion, the natural regime of surface and groundwater will be completely changed' (ibid: 13).

FIGURE PII.2 Geonyms derived from *treba,* with circles marking the hydronyms

FIGURE PII.3 Trebišnjica flowing through the town of Trebinje, courtesy of Krsto Mijanović

Complex religious streams likewise experience episodes of more or less systematic codification and alteration. Those like me, who endeavour to trace them, must be aware of their own capacity to (re)direct, define and simplify, impose order and disallow the enchanted strangeness of the hidden. This is why I am wary of (multi)national projects like the nomination of George's Day for inscription on the Representative List of the Intangible Cultural Heritage of Humanity (UNESCO 2014). Besides the obvious complexity (and probable infeasibility) of protecting and 'representing' the beginning of spring, the nation-state framework is an imposition upon religious streams. George's Day predates the nation-state world and continues to confront its fallacies, for example through the vernal movements of nomadic Gurbeti communities.

The anthropocentric projects on the Trebišnjica river system have devastated not just the flora and fauna, but the local *anthropoi* as well. Karstologist Ivo Lučić (2012a: 24) argued that what we have seen in the case of the Trebišnjica is the 'domination of a modernist mechanistic approach which emphasizes economic benefit and development', an approach that ignores the local cosmologies and traditions as important dimensions of cultural identity. Indeed, whole villages have been submerged under artificial reservoirs, while others continue to endure cyclical crop-destroying floods.

Delva told me how the spring of Brestovac (literally, 'Elm Creek'), beneath her house in the village of Kula, was regulated before the 1990s war. The source of the creek was altered and moved a few metres. Initially, it did not seem like a significant alteration, but, she said, everything changed. The water dried up. The birds stopped coming. The landscape was transmuted into an incomplete space, no longer recognizable to the Kula villagers. Delva's neighbour, Eno, took it upon himself to restore the spring to its original state. Soon after, the birds returned and their chirping could be heard again, Delva remembered.

The restoration of traditional festivities in the Field carried a similar hope for those few who returned from exile, that they would somehow reconstruct the place and lives familiar to them from the echoing voices of men as they pierced the landscape with their traditional bećarac songs for Elijah's Day. Belonging and hope, as Stef Jansen (2009) argued, are invested in this temporal dimension. As he noted, encounters with landscapes that no longer reflect 'home' have fashioned the refugees' hopes regarding return (see Chapter 2).

Birds and human beings were not alone in their struggle to remain. The whole environment, one of the most remarkable karst systems in the world (Lučić 2012a: 16), continues to be threatened by highly invasive damming and mining. An endemic species of cave fish, the peculiar-looking olm (*proteus anguinus*), also known as 'the human fish' (*čovječja ribica*), is seriously endangered (Milanović 2002: 20). Eno proudly told me about another endemic species:

> Our sinking river of Mušnica is famous for its *gaovica* fish, which is native to here. It is found nowhere in the world except in Gacko. Nowhere! Nowhere in the whole *dunjaluk!*[5] There are still some here, though. In summer, you will go fishing with Muhamed. It's a tiny fish, not very bulky, but sweet as sugar, it's a miracle really.

Even the famous seventeenth-century Ottoman travel writer, Evliya Çelebi, wrote a few lines about this particular fish. Although his descriptions are known for their occasional exaggeration, this one bears a striking resemblance to the fish Eno mentioned: 'There's a fish here that they call trout (*alabaligri*), colourful and speckled with golden patterns. This fish does not exist in any other country. They melt in the mouth of whoever is eating them and there is no fishy odour' (Çelebi 1996: 20). The Gacko gaovica (*parapphoxinus ghetaldi*) is, as a species, highly dependent on the natural karst rhythm of flooding. The damming of the river has brought this species to the verge of extinction (Milanović 2002: 20).

The current thermal power plant is a significant polluter of the air and water over an area much wider than just the Field of Gacko. Plans to build another station are well under way. According to a Devon Karst Research Society report, the second power plant will have a destructive anthropogenic impact involving at least a doubling of the discharge of pollutants and an extensive reorganization of the river courses (2006, section 13.1.4). Gračanica and Mušnica, the two main tributaries to the sinking waterway, were already completely redirected in 2013, because they lay over rich lignite deposits. And, since the Field of Gacko is the mainspring of a complex water system, the harmful impacts will doubtless be even greater for a much wider set of underground and overground terrains. Ashes from the plant would cover the Field, harming crops and cattle. The endangered species included those humans whose lives were antithetical to the programmes of the political and economic elites. Nationalism and industry, espoused by the same concentrated consortium, had systematically eroded the diversity of the local landscape: while working in Gacko, I had a persistent sense of an environment surviving at the limits of its strengths – a suffocated landscape – where diverse life manages against all odds to maintain basic functions.

With daring strength, the olm, the endemic 'human fish', has somehow managed to survive in its subterranean enclaves. Likened to humans primarily for its limbs and pale pink colour, its survival tactics make for another fitting analogy. Ill-timed and out of place, humans too have lived in distant pockets of the Field since the 1990s war, with the minimum habitat required. Uncertainty encountered by (human) returnees has occasionally been threaded with contained expectations of the future. The same villagers who once boasted proverbial sayings like 'God forfend a childless summer!' or teasing jabs like 'With them, it's one cabbage – one child', now emphasized the importance of Kanita Karailo, the only child born to a returnee family since the war.[6]

So, the questions facing me and other researchers into a Bosnian or any other sacral landscape are not easy. How to explore a system of belief, at times fragile, at others incredibly enduring, without disenchanting its secrecies, without making too violent an intervention? How to avoid moral, historical and cultural classifications? What can one ascertain about the contexts, sources and meanings of these landscapes, without inflicting violence upon the knowledge, practices and relationships to which they pertain? Most importantly, how to avoid informing future programmes of division and ruination? My answer to these difficult questions is to follow the lessons of the sinking river – to destabilize the many possible essentializations and generalizations by indicating the multiplicity of perspectives and the ultimate unattainability of bounded and complete temporal, spatial and experiential dimensions, as well as by acknowledging that substance in motion should never be forcefully accumulated into representations of stillness.

The source of our enigmatic river is, much like all sources, somewhere else, indiscernible beyond a certain point. What we see in the Field are only the first of the substantial overground streams. Before that, undocumented drops of rain fall onto riverbed and trickle down through the Dinaric mountain range – the largest karstland in Europe (Kranjc 2004: 591). Karst is the kind of landscape where water can erode and dissolve the rock, perforating it with caves and subterranean streams (Williams 2004: 1021). Above the cave system, on the surface, karst usually forms enclosed plains. From the depths, a hidden underworld fashions the exterior image – the Field of Gacko and other wide plateaus of the Dinaric mountain range.

There are two kinds of beginnings, karstologically speaking: 'autogenic recharge', where rocks receive the rain directly and end up with millions of fissures; and 'allogenic recharge', where the rain falls onto less soluble rock first and flows into organized streams (Williams 2004: 1022). The Field belongs to both kinds of beginnings. It contains countless invisible openings, where water and land meet, but also the more visible steady flows, which carve their way through the bed of limestone and brown coal.

Mirroring these Gacko creeks, winding through the landscape before joining and sinking, only to reappear elsewhere under another name, several streams of local sacral traditions appear as at once separate and part of the same substance. They too have countless internal meeting points – discursive and nondiscursive – some of which I have been able to record. These sacred streams maintain family relations with streams temporally and spatially far beyond the Field. Many religious remnants follow the sinking river.

As Lučić noted: 'It is evident that the length of the Trebišnjica and all the major changes along its course are expressed and measured in sacred places' (2012a: 18).

Ultimately, it seems to me, the 'success' of this work will lie in its uselessness for the various identitary and developmental projects on the Gacko horizons. The river, its fields and its humans have persisted primarily by evading the orderly depressions carved out for them by the states. Although James Scott (1990) was referring to the kinds of human resistance that come about in hegemonic situations, I would like to claim his concept of a 'hidden transcript' for the insurrectionary practices of both humans and nonhumans within and beyond the southeastern Bosnian highlands. The sinking river, the Field, and its humans are all empowered by a knowledge beyond the reach of modernist nationalist projects. Should this book be read by the key actors in those belated endeavours, I suspect that it will seem incomprehensible to them; should it be comprehensible, then a part of my plan will have already been successful. So, please forgive my erratic style and the long chapter to follow. Strategically wayward, I have tried to follow this river of many names in order to give you but a glimpse of its Elijah of many names.

Notes

1. It may even be the longest sinking water system in the world. Ivo Lučić (2012a) gives a more detailed description of the river. The length of its underground systems has been drastically reduced by damming and artificial accumulations. See Kazazić's (2006) reflection on the names of this river, which inspired the title of the Prelude.
2. Toponomastic research reveals the oldest layers of such reflective namegiving precisely in hydronyms (see, e.g. Peust 2011). The geographic determinant Bosnia (*Bosna*) similarly reflects the name of the River Bosna, whose source is in Sarajevo.
3. Two common contemporary words in Bosnia testify to this meaning. *Trijebiti* means 'to clean up' (usually a house), and *istrijebiti* means 'to cleanse', 'to purge' or 'to make extinct'.
4. My brief survey revealed the following toponyms: Trebinjčica, Trebolj, Trebečajski Potok, Triješanj, Trebačka Rijeka, Trebčica, Trebesin, Trebeda, Trebuša, Trijebovski Ponorac, Trijebinska Rijeka, Trebinja, Trebižat, Trebišnjica, Tribija, Trebunj, Trimuža, Trebešnjica, Trebević (2), Trebava, Trebova Planina, Trebiješ, Trebinjača, Tribljevina, Tribošić, Trebeško Brdo, Trebeševo, Trebeuša, Trebić Gore, Trebičina, Trebijovi, Trebimljska Brdo, Tribanj, Trijebanj, Trebinje, Trijebovo, Trebovljani, Trebačko Brdo, Trebečaj, Trebinjska Šuma, Zatrijebić, Trijebine, Trijebac, Tribunj, Trebišov, Tribić, Tribanj, Tribistovo, Trebče, Trepče, Trepča, Trepče-Šije, Trebečaj, Trebesinj, Trebac, Trebimlja, Trebiševo, Treboje, Trebovci, Tribošići and Trijepče.
5. In Bosnian Muslim cosmology, *dunjaluk* is 'this world' as opposed to *ahiret*, the 'afterlife'.
6. The sayings in Bosnian are: *Ne daj Bože ljeta bez djeteta!* and *U njih ti je kupus i dijete.*

CHAPTER 5

THE GEORGICS
An Extended Poetry of the Land

What tickles the corn to laugh out loud, and by what star
to steer the plough, and how to train the vine to elms,
good management of flocks and herds, the expertise bees need
to thrive – my lord, Maecenas, such are the makings of the song
I take upon myself to sing.

—Virgil, *Georgics*

An event can be described only participatively.
—M.M. Bakhtin, *Toward a Philosophy of the Act*

Historiographies are authoritative imaginings. They look for authentic evidence to structure narratives about the past, fleeing from innumerable analytical sources in its selective endeavours. Leaving behind the question of authority, this chapter plays with such imagination, attempting to trace the steps of the becoming of 'our' key cosmological characters, by taking you on a journey into the spaces and times of George and Elijah. The boundaries are so fuzzy that only an old-school ethnologist could make any sense of them. The plot appropriately starts off in the Field, but dares to make connections, from Palestine to Britain and Ireland, from Serbia and Hungary to the Indian subcontinent, with the discourses of 'farmers' and 'theologians' alike, to the immense body of practices and encounters that perpetually expand the plethora of Georgic images. This chapter argues for the relationship of language, words and naming to the affective and political lives of landscapes and their surprising continuities.

I begin with a reconstituted 'ethnographic' dialogue on George's Day in the Field, continue with a wide-ranging interrogation of George's and Elijah's identities and conclude with a return to the Field on Elijah's Day. The chapter, like the warm season in the Field, is at the same time temporally and spatially rooted and fluid, connected, extended. Like the sinking river, it is full of caveats, which may make for a difficult read. All of this I do not in provision, but in search, of the multifarious and partial contexts for the George and Elijah of the Field.

The claim, then, is not that the varied characters, times, spaces and discourses form some discrete cosmology with a common essential quality, but rather that, in many different ways, they are related. And, while the resemblances might at times be striking, their causes are at best a speculation about the affective, geographic, temporal and political proximities. Wittgenstein famously likened such similarities to 'family resemblances', which 'overlap and criss-cross' between the members (1997: 32). This concept helps to explain why the Palestinian and the Bosnian George might 'share' certain features, while the southeastern Bosnian and the southern Serbian George 'share' others. My claim is that they all inhabit an extended (although not necessarily discursive) unit of familiarity. Of course, a 'family', however defined, may often invite the observation of otherwise unnoticed 'physical' and 'social' resemblences, and so the act of comparison also 'constitutes a making of connections' (Strathern 2004: 51). The following pages are then at least two kinds of afterthought: those of my interlocutors, in their situated memories, and my own, through my choice of extensions and interpretations of their remembered acts.

In one of his early works, discovered in a pile of badly damaged notepads, Bakhtin (1999) distinguished between the act performed or lived (*postupok*) and the later consideration or representation of it, the afterlife of the act, as it were. The latter often amounts to 'theoreticism', which is in danger of escaping the answerability or responsibility that the lived act necessarily contains. The problem with Bakhtin's proposal is that the 'original' ritual act, the one remembered by my interlocutors, is also an afterlife, a performative memory of itself.

Take for example the lighting of bonfires on hilltops in the springtime. It is both a lived act and a memory. This is what Connerton (1989: 71) called 'bodily social memory'. It is habitual, sedimented in the body, he argued, and its hold over us stems from such bodily intimacy (ibid: 72, 94). So, every 'original' act may also be understood as a 'post-act'. The post-act is affectively and discursively related to, but different from, the original act and this process is perpetuated with every new reenactment. The post-act is not free from newer responsibilities, relations, desires and intentions. The act situated in the cyclical calendar is then always both a partial repetition and an original position. The act of narrated memory is simply a differently performed post-act. It also lingers between discursivity and affectivity. And it begs the same questions: Why are some remnants more durable than others? What novel relations and responsibilities are established by the post-act? In many moments, sitting beside my interlocutors, I knew that they were not simply narrating, but that their whole bodies, and many times also my own, were drawn into a landscape that wasn't there. The boundaries of participation and post-participative reflection are, to say the least, unclear.

The structure of this chapter should be understood as a lacework of George and Elijah through the post- (or post-post-) acts of my interlocutors' memories and George and Elijah as my own post- (or post-post-post-) act of extended analysis. It attempts to situate the two protagonists of the Field's warm season in Balkan and wider Indo-European traditional calendars and cosmological plateaux, in order to counterbalance the first part of the book and, at least partly, avoid the common academic tendency to analyse Bosnian religiosity through the context of nationalist governmentality since the 1990s.

I use the term 'Georgics' to name this unlikely family, a sea of resemblances in spite of the dissimilarities. It is no coincidence that this reflects the title of one of the major works of Virgil (2006), whose didactic poetry tackled the sacral, political and phenomenological character of 'work in the field' by describing the subtle signs of the land as it communicates to its godly and earthly beings, a landscape where practical tasks and cosmic meanings are never separate conditions. His Georgics were also reacting to the civil war and the destruction of the countryside and threaded with hope for its reconstruction. The extended 'Gacko Georgics', although situated in more than one historical and political context, do manage to speak to the destruction of the Field. They follow the ethos of the genre, taking the Greek etymology of 'working the land' and 'farmer' (see Fantham: xv) as indications not of an idealized landscape, but one which is necessarily enacted.

In this sense, Ingold's (1993) concept of the 'taskscape', which describes patterns of (dwelling) inter-activity, is useful. There is a need to surmount an epistemological and ontological obstacle by understanding that the 'identities' of George and Elijah are contained in the taskscape, the inter-activity of the Field. In fact, my interlocutors seldom spoke of Elijah or George at all. They employed the phrases 'George's Day' (*Jurjevo/Đurđevdan/Ederlez*) and 'Elijah's Day' (*Ilindan/Alidun*). The questions to be asked were not 'who?' and 'why?', but 'how?' and 'when?', I have learnt by trial and error – what to do in its appropriate time. Following Durkheim's argument, Ingold noted that 'rites, feasts and ceremonies are themselves as integral to the *taskscape* as are boundary markers such as walls or fences to the landscape' (ibid: 159). They are habituated navigation devices for human bodies and social activities, as informed by the landscape.

My Georgics of the Field are further inspired by the work of Hassan S. Haddad, and particularly his article '"Georgic" Cults and Saints of the Levant' (1969), in which he argued that the figures of George, Khidr and Elijah share a common 'agrarian' theme, that their resemblances relate to what I might now term 'a family of taskscapes', but also to an ancient deity of fertility. For Haddad, '[t]he term "georgic" emphasized the ecological aspect of the group. It comprises all those who are preoccupied with food production and the provision of living by coming into direct contact with nature' (ibid: 22).

Rather than doctrines and divine characters, the temporal and spatial coordinates of the Field as a lived space unlocked the meaning of the cosmos. During my fieldwork, many Muslims and Roma consciously reflected on their lack of knowledge about the biographies of George or Elijah. Beyond the enacted cosmology, Christians did make some use of theological narratives about these characters and their noble deeds, including the images of Elijah as a bearded old man and George as a young knight. Yet, asking anyone from the Field about the identities of these figures, or the definition of their feasts, would be likely to cause some initial confusion. Asking about the acts, memories and places that they entail would always be reciprocated with an abundance of narratives. As this chapter shows, the enacted Georgics of the Field show numerous similarities to the hagiographic expositions.

George and Elijah habitually have the potential to erupt into a life story. They may also draw into themselves the entirety of the Field. George is the first and Elijah the second of the three crucial temporal markers – the beginning of the fertile season, the end of the summer labour and the beginning of the infertile winter – so they may be related to virtually every single facet of life in the Field. As such, they are impossible to isolate from each other and the rest of the year. Nevertheless, I would like to collate some of my many conversations into a single summertime narrative – the Georgics of the Field. Following the division of drama into acts and scenes, these Georgics also reveal the structural performativity of the cyclical calendar. They point to the human and cosmic dramas, enacted simultaneously and elucidating each other.

These extended Georgics of the Field are informed by the narratives, images, acts, emotions and memories that bind George and Elijah. They venture beyond the Field, always looking back. I employ parts of the many conversations that I had in Gacko towards a reconstructed – or imagined – dialogue between my interlocutors, scattered around the Field and the world, drawn apart from each other, mostly by force. So, like the warm part of the year in the Field, the following pages begin with George. Then, they travel, sink, burst into and connect to places geographically distant. Finally, towards the end of the warm season and the chapter, they resurface in the Field again, with Elijah. Moreover, like the sinking river.

The Georgics: An Extended Poetry of the Land 179

FIGURE 5.1 George's Day in Visoko: dancing around fire on the hill of Križ

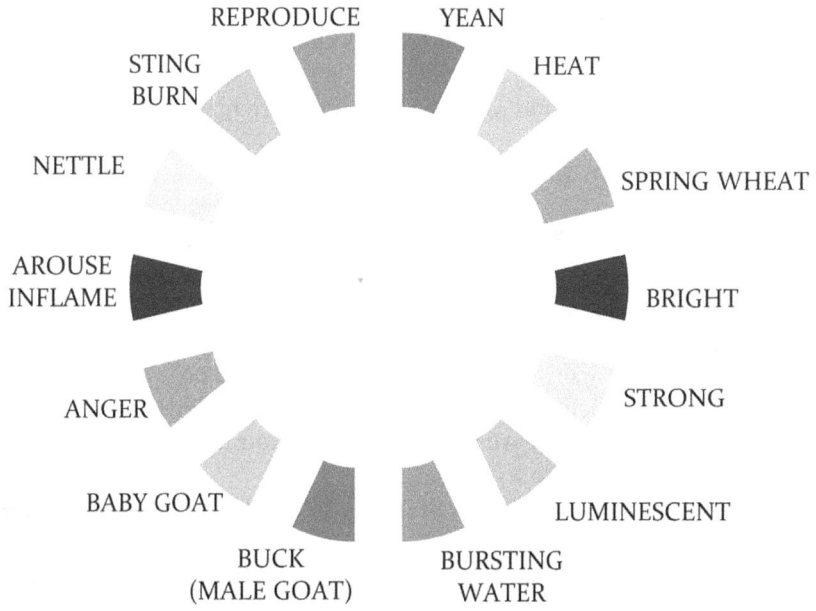

FIGURE 5.2 Meanings of Slavic derivatives from the root **yar*

The Georgics: (Post-)Act One

George of the Field

Scene One: The Origins

Nada: George's Day, we have celebrated it since we came into existence.

Nezir: It has been for thousands and thousands of years. Since I was four years old, my life has been connected to cattle and all those traditions of living. I have experienced it, I have lived it. I was a shepherd when young.

Lepa: It has been celebrated since the Creation.

Eno: Here in Gacko, we call it *Đurđevdan,* not *Jurjevo* [as in some other parts of Bosnia].

Safura: I learned of George's and Elijah's days from my parents. My father was very pious.

Edo: I learned it from my grandfather and my grandmother. I grew up with them.

Sejo: It must have been a Gypsy celebration adopted by the Serbs and the Muslims.

Eno: I don't know where it came from. You know, it's nowhere to be found in religion. It's like a Gypsy celebration, but [other] people paid a lot of attention to it.

Safura: What, George's Day? It was [celebrated by] Muslims and Serbs and Gypsies and all sorts!

Nezir: All of us, all of us, all of us! All of us embraced it as a shared festivity. It was in May.

Ahmo: Basically, Serb and Muslim traditions were ninety-five percent the same.

Osman: It was the creation of a shared tradition.

Scene Two: The Landscape Appears

Ana: You know the spring when the entire Field bursts with the scent and the whiteness of wild daffodils [*košuta*].

Nezir: One might say, if one took vegetation as a measure, that George's Day and Elijah's Day are the beginning and the end of a season. They say, 'Before Elijah's Day – drought, after Elijah's Day – mud'. It means that you are in the middle of summer and that autumn is approaching with its rains.

Eno: We say, Georgic rains [*đurđevske kiše*] and Elijan droughts [*aliđunske suše*].

Safura: The grass sprouts, vegetation appears. Rejoicing arrived of its own accord.

Scene Three: Lightning and Thunder

Fata: They say, watch out for the weather on George's Day. They say, if there are clouds or sunshine, that's what the summer will be like. But, they say, if you have thunder and lightning on George's Day, remember what day of the week it was and don't work with greens or potatoes, don't do anything in the garden that day. The kids would ask why, by God . . . People would say, because of the hail. If you go into the garden, the hail will fall and flatten everything. We would be wary of that. If it thundered on George's Day, I would never tend the garden that day of the week.

Mila: On George's Day, my father wouldn't allow any work on the land.

Safeta: We weren't allowed to braid our hair or to sew with a needle on George's Day, God forbid.

Delva: Neither Serbs nor Muslims worked on Procopius' Day [*Prokopov dan*]. It is on the twenty-seventh day of the seventh month. They would say, God forbid, do nothing, because of the lightning. The lightning would strike, for those who believed in these things, the lightning would strike a haystack or the hay wains. Raza [a local woman] was born on Procopius' Day.

Scene Four: Preparation

Zahida: On George's Day Eve, we would scatter ashes around the house. Three times you would circle the house with ashes, against harmful spells. And against witches.

Ružica: We would wake up early on the morning of George's Day.

Eno: My late grandmother would wake up very early on George's Day.

Mulija: Housewives would get up very early and draw a fire, so that there'd be smoke above the house. Nettles and smoked meat were cooked for the health of the household.

Ružica: On George's Day, a three-pointed candle is lit at noon, the youth sings, the holiday bread [*krsni ljeb*] is drenched in wine, the priest fumigates [the bread and the household] with incense.

Nada: It would happen that we would be fasting. It's not easy when it's for George's Day. It is much easier for Thomas' Day.

Ružica: My mother and grandmother would never break their fast. She lived for more than ninety years, but she would always fast, without a calendar.

Scene Five: The Tree, the Girl and the Swing

Mulija: Where there was a willow, the children would all gather to swing, for good health.

Fata: And then, in the evening, we would set up a swing underneath a walnut tree, but mostly it was under willows, wherever there was a willow. I don't know why, but mostly it was willows. There was something, but what – I don't know. It was mostly willows.

Delva: Willow ... Because a willow has some kind of power, something like that.

Fata: Because [the willow] was always somewhere near water.

Delva: Water, so that [the willow] is healthy, for us all to be healthy.

Eno: Well, the swings were swung. It was inevitable. Kids swing, bonfires are lit.

Hasan: There was organized swinging under a walnut tree. The young men and women would gather in fine clothes to flirt.

Safeta: Here, we would swing on a birch tree [*breza*]. Up to fifty lads and lasses would gather, and the women visit a bit too. The crowd was roaring. It was beautiful, my God ...

Fata S: Once, my father wouldn't let me go outside for George's Day. So, we stole a rope ... It was a truly joyful time [*rahatluk*].

Nura: As they were swung, the girls would sing: 'The dragon flew from the sea to the Danube ....' [*Zmaj proleće s mora na Dunavo ...*] I remember it. There were lots of other George's Day songs. When the lads would swing you, you would think you were flying somewhere far off ...

Safura: Girls would sing as they were swung. They would set up a swing where there was a mulberry tree [*murva*]. And there would be quite a gathering. A strong mulberry tree would be found, a rope fastened for swinging. And the lads and lasses ... The lad swings the lass. She would be in *dimije* [traditional baggy trousers] and a blouse.

Fata: Then, the lads, lasses, young married women of the house [*mlade i nevjeste*] and older people would gather. All would come together there – the whole neighbourhood [*mahala*]. If they didn't have a willow, they would go where there was one to gather. There was one down there, where the Zekić family lived. And they would have a party [*teferičili*]. Sing, dance, swing ... Swing, sing, dance ...

Fata S: We would swing near Studenac spring on a large oak tree [*dub*]. It was cut down by the butchers of the last war. You see that stump. It was thirty, forty metres tall. When it fell, it broke over two houses.

Scene Six: The Direction of Nettle

Eno: Nettles were burnt and cooked for the Annunciation and George's Day. I remember we cooked nettles. It was traditional.

Edo: Well, nettle [*žara*] is one of the first plants to grow in spring. You know, it's not exactly a harbinger, but one of the first plants. For *Đurđevdan,* which was a spring festival, it's cooked in a stew with beans, potatoes and meat. That's it.

Fata: Girls would wake up early, early in the morning. In the evening [before George's Day] they would plant nettles. Where will the nettle turn? Where will it fall?

Delva: If it turns in this direction, well the Sarići [family] are over there ... so you'll marry there, as it were. If it turns that way, towards the Bašići, or Džeci ... Then, over here it's [the village of] Fazlagića Kula ... Here, [the village of] Branilovići ...

Zahida: On George's Eve, the lasses would plant nettles. Where would the nettle turn? Where will the girls marry? They would observe the crawling bugs. What kind of bug is it, blond, black ... that's the lad who'll come.

Fata S: We got up at four or five in the morning to plant nettles in the manure in front of the sheds, where the cattle were. To see where we would marry!

Safeta: You might also put a piece of bread on the clean earth. If the bread were gone, it meant you would get married soon. That was the tradition.

Scene Seven: Water and Cornel

Eno: There was something to do with the water ... I don't know.

Nada: We would go down to the river and wash our faces in it, to ensure that the human [*insan*] is healthy.

Rade: For George's Day, the tradition was to go to the water spring and bathe.

Fata: So, we would take the cornel branches [*drijen*] and others ... It would be put in water and, in the morning, before sunrise, the girls would wash with it – to be as healthy as cornel wood! Some other herbs were put in too ... And, in the morning, before dawn, we would go to bathe. We go to bathe. Women and girls and the young newly weds, but mostly unmarried girls [*cure*]. You'd soak yourself! And some went where there was a mill. The mill would be turned on, water cascading down the wheel ... I had three brothers. They had their own watermill. The girls would go there, and the lads would follow. They want to see you, bless me, in the nude. Yes, yes, to see a girl nude. There was all sorts ...

Fata S: There was a watermill at the Ponor [where the river sinks], owned by Serbs, two brothers, Branko and Savo Radan. They would turn

	on the mill before six o'clock, before the sun warmed up. We would go to that mill to fetch water.
Delva:	They would say, don't answer anyone before the sun shines, because, they say, you'll sleep throughout the summer, drowse ... And, you would get some cornel and give it to someone and say: 'I give you this lazy cornel [*lijen drijen*], so that you may slumber for me and yourself, until this time next year', which meant from one George's Day to the next.
Safeta:	My late mother warned me: 'Be careful not to answer anyone'. But I forgot. Salko called me and said: 'I give you this lazy cornel. You will slumber. Slumber for me'. It was 6 May.

Scene Eight: Plants and Fertility

Safura:	We would sing: 'George's Day, when you come again, you'll not find me at my mother's – either married or in the black earth buried'.
Safeta:	A woman would put on a belt of willow branches. The newly weds would be told by their mother-in-law: 'Go on, put it around your belly'.
Fata:	Or, we would say, to an unmarried girl, take up your rakes [*grablje*] and, before the sun comes up, rake them around the house two or three times, to make, you know, the lads fight over who would get to rake in [*grabe*] the girls.
Delva:	We would pick branches of hornbeam [*grabovina*], to make the lads lock horns [*grabe*] over a girl.
Safeta:	And the male fern [*navala*] is to make the lads rush [*navale*] after her.
Zahida:	From George's Day on, we would pick herbs, all of them. Decorate the kids with male fern [*navala*], decorate the room with it ... It's a long, thin, serrated herb.
Mila:	Let me tell you now. A woman without children would go out on George's morning and pick willow branches and, excuse me, rub them a bit over her belly, saying: 'This year the withy, next year a belly'. That's how it is.
Ružica:	Yew. Do you know what yew [*tisovina*] is? It was used for amulets. It guards against the evil eye [*urok*]. It's good for the health too. Serbs and Muslims wore it alike and put it on cows and horses and everyone. The whole world wore it.
Zahida:	There is *izijes*. I used to put it ... for the children too.
Bećir:	*Izijes* is a sort of dust from old oaks.
Zahida:	It looked like [milled] peppercorns. And I would put it ... I would take a white handkerchief and put some *izijes* into the men's pil-

Fata S: There was a herb called *zdravac* [rock cranesbill], which we would put into water. And, my late mother would tell us: 'Wash your faces with that water, to stay healthy'. Even now, I would recognize *zdravac*. It was pinkish in colour and we would pick it from under a big cliff close to Ponor.

Zahida: Do you know what rock cranesbill [*zdravac*] is? It's a herb. They say it's very good. We would decorate ourselves with it.

Safeta: Mothers would garland their young children with flowers while they slept.

Scene Nine: Cattle and Bonfires

Mitar: We would gather enough supplies to last until George's Day, the basics.

Fata: I used to use as much meat in one day as some do in a month now. Slaughter a barren cow, slaughter fifteen/sixteen sheep and goats, and come spring I'd have nothing; the winter had eaten it all up . . .

Nezir: George's Day is a celebration for cattle and children, not your typical party. Cows celebrate leaving the sheds and the children going outside. All our traditions resembled Montenegrin ones.

Safura: The cows are let out, because they have spent the whole winter in the sheds, during the snows.

Sejo: The cows are beaten with Lenten roses [*kukurijek*] until the blood runs.

Fata: We would feed the cows [literally, 'break their fast'] on George's Eve. We used to put male fern [*navala*], feverfew [*povratić*], tansy [*koloper*], the cornel leaves and blossoms, all of it into water and bathe with it. We would also put in hyssop [*miloduh*]. And we would give that water to the cows to break their fast, to make them healthy.

Delva: For George's Day, I would find the spot with the best nettles and then find a *grudina*. A *grudina* is a place where the cattle waste is deposited. And you stick three nettles into it. And you watch where they fall.

Bećir: We lit fires for George's Day here . . .

Eno: Our village used to light bonfires up there on that ridge [*greda*]. There is still a bit of that in the Orthodox villages.

Mladen: Everyone lighted fires around the Field. They were competing to see whose would be the tallest. Large quantities of wood and old tyres were burnt.

Delva: I remember that we would light fires near the animal shed.

Zahida: Well, you know why that was... They were for the cattle, for some boon.
Nezir: Children gathered on George's Eve to light fires on hilltops.
Safeta: To encourage hair to grow, it's cut with a small axe. My late mother would chop off my hair at the place where we chopped wood. It was done before sunrise on George's Day.

Scene Ten: Meetings

Safura: Lads and girls would walk around, talk, and so on. Back then, they would each hold one end of a handkerchief. In some places, they even held hands.
Eno: The Gurbeti would arrive with the spring and start setting up their tents, tinning copper dishes, rejoicing and dancing...
Bećir: We would go, dance and sing with the Gypsies for George's Day.
Esma: We would arrange a get-together in one house, and everyone would come. Everyone would come, Serbs and everyone.
Dževad: In the village of Bahori, we had a big George's Day celebration and fair [*teferič*]. The whole landscape would be transformed with the pale buds of cranesbill [*zdravac*].
Rade: On the feast of the household patron saint [*krsna slava*], you would say: 'God be with this honourable home and may you have a happy feast day'.
Vlado: They say: 'George's Day – the outlaws' assembly. Demetrius' Day – the outlaws' parting'. The outlaws would go into the woods when spring came and return at the beginning of winter.
Osman: I remember from my childhood that Serb families used to come for George's Day. Even though they didn't live here, they would visit friends and sworn kin [*kumovi*].

George Beyond the Field

> George is said of geos, which is as much to say as earth, and orge [barley] that is tilling.
> —J. de Voragine, 'The Golden Legend or Lives of the Saints'

There are few characters as syncretic as George. This book has been conceived between two differently Georgic countries – Bosnia and England – with the occasional venture into others, such as Palestine. Writing its pages in England gave me yet another perspective on George's legacy. As the patron saint of England, he has been systematically woven into the national fabric, quite literally: his cross adorns the flag of England, as it does the textiles of various other existing and obsolete political formations. Georgic tales, symbols and folklore are always around the corner, whether it is a traditional George's Day dance in a public park, a football match or an imaginative springtime display in the window of a second-hand shop in Islington. George's cult is said to have become widespread in the British Isles only after the Crusades, when the saint was accorded patronage over the English Crusaders and, in the fourteenth century, patronage of England as a whole (Ng and Hodges 2010: 263). English George was a patron of warfare, health and rebirth, so to speak. He was primarily the advocate of the soldiers, knights, archers and armourers, but also of farmers, and a protector against the plague, leprosy and syphilis (see Farmer 2011: 182).

Bosnian George has a markedly disparate profile. He is 'pastoral' in nature, tied to fertility and vernal rituals. He enjoys no state recognition, though he may have had some presence in the mediaeval state. Some have even argued for a theory of George as the patron saint of mediaeval Bosnia. The historian Muhamed Hadžijahić has advanced this thesis in a short essay on Saints George and Elijah, building upon a 'logical' presumption by Friar Antun Knežević (1871) and a misreading of an article by the Russian historian Alexander Soloviev (1949), who had actually been referring to St Gregory.[1]

Knežević had put his claim of patronage in quotation marks, exclaiming: 'God willing, may Bosnians be united in everything as they are in their reverence for their "patrons", George and Elijah!'[2] His hopeful declaration is curious not only because of its deduction of 'patronage' from an apparent syncretic 'unison', but also because of the recognition that George and Elijah may serve as a model for overcoming the political divisions already observable with the advent of the nationalisms that would continue to polarize Bosnian communities through the twentieth and into the twenty-first century. It comes as no surprise, then, that George and Elijah are topics absent from the ethno-nationalist proclamations that have been a feature since the 1990s and which draw on other sources of sacralization (see Introduction). For such ideologies, they will always appear a pair of unacceptable crossbreeds.

Although the mediaeval Bosnian Church did accept the cult of saints (see Fine 2006: 483), George's patronage over the land seems to have remained an unofficial fact, a folk narrative, rather than an institutional matter. One processional song from the town of Drvenik in Croatia expresses George's saintly importance in Bosnia:[3]

Bosno slavna ti se raduj,	Rejoice famed Bosnia,
Svetog Jurja tvoga poštuj,	Honour your Saint George,
jer je on tvoj zaštititelj	For he is your guardian
i kod Boga obranitelj.	and defender with God.

This idea of George as the Bosnian patron saint also draws support from the founding of an Order of the Dragon under his patronage in 1408. To build ties with the Hungarian Emperor Sigismund (against the advancing Ottoman 'dragon'), two influential Bosnian feudal lords, Sandalj Hranić and Hrvoje Vukčić Hrvatinić, were admitted to the Order after attending a knightly congregation in Buda (see Fine 2007: 193). This crusading aspect of George could not have been long-lived, as the Kingdom had fallen to the Ottomans by 1463. Nonetheless, as late as 1708, Stipan Margitić Jajčanin, a Bosnian Franciscan, wrote:

> The feast of St George is great beyond description all over the world, but especially in the Bosnian Kingdom, in the golden kingdom, which chose him for its protector and intercessor with God almighty, not only the Catholics, but also the unbelievers, apostates from the Holy Church. Turks too feast on this day, bestowed upon the rectitude of Saint George, not only do they celebrate and call it *Jurjev dan* [George's Day] and abstain from work, but they also gather for a great fair in his honour. They dress up nicely, play games and lead the *kolo* and other dances. (From *Fala od sveti*, in Karamatić 2012)

When Stipan Margitić Jajčanin was writing of the 'Bosnian Kingdom', Bosnia had already been part of the Ottoman Empire for over two hundred years. He too reached the conclusion of George's patronage on the basis of widespread nature of the celebration; however, knowledge of the mediaeval Bosnian state and its Church is fragmentary and variously interpreted, so the extent of George's relation to it may never be fully deciphered.

In 1466, the testament of Radin, a vicar (*gost*) of the mediaeval Bosnian Church, mentions the names of several saints, including 'St George, of my Christened name'.[4] 'Christened name' relates to a tradition of household patron saints (*krsna slava*), common mostly (now perhaps only) to Orthodox Christian communities in the Balkans. Truhelka mentioned that Muslims, Catholics and Orthodox Christians in Bosnia celebrated the family patron saint day, arguing that the origins of this tradition are not to be found in the Orthodox Christian, but rather the 'Pataren' or Bosnian Church customs (1911: 370–71). Amongst these mediaeval relics shared by Muslims and Christians, he noted the celebrations of Christmas, George's Day and Elijah's Day (ibid).

One thing is certain. George is not an overtly political symbol in present-day Bosnia, nor is his legacy the subject of much scholarly attention. Yet, it would be difficult to find a single person in Bosnia who is not aware of George's Day. He is called Đorđe, Georgije, Jurje or Juraj, and many will be invoking his names and singing about him each spring. All the Bosnian communities, whether designated in religious, ethnic, national or local terms, have some tradition of celebrating his day.

George is a Christian, of both the Orthodox and Catholic persuasion; he is a patron of churches, depicted on icons, frescoes and banners. Since its emergence in the late antiquity, the cult of saints attained a central place for diverse strands of Christianity (see Brown 1981: 1). Mediaeval and early modern sources, however, reveal that both the Catholic and the Orthodox Church regarded as heretical some of the rituals that are still part of the Georgic traditions, including the veneration of the sun and the moon, 'dancing in village squares', the belief in nymphs and so on (see Fine 2007: 34–35).

Celebrations of George are traditionally central for the Bosnian Roma communities. Indeed, he has often been described as 'the Gypsy saint'. George is a Muslim, albeit outside of the Bosnian mosques, through the widespread springtime rituals. George is also a Bosnian Jew.[5] Tamar Alexander and Eliezer Papo (2011: 91–92) discussed one of the *prikantes* – healing ritual incantations of the Bosnian Jews – which summons help 'in the name of King Alexander, of green shoe, of green garment, who rode on a green horse'. As I argue later on in this chapter, Alexander the Great is one of the mythical Georgic heroes. George, like Elijah, may also be a socialist, or nonaligned: his day encapsulated the Yugoslav slogan of 'Brotherhood and Unity' (*bratstvo i jedinstvo*), particularly as a form of resistance in postsocialist times.

George is an integral, shared part of every Bosnian landscape. His life in the twenty-first century, after those landscapes were disrupted by war, began to attain certain counter-discursive qualities. Perhaps the unifying political image of the English George may stand as a warning against Bosnian George's direr potential. On the other hand, his 'shared' qualities are defining of his Bosnian identity, to the point where the construction of 'ethno-religiously clean' images seems impossible.

Georgic Life-giving Mysteries

The figure of George moves between canonical and apocryphal hagiographical and folkloric interpretations. He is usually depicted as a saintly knight originating in Cappadocia sometime in or around the third century and martyred in Lydda (Lod/al-Ludd) in Palestine (see Farmer 2011: 181–82). He achieved popular sainthood in the early days of Christianity. He was canonized in 494 by Pope Gelasius I, who, however, designated some of the extant writings as apocryphal and untrustworthy – the products of 'heretics and sectarians' – thus creating the grounds for a 'canonical George', the Christian martyr (Matzke 1902: 464). This Gelasian effort reshaped George's biography, Matzke noted: 'This form of the legend is characterized by the introduction of the name of Diocletian, due to the desire to connect the death of the saint with the tenth persecution of the Christians, and by the reduction of the tortures suffered by the saint and the wonders performed by him' (ibid: 481).

The canonical George, said to be of a Cappadocian father and a Palestinian mother, turned against Diocletian after witnessing his persecutions of Christians. He suffered many lurid and torturous trials and tribulations, yet remained unharmed. Provoked by Diocletian, he resurrected a dead man through prayer. He healed the diseased. He revived the dead ox of a poor peasant (ibid: 481–84); indeed, European Christians regarded him as one of the 'fourteen holy helpers', responsible for the protection of domestic animals (Guiley 2001: 110). He obliged a demon residing in a statue of Apollo to profess Christianity and other idols to self-destruct. Fragments of a fifth-century, apocryphal Greek text, known as the Vienna Manuscript or Vienna Palimpsest, note that, '[w]hen he prays to be baptized, George strikes the ground with his foot, and a fountain springs forth' (Matzke 1902: 489). According to this palimpsest, before his final death, George was killed and resurrected on three different occasions. He further resurrected hundreds of people, produced water to baptize them, turned a throne into a fruitful tree, and performed many other life-giving miracles (see Dickey 2012: 228).

In Muslim traditions, George appeared early on as a martyr named Jirjis. Again, he lived in Palestine and was resurrected three times, after having been killed by Diocletian (Newby 2002: 117). A detailed narrative of his life may be found in *Hayat al-Qulub,* or *Life of the Hearts,* a hagiography written by the seventeenth-century Persian scholar al-Majlisi (2002: 890–93). The narrative of Jirjis' martyrdom follows the Christian versions, except that his tortures have now been induced by the king of Syria and the resurrections confuse and infuriate his torturers, who taunt him to prove his claims. Two events are particularly interesting, as they reveal his fertile Georgic potency. In the first one, the king's companion tempts him to rejuvenate dead trees: 'He asked Jirjis to pray to his Allah so that He may turn that wood into original trees with branches and leaves and fruits to make him believe in him. Hearing this Jirjis sat up on his knees and prayed to Almighty Allah. Instantly the wood turned into trees bearing branches, leaves and fruits' (ibid: 892). The second situation extends the demonstration of his potency to cattle. A poor woman pleads with Jirjis to resurrect a cow, whose milk is her family's only sustenance: 'Jirjis gave her his staff and asked her to put it on the corpse of that cow and to say: O cow! Jirjis asks you to arise by the order of Allah. The woman did so and the cow became alive' (ibid: 892). A rather more elaborate version of Jirjis' life appears in Bosnia (Filan 2011b). This time, with divine guidance, he resurrects himself, fourteen human corpses and a cow's carcass, turns the king's dining chairs and serving dishes into fruit-bearing vegetation, and turns a wooden pillar standing in the centre of a poor woman's house into a 'tree so beautiful as no eyes have ever seen' (ibid: 5).

George's efficacy as an embodiment of virility is never explicitly narrated in the 'Gacko Georgics'; it is enacted. These acts make the whole landscape, the children, and even the human hair, grow strong and healthy. They increase the sexual potency and fertility of men, women and cattle. Rituals for these life-boosting miracles are usually said to be 'for the betterment of the household' (*radi napretka u kući*).

The Maiden's Girdle and the Control of Time

Jacobus de Voragine, a thirteenth-century Dominican friar and Archbishop of Genoa, wrote *Legenda aurea* or the *Golden Legend,* one of the most widely disseminated and copied books of the Middle Ages (Hamer 1998). De Voragine's (1998) compilation of saints' lives amalgamated various sources and portrayed George as a Roman army tribune, turned Christian, who preached against sacrificial rituals to the heathen gods and prayed for the destruction of their temples and idols. As I argue below, this anti-syncretic attitude on the part of George has also been attributed to our other, syncretic, figure – Elijah.

De Voragine's treatment of George (1998: 116–20) contains other, more interesting elements, however. Travelling through the province of Libya, George came upon the city of Silena, beside which lay a large lake, where a pestilential dragon had its lair. The citizens fed their sheep to the dragon, until their flocks ran scarce. Then, they offered it one sheep and one human being (making sure to avoid any gender bias). As mythic luck would have it, this tragic lot soon befell the king's only daughter. In the face of the king's offer of all his gold and silver and half his realm, the citizens retorted that it was only fair for him to follow his own decree. So, he agreed, struck by grief over his vanishing hopes of ever seeing her wedding feast or 'breast-fed' offspring. The chivalrous George 'happened to be passing that way' and, against all the maiden's best efforts to dissuade him, decided to mount his horse and confront the dragon 'in the name of Christ'.

One curious moment in the plot sheds light on the maiden as the protagonist who actually tames the beast: '[George] called to the princess: "Throw your girdle round the dragon's neck! Do not be afraid, child!" She did as he told her, and the dragon followed her as meekly as a puppy' (ibid: 117). George ultimately slew the dragon with his sword, claiming victory for himself, and the puzzling force of the maiden and her girdle were henceforth ignored. I, however, want to focus precisely on this seemingly unimportant detail, for the agency of the girdle helps elucidate the disposition of Bosnian landscapes to anchor their Georgic imagery through rituals involving young women.

In their persuasive analysis of the mediaeval English romance *Sir Gawain and the Green Knight,* Albert Friedman and Richard Osberg (1977: 303–5) argued that the girdle, dispensed from the umbilicus towards the genitalia, originally acted as an apotropaic item and a sign of initiation into the community. It protected and advertized virginity. The girdle of George's Libyan maiden is, thus, part of a long lineage:

> The great legendary girdles are all women's, and all seem to have originated as symbols of cosmic sovereignty that dwindled to narrower jurisdictions. The girdle of Ishtar, which, like the belt of the Jewish high priest, represented the peripheral ocean enclosing the universe, became a girdle of fertility. When she unfastened it in the underworld, reproduction ceased on earth. The girdle of fertility which Herakles wrested from Hippolyta as his ninth labor was once charged with Ares' numen, and the most famous of all girdles, the cestus (kestos) of Aphrodite-Urania, at one stage a symbol of life's continuity, became as early as Homer a 'gurdul of lecherie', exuding all the enticements of lust. (ibid: 304)

This is the same virginal girdle as was untied in the climactic moment of the wedding ceremony, one which prostitutes in mediaeval France were prohibited from wearing. Its substitution may be sought in the rural English tradition of bridesmen fighting over the brides' garters or ribbons from their bosoms (ibid: 305).

Similarly, 'Bosnian maidens' had their Georgic girdle of *miloduh,* the hyssop blossom. Although still green on 6 May, it matures into a fragrant and bright (blue or pink) shrub that grows abundantly in the landscapes of the Western Balkans. Its name is literally the binding of two words, *milo* ('kind', 'dear', 'pretty') and *duh* ('spirit', 'ghost'). This 'kindspirit' flower is an integral part of one ubiquitous Bosnian George's Eve ritual where young unmarried women would decorate the front doors to their houses with *miloduh*. As we have already seen, when night fell, the village lads would sneak out and 'steal' or 'scatter' the *miloduh* of the girls they liked. The girls knew, or at least hoped, it would happen, but had to pretend to be angry and complain of the loss of their 'virginal' flowers.

As a child, Subhija attended one such get-together (*sijelo*) of young women on George's Eve: 'I remember it well. All we saw was a bundle of *miloduh* thrown through the window. It was the lads sneaking about underneath and cutting the flowers. The girls would then hold vigils to protect the *miloduh*'. Isma, from the neighbouring town of Bileća, also told me that girls would use *miloduh* to decorate the front doors of their homes.

Sheikh Nurudin, the chief protagonist of Meša Selimović's novel *Death and the Dervish* (*Derviš i smrt*), describes these George's Day rituals with pious resentment as 'twenty-four hours of the lustful scent of hyssop and love', when girls go down to the mill to wash in the water spray 'believing in the magic of these flowers in the night' (1966: 17). Although the sexual connotations of the ritual are rather obvious, it is far from an explicit sexual encounter. Friedman and Osberg noted that the girdle has 'deep, ancient, "natural" psychic and cultural resonance; its meaning goes without saying and, in certain reaches, is too indelicate to be said' (1997: 315). I would argue that the impossibility of conversing directly about sexual desires was dealt with through the *miloduh* flower and the Georgic bathing rituals as it permits intense, open flirtation (*ašikovanje*). It reveals deeper roots, however, through its reference to ancient beliefs in the spirits inhabiting flora.

Water is central to the women's early morning Georgic rituals, usually known as *omaha*. But it is not just any water; it comes bursting and foaming from the river rapids or the turning wheels of watermills. The foaming water has obvious sexual references; the Greek 'Maiden of maidens', Aphrodite was born out of the seafoam stirred by Uranus' castrated genitals. The Greek word *aphros* (ἀφρός) indeed means 'foam'. When I asked Kana to give me a definition of *omaha*, she replied that 'it is where the water roars [*huči*]'. I think that such 'speaking water' is a probable residue of a belief in water spirits. We have already seen that fairies (*vile*) often take residence in water (see Chapter 4). Mokoš, the only recorded Slavic Goddess, probably of fertility, also resides and twists yarn on a spindle at water sources, which mark the boundary between world and underworld (see Belaj 2009: 178, Ivakhiv 2009: 1558).

Even Procopius' sixth-century *Gothic War*, considered to be the oldest source for the study of Proto-Slavic religiosity (Luján 2008: 105), mentions that the Slavs 'also worship rivers, nymphs and some other divine beings and they also sacrifice to them all' (ibid: 106). The mythology and toponymy of the Field confirm this. The fairies bathe at the Sopot spring, while the 'Fairy Cave' (*Vilina Pećina*) is located at Ponor, where the sinking river enters the earth, the same river which etymologically reveals its meaning as the 'sacrificial altar of cleansing'. Girls would go the mill near Ponor for *omaha*, to bathe on George's Day, receiving a kind of blessing from the running waters. The Slavic fairy often lives between this world and the underworld and negotiates between the two realms, but the waters and their surrounding caves are also where dragons reside.

A striking example for thinking about women as communicators with chthonic beings is the 'Maiden's Cave' (*Djevojačka Pećina*) near the village of Brateljevići in central Bosnia. It is the location of the last Muslim prayer (*dova*) in the Georgic cycle.[6] These prayers are performed on Tuesdays between George's Day and Elijah's Day. Sometimes, as in the case of the Maiden's Cave, the prayers have led to the evolution of pilgrimage sites visited by tens of thousands. Upon my visits in 2011 and 2012, I recorded versions of the mythic narrative about the site, which are outlined below.

A long time ago, a beautiful maiden decided at an evening get-together (*sijelo*) to prove her fearlessness by venturing into the deepest part of the cave to fetch some water from the well. She carried a pitcher and a spindle. She reached out to fetch the water and felt something there. She was so startled that she died on spot. Every year, people go to pray inside the cathedral-like cave and visit a small crevice in its depths, where there really is a well. In front of the well, there is a recently erected tombstone marked simply 'The Maiden' (*Djevojka*). The 'grave' is ritually covered with votive offerings for health. One of the offerings I saw was an ultrasound image of a fetus. Many of the women turned towards the cave walls to rub their palms over the moist surface and then on their faces. Those I asked were unwilling to tell me why they were doing it, which itself bore home the impoliteness of my question. After all, it was a Georgic ritual. It increased their fertility. I was told that nursing mothers in the Hrustovo Cave near the town of Sanski Most would drink from the stalactites to increase their milk.

This topos and the curious carved images of a maiden and a horseback rider on the cave walls imply a much older connection with our Georgic women's bathing rituals. The Maiden of the cave descended into the chthonic depths, where life and death draw near, into the dragon's lair, as I argue in the following pages. The pitcher would have been used to fetch water, but why the spindle? The Slavic Goddess Mokoš also spun near water. The fairies, also connected to water, have golden spindles in the epic songs (see, for example, Karadžić 1841: 111).

The spindle has been interpreted as a symbol of life, associated with deities in charge of vegetation, the moon and the earth, including the *Magna Mater*, the 'Great Mother Earth', and with cosmic renewal through sacrifice (Cirlot 2002: 305). The continuation of Time depends on the Maiden's offering: remember how Delva and Safeta described the potency of the George's Day 'lazy cornel', which can induce sleep (or drowsiness) for an entire year if a girl responds to someone before the sun comes out. In the famous European fairy tale, Sleeping Beauty's womanhood begins with a blood sacrifice and induces widespread slumber, suspending time. Knight noted: 'The girl "pricks her finger." She bleeds, as any girl of her age eventually must. The King was foolish to try to banish the spinning-wheels or spindles, for time cannot be suppressed – every girl will come of age and bleed, her cycle itself being among the most ancient of all clocks' (2004: 16).

The Maiden thus fits the 'Girardian' sacrificial model (see Girard 1989); her generalized maidenhood is offered in exchange for the well-being of the entire community, the fertility of its land, and all its Georgic maidens. She has successfully tamed the dragon.

Taming the Dragon

I found Nura's memory curious. As a girl, she used to swing on George's Day, singing 'The dragon flew from the sea to the Danube. . . .' What was this formula, repeated in the perfect affect of 'flying somewhere far away' by a Muslim Bosnian girl with no knowledge of George's defiance of the beast? Nura's song was recorded by Vuk Karadžić (1841: 163–64) in the early nineteenth century. It begins thus:

Zmaj proleće s mora na Dunavo	The dragon flew from the sea to the Danube
i pod krilom pronese djevojku,	And carried off a girl under his wing, –
pod jednijem lijepu djevojku,	A beautiful girl under one,
a pod drugim ruho djevojačko;	And bridal garments under the other.

The first image is thus of a maiden 'stolen' to be the dragon's bride. As discussed above, the ritual 'stealing' of brides was not uncommon in south Bosnia. Some of my interlocutors gave their accounts of performing this ritual. The song then narrates how the dragon grows thirsty and drops the girl to fetch himself some water. At the spring, the girl meets three merry lads, who express their desires to marry her or make love to her. She, however, has other plans:

Al' govori lijepa djevojka:	But the beautiful girl spoke:
„Prođ'te me se tri mlada bećara!	'Go away you three youthful lads!
Ja sam kćerca cara čestitoga,	I am the daughter of the noble emperor,
a sestrica paše bosanskoga,	And sister of the Bosnian pasha,
vjerna ljuba zmaja ognjenoga.	Faithful sweetheart of the fiery dragon.

Then, this mythic maiden 'flies away over the field, like a star over clear skies'. Nura, as a child, sang this song and imagined flying away in the same manner, before rushing over to the nettles to see where their leaves had turned. The myth was enacted affectively.

The dragon in her song is 'fiery' (*ognjeni*). His epiteth is the same as Elijah's, which means that he must be appeased in order to constrain his ability to destroy the crops. As a chthonic being, he takes sacrifices, ultimately in the form of a beautiful maiden – the only one who can truly tame him, which enables the continuation of life and the flourishing of the landscape. The dragon flies from the sea to the Danube, between two large bodies of water in the singer's cognitive map.

George's inheritance cannot be deciphered without a proper look at his victorious dragon-slaying episode. As turns out to be the case with other parts of his saintly biography, the antagonism with the dragon is old, 'preChristian' news both within and outside the Mediterranean. There is an abundance of similar characters in Indo-European mythologies, whose ability to merge into George rests on deeply ingrained symbols. To restore the fertility of the Maiden, George removes the threat to infertility. The dragon is thus a versatile representation of a number of specific threats, such as winter, drought, any major disease, inability to reproduce, tyrants and so on. It is no coincidence that dragons usually take residence at the most precious of locations – a local source of water, the 'well of life'. The Bible abounds with images of evil dragons which inhabit waters and bottomless pits. Pharaoh is compared to 'the great dragon that lieth in the midst of his rivers, which hath said, My river is my own' (Ezekiel 29: 3); dragon-like, the pharaoh thus renders the vital source of fertility inaccessible. Spaces where dragons settle for good are void of human life, and lands belonging to the enemies of God are destined to become the 'dwelling places of dragons' – desolate and ruined (Jeremiah 51: 37, Isaiah 34: 13).

The pattern of George's combat is strikingly similar to the Greek myth of Perseus and the sea monster. The beautiful virgin princess Andromeda is also given over by her father to be sacrificed near water to appease the monster Cetus. She is chained naked to a seaside rock when Perseus arrives and slays the monster with his sword, but not before he has made some 'last-minute' marriage arrangements with her parents (Bulfinch 1993: 144–46).

Similarly, the Hittite myth about the storm god and the dragon/serpent Illuyanka, starts with the image of a festival dedicated to the storm god, with obvious similarities to the vernal celebrations of George. In the introductory verses, the priests advise: 'Let the land grow (and) thrive, and let the land be secure [literally, 'protected']!' – and when it (indeed) grows (and) thrives, then they perform the festival of *purulli*' (see Beckman 1982: 18). The feast is used to lure out the serpent monster so that it may be slain by the storm god (ibid). Two badly damaged and less clear verses advise that the origins of the Hittite spring festival are related to the act of Inara, the storm god's daughter, who gave the king her house and 'the watery abyss'/underground spring (ibid: 19), which is reminiscent of the Georgic sinking rivers and abysses in the Field, as well as the deep underground well of the Maiden's Cave.

Hadaad/Baal, the Levantine deity of rain, storm and fertility, similarly defeats the sea god Yam and the sea dragon Lotan and travels to the underworld before his resurrection (see Colavito 2014: 26). Elijah, the inheritor of some of Baal's powers (discussed later in this chapter), paradoxically, also slays the prophets of Baal in the Biblical narrative (see 1 Kings 18). It might be ironic, but it is not unusual for the 'biographies' of highly syncretic characters to centre on such anti-syncretic acts, and Elijah is not the sole example of this simultaneous inheritance and denunciation. As I mentioned earlier, George is said to have made the statue of Apollo 'self-destruct'. Apollo, the god of light and sun, however, seems to be another one of George's older manifestations. Young women in Bosnia, according to Kovačević, would cast complex magic spells for George's Day, while praying to the sun for the attention of their lovers. They would turn towards the east and say: 'George's Day, my beautiful day, help me, I pray to you, bring back my most dear and most beautiful Mehmed' (Kovačević 1889: 119). Apollo slays Python, the dragon/serpent, which is in fact not a harbinger of infertility, but a product of 'excessive fertility'. Python, too, resides in a cave and threatens the existence of human beings (Bulfinch 1993: 23). He is the progeny of Gaia, 'mother earth' (Cotterell and Storm 2011: 21). Interestingly, Zeus punishes Apollo for killing Python by making him slave to a mortal (ibid). As I explain later, Zeus, or rather his Slavic counterpart Perun, was inherited by Elijah, who stands at the high point of the Bosnian summer.

Dragons have survived as part of Bosnian folklore. There are three words used to describe them *aždaha, ala* and *zmaj*. They are closely related to Alija Đerzelez and Prince Marko, the Georgic epic heroes of the Balkans (see Chapter 4). Two kindred narratives recorded in Bosnia relate the forming of the landscape to the arrival of a pestilent dragon (see Softić 2005: 30). In the first, the dragon wants to devour the people in the village of Umoljani, but is transformed into the local dragon-like rock, after the *hodža* (Muslim priest) makes a supplication. In the second narrative, a dragon attacks unmarried girls (*cure*) at their ablutions near a river. Their gathering corresponds to the George's Day ritual of *omaha* when women bathe in the waters at dawn. As the dragon is winding down to devour the young women, it creates gorges in the land. Again, there happens to be a priest to hand who leads the communal prayer, which ultimately turns the dragon into a landmark rock. In both stories, the *hodža* acts as a substitute for George. His appearance in these stories might be a later adaptation to make them more believable to specific audiences or simply an extension of Georgic powers, as with the epic heroes; Mircea Eliade (1959: 34-48), for example, argued that popular memory fuses past events and characters into 'archetypal categories'. The 'historical' elements in the biographies of the mythic characters are retained only when they express such archetypes.

Several images on Bosnian mediaeval tombstones (see Wenzel 1965: 376-9) reveal a peculiar juxtaposition of four figures: a dragon/serpent, a woman, a knightly figure on horseback (George) and a horse. On the tombstone from Visočica Mountain (see Figure PII.1), the woman is depicted with one hand connected to (or being devoured by) the serpent, while the other hand is holding onto the horse. Following Nura's song, we can imagine the woman as being saved by George in the moment of being 'stolen' into marriage by the serpentine monster. Wenzel (1965: 308) argued that this was a representation of the Goddess of the underworld. Whether the figure is a Goddess or some idealized maiden, it seems that the unpredictable infertility of nature and the fertilizing male virility are negotiated precisely through her. She balances out the two forces of the cosmos.

The horse on this tombstone is likely to be in some relation to Pegasus, the winged horse tamed by heroic Bellerophon with Athena's golden bridle, or by Athena herself in some accounts.[7] Bellerophon, 'the slayer', and Pegasus also fought the dragon-like Chimera (see Cotterell and Storm 2011: 71, 73). The sequence of characters in the tombstone scene is indicative of the centrality of the female symbol to Georgic traditions. The cycle in Bosnia is, after all, primarily marked by women's ritual descendance into caves and towards wells and rushing waters, as well as their flirtatious resistance of men's sexual advances.

In her discussion of Serbian oral traditions, Ljiljana Pešikan-Ljuštanović noted that dragons remained closely associated with water and chthonic features, particularly their cave habitat (2002: 8). The Bosnian tombstone image can thus also be read as a vertical relationship, where the battle of the chthonic creature and the supernal rain-giver is channelled through and settled by the woman/earth. Another Bosnian epic confirms this thesis.[8] It involves the transfer of George's characteristics to the equestrian epic hero Alija Đerzelez and those of the maiden to his beloved sister Ajka. That these two Georgic characters are siblings actually fits into the incestuous structure of the myth, explained in the next section. Ajka prays to the sun to bring her brother back, in the same manner as women used to pray on George's Day for their lovers (Kovačević 1889: 119). Alija then dreams that an enormous serpent has attacked his fortress, completely engulfing it. The serpent is intercepted by Ajka, who topples it, preventing it from devouring the fortress. The epic transfer contains all of the major Georgic features: the hero, the maiden (sister), the serpent/dragon and the horse. The salvaged fortress is equivalent to sustained life and fertility.

One of the most widespread and most noticeable images of Bosnian spring is a landscape dotted with bonfires. They were lit on elevated locations for the festival of the pre-Christian Jarilo (see Ivanov and Toporov 2001: 238). In Gacko, it was imperative that smoke from the hearth be visible above the roof of the house on George's Day morning. I was privileged to witness the ritual dance around the bonfire on the eve of George's Day in Visoko, the *lile* torches being carried around by children in the village of Mokro for Peter's Day and the enormous competitive bonfires lit for John's Day in Kreševo and Vitez. All of these fires have an apotropaic quality. They ward off evil spells, witches, spirits and chthonic beings. But, they also ward off snakes, as Eno told me: 'Snakes drink milk. So, in Gacko, we had to use smoke curtains to drive them out. We got good at it. We would catch one, stand on its head and take it by the neck and, once it opened its mouth, take out its teeth with a piece of wood and let it go'.

Lilek (1894: 632) also noted the Gacko George's Day tradition of lighting cattle manure to repel snakes. *Zmija* is the feminine noun for snake. *Zmaj*, the masculine version of the same noun, means dragon. One might argue that both the chthonic siblings are warded off by the Georgic fires – the snake because it endangers milk (the substance of budding life), and the dragon because it brings drought. There is no substantial distinction between the 'magic' and the 'pragmatic' fire, if one accepts that both *zmaj* and *zmija* are life-threatening. Yet another custom, noted by Frazer, implies that snakes were understood as a danger to fertility:

> Similarly, a Bulgarian wife who desires to have a child will strike off a serpent's head on St. George's Day, put a bean in its mouth, and lay the head in a hollow tree or bury it in the earth at a spot so far from the village that the crowing of the cocks cannot be heard there. If the bean buds, her wishes will be granted. (1993: 344)

The serpentine creatures of the Bosnian Georgic cosmology reveal the chthonic forces of death. They reside between the underworld and the world of humans, along boundaries such as caves, lakes and rivers. The maiden, with her bridling girdle, is crucial to the storyline. George is somewhat secondary; it is George's Day, but only after the maiden has 'saved the day'. She is the one who communicates with the chthonic and offers herself as bridal sacrifice to its creatures, allowing George to inseminate the earth and sweep up all the glory.

Georgic Residues: Spectres of Jarilo

It was a market day in the town of Gacko. Along a twenty-metre stretch of the central road, villagers displayed their produce. They were quite literally people in the midst of discursive formations. Their roadside market was wedged between the building site of the new Orthodox church and the reconstruction site of the Gacko mosque, both close to completion in 2012. The construction of the church, set to be the town's monumental centrepoint, however, seemed to be at a standstill. The marbled exterior looked finished, but the interior was completely empty. The clergy and the politicians, followed by townsfolk, would ritually circumnavigate the building on certain holidays. The courtyard, a raised concrete platform, was sometimes used for political or religious speeches. At other times, unlike the café of the nearby hotel Metohija, the church stood quite empty and was seldom approached.

Across the road, a dozen returnee men, led by Eno, were at work on the mosque. It was not the first destroyed mosque Eno had reconstructed: it was his third or fourth, depending on how you count – the one in the village of Kula had been burnt again, since its first postwar reconstruction. However, working on this mosque, in the town centre, was rather more precarious as of the approximately four thousand prewar Muslim inhabitants, not a single one had returned to live in the town. They were also working next to a 'symbol' of that change – the new church. Sadet, the imam (Muslim priest) for Gacko, was attacked next to the mosque on one occasion. So their relentless work, driven by Eno's hope for wider return, was conducted with a degree of caution, and the reconstruction work was paused during Orthodox holiday processions.

They would wake up around five in the morning, make their way from the villages to the town, while everyone was still asleep, and work until dusk. Labour would cease only for one long lunch break and the occasional cigarette pause. The townsfolk would pass by quickly. Sometimes, Eno would greet them, getting only silence in return. Danilo, a young Orthodox priest, was the exception. He would smile and greet as he passed. During his break, Eno would slip into the shade for a cigarette and a cup of coffee, half-filled with sugar, or a cigarette and some sweets. He spoke of the war only rarely and, even then, it was with a kind of Sisyphean optimism I soon got accustomed to. The stories were usually about traditions and plans to restore them.

On many of these sweetened breaks, he would tell me about the local toponyms. 'For example, this was always called Tennis', he said of the site of the church and the new Square of Count Sava. 'Most people don't know that it was where the Austro-Hungarian soldiers built their tennis courts, after the occupation, the first ones in the Balkans'. After this anectode, I found some unwitting dark humour in the words of the regional Orthodox bishop Grigorije, who described Tennis as an 'elevated place', which had finally been 'liberated from the oppressor' and graced with a new church, 'surely the most beautiful in recent Serb history'[9].

The villagers working at the market said nothing of either construction site, nor the ghost landscapes of Eno's memory. They kept to themselves just as much as the reconstruction team did. On one side of the market, a maker of *gusle* exhibited examples of his newly crafted instruments. They were made mostly from maple (*javor*) and walnut (*orah*). I was drawn to one particular piece, which I could not afford to buy. Its neck was skilfully carved into a sculpture of George, on his horse, in the moment of killing the dragon. Why was George there, occupying the dominant position on this masterpiece? It was, much like the *gusle* epics, an affective residue of an older formulation.

Beneath George, however, there was another, nationalized formula. On the body of the instrument, there was a carved image of Vuk Karadžić, the Serbian folklorist and language reformer of the nineteenth century. As noted, his authority over the national tradition has been claimed in more recent times by Radovan Karadžić, sentenced for genocide before the ICTY (see Chapter 4). Some eighty years ago, Milman Parry, a young Harvard professor, had a similar experience upon his arrival to Gacko, where he recorded these nationalizing tendencies in the making of *gusle*. With some frustration, he noted that the local people 'are unable to understand that the simple lines of the older *gusle* with its simplified stylization of the goat's head is a finer thing than a *gusle* which bears upon it the carved head of the ancient kings and heroes, the sovereign, and Vuk Karadžić' (Parry 1971: 449). Parry did not dwell on the reasons for the 'finer' ornament of the goat's head. Indeed, it is a residue of considerable value to my discussion of George. I propose to link the goat to a 'pre-Christian' ancestor of the very George who was carved onto the *gusle* I saw at the Gacko market.

The path from goat to George, as we shall see, takes some etymological and ethnographic reconstruction. The Slavic word for a male (billy) goat is *jarac*. It is composed of the root **jar* and *-ac,* a suffix for masculine nouns. A baby goat (kid) would similarly be *jare*. Of a goat birth, one says *ojarilo se* (it was yeaned/kidded). Now, if we wanted to construct an artificial agentive noun for that which brings forth/causes the birth of goats, in the sense of 'the yeaner', we would need to add the suffix *-ilo/-alo/-lo*[10] to the root **jar* – thus ending up with nothing less than the name of the Proto-Slavic spring deity – Jarilo (pronounced Yarilo).

Across the Slavic folk traditions, Belova (2001) noted, goats appear as a symbol of fertility. Some eastern-Slavic Christmas rituals include a re-enactment of dying and resurrection, followed by rhymes such as 'Where the goat walks, grain sprouts'.[11] This is even more interesting if we consider the symbolism of walking that Radoslav Katičić (1989) analysed in Slavic folk songs about George. He compiled a number of examples that embed George within the same composition: 'Where George walks, fields sprout',[12] leading him to argue that 'walking is equated with the stimulation of fertility' (ibid: 46). George's walk thus corresponds to the goat's walk, just as his image alternates with the goat's head on the carved neck of the *gusle.* Goats in the Balkans are conceived 'when the day shortens' and yeaned after about a half-year's time, at the wake of George's spring.

When I climbed to the ruins of the mediaeval fortress of Ključ on Gacko's Bjelasnica Mountain, a few goats guided me merrily to a clearing beneath the walls. There, they approached a peculiar piece of ornamented stone and drank water from the basin carved into its surface. None of the villagers knew what the stone was 'originally' for. Its ornaments resembled those on mediaeval tombstones and it might have been used as some kind of outdoors altar for specific occasions. As I observed, it was also water trough for goats roaming around the nearby cliffs.

Goats are another harbinger of life blossoming on Earth, so their associative vernal potential should not surprise. The root **jar* (pronounced *yar*) is to be found not only in the words *jarac* (buck), but also *jara/jarica* (wheat sown in the spring), *jarina* (spring and summer fruit, and a 'place where water foams'), *jarit se* (to reproduce – animals), *jariti se* (for bubbling/bursting water), *jara* (oven heat), *jarost* (heat, anger), *razjariti* (to anger), *najarcati* (to anger, arouse, inflame), *jarko/žarko* (bright, luminescent, strong), *žara* (nettle) and *ožariti* (to sting with nettle), amongst others.[13]

The diagram in Figure 5.2 reveals the functional and symbolic range of the spring cult. Each of the words derived from the root *yar expresses the bursting of springtime fertility – the heat, the light and the strength of the new season. In the Proto-Slavic language, the root *yar denoted the warm season in general, both springtime and summertime, and *jariti* meant 'to fertilize' and 'to ignite' (Belaj 2007: 153, Skok 1971: 755, Loma 2001: 238). Through the Indo-European verb *ai-lai-* (to warm up, to shine), the root *yar is also etymologically related to the English word *year* (Belaj 2007: 153, Skok 1971: 756). It becomes obvious that most elements of the Bosnian Georgic traditions are directly related to derivatives from the root *yar*, all expressing the movement and rebirth of organic matter. Bathing in droplets of 'bursting water' is the most distinctly Georgic of rituals. 'Bright flames' are lit on hilltops. The cattle are lashed with Lenten roses until their skin becomes 'inflamed'. Nettle appears in a variety of instances: children run around 'stinging' each other with nettle; girls predict future marriage proposals from the turning of the nettle leaves; they pick nettles to put into their bathing waters; nettle is burnt for the Annunciation and George's Day; finally, nettle is traditionally cooked into Georgic dishes.

George is thus heir to Jarilo's calendric and symbolic position. George comes from *geos* for earth and Jarilo from *yar for the spring; Jarilo was the Slavic vegetation and fertility deity. One recorded fertility ritual in Byelorussian folklore consisted of a girl pretending to be Jarilo, dressed up in white clothes and sitting on a white horse while people chanted a song about Jarilo, who, like the goat and George, walks through the fields and stimulates the crops (Zaroff 2002: 14, Ivanov and Toporov 2001: 237, Belaj 2007: 242). Such rituals focused on an idol called Jarilo and were prohibited as 'satanic games' by St Tikhon of Zadonsk, an eighteenth-century Orthodox bishop of Voronezh (Gimbutas 1971: 162). In one of his sermons to the people of Voronezh, St Tikhon noted that, while some respected Jarilo as a deity, others saw his day as playful folk festivity, a chance to wear their finery and commit to mischievous deeds (see Ivanov and Toporov 2001: 237).

Might the Jarilo–goat–George conundrum be related to the Greek Goat-Pan (Ae'gipan), who is the son of Zeus and a goat? In Roman mythology, Ae'gipan is said to be Silvanus, a deity who is the protector of woods, fields and farmers, and who was born of an incestuous relationship of Valeria of Tusculum and her father Valerius (Smith 1844: 26). The connection between incest and fertility appears in Slavic mythology as well. Belaj (2009: 173) attempted to reconstruct Jarilo's biography from the few available historical sources and the breadth of Slavic folklore. He noted that Jarilo is the son of god Perun and goddess Mokoš and that he was abducted and taken to Veles, the chthonic protector of animals (and dragons), where he lived as the protector of wolves. Returning from the underworld, he crossed a sea, revived vegetation and engaged in an incestuous relationship with his sister Mara. The continuation of their relationship ensures fertility, as was the case with Osiris, the Egyptian deity of the underworld and vegetation, who engaged in a relationship with his sister Isis – an incest that made the vernal renewal possible (see Belaj 1989: 74).

Arguing that this set of relationships amongst ancient fertility deities might have been the model for 'St George and the Maiden', Ali Qleibo noted: 'Baal and Anat, his consort, ally, sister, and wife are bound in the same primordial holy couple relationship as that of Osiris to Isis in Egypt and of Ashtar to Tammuz in Babylonia' (2011: 5). Why is incest allowed when it comes to fertility deities? It seems to underscore the notion that the fertilizer and the fertilized are within each other, inseparable. Claude Levi-Strauss' famous argument on the 'universality' of the incest taboo suggests that its introduction is the beginning of a crucial shift, the formation of human identity and culture itself, as, with this change, 'nature's sovereignty over man is ended' (1969: 25). If one were to follow this argument, cosmological incest would then appear to have been a human reminder of the ultimate sovereignty of nature.

The reconstruction of Jarilo–George conundrum bears a striking similarity to the image of Dionysus, the Greek god of winemaking and vegetation. Many Dionysian festivals announce the spring, and one of Dionysus' two main incarnations is a goat. His names and titles include 'kid' (for example *jare*), 'teeming' or 'bursting' (similar to *jariti se*) and 'he of the green fruit' (similar to Zeleni Jurje/Khidr). Like George, he suffers a violent death and experiences a resurrection, which is reenacted in spring rituals. The parallels become even more interesting. Jarilo is the son of Perun, the Slavic god of sky and thunder; Dionysus is the son of Zeus, the Greek god of sky and thunder. Jarilo descends to Veles, the Slavic god of the underworld and his return in the spring is celebrated as his resurrection; Dionysus descends to Hades, the Greek god of the underworld, and his return/resurrection is also celebrated annually, most likely in the spring.[14]

In one version of this myth, Dionysus returns from the underworld through a lake, and festivals in his honour are marked by the sacrificial throwing of a lamb into the lake (Frazer 1993: 389–90). On George's and Elijah's days, Muslims and Christians visited the lakes on mounts Šar and Korab, where they sacrificed lambs together and let the blood spill into the lake (see Špiro et al. 1970: 170). On the Pešter plateau, in the Serbian karst highlands not far from Gacko, Muslims and Christians also slaughtered lambs and poured blood into the lake during the George's Day celebrations, explaining that a dragon had been wont to appear from the lake before George slew it (Čajkanović 1973: 177–78).

So, across the Indo-European mythologies, dragons – the underworld creatures who guard the source of water – represent the death or withdrawal of vegetation, which endangers all fertility, but particularly that of human beings, as symbolized by the virginal maiden. Georgic springtime heroes are celebrated for their power to conquer frightening infertility (winter or drought) and unleash the reproduction of life upon the landscapes. They are the embodiment of sexuality, warmth and rupture. They recall the omni-resurrection, the forces of new beginnings, like the rush that Bosnian girls feel when they are pushed high up on their swings by boys on the morning of George's Day. George and his fellows promise abundant vegetation, the multiplication of human and animal life. The maiden and her sisters make sure that the promise is kept by communicating with the underworld. Together, they bring to life what seemed dead during the dark months of the cold winter.

Ethnographic, ethnological and etymological reconstructions indicate the antiquity of these spring rituals, although there is, of course, no way to establish a linear 'historical' narrative. Perhaps the strongest trace to follow is not to be found in the archaeology of material remains, but in the affective residues, in our bodies confronted with the changing seasons and the enormity of the unknown.

Khidr, the Verdant One, in Whom the Rivers Meet

The colour green is one of the most common symbols of fertility. It signals life in the desert plains, as much as it does in the snow-covered highlands. One could travel from India to the Atlantic coasts of Europe by way of 'green' and life-giving springtime characters. Greenness is inseparable from water, which is why these characters never appear without some kind of relationship to a well, lake, river or sea.

There is a plethora of 'green' characters in Britain. Although the May Day rituals and associated festivities point to a strong and old bond with their Indo-European counterparts, some doubt has been cast over the age of the famous Jack-in-the-Green, who is said to date from the seventeenth century (see Judge 1979, Hutton 2001: 241–43). The Green Man, sometimes associated with Jack-in-the-Green, was just a nickname given by Lady Raglan, a member of the Folklore Society, in 1939 to the carved faces on sacral architecture dating to the mediaeval times (Hutton ibid). Another 'green' character associated with May Day is Robin Hood (ibid: 270). As with the outlaws and heroes from the South Slavic epics, Robin seems to have attained some Georgic characteristics of his own. The Western Balkans have a tradition of Green George (*Zeleni Jurje/Juraj*). In a manner similar to some May Day festivities in Britain, a man completely covered in green garlands would lead the village processions on George's Day (Agapkina 2001: 174). George is, of course, profoundly green even without such titles. Where he walks, greenery sprouts...

One of the most perplexing and elusive figures of the Georgic mythology takes for his name just that – the colour green. He is the Green One, the Verdant. He appears as a prophet, a saint and a deity. Although his name has countless local variations, he is most commonly known as (al-)Khadir and (al-)Khidr, which likely comes from the Arabic word for green – *akhdar* (see Haddad 1969: 25). Throughout the Indian subcontinent he is known to Muslims and Hindus as Khwaja Khizr (Khadir), Pir Badar or Raja Kidar, celebrated with fire rituals at lakes, rivers and wells (see Coomaraswamy 1989: 157–67). In Twelve Imam Shi'ism, Khadir is closely associated with the twelfth imam, the Hidden, the *Mahdi,* and pilgrims visit shrines to seek help from both of them (Sahibzada 2009: 429). Like George, the earth becomes green where he stands or prays (ibid: 428).

Yezidis celebrate the Green One on two separate occasions in February, as Khidr Ilyas – the saint of life, water and health – and as Khidr Nebi (in Armenia and Georgia), the deity of love (Acikyildiz 2010: 111). As part of the Khidr Ilyas festivities, he is awaited with an offering in the form of a meal, which is similar to the Passover Seder traditions when awaiting Elijah. For Khidr Nebi, the Yezidis fast for three days without showering or cleaning their homes (ibid). I have noted the ritual avoidance of specific actions between George's Day and Elijah's Day in Bosnia, which act as a way to control the temper of the saints and thus protect the household, the crops or the cattle. Druze communities also celebrate al-Khidr and visit shrines dedicated to him (Swayd 2006: 98). He holds great importance for the Alawites of northern Syria, who invoke his name before any action (Haddad 1969: 25–26). By most Turks and the Alevis in particular, as Walker and Uysal (1973) noted, he is known as Hizir, the patron saint of travellers. He is associated with fertility and vernal renewal and celebrated on 6 May, which is George's Day under the Julian calendar.

The first time I heard of Khidr was from dervishes in the Qaderi tekke of Hadži Sinan in Sarajevo.[15] It was not surprising, because, as master of esoteric knowledge, Khidr remains important for Sufi paths and is purported to be the founder of many of them (Newby 2004: 122). Khidr is also said constantly to circumnavigate the tekke in the Bosnian town of Blagaj, as though circling around the Ka'aba (see Omerika 1999).

Outside of Sufi and academic circles, Khidr is rarely mentioned explicitly. Roma celebrations of George's Day as a rule include the famous *Ederlezi* song. Usually sung or blasted from speakers for the dancing crowds, it tells of the *Ederlez* festivities, the name of which is a compound of Khidr and Elijah (like *Khidrellez, Khidr Ilyas* and other variations). My Roma interlocutors, however, usually referred to it as *Đurđevdan* (George's Day). As usual, the 'absence' of a doctrinal narrative was juxtaposed to an extensive cosmological enactment. This knowledge was embodied in the ritual process, but also in everyday action, life-stories and transgenerational memories. Before all the site-specific and individual agencies seep in, the Georgic calendar acts primarily as a mnemonic for a life which would otherwise require another structure. It is there to remind of when and how to sow and harvest the crops, lead animals to pasture, collect medicinal herbs, shift a nomadic settlement, trade with neighbouring communities, circumcise sons, transition to adulthood, flirt, fall in love and become a fully fledged member of the community.

In that sense, calendric structures could also be understood as a snapshot of the dominant discourses on life and death. What happens when such positionality is disturbed? How are we to understand what the Georgic calendar is, after the most violent of technologies, migrations, wars and hegemonic discourses have taken their tolls? Here, the Bosnian landscapes give different answers. In one place, the calendric story makes sense as it was. In another, it is given a tweak, to follow a contemporary development. And, in places like the Field, it seems to linger between a hope that 'reconstructing traditions will reconstruct the village' and nostalgia for bygone days.

Various actors are tipping the scales in their own directions. On one side, there is the obvious hegemonic culprit materialized in nationalism. My position against it needs little introduction beyond the destruction it continues to produce. It is somewhere on the other side of the scales that I have to position the ethical justification for my work. The apparent potential of the syncretic traditions to develop into a strong challenge to anti-syncretic agents is one of the possibilities open to the Field's communities. After all, George and Elijah have entered a similar battle on other fronts.

Khidr is not mentioned explicitly in the Qur'an, but is often understood to be the anonymous servant of God, whose meeting with Moses is recounted in the surah 'the Cave' (18: 60–82).[16] Moses decides to travel to the 'confluence of two rivers [also translated as 'seas']'. After they have arrived there and travelled onwards, he and his servant discover that a fish they were carrying for food has come back to life and slipped into the river (sea). Moses exclaims that this is exactly what they were searching for, so they decide to trace their way back to the meeting place of the two rivers (seas). There, they find 'a servant of God', whom God has granted mercy and taught knowledge. Moses asks to follow this person and be taught what he knows. The mysterious riddler gives him quite the epistemological quandary: 'He said, "Indeed, with me you will never be able to have patience. And how can you have patience for what you do not encompass in knowledge?"' (Sahih International 18. 67–68). Moses promises patience and embarks on a journey with this man, but succumbs to disbelief each time the man commits an inexplicable act. So, he scolds the man for the acts of piercing a ship with many travellers on board, killing a boy and repairing a wall without asking for payment. Finally, the man decides to part ways with Moses, but first explains the reasoning behind his acts. He pierced the ship to save it for its poor owners from the king who wanted to seize it; the boy was killed because he would grow up to be violent towards his parents; and, the wall was repaired because some orphans were destined to find treasure their father had hidden beneath it.

This story of divine guidance is mentioned and elaborated upon in ahadith.[17] At the confluence of the two seas, according to this tradition, Moses has found none other than Khidr, a bearded man covered in a cloak (see Juynboll 2007: 569–72). When the two of them are on board ship (the one about to be pierced), one version of this story notes that: 'A bird came and having perched on the board of the ship it took one or two beaks full (of water) from the sea. Al-Khadir said: "Musa [Moses], my and your knowledge as compared with God's knowledge are like that beak full of water scooped up [by that bird] with the sea"' (ibid: 571). Thus, the vast knowledge that Khidr, the Verdant, imparts to Moses on their journey is the understanding of human knowledge as bounded, fragile and fallible. He, the embodiment of cyclical life, together with other Georgic characters, expresses the human thought that all of earthly existence is utterly unpredictable and that its stability may only be achieved by pleasing the Divine.

In some traditions, Khidr's knowledge is attributed to his discovery of the Fountain of Life, a magical spring from which he has drunk (see, for example, Hasluck 1929: 319). This finding is part of many versions of the 'Alexander Romance', the popular mediaeval stories of the miraculous and heroic journeys of Alexander the Great. Khidr is often associated with Alexander, sometimes as his or cook or the leader of his army (see Hasluck 1929: 319). 'The Water of Life', as Aleksandra Szalc (2012: 327–28) argued, only appeared as part of the Alexander Romance from the fifth century onwards. She further notes two versions of the story that are very similar to that of the Qur'anic/hadithic meeting between Moses and Khidr (ibid). In a Byzantine version, Alexander, travelling through the Land of Darkness, stops near a bright stream and orders his cook to prepare a dried fish for a meal. The fish comes alive while being washed in the stream. The cook does not disclose this miracle to Alexander, but drinks the water himself and seduces Alexander's daughter Kalē ('Beautiful') with it.

The story appears in slightly different form in the sixth-century sermon by Jacob of Seroug attached to a Syriac Alexander Romance. Journeying beyond the Land of Darkness to find the Water of Life, Alexander receives instruction from an old man that he would be able to recognize it in a place with many wells and springs by immersing a dead fish in each of them until it came to life. In this version, too, Alexander fails to attain eternal life and his cook is lost after jumping into the miraculous waters to catch the fish (ibid).[18]

Travelling through the Land of Darkness to reach the ultimate Source of life bears a striking resemblance to the journey of George and his predecessor Jarilo, who descends into the underworld before resurfacing and spreading vernal fertility over the earth. Coomaraswamy (1989: 160) noted this dual potential of Khidr:

> Khizr is at home in both worlds, the dark and the light, but above all master of the flowing River of Life in the Land of Darkness: he is at once the guardian and genius of vegetation and of the Water of Life, and corresponds to Soma and Gandharva in Vedic mythology, and in many respects to Varuna himself, though it is evident that he cannot, either from the Islamic or from the later Hindu point of view be openly identified with the supreme deity.

Alexander's daughter, who drinks the Water of Life in the Byzantine version of the Romance, is the quintessential maiden, akin to the king's daughter saved by George from the chthonic creature that guards the source of water. As the indispensable elements of fertility, their paradigmatic images inhabit the same symbolic axis. As such, the maiden exists regardless of her historical versions and pronunciations. Her full meaning can only be understood in flesh and blood, in the ritual of *omaha,* when young Bosnian women wake up before dawn on George's Day, rush to the nearest rapids or water mills, spray themselves with dispersed droplets and carry some of the water home to mix with spring herbs and wash their faces with later on. The salted dried fish, which comes to life at the confluence of the two seas for Moses and Khidr, is the same fish which escapes Alexander and his cook. The possible reasons for the supernatural properties of the water, apart from its obvious necessity for all life, may be traced in Indian and Slavic mythologies.

It is difficult to speculate upon the junctures of myths, points in time and space where one big narrative becomes acquainted with another to form a new expression, or why certain traditions so persuasively cooperate. The spectral varieties of the Green One are geographically wide, diverse and sometimes incoherent in terms of signifiers. The *signified,* however, travels much further. Beyond the many pronunciations and depictions, there is the Green, by any other name...

Some have suggested Khidr's and Alexander's connection to the Mesopotamian Epic of Gilgamesh (Wheeler 2002: 26, Szalc 2012: 328). As Kovacs (1989: xvii–xxxiv) noted, Gilgamesh was a partly human and partly divine monster-battling hero. His story begins when Enkidu, a personification of natural forces, a man raised by beasts in the wilderness, is sent by the gods to confront Gilgamesh's tyrannical kingship over the people of Uruk. They wrestle and, after Gilgamesh's victory, become friends. To achieve fame, they venture to the Cedar Forest to cut down a sacred cedar. Their transgressions, the killing of the Guardian of the Cedar Forest and the Bull of Heaven sent by the goddess Ishtar, are punished by the gods, who take Enkidu's life.

Gilgamesh decides to discover the cure for immortality and travels over the Waters of Death to seek advice from the only immortal man ever known, Utanapishtim the Faraway, the survivor of the Flood, who lived at the 'the mouth of the rivers' (ibid, Tigay 2002: 4). Utanapishtim, who was granted eternal life by his God for his piety, gives him two chances to attain eternal life. Both chances are squandered by Gilgamesh. Firstly, he fails the test of immortality. Secondly, he dives to the bottom of the river to fetch the 'plant of rejuvenation', but it gets stolen by a snake (ibid, Szalc 2012: 328).

Again, we have a hero who travels through the underworld towards the source of life hidden in miraculous waters and guarded by a chthonic creature.[19] Yet, neither Alexander nor Gilgamesh ever achieve immortality. Khidr's stories perhaps make him seem more like the immortal Utanapishtim, the former residing at 'the confluence of the two rivers [seas]', the latter at 'the mouth of the rivers'. Al-Majlisi, the Safavid-period Persian scholar who recorded the lives of Muslim prophets, noted that this toponym had been explained as the two rivers of knowledge, one of apparent knowledge, as represented by Moses, and the other of hidden knowledge, as represented by Khidr (2002: 493). The fact that our earliest record of this mythical toponym appears in Mesopotamia, literally translated as 'the land between rivers', places the immortal Verdant One at the confluence of Tigris and Euphrates.

I think that the widespread image of the confluence of the rivers might be best understood as the boundary between life and death, the same as the *ponors* visited in Georgic Bosnian rituals. As so often, the most developed narrative is to be found in the cosmology of ancient Greece. The river Styx is the boundary between Hades – the underworld and the aboveground world of the living. Five rivers merge in the Styx. Human souls are ferried across it by the old man Charon and then confronted by the many-headed dog-monster Cerberus (see Felton 2010: 92). Heracles, the hero son of Zeus, who manages to defeat Cerberus, also achieves immortality. George/Khidr, as the immortal human hero, is thus witness to the knowledge otherwise unknown to the short-lived.

Al-Majlisi's explanation of Khidr's greenness is remarkably similar to the stories about Jirjis/Đirđis (George):

> His miracle was such that whenever he sat on earth that piece of earth became green and grass grew on it. If he sat on a wooden plank or inclined over a dry piece of wood that wood would also become green and leaves would sprout from it as well as buds. That is why he was called al-Khidr (green). (2002: 499)

Al-Majlisi then revealed Khidr's real name as Taaliyaa and traced his lineage to Noah himself.[20] It is a phononym of Thalia, a spring-related character from Greek mythology, variously mentioned as one of the Muses, Charites

(Graces) or Nereids related to fertility (Cancik and Schneider 2006). Her name comes from the Greek *thállein,* 'to sprout', 'grow', 'thrive', particularly in reference to fruit trees (ibid).

Thallo, related to the same Greek root, is one of the Horae, goddesses of the order of nature and the seasons (Anthon 1884: 379). She is the Hora of spring and Carpo is the Hora of autumn; together they promote the fertility of the earth (ibid). They correspond to George and Demetrius in the contemporary Bosnian folk calendar. Thallo is tasked with accompanying Persphone during her descent into the underworld (Daly 2009: 43). Persephone, the daughter of Earth Mother, Demeter and Thunder God Zeus (Slavic Mokoš and Perun), is promised by her father to the God of the underworld. She is casually picking flowers in a meadow when the earth opens up and she is abducted by Hades, just like the Bosnian maiden abducted by the dragon. Distressed Demeter stops inducing fertility on earth, until the Sun, Helios, reveals her daughter's whereabouts. Persephone is allowed to leave Hades, but, thanks to her mistake in eating a single pomegranate seed in the underworld, she must return there each winter. The spring festivities mark her return (ibid).

Khidr as the 'verdant' and Thalia as the sprouting/growing/thriving are spectres of the same cosmic meaning.[21] Jarilo, the Slavic predecessor of George, as I have already demonstrated, is etymologically within the same semantic group. They all stand at the beginning of the warm season, after descending into the underworld and bringing forth fertility with their return. It would be impossible to establish the 'source' in this intricate web of mythologies. Their epicentre does seem to be the Mediterranean, where they approach each other, merge, collide and produce thousands of variations. Within this immense complexity, their common identity becomes apparent in the perduring, paradigmatic narrative, sufficiently simple and persuasive to be read anew from life and landscape alone.

Our Day: A Georgic Extension into Visoko

Roma traditions keep alive the memory of Khidr's and Elijah's peculiar connection through *Ederlez,* one of the words for George's Day. Unlike the Field of Gacko, to which the thriving Gurbeti communities have not returned after the 1990s war, the Roma of the central Bosnian town of Visoko have maintained their sacral landscape. And, this landscape comes to life on George's Eve. When I arrived to Visoko, small groups of families and friends were already ascending the hill to congregate at the Carica spring and make wishes for the coming year. It was their day, *Đurđevdan,* the beginning of a new season, but in the words of Hasiba, it is everyone's day and all Bosnians celebrate. Indeed, I met many Muslims and Serbs who eagerly participated. When I asked someone whether non-Roma 'shared' their day, one woman abandoned the face-washing ritual, turned to me and, with some resentment, said: 'I am a Serb!' Melina, my host, a young Roma woman who worked for a local NGO, was happy for everyone to participate, but thought that describing it as 'everyone's day' was wrong: 'It is a Roma day. We should be proud of our heritage, say that we are Roma and that it's our festival'. Her words recall a famous Roma song, which goes: *Romano dive, amaro dive, Ederlezi* (Romani day, our day, *Ederlezi*). But even that song has been translated into virtually all the languages of the Balkan Peninsula. It is a Roma day and a Roma song, but everyone else's too.

The tradition of George's Day is embedded in the earliest memories of the Visoko Roma. Hydronyms like Vrelo Carica (the Empress Spring) argue for mediaeval sources, as the town was then a seat of Bosnian royalty. The narrow pass around Carica, bursting with greenery, led towards a grand field which spread like an atrium to hold the merry congregation. The elderly attempted to keep up with the children in their mountaineering efforts to find just the right sprigs of cornel and nettle. Melina and Hasiba taught me to tie small red ribbons to unoccupied branches of cornel, repeating, 'I take health, forsake malady' (*Uzimam zdravlje, ostavljam bolest*). Each additional ribbon was a well-defined wish for loved ones imparted onto the thriving shrubs. Children ran around stinging each other's legs with nettles. Their games were sometimes interrupted by a quick visit to the spring, where they disappeared into a crowd of women splashing their faces with water and throwing three driblets over their backs, 'for luck'. Young married women wanting to get pregnant, gently lashed themselves with willow withies. 'This year with withy, next year a belly!'; they repeated the rhyme that was only a memory in the Field of Gacko.

A short visit home and then dusk began to settle over the Roma neighbourhoods on the hill of Križ. A synthesizer and a couple of large speakers were placed at the central intersection and the crowd slowly grew. 'I don't know why Roma people always live on hills', Melina reflected on her native landscape, 'but we always do'. I concluded that it's a culture of 'basking in the sun', but the moon soon had its own comment upon my thoughts. The next day, I read in the news that it was the night of perigee, when the moon is closest to the Earth and thus seems substantially brighter and larger than usual.

Some men started up a fire, which instantly created a circle of focused onlookers. One woman in a blue shirt and a few girls with clusters of fake ducats around their waists awaited no invitation. It was not long before my friend Alma and I were dragged into the circle to participate in the synchronized *kolo,* the 'wheel dance', as another full moon attended hopes for another good season.

I am well aware of the problematic romanticized images of Roma people, imagined as dancing and signging their way through life. Please remember that this is a description of a feast, for the most part given without its wider, everyday contexts.

From the Bosnian Roma Dance to the Palestinian Shrines

My search for the link between the Bosnian Green George and Khidr, the Indo-European Green One, took me to the eastern edge of the Mediterranean Basin. In the winter of 2013, I travelled to Palestine, where Khidr/George is said to have suffered, lived and died, and yet another part of the world where he maintains his vernal resurrections and grants miraculous fecundity.[22] The connection between the Balkan and Palestinian characters has already been observed by the Croatian ethnologist Vitomir Belaj, in his article on 'Green George in the Holy Land' (1989), where he raised some interesting questions on the connections between George, Khidr and Elijah. He argued for much older roots to their relationship:

> There are many elements at play, too many to explain them through simple coincidence. If it is ever possible to prove a cultural and historical connection between the Proto-Slavic myth of (the green) Jurje [George] and the folk traditions of the 'Green One', El-Khader in the Holy Land, I suspect that it will be possible only somewhere in the very deep past, in a pre-Sumerian and pre-Indo-European cultural horizon, someplace at the very beginnings of land cultivation. (1989: 75)

Belaj does not seem to take into account that Khidr belongs to the Balkans just as much as any of his Slavicized or Christianized versions. Khidr is present in the Balkans through Roma and Muslim (Sufi) traditions. Belaj's omission seems to rest upon the presumption that the Roma *Ederlez* should not be investigated as a 'native', 'Slavic' layer of the Georgic story. This is, however, a crucial pitfall. It is problematic not only because of the unwitting racism such a selective approach entails, or because it fails to account for the long and culturally rich presence of Roma and Sufi communities in the Balkans: the main shortcoming is the presumption that there could be anything 'autochthonous' about George, Khidr or Elijah. Their syncretic messiness appears out of multiple temporal and spatial proximities. I would, however, agree that these three characters, along with many others, share a much deeper connection, one that is oriented towards certain early religiosities shaped by life with the earth and its seasons. The following extensions are a glimpse into another space where George, Khidr and Elijah are 'shared' and 'syncretic', but also imbued with political agency.

Hybrid Geometries: A Georgic Extension into Palestine

The Palestinian George and Khidr are rarely found without each other. They are but two names for one person, as attested by their 'cohabitation' in a large number of shrines throughout Mesopotamia and the Levant. Perhaps the most prominent of such sites is the Biblical town of Lod in contemporary Israel/Palestine, known as al-Ludd in Arabic and Lydda in Latin. I have already mentioned it as the place where George is said to be buried. It is a town divided by an intra-Israeli concrete curtain, between 'Arabs' and 'Jews', and inhabited by only a fraction of those who were there before the conflicts.

Hidden amongst the dilapidated buildings of the 'Arab' part of al-Ludd lies an intricate mesh of synchronic and diachronic Georgic syncretism. Several qualitatively different kinds of sharing form part of this site. At first, one approaches a 'vertical' hybrid. Embedded on top of an old Byzantine church and the tomb of St George, and within the remains of a monumental twelfth-century Crusader Church of St George, there are two adjoining and actively used temples, the nineteenth-century Greek Orthodox Church of St George next to the thirteenth-century al-Khader mosque.[23]

These structures were partly built with *spolia* from the older temples (see Sharon 1983: 800–2). Buildings on top of each other and within one another may, at first, resemble a chronological chart of the sacro-political currents that have seeped over the site. Yet, the geometry of relationships within al-Ludd is far messier than a mere succession of historical periods. Through their contributions to the site, the various layers have spoken to each other and formed a new, hybrid language. They have seeped through each other's ontological boundaries to the point where one contributing layer can no longer be singled out, without losing some of its defining qualities. It is only with the rise of particular exclusive imaginaries that places like al-Ludd become 'strange creatures'. They become points of reference for outsiders and are turned into havens of pluralism, bastions of resistance, or obstacles to nationalisms and religious fundamentalisms. They are destroyed or memorialized due to their capacity to reconcile what is otherwise presented at odds. The story of ontological mixture is more complex than the overlapping traditions of the Palestinian/Israeli 'Muslims, Christians and Jews'. Syncretism is more readily apparent when narrated along with the protracted conflicts of identitary politics.

Yet, no telling of the Georgic story of al-Ludd should leave out the traces of earlier religious systems. Ali Qleibo (2011) argued that George and Khidr in the Palestinian sacral calendar and geography show a strong connection to Canaanite ritual. These remnants are attested in the very transposition of the deities El/Dagon and Baal into George/Khidr and Elijah, in the continued sacral use of high-altitude locations, and in apotropaic blood sacrifices. Several toponyms in and around al-Ludd are related to the fertility god Dagon (see Smith 1901: 164), sometimes conflated with the principal deity El (see Fontenrose 1957).[24] Dagon was also possibly revered and represented as a fish god (ibid: 278). The resurrected fish is not only the sign of Khidr in all the various versions of his story; he is also often depicted as a man dressed entirely in green, traversing the waters of life atop a fish as his vehicle (see Coomaraswamy 1989: 157).

Chapters of this history, from the Canaanite to the Israeli, have created their specific contexts for syncretism. Beyond those contexts, the inhabitants, the daily visitors and the pilgrims have continued to define and erase the boundaries between doctrines. Through their inter-penetrative cosmologies, the inherently political, vertical layers of sacra are made to permeate each other. They trasnform the compound around George's tomb into a place with sacral meaning as a whole. The story of the site's layers thus appears multifaceted, simultaneously syncretic and anti-syncretic. The redefinition of the space is an ongoing process. While the church and the mosque are understood as part of the same sacred place, the recent addition of a fenced-up synagogue is read as an intrusion by some Palestinians I talked to. Perhaps that's how all the Georgic structures in al-Ludd began, before being joined together by the rhythm of the seasons.

George's Tomb

To reach the grave of George in al-Ludd, one must descend into the crypt beneath the altar. In this small chamber, on top of a stone sarcophagus, lies a recognizably knightly figure carved in a marble panel relief, illuminated by pilgrims' candles. The inscription around the panel reads *Ο ΑΓΙΟΣ ΓΕΩΡΓΙΟΣ ΟΤΡΟΠΑΙΟ ΦΟΡΟΣ,* 'Saint George the Trophy-bearer'. As I contemplated this (with my camera), a woman entered the chamber and approached the grave. It was a profoundly intimate meeting in which my presence was uncalled for, but also completely ignored. In what seemed like trembling excitement, she leant over the relief with her entire torso and murmured supplications I could not make out. When she stood up, the clumsy gesture I made towards her with my camera went unnoticed. She kissed the golden mosaic image of George on the wall and then returned to the sarcophagus once more. Perhaps she was used to the occasional tourist taking photos, I thought, to excuse my voyeurism. She soon hurried out in the manner of her arrival. Based on the analogy between my Bosnian research and the Palestinian Georgic traditions, it would not have been surprising to find she was praying for fertility or the health of her household. The group of pilgrims that arrived after she had left placed small souvenir icons of George

The Georgics: An Extended Poetry of the Land 215

FIGURE 5.3 The syncretic complex of George/Khidr in al-Ludd, Palestine

FIGURE 5.4 Prayer at the tomb of George in al-Ludd, Palestine

on top of the sarcophagus and knelt in brief prayer. The icons would have eventually been given as gifts, retaining something of the sanctified 'aura' of George's presence.

George/Khidr performs two basic functions. He ensures health and provides general protection from evil; he also aids the reproduction of people, vegetation and cattle. In spite of the geographical and contextual distance, this is very consistent with the 'health/fertility' formula found in the two previously discussed George's Day chants from Bosnia: 'I take health, forsake malady' and 'This year with withy, next year a belly'. Within a wider discussion of George as the patron of fertility, Frazer described his importance for Muslim and Christian 'barren women' in 'the East', with particular reference to Syria: 'Childless women of all sects resort to it in order that the saint may remove their reproach. Some people shrug their shoulders when the shrine is mentioned in this connexion. Yet many Mohammedan women who desired offspring used to repair to it with the full consent of their husbands' (1911: 346).

The other aspect of the life-endorsing George/Khidr is his apotropaic potency. The facades of many Palestinian homes are decorated with small reliefs of the saint, particularly above the house doors. He functions as the protective patron of the household, ensuring that the family is healthy and prosperous. Walking down one street in Bethlehem, I noticed that this image was on virtually every building. George was the same symbol for Hasiba from the town of Visoko in central Bosnia, who spent considerable time tying red ribbons to branches of cornel on George's Eve, mentioning by name each of her children and grandchildren, wishing them health, summoning protection over them and making even more specific plans, like their successful enrolment into university.

The Battle of al-Ludd and the Four Immortal Characters of the Last Hour

One character related to George's burial town is Dajjal. In Islamic eschatology, framed through hadithic narratives, Dajjal is the antichrist, the false messiah.[25] He will appear as one of the signs in the Last Hour and be slain by Jesus at the gate of al-Ludd.[26] While his characteristics are expounded in a hadith, I deal only with those directly related to our Georgic narratives.[27] Thus, according to the Prophet Muhammad, Dajjal's presence is related to a falsification of nature and two 'contradictory rivers':

> I know what the Dajjal will have with him. He will have two flowing rivers, one that appears to the eye to be clear water, and one that appears to the eye to be flaming fire. ... He will have water and fire with him, but his fire is cool water and his water is fire, so do not destroy yourselves. (Sahih Muslim 54. 131)

This deceptive creature, slain at the gates of the town where the dragon slayer's remains lie, is connected to the dragon on a symbolic level. He brings with him that confluence of the two rivers, the primary location of all our other Georgic characters. The rivers are deceptive because, again, they are symbols of life and death. What makes Khidr's knowledge greater than that of Moses is his ability to comprehend and safely make the choices which seem the least obvious to humans. The appealing choice of worldly life in Dajjal's cool water is the short-sighted one that is eventually revealed as fire. Death is the beginning and the true life lies beyond its gates. As Juynboll (2007: 34) noted: 'Dajjal causes natural phenomena to appear as the opposite of what they really are'.

According to another hadithic narrative, Dajjal should appear near the gates of Medina, where he will be confronted by a mysterious person, who is 'the best of men or one from amongst the best of men'. They engage in a curious battle to prove who they are. Firstly, Dajjal kills the good man and brings him back to life. Then he tries to kill him again, but this time he fails (Sahih Muslim 54: 138, Sahih al-Bukhari 29: 16). This performance of mortality, resurrection and immortality is perhaps best understood through the brief note which follows the hadith in Sahih Muslim (ibid): some understood this person to be Khidr.

Some exegetical texts dedicate ample attention to Khidr's lifespan. The *tafsir* (Qur'anic commentary) of the thirteenth-century scholar al-Qurtubi thus lists four characters endowed with immortality: Khidr, Jesus, Elijah and Dajjal (see Sands 2006: 82). All of these characters are part of the Georgic model and there is some overlap between them all. Jesus, as noted, will slay Dajjal in al-Ludd, where George the dragon-slayer is buried. George is venerated simultaneously with Khidr, the Verdant – on the same days, in the same places, through the same rituals. The last immortal from this Georgic quartet is Elijah. His 'identity' in the story has been deemed so important that he earns a mention in many versions of the spring ritual, alongside George-Khidr. They are known as Khidr-Elijah, or Khidr-Ellez. In Bosnia, George/Khidr and Elijah come together in the Roma feast of *Ederlez/Đurđevdan* and the entire warm season between George's and Elijah's days.

The Intimacy of George, Khidr and Elijah

George (Khidr) is intimately related to Elijah. Between them stand the rituals of the Bosnian summer. According to a Palestinian belief recorded in the mid nineteenth century, George possesses Elijah's spirit (Belaj 1989: 69). Like George, Elijah sometimes rides a horse through the air (ibid). Indeed, one the most popular icons in Palestine, as Qleibo (2011: 7) noted, is of Elijah (Mar Elias) seated behind George and holding a bucket of water as a sign of his capacity to bring forth the rain. Their alliance is indispensable to fertility of land, as in this Palestinian song (Qleibo 2011: 7):

> Oh master Khader, the green one
> Water our green plants
> Oh master Elias
> Water our drying plants

The overlapping characteristics of Khidr and Elijah were mentioned by the Byzantine Emperor Cantacuzenus in the fourteenth century (see Hasluck 1929: 322). According to various Mediterranean traditions, Khidr and Elijah meet every year for a feast on a shore that divides land from water and together make the pilgrimage to Mecca, where they say a prayer.[28]

A meeting similar to the Qur'anic narrative of Moses and the man recognized as Khidr appears in the Jewish rabbinical tradition – only, this time, the puzzled questioner is not Moses but a third-century Rabbi, Joshua ben Levi, born in Lydda/Lod, which has already been mentioned as the burial place of George, and the instruction on divine knowledge comes not from Khidr but from the Prophet Elijah (Segal 1935: 88–91). Khidr, George and Elijah are often conflated into the same character (see Hanauer 1907: 51–52).

Many sacred places are related to both George/Khidr and Elijah. For example, the Greek Orthodox Church of George in Al-Salt in Jordan is also considered to be a place visited by Elijah (Belaj 1989: 70). Their most striking meeting is at a festival celebrated across the Mediterranean on the same date as George's Day according to the Julian calendar (6 May). There are various titles for this festival, but they always combine the names of Khidr and Elijah. In Bosnia, it is *Ederlez*; in Turkey, it is *Hizir-Ilyas* or *Hidrellez*; as already mentioned, the Yezidis also celebrate Khidr Ilyas festivities and wait for him with the offering of a meal (Acikyildiz 2010: 111). Alija Đerzelez, the most prominent of the Bosnian Georgic epic heroes, makes this meeting even more prominent.[29] His name can be read as 'Elijah Khidr-Elijah', because Alija is the Bosnian Muslim incarnation of Elijah, while I would argue that Đerzelez is the same compound as *Ederlez* ('Khidr-Elias' or 'Đirđis-Elias'). Alija Đerzelez is said to be buried in the Bosnian village of Gerzovo, where the famous 'shared' Elijah's Day gathering was held.

George's Intimacy with Demetrius and the Guardians of the Key

While George and Elijah define the Bosnian fertile season, there is another character intimate with them – Demetrius. His day, 8 November according to the Julian calendar, is known as Demetrius' Day (*Mitrovdan*) or the Day of Kasum. Serbs in Gacko use the former name, Muslims both of them. Kasum derives from the Arabic *qasim* which means 'dividing' or 'divider'. Kasim is also a Muslim and Mitar/Dimitrije a Serb male name in Bosnia. Mitar or Kasim thus divides the warm part of the year from the winter. One Bosnian saying plays on the similarity of the word *Kasum* to the word *kas* (horse trot): 'As Kasum trots in, summer trots away' (*Kasum dokasa, ljeto prokasa*).

There are two feasts of George/Khidr in Palestinian al-Ludd, one in the springtime, when George was born, and the other in the autumn when he died or when his relics were interred (Sharon 1983: 802). This double annual celebration of the saint is particularly interesting, as it follows the repetitive fertility journey of all our other Georgic characters – birth in spring – death (or descent into the underworld) in autumn. The latter feast corresponds to the Demetrius' Day of the Bosnian calendar. George-Khidr thus descends into hiding during the 'infertile period' and reappears in all his splendid greenness for the fertility celebration.

Khidr is also celebrated twice a year by Christians and Muslims in his eponymous Palestinian town of al-Khader, firstly to mark his arrival (resurrection) in the springtime and then the time of his death during the harvest festivals, when sheep are slaughtered behind Saint George's Monastery. The sacrificial blood is considered to have apotropaic qualities and is sometimes drunk or taken home to be daubed on the front door (Qleibo 2011: 8–9). People in this town say that George's family was from al-Khader and that his mother lived near the monastery.

When I visited al-Khader Monastery, I noticed a beautiful fresco of George and Demetrius in a loving embrace, almost as if they are sharing a torso. A copy of the image stood by my desk as I was writing this book, reminding me how the spatial and temporal extensions of the Field's religiosities are simultaneously very complicated and very simple. The Bosnian and Palestinian characters have grown into different narratives and practices, yet they mark the same inevitable turning of the seasons and continuously 'shared' cosmic trajectories. Both Muslims and Christians hold al-Khader Monastery sacred, during the George's Day festivities and otherwise: they seek prosperity, mental health and fertility there. I saw people passing through some iron chains. Some of the visitors explained that it was the bridle of George's horse. They kissed it three times and put it over their heads. The third time, the whole body passed through.[30]

With his son seated on top of his shoulders, the Muslim caretaker of the monastery guided me into the dark space adorned with icons. His family has always guarded the monastery, he told me. I recalled the traditions of Muslims who guarded the keys of churches and Christians who guarded mosques in Bosnia and Kosovo. Such guardianship was part of the In-Other relationship. The minaret of the mosque in Kazanci near Gacko is still standing reportedly because an elderly Serb man living there pleaded with soldiers not to destroy it.

Al-Khader, like al-Ludd, was enveloped both within and outwith the Israeli concrete curtain. Its Georgic traditions remarkably resembled the syncretism and sharing so abundant in Bosnia. They too have survived against the odds of the destructive anti-syncretic aspirations of nation-state homogenization.

The Intimacy of Elijah and Perun

Then Jupiter, squire of the sky, straddling the night clouds, dispatches
from his gleaming hand a thunderbolt and makes the whole world quake.

—Virgil, *Georgics*

Elijah's Day, 2 August, is the culmination of the season introduced by George. There is ample cause for celebration: the crops, the cattle and the humans have survived the season. Before white winter locks the Field into its embrace, numbs the crops under ice and confines humans to their households and cattle to the sheds, one more joyful *teferič* is in order. According to one legend, even the king of mediaeval Bosnia would come down from his fort of Visoki for Elijah's Day to join the folk fair in Arnautovići, where he would dance with young women (Filipović 2002: 531). Christians and Muslims have 'shared' these celebrations for centuries. In 1708, Friar Stipan Margitić Jajčanin noted that Elijah was revered in Bosnia, not only by God, the Church and the Christian folk, but also by the heathen Turks, who held him for a great saint, calling him 'Fiery Elijah' (*Ognjeni Ilija*) and abstaining from work in fear of fire from the heavens (in Karamatić 2012).

Like George and Khidr, Elijah is associated with fertility and rain. The Biblical Elijah brings fire from the sky and controls precipitation. He tells Ahab: 'As the Lord God of Israel liveth, before whom I stand, there shall not be dew nor rain these years, but according to my word' (1 Kings 17: 1). He goes up in the whirlwind into heaven (2 Kings 2: 11). He strikes his mantle over water and makes the land dry (2 Kings 2: 8). In al-Majlisi's *Stories of the Prophets* he appears under the name of Ilyas (2002: 567–73). He is an old, hundred-metre tall man with white hair, who sends his curse of drought and famine for seven years and shares a meal with Prophet Muhammad. According to one rabbinical legend, Elijah became immortal by discovering the Fountain of Life (Washburn Hopkins 1905: 19). In Bosnia and other countries in the Balkan Peninsula, Elijah is known and often depicted as 'Elijah the Thunderer' (*Ilija Gromovnik*) and 'Fiery Elijah' (*Ognjeni Ilija*). In the summer of 2012, the Catholic community in the town of Stolac sanctified a large statue of Elijah with a lightning bolt in his hand.

Elijah is heir to Slavic Perun, the God of thunder, law and war and a major character of the Proto-Slavic pantheon (Ivakhiv 2009: 1558). 'His actions', Gimbutas noted, 'were perceived by the senses: he was seen in the thunderbolt, he was heard in the crackling rattle of stones or the thunderous bellow of the bull or he-goat, and he was felt in the sharp touch of an ax blade' (2005a: 7052). He was obviously the Slavic counterpart of the Greek Zeus, the Germanic Thor and the Roman Jupiter. Procopius' sixth-century treatise noted that the Slavs 'believe that one god, the maker of the lightning, is the only lord of everything and they sacrifice to him cattle and all kinds of victims' (in Luján 2008: 105). He also appears in the Russian *Primary Chronicle,* amongst the Slavic gods worshipped in tenth-century Kiev (Gimbutas 2005a: 7062, Ivakhiv 2009: 558).

Perun's name is derived from *per-/perk-,* which means 'to strike' or 'to splinter', and is related to 'oak, oak forest' and 'mountaintop' (Ivakhiv 2009, Gimbutas 2005a). He was indeed venerated in oak forests and on mountaintops (see Vasiljev 1996: 32). Thunder and lightning were generated when he threw his axe, and the struck objects attained apotropaic qualities (Dundzila 2005: 156). I believe that the chipped pieces of the peculiar split rock at Ajvatovica have apotropaic qualities because Ajvaz Dedo embodies some of Elijah's agency. Similar powers have been attributed to chips of yew and oak. Georgic fertility rituals in the Field related to yew amulets and oaks or oak dust were mentioned earlier in this chapter.

Perun's temples were in forests and mountains. The primeval forest of Perućica, the Prenj mountain range, and other toponyms in the vicinity of Gacko, reveal traces of the Perun cult. The apotropaic quality of oaks in Gacko and, indeed, their sacred meaning in most of Europe, owe something to the peculiar propensity of oaks for being the foremost arboreal attraction for lightning (see HadžiMuhamedović 2013). Perun's main adversary is Veles (also Volos, Chernobog), the chthonic three-headed serpentine or dragon-like deity.[31] Along with the Bosnian Elijah, it is clear that George also inherited some of Perun's position. Haddad (1969: 27) argued that the common origin of George, Khidr and Elijah might be found in the Baalic cults. Elijah, however, is in explicit conflict with the prophets of Baal and their followers,[32] although Baal is also a thunderbolt-carrying god riding a white horse, like Perun.

To arrive at the central occasion of the Gacko calendar, this chapter has taken a long and meandering path through its summer, venturing into narratives, practices, times and spaces far distant from its starting point. Now, the 'Gacko Georgics' have returned to the Field for their most important occasion. The memories of my interlocutors continue their conversation with Elijah's Day.

The Georgics: (Post-)Act Two
Elijah of the Field

Scene One: She Did It before Me

Fata: Why is it celebrated? I don't know. I don't know.

Nada: Well, Elijah is the protector of Nadanići.

Edo: So, there is a story about how the Greeks used to live here and how they left this place, in fact ran away, because snow fell on Elijah's Day in the eighth month.

Osman: I heard of Elijah's Day as a child. It was a treat to go to the fair, because you were usually taking care of the cattle, you know.

Eno: This fair, this Elijah's Day ... I can't find it the religious books, or anywhere else. It is typically considered a ... how should I put it, folk celebration ... I can't get to the bottom of it. There wasn't even a *mevlud* [celebratory Muslim prayer meeting] on that day. It doesn't exist anywhere in religion. The Orthodox won't be able to give you a definition either. But, everyone recalls certain traditions.

Ružica: It was the most important day for Nadanići.

Delva: Why is it celebrated? Well, it was simply a date for the nation to gather.

Mila: I learnt it from my mother. That's how it was. Whatever I used to do, she did before me. It was passed down from generation to generation [*s koljena na koljeno*].

Scene Two: The Last Release

Eno: Elijah's Day is the last celebration of the year to give people some light relief. After that, all such get-togethers cease. Winter is coming; all the work is hastily finished, wood hauled in and the summer crops collected. Winters are long. Elijah's Day was their last release.

Nezir: It was our biggest celebration – a gathering of villagers, their children and families.

Osman: It was the biggest festival and gathering. The *Bajrams* [Eids] were something different.

Nezir: It was a gathering of all the strata of the community, children, adults, men and women.

Eno: The biggest holiday, by far. Not even George's Day came close to it. There was nothing like it. Elijah's Day was the biggest fair.

Drago: They were considered religious, but were folk gatherings. People wore festive clothes. The youth got a chance to meet.

Osman: A few days before, the youth would start preparing; even as much as ten days before. The girls would begin to dress up. The richer

	ones would order *dimije* and *anterije* from tailors, folk attire made from expensive fabrics. The lads would also get traditional clothes and, later, suits.
Eno:	People, especially children, would get their hair cut before Elijah's Day and buy new clothes. Even though there weren't many occasions for buying clothes in the village through the year, they did buy special clothes for Elijah's Day. People would wear the most festive garments they had.
Safeta:	People would come, up to a week before Elijah's Day. Each household had up to thirty children. And the women would wake up, milk the cows, prepare the children and lock up the cows and sheep. And, all day long, people would be coming over.
Bećir:	The fair. There was *kolo* dancing, singing, live music, food, drinks . . .
Eno:	I remember the horse waggons. Older women and children from villages further away would arrive sitting on top of them, all decorated with flowers, in festive clothes.
Mitar:	A real folk fair, a universal celebration.
Safeta:	The whole world came. The fair was on the second day and second night of August. There was no electricity, so we would light lanterns. But the weather would be nice, lots of moonlight. Five thousand souls would come.

Scene Three: Saying Time

Nezir:	Elijah's Day and the *teferič* are eagerly awaited all year. As soon as it's over, the whole story is steered towards the next year's fair.
Eno:	God forbid, but when cursing children or cattle, people would say, 'May you not await [to see the next] Elijah's Day! [*Aliđuna ne dočeko!*]. I remember how the women would scold the children. That's how important Elijah's Day was.
Sejo:	Well, in reckoning the seasons, they would say: 'Through dust 'till Elijah's Day, through mud after Elijah's Day' [*Do Aliđuna po prahu, od Aliđuna po kalu*]. As soon as 2 August passes, they say, the weather starts to change.
Fata:	It means that up until Elijah's Day, you can walk around in your slippers. After Elijah's Day, you can't go out without boots. After Elijah's Day here, you have to prepare for when the snows begin. You have to stock up on flour, sugar, coffee, cattle feed . . .
Mladen:	There is also the saying: 'Before noon Ilija, after noon Alija'. Ilija was celebrated in Nadanići and Alija in Kula.
Eno:	They also say, 'Georgic rains' and 'Elijan droughts'.

Safeta: One year, they banned the Elijah's Day fair in Kula. It was perhaps two years before I got married, in 1957. Another year, I remember from my childhood, the Partisans crossed hands and danced the *Kozaračko kolo* with us at Bare.

Rade: We got married. It was Elijah's Day. When we came to my village, the wheat was already ripening and it was the custom to enter the wheat fields. My father said: 'My Radojica is getting married. Everyone, run into the wheat!'

Eno: The mowing starts before Elijah's Day, on 1 July. That was the time for hard work.

Sejo: By Elijah's Day, the grass has been mown. Only those with no manpower would still have any haystacks outside the barn.

Scene Four: Similarities and Meetings

Nada: Muslims celebrated it too. People would come from Bileća and Nevesinje, the lads would go to other municipalities.

Nezir: Serbs would come to Kula to celebrate, in those golden times, together with Muslims.

Safet: On the same day as *Aliđun,* the Serb neighbours had their *Ilindan* fair in Nadanići.

Osman: Well, the Serbs have that too, the same traditions. People went from one gathering to another. The Orthodox celebrate next to the church in Nadanići. But, it was the same – as they say – an exact copy.

Lepa: Elijah's Day was celebrated in the Muslim villages too, around Kula. Before the war, when we worked in the thermal power plant, they would tell us about the celebrations in Kula.

Eno: After all, this is a farming area. The villages are remote, so Elijah's Day would be used for such meetings and family connections. Memories are evoked, and so on. People have a bit of fun.

Fata: And, for Elijah's Day, everyone would gather here. More of them [Serbs] than us. And our folk [Muslims] would go to Nadinići ... The lads, not the girls, but the lads ...

Osman: Elijah's Day influenced the creation of friendships and unity.

Bećir: Serbs would do the same things on that day, near the Church.

Zahida: By God, the same as we did: drank, danced, sang ...

Scene Five: The Church, the Mosque and the Aspens in-between

Drago: The Serbs would congregate around the church, where the young people and the adults would come. The church was visited by people from other towns, from Nevesinje, Kalinovik, even from Montenegro.

Rade: The fair is held next to the church. The banners are carried around it. Whoever pays the most has the privilege of carrying the banners with the image of the saint.

Nada: They carry the banners around our church.

Drago: The one who pays the most gets to carry Elijah's banner around the church.

Nezir: Our festival route was to walk around the Studenac spring and the mosque.

Eno: People gather around the mosque in Kula. Electricity would be hooked up for the fair from the mosque.

Osman: Because Muslims celebrated near the mosque in Kula, it was thought of as something religious, but it wasn't such. It was traditional.

Safeta: The party was in Jasike [The Aspens] before. Then, later, we started having it here, in Kula.

Bećir: The oldest place for the Elijah's Day gathering was deeper in the Field. There were ten to fifteen aspens and a source of water at that place. It was called Jasike [Aspens].

Eno: I used to go there with my grandmother. Huge aspen trees threw comfortable shade. The place, sadly, doesn't exist anymore. It was buried by the waste from the thermal plant.

Scene Six: The Guests Must Eat

Mladen: A thousand vehicles arrive for Elijah's Day. Bread is baked. There's a whole marketplace of young men and women.

Ljubica: The ornamented bread is not made with yeast. It is [ceremonially] broken when the candle is lit. We slaughter something. Then, we pray to God.

Nezir: And our favourite Elijah's Day drink was *Cockta* [a popular Yugoslav carbonated beverage].

Fata: When I came here as a young bride, they were preparing for the fair. My father-in-law told me: Come on daughter-in-law, prepare the meals'. 'Tomorrow,' he said, 'is Elijah's Day. There will be guests. They must eat'. So it was: bake pies, cook meat ... Cook, bake, cook ... To have enough bread. And, everything was prepared.

Osman: Every household prepared meals for guests from the towns of Bileća, Foča, Nevesinje and others. Pies were prepared, mostly with cheese or meat. Meat was baked. Baklava was prepared.

Eno: There would be stalls selling spit-roasted lamb, baking cookies [*gurabije*], fresh juices, Turkish delights [*rahat lokum*], and so on ... There were shoemakers, craftsmen with horse equipment, textile sellers, all kinds ... a real village fair. A few thousand people would come to buy things.

Scene Seven: Love and Flirtation

Eno: After all, many loves began and marriages were made there.

Osman: Walking around that fair in the meadow, people would meet. There were those who would come intending to meet a girl, groups of lads from the neighbouring towns. They would stay for a week, singing and dancing with the girls. They would interrogate friends and cousins to find out which girls were fine and then let slip that they would like to marry one, and so on.

Zahida: Lads would come here for Elijah's Day from the surrounding towns, and lads from Gacko would go to other places.

Drago: For Elijah's Day, you could walk up to a girl and ask for her hand. Either she would accept or she wouldn't. But those marriages would last.

Ljubica: Before, Elijah's Day used to be like this: I would be walking around with one lad. It would be like love. Then along comes another one ... Then, a third asks: Will you give her over to me [*prepustiti*]? The girl who collects the most proposals is a *namuša*. She is reputable as a beauty [*na namu*]. *Namuše* would sing and many songs were sung about them. For example, there's one about Desa Milinkuša, who was a famous *namuša*: 'The scorching sun shines down from the heavens, just as Milinkuša Desa does here on earth' [*Žarko sunce sija sa nebesa, a sa zemlje Milinkuša Desa*].

Eno: Well, there was always some family lobbying. Gacko is that type of area, with the tribes keeping track of families' reputations. There was always some lobbying and there still is. If two girls got married that Elijah's Day, hundreds dreamt of doing the same the next year.

Fata: During the fair at Kula, if someone had a diligent wife, the men would gather and talk: 'Wow, she's good, the best'. And then, in the evening, they would meet in some house and discuss the details, who was good, who she was related to, and so on. Then, their wives would protest: 'I am going to smack you now!'

Scene Eight: Fistfights and 'Rock from the Shoulder'

Lepa: The men compete at 'rock from the shoulder' [*kamena s ramena*] and the long jump.

Mujo: More recently, there was a football tournament in Kula near the mosque. There were twenty teams ...

Eno: There were many sport activities on Elijah's Day, especially horse races, sprinting, athletic disciplines like 'rock from the shoulder', tug-of-war, the long jump ... Sometimes, there were fistfights.

Mirso: Fights are traditional for Elijah's Day get-togethers. Between one and two hundred people might get into a fistfight. People haven't seen each other for a long time and arguments break out. It was a kind of communication. A bit of alcohol, a bit of tribal competition. Women dance the *kolo*. Sometimes, the police get called. We witnessed a fight in another village and said: 'Look, it's the same as in our place!'

Nada: The sound lads would gather to throw the javelin or 'rock from the shoulder', pull rope or play football in the field next to the church.

Osman: These Elijah's Day performances sometimes include horse races, with the best horses. There was also a high jump.

Rade: There was also the log carrying [*klipa se tegli*], log lifting [*dizanje klipa*], climbing the greasy pole, jumping on inflated animal skin bags [*skok na napuhanu mješinu*], and so on.

Scene Nine: The Harmonies

Ljubica: When a group of lads sings together for a while, somehow or other they harmonize.

Mladen: The Serbs sing *ganga* and Muslims *bećarac*. But, Serbs in other places sang *bećarac* too.

Lepa: The men sing *ganga*, which can be heard far off.

Mirso: The leader of the *bećarac* will sing for up to five hours and the veins on his neck will swell. The basses [*basovanje*] and the strength of the *bećarac* would extinguish the flames in the lanterns.

Osman: Folk songs were sung. Accordion players would come from Sarajevo or Mostar and spend the night in someone's house. Mostly, people played the flute and the harmonica.

Eno: We also played the bagpipes [*diple na mijeh*] and the *gusle*. The last bagpipe player in this area was the late Zejnil Zekić. The instrument is quite rare now.

Eno: *Bećarac* singing was inevitable. Any gathering of men in the village would be unimaginable without it. There were even singing competitions. According to one anecdote, the bass of the *bećarac* would be so strong that it would blow out the lanterns.

Lejla: We would sing: 'Pots and pans flirt, and so do lads and lasses' [*Ašikuju kašike i lonci, a da ne bi djevojke i momci*].

Delva: I haven't heard *bećarac* here for twenty years.

Rade: The *kolo* dance would be joined [hands]. The *trojanac*, for example.

Eno: We would dance the *sremica* and the ordinary *kolo*. As they say, one step forward, two steps back.

Scene Ten: Like the Swallow

Osman: After the war, the tradition of fair has been continued around the mosque, which has been burnt down more than once, however. A

	couple of thousand come for the day. But, there is little communication with the Serbs. Only the police come to observe. Individually, people might be friends, though.
Šejla:	Some will spit-roast lamb, usually the diaspora with money, and the returnees will bring cheese and *kajmak*.
Sejo:	They organize these festivities in the diaspora as well, in Chicago …
Eno:	Well, a lot has changed. People are scattered around the world. It was easy to organize Elijah's Day when you had five thousand Muslims in Gacko, two and a half thousand in Kula. Now we change the dates to suit the diaspora. Elijah's Day is important for return, in every sense. Everything that gets revived contributes to return.
Lepa:	It is still happening. We still have the Elijah's Day feast.
Drago:	There will be 'stone from the shoulder' games near the church. It happens every year.
Ružica:	And the peasant songs and the *gusle* and the traditional costumes, it'll all be there.
Eno:	Elijah's Day is a phenomenon. As the swallow returns each spring, so the traditions return too. Emperors and occupying powers have changed, but tradition remains. It hasn't been easy to come back. The first postwar Elijah's Day was in 2000.
Virgil:	Why, even when you've chopped an olive tree – can you believe it? – buds burgeon from its seasoned stump. (2006: 28)

Recapitulation: Lives of Seasonal Order

Explaining a symbol, like tracing one life, is a lost endeavour. It is always inherently ineffable. Whatever one assembles into a single description is no more than a tale, a didactic selection of images and connections. These 'Georgics of the Field' have been written to counterbalance the first part of the book, to explore the inheritance of my interlocutors – a composition of cosmological practices far richer and more complex than their dealings with the 1990s war in Bosnia. Georgic characters do find a way to connect the cosmologies of most of the religious communities in Bosnia, but they do so because of the immense and deep interaction of the Indo-European paths with the major themes of the Georgic phenomena. Another reason is that, regardless of religion, these communities continue to inhabit what Maureen Korp has called 'landscapes of seasonal order', whose humans and nonhumans align 'with the land in response to regular changes of season and other cosmic forces' (2005: 112). In that sense, this chapter is a turn towards the cosmology of the peasants from the Field, whose chores, again in Virgil's words, 'come round in seasons and cycles, as the earth each year retraces its own tracks' (2006: 41).

FIGURE 5.5 Elijah's Day service next to the church in Nadanići

FIGURE 5.6 Elijah's Day congregation next to the mosque, at the spring of Sopot in Kula

The performative structure of these 'Georgics' attempts to reflect the temporal rhythm and excitement of the warm season in the Field. Sometimes, images are repeated to accentuate the commonness of the rituals. At other times, different elucidations of the same ritual are juxtaposed to show the internal variations and inconsistencies. The strangeness of the 'constructed' dialogues between those who could easily have had such conversations before the 1990s is an argument of its own: the Field exists in modes away from the nationalist chronotope. It is sung in the unison of desire even after its ruination. Even in each other's absence, there is a remarkable conversation with In-Other, occurring across the so-called 'ethno-religious' boundaries. When *Gačani* begin to speak about the calendar, they inevitably reference the proximities with the Other and the recent historical changes sculpting their distances.

Jasike, the aspen-sheltered part of the Field, was the old locus of the festivity, destroyed by the introduction of the thermal power plant. In Slavic traditions, as Agapkina (1996) pointed out, the aspen was related to certain magic rituals. Enveloping something, like a cradle, with aspen was an apotropaic method (ibid). As Jasike were located towards the middle of the Field, it is possible to suppose that it may originally have been a sacral focal point of the Slavic God Perun's feast and that it later constituted a 'shared' place for both Christians and Muslims.

We have seen that yew (*tisovina*) has an apotropaic meaning for the Muslims and the Christians alike. It was not present only in narratives, but sold in abundance at makeshift stalls during the festivities. I saw one such stall on the road outside St Elijah's Church in the Field and many others along the Maiden's Cave and Ajvatovica pilgrimage paths. At Ajvatovica, one seller had a laminated piece of paper explaining the rather similar powers of the yew:

YEW
- makes happy
- protects from various trouble,
- black magic,
- evil eye (*urok*),
- magic curse (*sihir*)
- it is even used an amulet

Lilek (1894: 369) noted that in Gacko, particularly in the villages, people believed that the yew has more power than any other wood. They used to place it around the neck of rams and bulls and stitched it into the garments of children. Yews, these 'natural temples', these 'living things', as Wordsworth described them (in Curtis 2012: 49–50), often grow for thousands of years (Bevan-Jones 2017). Their perdurance is symbolically attached to the body and the Field's tradition in search of survival.

We have seen that George is not the central character on his day. The figure of the Maiden, which has been downplayed in the expositions and depictions of the Georgic myth, is here revealed as central to the rituals within and beyond the Field. The connections made between Proto-Slavic religiosity and the folk calendar in Gacko are not a claim of stable continuity, but rather of an important instance of diachronic syncretism. The image of the sacred sinking river from the Prelude to Part II of this book is not just my metaphor. It is a symbol strongly related to the content of my discussion. Elijah, as the heir to Perun and other beings in charge of thunder and lightning, is revered and feared in the Dinarides for a very real reason, one that 'science' has apparently come to some kinds of terms with. As Lučić (2012a: 18) noted, a 1958 study of atmospheric discharge over the course of the sinking river revealed double the number of strikes compared to other spaces. Oaks, Elijah's trees, also tend to attract more lightning that other flora. All of this has already been deeply embedded into the Georgic cosmology. Turns of the seasons, movements in the landscape and all other spatial and temporal knowledge – the wealth of being in the world – are inseparable from the body; this made so violent their unravelling.

My arguments and extensions are not given as definite interpretations, but possible journeys into the questions of Georgic encounters. Although substantially speaking to the lives of isolated individuals and fragments of traditions, they still reveal remarkable similarities, connections and continuities. The voices that constitute this chapter are singing an ever more intricate poetry of the land and time of Elijah in the *vakat* (epoch) when his entitlement to the Field is being systematically unimagined.

Notes

1. On Saint Gregory (Grgur) in the charters of mediaeval Bosnia, see Soloviev (1949) and Fine (2007: 149).
2. This is my translation of '*Bog bi dao, te se Bošnjaci u svem tako složili, kako su složni u štovanju "otaca" Jurja i Ilije!*' (Knežević 1871: 347)
3. This song was recited by Neda Rušinović (Vulas) to Ivana Meštrović in 2008 (cited in Dragić 2013: 294).
4. The testament gives a list of 'big feasts' (*velike blage dni*) when charity should be handed out to the poor: 'Holy Sunday, St Petka (or Holy Friday), Christmas, Annunciation, Easter, St George, Ascension, St Peter, St Paul, St Stephen the Protomartyr, Archangel Michael, St Virgin Mary and on the All Saints Day' (Truhelka 1911: 369). Interestingly, Elijah's Day is missing from this list.
5. Jewish Sephardic and Ashkenazi populations have been almost completely cleansed from Bosnian landscapes. About one thousand Jewish people still live in Bosnia today, mostly in Sarajevo. Only a small part of my ethnographic research related to the Sarajevo area, so I am not in a position to make assumptions about their possible participation in or exclusion from Georgic festivities.

6. *Dova* is a Bosnian Muslim word for prayer and it comes from the Arabic word *dua*, meaning 'prayer' or 'supplication'. Accordingly, the Maiden's Cave and many other places are referred to as *dovište*, which literally means 'place where *dova* is made'. For more on the Maiden's Cave, see HadžiMuhamedović (2012) and Mulaomerović (1997).
7. Zephyrus, the equine Greek god of the west wind and father of immortal horses is another possible relative.
8. This is in the song 'Đerzelez Alija i Vuk Jajčanin' (see Buturović 1995: 110–20).
9. See 'Gacko – Povratak iz zaborava grofa Save', retrieved 2 January 2011 from lat.rtrs.tv/vijesti/vijest.php?id=9228.
10. Construction of the agentive noun from the verb would be similar to *sušiti–sušilo* (to dry-dryer), *cijediti–cjedilo* (to strain-strainer), *guditi-gudalo/ilo* (to bow a string instrument-bow), etc.
11. '*Kud koza hodi, tam žito da rodi*', and others.
12. '*Kuda Jura odi, tud vam polje rodi*', and others.
13. See in Vasiljev (1996: 65), Skok (1971: 755), Belaj (2007: 240) and Loma (2001: 238).
14. Descriptions of Dionysus and Dionisian rituals may be found in Frazer (1993: 385–92, 464–69).
15. A *tekke* (Bosnian, *tekija*) is a Sufi monastery.
16. See, for example, Sahibzada (2009) and Newby (2004: 122)
17. 'Hadith' (plural 'ahadith') is basically any passed-on story about the sayings and deeds of Prophet Muhammed. There are various sources, and their credibility is variously judged by different 'authorities'. 'Hadith qudsi' is any hadith considered to be divine knowledge as told by the Prophet, but which does not form part of the Qur'an.
18. Desmond Maurer kindly drew my attention to the Celtic version of this story, whereby the archetypal Georgic hero Finn MacCumhail attains the knowledge of the world after tasting the 'salmon of knowledge' meant for his master.
19. Snakes and dragons are related chthonic symbols, as argued earlier in this chapter.
20. He noted that Khidr is the son of Malkaan [?] who is the son of Ghaabar [?] who is the son of Arfahshad [Arpachsad] who is the son of Sam [Shem] who is the son of Nuh [Noah]. Another name he used for Khidr was Khaleeaa (Al-Majlisi 2002: 499, 508).
21. Al-Majlisi (2002: 508–9) also narrated an episode when Khidr gets married to a virgin girl. He does not wish to consummate his marriage and asks the girl to keep it a secret. When questioned, she replies that Khidr is a woman. He is locked into a room, but escapes from it by shapeshifting and joins the army of Dhu'l Qarnayn (Alexander the Great).
22. Al-Khader is the Palestinian variant of Khidr's name.
23. This mosque is also known as the Friday or al-'Umari mosque.
24. Smith (1901) also noted that Dagon may be related to Dajjal, the antichrist who, according to Muslim eschatology, will be slain by Jesus in al-Ludd. I discuss the narratives on Dajjal later in this chapter. The Canaanite deity El (as the 'God Most High') is etymologically related to the names of Elijah (see Qleibo 2011: 7).
25. Most of these ahadith may be found in the two widely recognized compilations from the ninth century, Muslim ibn al-Hajjaj's *Sahih Muslim* (2014) and Muhammad al-Bukhari's *Sahih al-Bukhari* (2014). For purposes of clarity, they will henceforth be

referenced only as Sahih Muslim and Sahih al-Bukhari with the appropriate book and hadith numbering.
26. Hadith on Dajjal's appearance in the Last Hour (Sahih Muslim 54: 51, 54: 120); Hadith on Dajjal being slain by Jesus at the gate of al-Ludd (Sahih Muslim 54: 136)
27. Smith (1901: 164) noted that the name Dajjal, as well as some local toponyms near al-Ludd, might have their origins in Dagon, the Mesopotamian deity of fertility.
28. See Walker and Uysal (1973: 288), Sands (2006: 82) and Al-Majlisi (2002: 512).
29. For a discussion of Alija Đerzelez as a Georgic character, see Chapters 3 and 4.
30. A smaller version of St George's chains is also to be found in Lydda, albeit protected by a glass casing and the stern gaze of the resident nun.
31. See Gimbutas (2005a: 7052), Ivakhiv (2009: 558) and Belaj (1989: 65).
32. See 1 Kings 18: 21–27 and al-Majlisi (2002: 567).

CONCLUSION

WAITING FOR ELIJAH

> The deeper experience of waiting is not in its quantity, not in how long I have to wait, but in the fact – the existential fact – that I am enduring.
> —H. Schweizer, *On Waiting*

Through the close consideration of one Bosnian landscape, the Field of Gacko, this book has discussed the relationship between encounter and time. Broadly understood, encounters include exchanges, alliances and intimate proximities between the bodies of 'different' characters, their communities and bodies of religious thought and practice. I have looked into encounters between 'humans' and 'nonhumans', as well as between 'different' kinds of nonhumans. All of these encounters, I have argued, were deeply implicated in the Field's times and temporalities and the definition of cosmological and political approaches, economies, social structures, fears, hopes and affinities. After the Field experienced forceful social change through the 1990s war, the past became synonymous with the landscape of a specific time-reckoning. There thus occurred another kind of encounter, between space and time of a specific quality (a chronotope). Lastly, there were encounters between two dominant chronotopes, indicating an active conversation (sometimes through silence) about the future. I put into conversation the isolated voices of the Field and particularly their struggle against segregating essentialisms.

Despite arguing for an abundance of encounters of the Field, this book has refused to resolve the existing conceptual confusion between religious 'syncretism', 'hybridity', 'sharing' and 'mixture'. These designations have been taken as problematic, on the one hand, that is as a (by-)product of ethno-national and anti-syncretic boundary making. On the other hand, encounter as a human condition indicates that there are always circumstances of social differentiation and that any outcome of conversation, including the situated Self, is inherently syncretic. In the first part of the book, I provided a general idea of the chronotopic rift (Chapter 1), and then proceeded to explain the temporality of the *homely* and the *unhomely* (Chapter 2) and the filtered images of the Field through the calendric ritualization of face-to-face encounters with intimate Others (Chapter 3). I have argued that the intentional structures of the Field's rituals become more apparent through the reorientation that follows moments of disorientation. Formed into powerful filtered images, home has been retained as didactic narrative. I have demonstrated how syncretic conversations may be nonconscious (Chapter 4); the anti-syncretic nationalist discourse has been a powerful locus of hybridity, unwittingly and affectively inclusive of the religiously plural landscape, in spite of its exclusive claims. The second part of the book presents only a snippet of the temporally and spatially immense terrains of encounter that result in the syncretism of the Field. That is to say, if we take syncretism seriously, there is no end in sight; new interactions and connections constantly emerge. Most readers of Chapter 5 will be able to argue for possible further extensions.

I have provided evidence of the ways in which ethno-nationalism in Gacko confronted religious fluidity and mixture. My focus was, however, primarily on the specific orientation that delegitimized nationalism through memories of the shared Field. These memories were chiefly founded in the shared sacral annual cycle and its main protagonist, Elijah. His two names – Ilija and Alija – defined the social and cosmic meanings of the Field. The traditional waiting for his harvest festival took on an additional meaning in the postwar context: the possibility of social reconstruction. He became a sign of one temporality in desire of another, of a waiting to wait. Waiting for Elijah was also a practice of extending or maintaining Elijah and ensuring that his place in the Field is reserved until such time as it can again be occupied by the society he has been taken to represent.

Two Turns for the Anthropology of Bosnian Landscapes

The arguments presented in this book have wider implications for the study of Bosnian landscapes, particularly enquiries that deal with the qualification of communal (religious, ethnic or otherwise conceived) relationships. In that sense, I have argued for two anthropological 'turns', toward affect and proximity. In combination, they have the potential to bridge some of the perilous fissures opened up by ethno-nationalist articulations.

As mentioned in the introduction, Joost Fontein's (2011) article 'Graves, Ruins, and Belonging: Towards an Anthropology of Proximity' proved enlightening for my own methodological direction. Whilst the methods for such an anthropology still need refinement, I found numerous ways of understanding the Field's orientation towards trajectories, overlapping and shared practices, intimacies and encounters. In landscapes where discourses of division have powerful stakeholders, a proximity turn complicates the fields of political imagination simply by finding out their inevitable inconsistencies. I see it not as a partial view, but one reaching across identity politics. As Fontein (ibid: 721) noted, an 'analytic of proximity does not eschew difference or change in favour of similarity or continuity; rather it seeks to provide a framework for understanding both at the same time'. The Field of Gacko has been an arena for overt violence, and so the strong 'chronotopic' contrasts that I encountered there are not necessarily applicable to other, more politically plural contexts.

My second, affective, turn posits that the Field's body/landscape also has a nonintentional capacity to communicate its orientations. Following Navaro-Yashin (2009, 2012), I have looked at the affectivity of remnants and ruins in order to understand home and belonging in their different modes of being. One such analytical source was the language of my interlocutors, informative through its affective perpetuation of meanings, attachments to time and space, and even its 'thick' silences. I found that the reluctance to 'give language' to certain social processes was a political position of the body. Silence was but one of the 'colours' of language; invigorated moments of social communication filtered from the landscape of the past were yet another. The traditional life of the Field was condensed within proverbs and sayings, which appear throughout the book as an indication of the learned modes of landscape-reckoning.

Understanding the formative modes of intimacy and otherness has been a pre-requisite for any discussion of shared and syncretic religion in the Field. I have shown how various kinds of habituated encounters maintained one landscape by lingering after the destruction that occurred in the 1990s. Although meetings and visits between (ethno-religious) communities have been discussed as part of these encounters, they are also portrayed within the layered cosmological framework of the Field. These were not simply encounters that might be of interest to an anthropology of political history; they are pertinent to the studies of Proto-Slavic and Proto-Indo-European religiosity and syncretism, as well to the phenomenological approaches to landscapes.

Forced into the unhomely, the Field dwelt on home. It turned towards typical images of the social, encounters during summer feasts between members of the 'different' communities and with 'super-natural' beings. Home started to crystallize and gain stronger discursive outlines. It was voiced in distinction to the present. The focus on the shared Field and its remnants was a resistance to the dominant ethno-national logics. As a dwelling that continued to dwell in its own absence, the Field offered a comprehensive discussion of its time, place and space. A different methodological approach might have obscured the phenomenon of 'sharing', locked it into the 'past' of the landscape. I argue that, precisely by turning towards its past, the Field spoke to its futurities.

Looking into the cosmology and social structures encapsulated by the Field's summer, I discovered 'encounter' as one its main stipulations: Ilija and Alija, the two faces of Elijah met in the sun of noontime; the world and the underworld met in the enigmatic figure of the Maiden; George and Elijah met in the equally enigmatic, far-reaching figure of Khidr; and Georgic heroes traversed the world to embrace each other. The ritual meaning of the institution of sworn kinship (*kumstvo*) served as a catalyst for encounters between members of 'different' religious communities. Sworn kinship was also a meeting with other beings in the Field – saints, animals and fairies. Finally, the bodies of Ilija and Alija met in a mass grave. Their histories were bound to each other every step of the way. As Ljubica said about the Elijan voices: 'When a group of lads sings together for a while, somehow or other they harmonize'. This intriguing 'somehow or other' capacity of proximity to fashion shared worlds of meaning has been the connecting thread of the previous chapters.

The 'In-Other' was used as an orientational and disorientational device. A sudden change in the landscape engaged the bodies; the meeting was new, but it was also cyclically new – these relationships were habitual (see Chapter 3). They structured the time of the place. George's Day was not only an encounter between winter and the warm season, but also between the settled community and the Gurbeti. The Gurbeti signalled the beginning of spring and a celebration after which work would commence. Sworn kinship was maintained as part of the festivities and other important occasions, but it also had an important function in the economic and social life of the Field. The postwar absences that were at first disorientational have produced an even stronger orientation towards encounters and revealed some of the 'original' intentional structures.

My arguments about intimacy and otherness will have to be taken with a degree of caution by researchers looking into other Bosnian locales. Firstly, there are significant particularities of the Field's geographic and sociopolitical circumstances. Unlike many other parts of Bosnia, the Field's economy was shaped much more by pastoral farming than by tillage, which was reflected in its cosmological inflections. For example, in spite of the rich George's Day traditions, the rituals do not seem to have taken the form of large communal festivals for the 'settled folk', except when they joined in the *teferič* fairs of their nomadic Gurbeti neighbours. There are also differences to be found in the particularities of the urban/rural configuration and the spatial relations of households. The calendar had been traditionally preserved in the villages and hamlets. The severity of the winter snows, the karst topography, the introduction of the thermal plant in the 1970s and the political hegemony in the town since the 1990s have shaped physical and symbolic distances between the Field's households and the 'religious' communities.

The expulsions of the 1990s were followed by the small-scale Muslim return and an absence of Gurbeti. In more urbanized spaces, like the towns of Visoko and Zenica, Elijah's and George's Day have taken on the form of a more active postwar 'mixture'. However, during Elijah's festivities, the hamlets in the Field gravitated towards larger villages with a church or a mosque, so that the 'inter-religious' mixture was limited to 'visitations'. The old location of the festivities in Jasike indicates the possibility that Elijah's Day was at one time an actively 'shared' and 'mixed' event and on George's Day itself, active 'mixing' with the Gurbeti was facilitated by the proximity of their seasonal settlements.

Many other aspects of these encounters are considered in the discussion of home, including 'lucid dreams' about past meetings, recollected encounters in exile, encounters with ruins of home and through the hybridity of the Gacko epics. I have argued that they furnish time with its qualitative content, but also with its structure – that they are a way of *telling* time. However fragmentary, these encounters have been employed to write a kind of genealogy of the Field as home.

The focus on encounters, in their material, historical and affective dimensions, reveals the analytical potential in the methodology of proximity. This book rests on the relationship between the 'morning Ilija' and the 'afternoon Alija', considered as a point of encounter rather than a point of divergence into 'ethno-religio-national' polarities. A different methodological model might have obscured the breadth of proximities and their importance to religiosity of the Field.

In terms of the syncretic layering of Bosnian religion, contributions from various directions have been traced. Calendric religiosity was inclusive of Illyrian, old Slavic, Christian, Gurbeti, Muslim and communist elements. Because of their shifting spatial and cultural trajectories, the contribution of the nomadic Gurbeti to this complex religious system in the Field is probably far greater than anything this study has been able to ascertain. This difficulty arises not simply out of their postwar absence, but also out of the lack of historical data on the influence of the various 'Roma' communities on Balkan religions. The richness of their cosmologies certainly deserves much more anthropological attention. A further investment in analogies drawn between language and ethnography would be useful in that sense.

The powers of old Slavic deities have been dispersed across a collection of Christian saints and into Muslim and Gurbeti cosmologies. The problem of defining Bosnian syncretism is multifaceted; there is a clear danger of taking ethnicity as the starting point for a discussion of converging practices and beliefs. I have partly used the vocabulary of ethnicity, but only because of the common self-referential names for the communities in the Field. Syncretic practices were the product of 'diachronic' layering as much as of 'synchronic' proximities. The boundaries of religious differentiation were increasingly introduced into the Field by the nationalizing processes of the nineteenth century and after. There might come a time when my discussion of 'Serbs', 'Muslims' and 'Gurbeti' appears anachronous, in some ways similar to what I felt when reading Crapanzano's (1985) discussion of 'whites' and 'blacks' in the contexts of South African apartheid. Reading contemporary Bosnian 'ethnonyms' this way is problematic, I have argued as whilst accommodating the inevitable political discourses, they often signify the local community with some distinction. Although the conflation of 'Orthodox Christian' with 'Serb' developed earlier on, the current tendencies are to reshape communities such as Muslims into 'Bosniaks' (rather than the historically synonymous 'Bosnians') and Gurbeti into 'Roma'. These politics of identity seldom imply that the words and practices related to living identities are lost. Most often, they are interchangeably employed, depending on the audience, but the habits remain resilient to change.

This book would have benefited from further ventures 'across the borders'. I have navigated the topic over boundaries of various kinds, including the political separations within the Field, Bosnia and the region. I have also conducted 'cross-temporal' comparisons and included stints of fieldwork in Palestine/Israel. My incomplete ventures have demonstrated the problematic of the nation-states' claims to Georgic traditions. There are some further logical spaces for such exploration, particularly the pastoral sacral traditions along the Dinaric chain, which stretches from Albania in the south, through Kosovo, Serbia, Montenegro and into Bosnia and Croatia. As these traditions are actively negotiated, I expect that future research will encounter significant changes in the Field as well. With some regret I decided to abandon, temporarily at least, a number of related phenomena witnessed during my fieldwork outside of Gacko. This has resulted in the absence or mere marginal inclusion of various season-specific rituals and pilgrimage sites that I was fortunate enough to observe, such as prayers on Mount Ratiš, at Ajvatovica and in the *Djevojačka Pećina* (Maiden's Cave), the Peter's Day rituals in Mokro, the John's Day rituals in Kreševo, the Elijah's Day and the George's Day festivities in Stolac, Zenica and Visoko, and so on.

Throughout this work, I have attempted to destabilize it at the same time by leaving arguments open-ended and juxtaposing them to other, different perspectives. Perhaps most obviously, Chapter 5 takes the form of an unfinished reading and many of its parts will be burdened by a lack of conclusion. This decision relates to the already discussed problem of extensions, the choice of spaces and data through which analysis is supposed to ensue.

Those etymological discussions, which may strike the linguist as a result of their undeveloped simplicity, may prove a difficult read for others. What is an anthropologist to do with toponyms? Is not the assumption of their connection to the 'contemporary' Field a wide stretch? Explanations of these choices are to be found in the words of my interlocutors and my attention to the so-called ethnographic analogies. They show how place names are constructed according to and often indivisible from the function and memory of the place. For example, the old locus of Elijah's Day celebrations in the Field was called Jasike (Aspens). In this place, there were many aspen trees providing comfortable shade, but also indicating a connection to Proto-Slavic cosmology. The newer location of the Elijah's Day celebration is the spring of Sopot and the villagers still use it for shade and to quench their thirst during the very hot August celebrations. Etymological reconstruction shows that *sopot* and the root *sop* had a Proto-Slavic meaning of 'water spring' (Skok 1972: 307). Building upon this ability of the Field – to diachronically link loci through words – I made use of etymology in my attempts to understand the traditional calendar. I also employed old maps for the elicitation of detailed memories and discussions about the landscape.

The same question might be asked about my references to epic poetry. What can they tell us of the Field from 2011 and 2012, or should they be seen as my own imagined connections? My interlocutors often pronounced their existing knowledge of the same songs, which are to be found in the anthologies of Balkan epics. The Field was indeed famous as a particularly rich space for research into the epic (see e.g. Lord 1991, 2000; Parry 1971 and Vidan 2003a). By employing epics as a reference, I am not relying on something 'extinct' or discarded, but on a body of knowledge intimately transmitted in the Field, at the time when I conducted my research.

Another problem, already indicated in Chapter 1, is of contrasting stories. The book may give the impression that there are no chronotopes besides the two presented. 'What if there are hundreds of chronotopes?' one of my colleagues has asked. Indeed, there sure are, which is why I have called the ethnoscape and the sacroscape the 'grand' chronotopes, or the 'dominant collective themes': they oriented the Field and became the substance of most of my conversations. The social, political and physical changes shaping the lives of my interlocutors provided for these contrasting spaces.

I have argued toward an anthropology of affect and proximity. These are theoretical concepts. They approach the Field, but are not equal to its lives. My foremost concern was to avoid over-theoreticizing intimacy. While this is an anthropological endeavour, it is also a work bearing the full weight of human lives. Dealing with this responsibility, I have transcribed and translated large portions of my conversations, which in themselves made many connections.

TimeSpace to Remember/Forget

Places reveal their complexity, the messiness of being, longing and belonging when the observer starts to understand their alliances with various times of particular qualities. These alliances become vivid in places which have undergone sudden and profound change. They tell time through an unresolved tension between different pasts, presents and futures. Being in such places, one may acquire the ability to move through different lifescapes in a single landscape and see how these collective notions of living stick to tangible and intangible remains, to memorials and memories, to public and intimate geographies, spatial design, ruins, conversations, absences and desires...

These alliances between time and place, inaugurated by humans and nonhumans alike, I have called 'chronotopes', employing Bakhtin's term (see Chapter 1). They speak to the continuities and ruptures of a Bosnian landscape – the Field of Gacko – on historical and intimate planes. They are populated with actors, times and places committed to markedly different tasks. These chronotopes offered a reading of what occurred in the past, but also of what the landscape should be in the future. The 'friction' (see Tsing 2004) between the alliances in the Field was dialectical. It was a discussion of the 'truth' of the place towards an imagined solution. At the same time, it pointed towards the problem of defining the truth of the place. Those people who desired the old chronotope also (willy-nilly) participated in the making of the new one.

So, the Field of Gacko, like its humans, cannot be depicted either as solely the ground for nationalist endeavours and anti-syncretism or as a space of inter-religious conversation and syncretism. Instead, the Field exhibited two grand discourses and timespace relationships at once, in a state of what I have termed 'schizochronotopia' – a split occurring within the same body/landscape. The problem lies in the fact that the two chronotopes have led paradoxical lives; they were fashioned against each other, yet they have striven to forget each other. Forgetfulness had been possible, but only temporarily. There was always a slip, a fracture, a moment that led into face-to-face encounter with the other chronotope.

Paul Connerton argued against the notion of forgetting as a unitary phenomenon, outlining several possible 'types' (2008). This book discusses only those types of forgetting that are a qualification of certain types of memory. Such forgetting is never 'accidental'. As Mary Douglas (1995: 13) noted: 'Forgetting includes different kinds of selective remembering, misremembering and disremembering and it is quite different from ignorance'. Schizochronotopia, however, reveals their messiness and interconnectedness. It speaks not only to the varieties of memory and forgetting, but also to what happens when one person or landscape enacts disparate forms of remembrance and forgetting. Forgetting was the substitution of one memory by another, where the outlines of what we might call a 'political strategy' seem rather clear. But, forgetting is also the absence of spoken or enacted memory, which may be read at once as an inability and a strategy of the body.

To understand the Field's types of forgetting, I have pointed towards their coupling with certain types of remembering. The first couple was most strongly embodied in the new design of the small town of Gacko and its official internet presentation (see Introduction), which omitted all traces of the shared Field and filled the empty lines with 'history', memorials and spray-painted slogans. Signs of these alliances were, most often, textual; they offered a reading of themselves. Graffiti declared that Mladić, Mihailović and Šešelj are heroes, not war criminals or that Kosovo is the soul of every Serb man. The Field's dead were slowly turned into martyrs. The 'shared' mass grave in Korita was turned into a sign of Serb victimhood, while a large memorial to Bosniak martyrs of the war was erected in the village of Kula (see Chapter 1).

Even though more overtly violent, Gacko's nationalism was not significantly different from any other nationalism. As an exclusionary political programme, it defined itself against fluidity and mixture (of religion, language, space and so on). It worked to forget shared lives, instituted new toponyms and held a tight grip over public events. Its forgetting was part of a new regime of memory. The nationalists worked to memorialize Gacko as a place that belongs to a pure state of affairs, but, to do so, they had to resort to the 'shared' traditions.

Even more recent to the Field, however, was a renewed discourse of 'sharing' and 'coexistence'. I say 'renewed discourse' because not only did 'sharing' exist before the nationalist projects of the 1990s, but it also already had certain discursive outlines, as the First and the Second World War had both created distances between the 'religious communities'.[1] This research was concluded at times when distances and proximities were being actively remembered and rethought by my interlocutors. 'Sharing' had become the primary memory of the prewar Field and it corresponded to a general 'lack of words' about the period of war and the constitution of the 'new' Gacko. The abundant memories of a shared, peaceful and pastoral landscape postponed dealing with political and social changes. The fixation of memory on the ideal rhythm of the seasons and their ritual festivities relegated the nationalist processes to a domain outside of home.

These 'shared' rituals were the most important temporal markers for the Field. They transferred the traditional logic of landscape regeneration from the seasonal budding of life in the Field to a hope for the regeneration of the postwar Field through the return of the sacral calendar. Beyond reconstruction of a few buildings, waiting for Elijah's return had been a form of investment towards a comprehensive and integrated reconstruction of the community. The Field had been temporally and cognitively divided into two places in order to allow for the possibility of return.

(Power) Plants and Home (Lands)

This book discusses the temporal aspects of 'inter-religious' proximity in one of the most divided landscapes in Bosnia, or perhaps even the world – the Field of Gacko. In outlining the two dominant chronotopes, I have also argued that they have their respective means of perpetuation. Although qualitatively very different, they can be understood as political endeavours; they cared to guide the Field into specific socio-political directions and indicated its possible futurities. A survey of the political currents in the Field might be summarized through two opposing alliances of, firstly, plants and home and, secondly, power plants and homelands. In explicating these oppositions, I wanted to draw attention to the potentialities of the Field and a political battle hardly noticeable to most spectators. These metaphoric and real distinctions reveal the 'internal' confrontations of the chronotopic, bi-directional Field. They are exclusive of each other, not in a single body/landscape, but in a body/landscape interchangeably situated in different times. The reasons for these connections should be clear enough by now. If not, I offer a reminder.

Plants and Home

The Field as home was condensed into its warm seasons (from George's to Demetrius' Day). Such home was cognitively mapped through the variety of flowers, herbs, trees and shrubs, in their succession. The colours and scents all had the affective possibility to awake the multiple dimensions of social life before the war. Their functions were interlaced with symbolic meanings. The knowledge of the plants belonged to the related domains of medicine, fertility, survival, sexuality, beauty, economy and cosmology. Plants encapsulated the sacroscape, the pastoral landscape of seasonal order and its religiosity. Because of the general presence of plants in my interlocutors' narratives about the desired past times and their cyclical making of place, I employ them here as a metaphor for the diverse intimate portraits of the prewar chronotope.

In teaching her grandson Edo the usefulness and meanings of plants, Zahida was projecting a chronotopic image to her posterity (see Chapter 2). She was successful in her temporal transfer – I learned from Edo even more than I did from his grandmother. However, if her project was to work, she

FIGURE 6.1 Extent of damage caused by the thermal power plant and the mines in the Field, CNES/Airbus, Map data © 2017 Google

FIGURE 6.2 The Field in summer

explained, the Field needed more people of Edo's age. For her, this generation would be a classroom and her vivid lectures on myths would also be life lessons; the functional and the sacral aspects of the Field that she perpetuated were inseparable.

Zahida once told me about a hill near to her house in the village of Hodinići that was haunted by *utvare* (apparitions). On this hill, there was said to be a *gradina,* an Illyrian hillfort. People were reluctant to go there and refused to cut its trees. Bećir, Zahida's husband, supplied a further explanation: the wooded hill was preserved for women and children to hide in during wars. The two reasonings, much like the relationship of lightning and Elijah, were part of the same knowledge of living in the Field. Zahida and Bećir, in their conversation about the nearby hill, also preserved the Field's history. Recent research has revealed that *gradine* were constructed on regional hilltops during the last two millennia BC as, amongst other functions, *refugia* (places of refuge, hideaways) and ritual foci (see Forenbaher and Rajić Šikanjić 2006: 467). The fascinating potential of sacral knowledge about the Field thus deserves much more attention; the seemingly simple stipulation 'not to cut the trees' was layered with meanings that are not only of the past. The myths were didactic; they provided a comprehensive knowledge of how to dwell in the Field.

Being at home implied a knowledge of the plants. On a visit to his late grandmother's house, Elvedin found her flowers still growing in the rubbles (see Chapter 2). He recognized each of them, telling me that his home could not be contracted into words. I have written about it through the theory of affect, attempting to convey my sensing of the uncanny encounter, but I am sure that I have not succeeded in the task. There can only ever be partial translations of its meaning. And that not-fully-translatable meaning of home is between the personal and the communal, between anchors and loss; its trajectories, however strongly fixed to specific images, are immense.

If home is not compatible with any synthetic account, it is obvious that a historiography of home must be impossible. Anthropological endeavours like this one, whilst themselves unable to *convey* home, point to the problem of writing a social and political history of the Field without a *sense* of home. Plants, like encounters, thus work on different levels to indicate the complexity of place and time, without imprisoning them into documentary narration about the past.

Home in the Field was not simply a place to return to. It was designated by time-specific qualities. Returning home meant, in a more-than-metaphoric sense, the possibility of Elijah's return and the continuation of an active economic, religious and social symbiosis with the landscape. Plants structured the time-specific relationships in the Field, which is evident throughout the discussion of George's Day (see Chapter 5). From the pre-bridal nettles to *izijes*, the post-bridal 'oak dust' and the child-anticipating willow, plants attuned the time of the body and the community to the time of the Field and the Cosmos. Hundreds of other examples have been given throughout this book. They can be springboards for future researchers of Bosnian and wider religiosities. Due to my focus on time and temporality I am certain that I have not given the interpretation of plant usage sufficient attention. I hope, however, that I have provided a glimpse into the fact that the knowledge of plants, their times, functions and symbolic meanings, was synonymous with knowledge of the community abiding by the traditional calendar, one shared by In-Other, the neighbours, sworn kin, fairies, wolves, epic heroes, ghosts, lightning...

Power Plants and Homelands

I have mentioned the political entity called 'Republika Srpska', usually translated as 'Republic of Srpska', although it means 'Serb Republic'. Like its twin, the Federation of Bosnia and Herzegovina, it was forged through the 1990s war and instituted through the Dayton Accords in 1995. The whole of the Field is currently part of the 'Serb Republic' and the political structures that govern this entity also govern the Municipality of Gacko and its gigantic corporation, The Gacko Mine and the Thermal Power Plant (RiTE Gacko). The plant has been a violent intervention in the sacroscape from its inception in the 1970s, displacing the 'original' location of Muslim Elijah's Day gatherings and fashioning a physical obstacle between 'Muslim' and 'Serb' villages. Humans and nonhumans, especially in the pastoral Georgic Field, are inseparable and any damage to nonhumans was always reflected in the lives of my interlocutors. Within and beyond the Field, the mine and the plant continue to be calamitous polluters of the endemic flora and fauna and the unique and sacred water system, as well as of the wealth of cultural and human remains.

In spite of this, the Power Utility of the Republic of Srpska plans to add a second block to the thermal plant. The corporation is owned by members of the nationalist parties and employs people on the basis of their ethnic and political affiliation. Not surprisingly, the same corporation is thus oblivious to anything but the nationally homogenized town of Gacko:

> In the area of Gacko Field, the town of Gacko is *the only inhabited place,* with around 10,000 residents, and since there are no industrial facilities except for the Gacko Mine and Power Plant, there is *an imposed logic of essential need* for further research and investment into the development of this mining basin. On the basis of confirmed reserves of lignite, further construction of thermal energy blocks has been planned in Gacko. This primarily refers to the 'Gacko II' Mine and Thermal Power Plant (RiTE),

which would round up the energetic potential of the basin to 2 x 300 MW. As regards the planned construction of the 'Gacko II' thermal power plant, extensive research has been conducted and a comprehensive study made and revised as to the choice for the location of the second phase of the Gacko mine, as well as the technical project for the 'Gacko II' thermal power plant. (ERS 2009, emphasis mine).

These plans are an imminent threat to the lives of all of my interlocutors. Any changes that they make to the Field will be the implicit outcome of crimes committed during the 1990s. When the first power plant was built in the 1970s, the landowners were silenced by the provision of some monetary compensation. Many of the people in the Field have sworn 'never to sell off any of their land', but the situation in the town spoke against this claim. Not a single 'non-Serb', according to my knowledge, owned a flat, house or business in the town. There were only the partially reconstructed mosque and the adjacent offices of the Islamic Community. The returnees no doubt had a dedication to the Field that differed from that of the diaspora, but many of them were already elderly when I conducted my research and their property will be inherited by descendants who are used to living elsewhere. A large part of the land in the Field is owned by the 'state', which makes its future use even less secure.

Muslims are not the only religious community dispossessed by the plans for the new power plant. The rural Serb communities, which were likewise oriented towards the Georgic chronotope, are also being erased by these projects. The small town of Gacko has accumulated all the representational, national power and the villages have become both discursively and physically peripheral to it. When Milorad Dodik, the president of the Republic of Srpska, visited the power plant in 2014,

> [h]e spoke to Milan Radmilović, the mayor of Gacko Municipality, who, along with the management of the 'Mines and Thermal Power Plant', escorted him, as he visited the Church of the Holy Trinity currently under construction in Gacko, for whose completion he promised financial assets of 100,000 KM, to be paid by his cabinet by September. (RiTE Gacko 2014)

The connection between the power plant and the new church, made a few months before general elections in Bosnia, was a symbolic promise of a 'homeland-in-becoming'. It propagated the image of a landscape that was thriving, not struggling to survive. Like legitimation through bodily remains and other symbolic geographies, the new church designated the political opposition as blasphemous. The politician in question won another term. In 2015, the media reported that the Power Utility of Republic of Srpska was still planning to build the new block, that negotiations were taking place with Dongfeng Electric, a Chinese investor, and that the project of extension 'had been incorporated into the strategic documents of the Republic of

Srpska' (Salapura 2015). These agreements, which would make the Field but a tiny spot in the wider course of global 'dependent development', need to be confronted through a critique of the acute dispossession of land and energy resources, as well as the systematic destruction of habitat and cultural heritage in the Field.

The promise of a 'homeland' in the Field stands in stark contrast to the possibility of retaining 'home' and 'land'. As indicated throughout this book, such political programmes count on local religiosity only by imagining its 'purity', all the while constructing new histories, sacred places and traditions along the way. The Field, however, has found ways to survive around the first power plant and even to construct stronger discourses of shared life (see Chapter 1). Power is anything but clear.

George Killing the Dragon?

> Where there is dirt, there is a system.
> —M. Douglas, *Purity and Danger*

> Where there is power, there is resistance...
> —M. Foucault, *The History of Sexuality*

At the very end, I want to suggest that the Field's orientation toward encounters experienced and structured through the shared calendar may also speak to a wider Georgic potential of resistance. George and Elijah, the two chief Bosnian syncretic characters, belong to many other landscapes of shared religious systems; some of their temporal and geographic coordinates have been indicated in Chapter 5. Like in the Field, they may also increasingly be followed through overtly violent anti-syncretic interventions. As part of the widespread cleansing of syncretic and 'impure' sites, the so-called 'Islamic State' (or 'ISIS', 'IS' and so on) has destroyed many shrines, mosques, monasteries and churches dedicated to George, Khidr and Elijah, which were considered sacred by the various Muslim, Christian, Yezidi (and so on) communities in Iraq, Syria and elsewhere.[2] Propaganda released by the militants and reported by the media (see, for example, Freeman 2015) shows the obliteration of George's images. These were not simply attacks on an Other, but on the fluid boundaries between Self and Other, attacks on In-Other.

The act of destruction (or 'cleansing') itself recognizes that human geographies are concentrated around particular symbols; it accentuates their meanings. The political potential of George and Elijah was thus already located through their exclusion; the opening quotations from Douglas and Foucault are illuminating for this discussion. The construction of impurity is the construction of systemic boundaries and power. Resistance, however, is inherent to power and, as the remainder of Foucault's sentence goes, it is 'never in a position of exteriority in relation to power' (1990: 95). The designated areas of interference to power are often (or always?) the ones through which resisting claims are formed. The makings of boundaries and purities are subverted through 'transgressive' and 'mixed' positions. Of course, when such subversions gain power, they may set up new purities to be answered by new kinds of resistance, but that is not the matter discussed in this book. Hegemony in the Field, as in Syria, lay with the (aspirant) states, not the traditional calendar.

The battle between the shared George and the politics of anti-syncretism has been occurring on another 'front'. As part of the Saint George Art Competition in 2007, children in Palestine illustrated one recurring situation: with his spear, George pierced a dragon whose tail extended into the concrete slabs of the Israeli separation wall covered with barbed wire.[3] I want to make only a partial analogy between the discursive spaces inhabited by George in Palestine and the orientation of the 'shared' festivities in Gacko. George and Elijah, heralding a chronotopic image of the Field, have been positioned as antithetical to the political outcomes of the 1990s war and particularly the distances between the 'religious' communities. Not fully achievable in the ethnoscape, they have harboured a potential of direct political resistance.

Although revolt against the structural espousal of nationalism and production of inequalities has proved infeasible, the Field had a repertoire of creative subversive modes. The cosmologic of waiting and encounter has been 'updated', furnished with an ability to respond to new political pressures. Through the focus on the eternal, cyclical return of nature, *Gačani* have oriented their landscape toward social restoration as well. As Mircea Eliade noted:

> What is important is that man has felt the need to reproduce the cosmogony in his constructions, whatever be their nature; that this reproduction made him contemporary with the mythical moment of the beginning of the world and that he felt the need of returning to that moment, as often as possible, in order to regenerate himself. (1959: 76–77)

Although propelled primarily by women (rather than Eliade's 'man'), the re-enactment of springtime cosmogony was already constructed as the promise of social regeneration (see Chapter 5). Waiting was also naturalized; the rich yields of summer and the fullness of communal encounter were celebrated as part of the same meaning. 'The method of hope', Miyazaki noted, 'is a performative inheritance of hope' (2004: 128); waiting was the Field's inherited method of hope. Through the consolidation of memory and the corresponding counter-discursive silences, a response has been in the making. The Field has been strengthening its past into a 'golden age' against the darkness of exclusionary politics, sending old epic heroes to battle the martyrs and heroes of the state. It sought to be haunted by familiar ghosts of the Good, and declared that body and landscape cannot be separate. The tongue pursued its grammar of Intimate Others.

As I bring to a close these meandering courses, I think of two lines from Mak Dizdar's poem: 'It is time to think of time ... Lo it is time to think in time'.[4] What could be the difference between the thinking *of* and thinking *in* (time)? To me, it seems like an ontological and political puzzle. Seasonal, landscaped time appears different from nationalist time. They ask to be differently embodied, but sometimes, as in Gacko, have to be negotiated in the same body. The Field points to the chasm: in seeking to live in time, it is made to think of time. Familiarized through the body and alienated through territorial politics, time is made to speak in and of itself, to wait for itself.

The Field has been waiting for its own promise of the past, for George to awaken, with trees full of swings, the falling of Gurbeti, droplets of water on girls' breasts before dawn and the wind, full of inherited future, in the nettle leaves. The Field has been waiting for the making of stories to be told in winter, the summer crops festively shared with 'kin and sworn kin', the sweet offerings to guests, for strangers on crossroads invited inside. The Field has been waiting for its fullness in a transcendent feast, for its august day and the shared intensity of the noon sun. The Field has been waiting. The Field has been waiting for Elijah to come.

Notes

1. Earlier types of distance-production in Bosnian may be attributed to the identity politics of the Austro-Hungarian Empire and religion-based structural differences in the Ottoman Empire.
2. In the continuing rampage of these religious nationalists, it is difficult to ascertain the full scope of destruction. In and around the Iraqi city of Mosul alone, the following 'Georgic' sites have been destroyed, amongst many others: the Prophet Jirjis Mosque and Shrine (see http://www.theguardian.com/world/2014/jul/28/islamic-state-destroys-ancient-mosul-mosque, retrieved 25 July 2015), St George's Monastery (see Mezzofiore 2015), the Shrine of Khidr-al-Elias in Tal Afar (see Human Rights Watch 2014) and Mar Benham (or Tell al-Khidr) Monastery (see Hall 2015).
3. For these and further images, see the Leicestershire Holy Land Appeal (2007).
4. See Dizdar's (1999) poem 'The Fourth Horseman'.

Bibliography

Anonymous. 1875. 'A Ride through Bosnia'. *Fraser's Magazine: July to December 1875, New Series* 12: 549–50.
Acikyildiz, B. 2010. *The Yezidis: The History of a Community, Culture and Religion*. London: I.B. Tauris.
Adorno, T.W. 1981. 'Cultural Criticism and Society', in R. Tiedeman (ed.), *Prisms*. Cambridge, MA: MIT Press, pp. 17–34.
Agapkina, T.A. 1996. 'Symbolism of Trees in Traditional Slavic Culture: Aspen' (article in Russian, abstract in English), *Codes of Slavic Cultures* 1(Plants): 7–22.
———. 2001. 'Đurđevdan', in S.M. Tolstoj and Lj. Radenković (eds), *Enciklopedija: Mitologijski rečnik*. Belgrade: Zepter Book World, pp. 173–75.
Agar, M. 2007. 'Culture Blends', in L. Monaghan and J.E.A. Goodman (eds), *Cultural Approach to Interpersonal Communication: Essential Readings*. Malden, MA: Blackwell, pp. 13–24.
Agency for Statistics in Bosnia and Herzegovina. 2013. 'Preliminary Results of the 2013 Census of Population, Households and Dwellings in Bosnia and Herzegovina'. Retrieved 20 March 2016 from http://www.bhas.ba/obavjestenja/Preliminarni_rezultati_bos.pdf.
———. 2016. 'Census of Population, Households and Dwellings in Bosnia and Herzegovina, 2013. Final Results'. Retrieved 3 August 2017 from http://www.popis.gov.ba/popis2013/doc/RezultatiPopisa_BS.pdf.
Ahmed, S. 2006. *Queer Phenomenology: Orientations, Objects, Others*. London: Duke University Press.
Al-Ali, N. 2002. 'Gender Relations, Transnational Ties and Rituals Among Bosnian Refugees', *Global Networks: A Journal of Transnational Affairs* 2(3): 249–62.
Albera, D. 2008. '"Why Are You Mixing What Cannot Be Mixed?" Shared Devotions in the Monotheisms', *History and Anthropology* 19(1): 37–59.
al-Bukhari, M. 2014. *Sahih al-Bukhari,* trans. M.M. Khan. Retrieved 12 June 2014 from http://sunnah.com/bukhari.
Alexander, T., and E. Papo. 2011. 'On the Power of the Word: Healing Incantations of Bosnian Sephardic Women', *Menorah* 2: 57–117.
al-Hajjaj, M. 2014. *Sahih Muslim,* trans. A.H. Siddiqui. Retrieved 10 September 2014 from http://sunnah.com/muslim.
al-Majlisi, A.M.B. 2002. *Hayatul Qulub. Volume 1: Stories of the Prophets,* trans. S.H. Rizvi. Qom: Ansariyan Publications.
Althusser, L. 1971. *Lenin and Philosophy and Other Essays*. London: Monthly Review Press.

Anderson, B. 1991. *Imagined Communities: Reflections on the Origin and Spread of Nationalism*. Revised Edition. New York: Verso.
Anthon, C. 1884. *A New Classical Dictionary of Greek and Roman Biography, Mythology and Geography*. New York: Harper and Brothers Publishers.
Antze, P., and M. Lambek. 1996. 'Introduction: Forecasting Memory', in P. Antze and M. Lambek (eds), *Tense Past: Cultural Essays in Trauma and Memory*. London: Routledge, pp. xi–xxxviii.
Appadurai, A. 1990. 'Disjuncture and Difference in the Global Cultural Economy Theory', *Culture and Society* 7: 295–310.
———. 1991. *Modernity at Large: Cultural Dimensions of Globalization*. Minneapolis, MN: University of Minnesota Press.
ASA. 2012. *The Ethical Guidelines for Good Research Practice*. Association of Social Anthropologists of the UK and Commonwealth. Retrieved 1 September 2013 from http://www.theasa.org/ethics/guidelines.shtml.
B92. 2015. 'Rehabilitovan Draža Mihailović'. Retrieved 14 May 2015 from http://www.b92.net/info/vesti/index.php?yyyy=2015&mm=05&dd=14&nav_id=991709.
Bajraktarović, M.R. 1961. 'Jedan primjer srodstva po kumu (u gornjem Polimlju)', *Glasnik etnografskog muzeja u Beogradu* 24: 99–100.
Bakhtin, M.M. 1981. *The Dialogic Imagination: Four Essays*. Austin, TX: University of Texas Press.
———. 1986. *Speech Genres and Other Late Essays*. Austin, TX: University of Texas Press.
———. 1999. *Toward a Philosophy of the Act*. Austin, TX: University of Texas Press.
Banac, I. 1984. *The National Question in Yugoslavia: Origins, History, Politics*. Ithaca, NY: Cornell University Press.
Banks, M. 1996. *Ethnicity: Anthropological Constructions*. London: Routledge.
Barkey, K. 2008. *Empire of Difference: The Ottomans in Comparative Perspective*. Cambridge: Cambridge University Press.
Baskar, B. 2012. '*Komšiluk* and Taking Care of the Neighbor's Shrine in Bosnia-Herzegovina', in D. Albera and M. Couroucli (eds), *Sharing Sacred Spaces in the Mediterranean: Christians, Muslims, and Jews at Shrines and Sanctuaries*. Bloomington, IN: Indiana University Press, pp. 51–68.
Basso, K.H. 1970. '"To Give Up on Words": Silence in Western Apache Culture', *Southwestern Journal of Anthropology* 26(3): 213–23.
Bečić, S. 1965. 'Vjerska svečanost u Kuli kod Gacka'. *Glasnik VISA* 11–12: 453–55.
Beckett, S. 2010. *Waiting for Godot*. London: Faber & Faber.
Beckman, G. 1982. 'The Anatolian Myth of Illuyanka', *Journal of Ancient Near Eastern Society of Columbia University* 14: 11–25.
Belaj, M. 2012. *Milijuni na putu: Antropologija hodočašća i sveto tlo Međugorja*. Zagreb: Naklada Jesenski i Turk.
Belaj, V. 1989. '"Zeleni Juraj" u Svetoj Zemlji', *Studia Ethnologica* 1: 65–78.
———. 1998. *Hod kroz godinu: Mitska pozadina hrvatskih narodnih običaja i vjerovanja*. Zagreb: Golden Marketing.
———. 2007. *Hod kroz godinu: Pokušaj rekonstrukcije prahrvatskoga mitskoga svjetonazora*. Zagreb: Golden Marketing.
———. 2009. 'Poganski bogovi i njihovi kršćanski supstituti', *Studia Ethnologica Croatica* 21:169–97.
Belova, O.V. 2001. 'Koza', in S.M. Tolstoj and Lj. Radenković (eds), *Enciklopedija: Mitologijski rečnik*. Belgrade: Zepter Book World, pp. 272–73.

Bender, B. 1993. 'Introduction: Landscape – Meaning and Action'. In B. Bender (ed.), *Landscape: Politics and Perspectives*. Oxford: Berg.

Berber, N. 2010. *Unveiling Bosnia-Herzegovina in British Travel Literature (1844–1912)*. Pisa: Pisa University Press.

Bergson, H. 1911. *Matter and Memory*. London: G. Allen & Unwin.

———. 2002. *Henri Bergson: Key Writings,* ed. K.A. Pearson and J.Ó. Maoilearca. London: Bloomsbury.

Bevan-Jones, R. 2017. *The Ancient Yew: A History of Taxus baccata*. Oxford: Windgather Press.

Bilušić Dumbović, B. 2014. 'Prilog tumačenju pojma krajolika kao kulturne kategorije', *Sociologija i prostor* 52(2): 187–205.

Bloch, E. 1996. *The Principle of Hope*: *Volume 1*, trans. N. Plaice, S. Plaice and P. Knight. Cambridge, MA: MIT Press.

Bloch, M. 1973. 'The Long Term and the Short Term', in J. Goody (ed.), *The Character of Kinship*. Cambridge: Cambridge University Press, pp. 75–87.

Bodewitz, H.W. 2002. 'The Dark and Deep Underworld in the Veda', *Journal of the American Oriental Society* 122(2): 213–23.

Bogdanović, B. 2008. *Tri ratne knjige: Grad i smrt, Srpska utopija, Grad i budućnost*. Novi Sad: Mediteran Publishing.

Bogišić, V. 1874. *Zbornik sadašnjih pravnih običaja u Južnih Sloven*a: *Knjiga prva*. Zagreb: Jugoslavenska akademija znanosti i umjetnosti.

Bojić, N. 1992. 'Ko ste vi, Vojislave Šešelju?'. Retrieved 7 December 2012 from http://www.vseselj.com/index.php?a=107.

Bougarel, X. 1999. 'Yugoslav Wars: The "Revenge of the Countryside" Between Sociological Reality and Nationalist Myth', *East European Quarterly* 33(2): 157–75.

———. 2004. *Bosna: Anatomija rata,* trans. J. Stakić. Belgrade: Fabrika knjiga.

Bougarel, X., E. Helms and G. Duijzings (eds). 2007. *The New Bosnian Mosaic: Identities, Memories and Moral Claims in a Post-War Society*. Aldershot, England: Ashgate.

Bourdieu, P. 1990. *The Logic of Practice*. Stanford, CA: Stanford University Press.

———. 2000. *Pascalian Meditations*. Cambridge: Polity Press.

———. 2002. *Distinction: A Social Critique of the Judgement of Taste*. Translated by Richard Nice. Cambridge, MA: Harvard University Press.

Bowman, G. 2012. 'Introduction: Sharing the Sacra', in G. Bowman (ed.), *Sharing the Sacra: The Politics and Pragmatics of Inter-communal Relations*. New York: Berghahn Books, pp. 1–10.

Bracewell, W. 1992. *The Uskoks of Senj: Piracy, Banditry and Holy War in the Sixteenth-Century Adriatic*. London: Cornell University Press.

———. 2000. 'Frontier Blood-Brotherhood and the Triplex Confinium', in D. Roksandić and N. Štefanec (eds), *Constructing Border Societies on the Triplex Confinium*. Budapest: Central European University, pp. 29–45.

———. 2003. '"The Proud Name of Hajduks": Bandits as Ambiguous Heroes in Balkan Politics and Culture', in N.M. Naimark and H. Case (eds), *Yugoslavia and Its Historians: Understanding the Balkan Wars of the 1990s*. Stanford, CA: Stanford University Press, pp. 22–36.

———. 2016. 'Ritual Brotherhood across Frontiers in the Eastern Adriatic Hinterland, Sixteenth to Eighteenth Centuries', *History and Anthropology* 27(3): 338–58.

Braudel, F. 1972. *The Mediterranean: And the Mediterranean World in the Age of Philip II. Volume 1*. Translated from the French by Siân Reynolds. London: Collins.

Brewer, J. 2000. *Ethnography*. Buckingham: Open University Press.
Bringa, T. 1995. *Being Muslim the Bosnian Way: Identity and Community in a Central Bosnian Village*. Princeton, NJ: Princeton University Press.
Brown, P. 1981. *The Cult of Saints: Its Rise and Function in Latin Christianity*. Chicago, IL: University of Chicago Press.
Bryant, R. 2016. 'Introduction: Everyday Coexistence in the Post-Ottoman Space', in R. Bryant (ed.), *Post-Ottoman Coexistence: Sharing Space in the Shadow of Conflict*. New York: Berghahn Books, pp. 1–38.
Buka. 2015. 'Dodik o 1. martu: Nijedan zajednički praznik koji slave tri naroda u Bosni i Hercegovini nije moguć'. Retrieved 1 March 2015 from http://www.6yka.com/novost/75830/dodik_o_1._martu:_nijedan_zajedni%C4%8Dki_praznik_koji_slave_tri_naroda_u_bosni_i_hercegovini_nije_mogu%C4%87.
Bulfinch, T. 1993. *The Golden Age of Myth and Legend: The Classical Mythology of the Ancient World*. London: Wordsworth Editions.
Bureau of Statistics of the Republic of Bosnia and Herzegovina. 1993. 'Popis stanovništva, domaćinstava, stanova i poljoprivrednih gazdinstava 1991. Etnička obilježja stanovništva. Rezultati za Republiku po opštinama', *Statistički bilten* 233.
Buturović, Đ. 1995. *Usmena epika Bošnjaka*. Sarajevo: Preporod.
Čajkanović, V. 1973. *Mit i religija u Srba*. Belgrade: Srpska književna zadruga.
Čajkanović, V., and R. Cajić. 1995. *Stara srpska religija i mitologija*. Belgrade: Srpska akademija nauka i umetnosti.
Cancik, H., and H. Schneider. 2006. 'Thalia', in H. Cancik and H. Schneider (eds), *Brill's New Pauly: Antiquity Volumes. Brill Online, 2014 Reference*. Retrieved 25 August 2014 from http://referenceworks.brillonline.com/entries/brill-s-new-pauly/thalia-e1206280.
Caplan, P. 2003. *The Ethics of Anthropology*. New York: Routledge.
Carsten, J. 2004. 'The Substance of Kinship and the Heath of the Hearth: Feeding, Personhood, and Relatedness Among Malays in Pulau Langkawi', in R. Parkin and L. Stone (eds), *Kinship and Family: An Anthropological Reader*. Oxford: Blackwell, pp. 309–27.
Carter, P. 2010. *The Road to Botany Bay: An Exploration of Landscape and History*. Minneapolis, MN: University of Minnesota Press.
'Case of Sejdić and Finci v. Bosnia and Herzegovina', European Court of Human Rights Decision. Retrieved 1 September 2014 from http://hudoc.echr.coe.int/sites/eng/pages/search.aspx#{"dmdocnumber":["860268"],"itemid":["001-96491"]}.
Çelebi, E. 1996. *Putopis: Odlomci o jugoslovenskim zemljama*, ed. S. Zahiragić. Sarajevo: Sarajevo-Publishing.
Ćimić, Z. 2006. 'Gacko moje, moja rano ljuta...'. Retrieved 2 March 2016 from http://www.gacko.net/zaim_cimic_2.htm.
Cirlot, J.E. 2002. *A Dictionary of Symbols*. Mineola, NY: Dover Publications.
Cohen, A.P. 1985. *The Symbolic Construction of Community*. London: Routledge.
Colavito, J. 2014. *Jason and the Argonauts through the Ages*. Jefferson, NC: McFarland.
Coleman, L. 2009. 'Being Alone Together: From Solidarity to Solitude in Urban Anthropology', *Anthropological Quarterly* 82(3): 755–77.
Coleman, S., and P. Collins. 2006. *Locating the Field: Space, Place and Context in Anthropology*. Oxford: Berg.
Connerton, P. 1989. *How Societies Remember*. Cambridge: Cambridge University Press.
———. 2008. 'Seven Types of Forgetting', *Memory Studies* 1(1): 59–71.

Convention on the Prevention and Punishment of the Crime of Genocide (adopted 9 December 1948, entered into force 12 January 1951). Adopted by General Assembly Resolution 260 A (III).
Coomaraswamy, A.K. 1989. *What is Civilization? And Other Essays*. Great Barrington, MA: Lindisfarne Press.
Cotterell, A., and R. Storm. 2011. *The Ultimate Encyclopedia of Mythology*. Leicestershire: Hermes House.
Couroucli, M. 2012. 'Introduction: Sharing Sacred Spaces – A Mediterranean Tradition', in D. Albera and M. Couroucli (eds), *Sharing Sacred Spaces in the Mediterranean: Christians, Muslims, and Jews at Shrines and Sanctuaries*. Bloomington, IN: Indiana University Press, pp. 1–9.
Crapanzano, V. 1985. *Waiting: The Whites of South Africa*. New York: Random House.
———. 2004. *Imaginative Horizons: An Essay in Literary-Philosophical Anthropology*. Chicago, IL: University of Chicago Press.
Crowley, S., and D. Hawhee. 2004. *Ancient Rhetorics for Contemporary Students*. New York: Pearson/Longman.
Cruikshank, J., et. al. 1990. *Life Lived Like a Story: Stories of Three Yukon Native Elders*. Lincoln, NE: University of Nebraska Press.
———. 2005. *Do Glaciers Listen? Local Knowledge, Colonial Encounters, and Social Imagination*. Vancouver: University of British Columbia Press.
Curtis, J. (ed.). 2012. *An Addendum to The Poems of William Wordsworth: Collected Reading Texts from the Cornell Wordsworth, In Three Volumes*. Penrith: Humanities-Ebooks.
Cvijić, J. 1922. *Balkansko poluostrvo i Južnoslovenske zemlje: Volume 1: Osnovi antropogeografije*. Retrieved 3 February 2016 from http://ebooks.antikvarne-knjige.com/cvijic-balkansko-1/.
———. 1931. *Balkansko poluostrvo i Južnoslovenske zemlje: Volume 2: Osnovi antropogeografije*. Retrieved 3 February 2016 from http://ebooks.antikvarne-knjige.com/cvijic-balkansko-2/.
Čvorović, J. 2010. *Roast Chicken and Other Gypsy Stories: Oral Narratives Among Serbian Gypsies*. Frankfurt: Peter Lang.
Daly, K.N. 2009. *Greek and Roman Mythology A to Z*. New York: Chelsea House Publishers.
De Certeau, M. 1984. *The Practice of Everyday Life*. Berkeley, CA: University of California Press.
Dedijer, V. 1992. *The Yugoslav Auschwitz and the Vatican: The Croatian Massacre of the Serbs During World War II*. Translated by Harvey L. Kendall. Freiburg: Ahriman-Verlag.
de Genova, N. 2002. 'Migrant "Illegality" and Deportation in Everyday Life', *Annual Review of Anthropology* 31: 419–47.
De Vaan, M. 2008. *Etymological Dictionary of Latin and the Other Italic Languages*. Leiden: Brill.
de Voragine, J. 1900. *The Golden Legend or Lives of the Saints*, trans. W. Caxton. London: Temple Classics.
———. 1998. *The Golden Legend: Selections*. London: Penguin Books.
Derksen, R. 2008. *Etymological Dictionary of the Slavic Inherited Lexicon*. Leiden: Brill.
Devon Karst Research Society. 2006. 'Fatnica Polje: Anthropogenic Impact'. Retrieved 20 March 2015 from http://www.devonkarst.org.uk/Fatnicko%20Polje/FP13.htm.
———. 2007. 'Gatačko Polje'. Retrieved 4 September 2013 from http://www.devonkarst.org.uk/gatacko%20polje/gatacko%20polje,%20eastern%20herzegovina_hp.html.

Devrnja Zimmerman, Z. 1986. *Serbian Folk Poetry: Ancient Legends, Romantic Songs*. Columbus, OH: Kosovo Publishing Company.
Dickey, C. 2012. *Afterlives of the Saints: Stories from the Ends of Faith*. Columbia, MO: Unbridled Books.
Đilas, M., and N. Gaće. 1994. *Bošnjak: Adil Zulfikarpašić*. Zürich: Bošnjački Institut.
Dizdar, M. 1969. *Stari bosanski tekstovi*. Sarajevo: Svjetlost.
———. 1999. *Kameni spavač/Stone Sleeper*, trans. F.R. Jones, with afterwords by R. Mahmutćehajić and F.R. Jones. Sarajevo: Kuća bosanska.
Donnan, H., and T.M. Wilson. 1999. *Borders: Frontiers of Identity, Nation and State*. Oxford: Berg.
Douglas, M. 1966. *Purity and Danger: An Analysis of the Concepts of Pollution and Taboo*. London: Routledge.
———. 1995. 'Forgotten Knowledge', in M. Strathern (ed.), *Shifting Contexts: Transformations in Anthropological Knowledge*. London: Routledge, pp. 13–30.
———. 2002. 'Foreword: No Free Gifts', in M. Mauss *The Gift: The Form and Reason for Exchange in Archaic Societies*. London: Routledge, pp. ix–xxiii.
Dragić M. 2013. 'Sveti Juraj u tradicijskoj baštini Hrvata', *Croatica et Slavica Iadertina* 9(1): 269–313.
Du Bois, W.E.B. 2007. *The Souls of Black Folk*. Edited with an Introduction and Notes by B.H. Edwards. Oxford: Oxford University Press.
Duijzings, G. 2000. *Religion and the Politics of Identity in Kosovo*. New York: Columbia University Press.
———. 2003. 'Ethnic Unmixing Under the Aegis of the West: A Transnational Approach to the Breakup of Yugoslavia', *Bulletin of the Royal Institute for Inter-Faith Studies* 5(2): 1–16.
Dundzila, V.R. 2005. 'Baltic Indigenous Religions', in B. Taylor (ed.), *Encyclopedia of Religion and Nature, Volume I*. London: Continuum, pp. 155–58.
Džogović, A. 2013. 'Alija Đerzelez: mit i stvarnost'. Retrieved 7 May 2013 from www .avlija.me/eseji/alija-dzogovic-alija-derzelez-mit-stvarnost.
Edwards, C.C. 1983. 'The Parry-Lord Theory Meets Operational Structuralism', *Journal of American Folklore* 96: 151–69.
Eliade, M. 1959. *Cosmos and History: The Myth of Eternal Return*, trans. W.R. Trask. New York: Harper Torchbooks.
Errante, A. 2000. 'But Sometimes You're Not Part of the Story: Oral Histories and Ways of Remembering and Telling', *Educational Researcher* 29(16): 16–27.
ERS (Elektroprivreda Republike Srpske). 2009. 'ZP RiTE Gacko a.d. Gacko'. Retrieved 5 July 2015 from http://www.ers.ba/index.php?option=com_content& view=article&id=7:rite-gacko&Itemid=26&lang=en.
Evans, A. 1876. *Through Bosnia and the Herzegovina on Foot During the Insurrection, August and September 1875; With an Historical Review of Bosnia, and a Glimpse at the Croats, Slavonians, and the Ancient Republic of Ragusa*. London: Longmans, Green and Co.
Evans-Pritchard, E.E. 1939. 'Nuer Time-Reckoning', *Africa: Journal of the International African Institute* 12(2): 189–216.
———. 1940. *The Nuer: A Description of the Modes of Livelihood and Political Institutions of a Nilotic People*. Oxford: Clarendon Press.
———. 1951. *Social Anthropology*. London: Cohen and West Ltd.

Ewing, K.P. 1994. 'Dreams from a Saint: Anthropological Atheism and the Temptation to Believe', *American Anthropologist* 96(3): 571–83.
Fabian, J. 1983. *Time and the Other: How Anthropology Makes its Object*. New York: Colombia University Press.
Fantham, E. 2006. 'Introduction', in Virgil, *Georgics*. Oxford: Oxford University Press, pp. xi–xxxiii.
Farmer, D.H. 2011. *Oxford Dictionary of Saints*. Oxford: Oxford University Press.
Federal Bureau of Statistics of Bosnia and Herzegovina. 1998a. 'Popis domaćinstava/kućanstava, stanova i poljoprivrednih gazdinstava 1991. Stanovništvo: uporedni podaci 1971, 1981 i 1991', *Statistički bilten* 265. Retrieved 20 March 2016 from http://fzs.ba/wp-content/uploads/2016/06/stanovnistvo-uporedni-podaci-1971_1981_-1991-bilten-265.pdf.
———. 1998b. 'Popis domaćinstava/kućanstava, stanova i poljoprivrednih gazdinstava 1991. Stanovništvo po naseljenim mjestima'. *Statistički bilten* 257. Retrieved 20 March 2016 from http://fzs.ba/wp-content/uploads/2016/06/stanovnistvo-prema-starosti-i-spolu-po-naseljenim-mjestima-bilten-257.pdf.
Felton, D. 2010. 'The Dead', in D. Ogden (ed.), *A Companion to Greek Religion*. Malden, MA: Wiley-Blackwell, pp. 86–99.
Filan, K. 2011a. 'Određivanje vremena u prošlom vremenu: od doba godine do doba dana', *Riječ Bošnjaka* 21: 12–32.
———. 2011b. 'Ova priča govori o doživljajima pejgamber Džerdžisa'. Unpublished translation, on file with the author.
Filipović, M.S. 1969. *Prilozi etnološkom poznavanju severoistočne Bosne*. Special issue of *Građa* 16(12).
———. 1982. *Among the People: Native Yugoslav Ethnography: Selected Writing of Milenko S. Filipović*, ed. Eugene A. Hammel. Ann Arbor, MI: University of Michigan Press.
———. 2002. *Visočka nahija*. Visoko: Mak.
Fine, J.V.A. 2006. *The Late Medieval Balkans: A Critical Survey from the Late Twelfth Century to the Ottoman Conquest*. Ann Arbor, MI: University of Michigan Press.
———. 2007. *The Bosnian Church: Its Place in State and Society from the Thirteenth to the Fifteenth Century*. London: SAQI & The Bosnian Institute.
Foley, J.M. 1990. *Traditional Oral Epic: The Odyssey, Beowulf, and the Serbo-Croatian Return Song*. Berkeley, CA: University of California Press.
———. 2004. 'Comparative Oral Traditions'. Retrieved 14 July 2015 from http://bdb.bertsozale.eus/uploads/edukiak/liburutegia/xdz4_ld_000169_01.pdf.
———. 2005. 'South Slavic Oral Epic and the Homeric Question', *Acta Poetica* 26(1–2): 51–68.
Fontein, J. 2011. 'Graves, Ruins, and Belonging: Towards an Anthropology of Proximity', *Journal of the Royal Anthropological Institute* 17(4): 706–27.
Fontenrose, J. 1957. 'Dagon and El', *Oriens* 10(2): 277–79.
Forenbaher, S., and P. Rajić Šikanjić. 2006. 'The Prehistoric Hillfort at Grad (Pelješac, Dalmatia) – Preliminary Results of Intensive Surface Survey', *Collegium Antropologicum* 30(3): 467–73.
Foucault, M. 1990. *The History of Sexuality: An Introduction*. London: Penguin Books.
Fraser, J.T. 1987. *Time: The Familiar Stranger*. Amherst, MA: University of Massachusetts Press.

Frazer, J.G. 1911. *The Magic Art and the Evolution of Kings, Vol 2*. London: Macmillan and Co.

———. 1993. *The Golden Bough: A Study in Magic and Religion*. Hertfordshire, UK: Wordsworth Editions.

Freeman, C. 2015. 'Islamic State Defaces St George in Assault on Christian Churches in Iraq'. Retrieved 25 July 2015 from www.telegraph.co.uk/news/worldnews/middleeast/syria/11476676/Islamic-State-defaces-St-George-in-assault-on-Christian-churches-in-Iraq.html.

Freud, S. 1955. 'The "Uncanny"', in J. Strachey (ed.), *The Standard Edition of the Complete Psychological Works of Sigmund Freud: Volume XVII (1917–1919)*. London: The Hogarth Press, pp. 219–52.

Friedman, A.B. and R.H. Osberg. 1977. 'Gawain's Girdle as Traditional Symbol', *Journal of American Folklore* 90(357): 301–15.

Gavazzi, M. 1939. *Godina dana Hrvatskih narodnih običaja*. Zagreb: Izdanje Matice Hrvatske.

Geertz, C. 1983. *Local Knowledge: Further Essays in Interpretive Anthropology*. New York: Basic Books.

———. 1993. *The Interpretation of Cultures: Selected Essays*. London: Fontana.

Gell, A. 1985. 'How to Read a Map: Remarks on the Practical Logic of Navigation', *Man*, New Series 20(2): 271–86.

———. 1996. *The Anthropology of Time: Cultural Constructions of Temporal Maps and Images*. Oxford: Berg.

Gellner, D.N. 1997. 'For Syncretism: The Position of Buddhism in Nepal and Japan Compared', *Social Anthropology* 1(3): 277–91.

Georgieva, C. 1999. 'Coexistence as a System in the Everyday Life of Christians and Muslims in Bulgaria', *Ethnologia Balkanica* 3: 59–84.

Gilbert, A., et al. 2008. 'Reconsidering Postsocialism from the Margins of Europe: Hope, Time and Normalcy in Post-Yugoslav Societies', *Anthropology News* 49(8): 10–11.

Gimbutas, M. 1971. *The Slavs*. London: Thames & Hudson.

———. 2004. *Sloveni sinovi Peruna*. Belgrade: Centar za paleoslovenske studije.

———. 2005a. 'Perun', in J. Lindsay (ed.), *Encyclopedia of Religion. Volume 10*. New York: Macmillan Reference, pp. 7062–63.

———. 2005b. 'Slavic Religion', in J. Lindsay (ed.), *Encyclopedia of Religion. Volume 12*. New York: Macmillan Reference, pp. 8432–39.

Girard, R. 1989. *Violence and the Sacred*. London: Johns Hopkins University Press.

Grabeljšek, D., et al. 1983. *National Structure of Population in SFR Yugoslavia. Volume 1: Data on Localities and Communes*. Belgrade: Federal Bureau of Statistics of Yugoslavia.

Grandits, H. 2014. *Multikonfesionalna Hercegovina: Vlast i lojalnost u kasnoosmanskom društvu*. Sarajevo: Institut za istoriju.

Gross, D.R. 1984. 'Time Allocation: A Tool for the Study of Cultural Behavior', *Annual Review of Anthropology* 13: 519–58.

Guiley, R.E. 2001. *The Encyclopedia of Saints*. New York: Facts on File.

Gupta, A., and J. Ferguson. 1997. 'Beyond "Culture": Space, Identity, and the Politics of Difference', in A. Gupta and J. Ferguson (eds), *Culture, Power, Place: Explorations in Critical Anthropology*. Durham, NC: Duke University Press, pp. 33–51.

Haddad, H.S. 1969. '"Georgic" Cults and Saints of the Levant', *Numen* 16(1): 21–39.

Hadži Vasiljević, J. 1924. *Muslimani naše krvi u južnoj Srbiji*. Belgrade: Štamparija 'Sv. Sava'.
Hadžibegović, I., and H. Kamberović. 1997. 'Građansko društvo u Bosni i Hercegovini', *Revija slobodne misli* 9–10: 48–56.
Hadžijahić, M. 1974. 'O jednom manje poznatom domaćem vrelu za proučavanje crkve bosanske', *Prilozi Instituta za istoriju BiH* 10(2): 55–107.
———. 1978–79. 'Sinkretički elementi u islamu u Bosni i Hercegovini', *Prilozi za orijentalnu filologiju* 28–29: 301–29.
———. 1981. 'Još jedno bogumilsko-islamsko kultno mjesto', *Glasnik Vrhovnog islamskog starješinstva* 3(81): 258–74.
Hadžijahić, M., and A. Purivatra. 1990. *ABC Muslimana*. Sarajevo: Bosna/Muslimanska Biblioteka.
Hadžijahić, M., M. Traljić and N. Šukrić. 1977. *Islam i Muslimani u Bosni i Hercegovini*. Sarajevo: Starješinstvo Islamske Zajednice.
HadžiMuhamedović, S. 2012. 'Bosnian Sacral Geography: Ethnographic Approaches to Landscape Protection', in J-M. Mallarach (ed.), *Spiritual Values of Protected Areas of Europe*. Bonn: German Federal Agency for Nature Conservation, pp. 55–62.
———. 2013. 'The Tree of Gernika: Political Poetics of Rootedness and Belonging', in P. Dransart (ed.), *Living Beings: Perspectives on Interspecies Engagements*. Oxford: Bloomsbury, pp. 53–72.
———. 2016. 'Grid Desires, or How to Tame a Three-Headed Dragon'. *Anthropology Book Forum* 2(1). Retrieved 23 March 2016 from http://journals.sfu.ca/abf/index.php/abf/article/view/43/59.
Hage, G. 2009. 'Introduction', in G. Hage (ed.), *Waiting*. Melbourne: Melbourne University Press, pp. 1–12.
Halbwachs, M. 1992. *On Collective Memory*. London: University of Chicago Press.
Halilovich, H. 2011. 'Beyond the Sadness: Memories and Homecomings among Survivors of "Ethnic Cleansing" in a Bosnian Village', *Memory Studies* 4(1): 42–52.
———. 2013. *Places of Pain: Forced Displacement, Popular Memory and Trans-local Identities in Bosnian War-Torn Communities*. New York: Berghahn Books.
Hall, J. 2015. 'Another Blow to Christianity and Civilisation: ISIS Destroy 4th Century Mar Benham Monastery in Iraq', MailOnline, 19 March. Retrieved 25 July 2015 from www.dailymail.co.uk/news/article-3002530/Another-blow-Christianity-civilisation-ISIS-destroy-4th-Century-Mar-Benham-monastery-Iraq.html.
Hamer, R. 1998. 'Introduction', in J. de Voragine, *The Golden Legend: Selections*. London: Penguin Books, pp. ix–xxxi.
Hammel, E.A. 1968. *Alternative Social Structures and Ritual Relations in the Balkans*. Englewood Cliffs, NJ: Prentice-Hall.
Hamzić, V. 2015. 'The *Dera* Paradigm: Homecoming of the Gendered Other', *Inter-Congress of the International Union of Anthropological and Ethnological Sciences, Bangkok, 20 July 2015*. Bangkok: IUAES.
Hanauer, J.E. 1907. *Folk-lore of the Holy Land: Moslem, Christian and Jewish*. London: Duckworth and Co.
Hangi, A. 1906. *Život i običaji muslimana u Bosni i Hercegovini. Drugo znatno povećano i ispravljeno izdanje*. Sarajevo: Naklada Daniela A. Kajona.
Hanuš, J.I. 1860. *Bajeslovný Kalendár Slovanský čili pozustatky pohansko-svatečnych obraduv slovanskych*. Prague: Kober & Markgraf.

Hasanbegović, S.O. 2000. 'Stabla što nebo ljube: 380 godina genealogije rasta i stradanja porodica Hasanbegović i Pašić: Avtovac – Mulji – Gacko'. Retrieved 4 April 2016 from http://www.gacko.net/safet_hasanbegovic_2.htm and http://www.gacko.net/safet_hasanbegovic_3.htm.

Hasluck, F.W. 1929. *Christianity and Islam under the Sultans. Volume 1.* Oxford: Clarendon Press.

Hayden, R. M. 2002a 'Antagonistic Tolerance: Competitive Sharing of Religious Sites in South Asia and the Balkans', *Current Anthropology* 43(2): 205–31.

———. 2002b. 'Intolerant Sovereignties and "Multi-Multi" Protectorates: Competition over Religious Sites and (In)Tolerance in the Balkans', in C. Hann (ed.), *Postsocialism: Ideals, Ideologies and Practices in Eurasia*. London: Routledge, pp. 159–79.

———. 2007. 'Moral Vision and Impaired Insight: The Imagining of Other Peoples' Communities in Bosnia', *Current Anthropology* 148(1): 105–17.

Henig, D. 2011. 'The Embers of Allah: Cosmologies, Knowledge, and Relations in the Mountains of Central Bosnia', Ph.D. dissertation. United Kingdom: Durham University. Retrieved 20 April 2015 from http://etheses.dur.ac.uk/915/.

———. 2012a. '"Knocking on My Neighbour's Door": On Metamorphoses of Sociality in Rural Bosnia', *Critique of Anthropology* 32(1): 3–19.

———. 2012b. '"This is Our Little Hajj": Muslim Holy Sites and Reappropriation of the Sacred Landscape in Contemporary Bosnia', *American Ethnologist* 39(4): 751–65.

———. 2015. *Contested Choreographies of Sacred Spaces in Muslim Bosnia*, in E. Barkan and K. Barkey (eds), *Choreographies of Shared Sacred Sites: Religion and Conflict Resolution*. New York: Columbia University Press, pp. 130–60.

Heywood, C. 1996. 'Bosnia Under Ottoman Rule, 1463–1800', in M. Pinson (ed.), *Bosnia-Herzegovina: Their Historic Development from the Middle Ages to the Dissolution of Yugoslavia*. Cambridge, MA: Harvard University Press, pp. 22–53.

Hirsch, E. 1995. 'Introduction: Landscape – Between Place and Space', in E. Hirsch and M. O'Hanlon (eds), *The Anthropology of Landscape: Perspectives on Place and Space*. Oxford: Clarendon, pp. 1–30.

Hirsch, E., and C. Stewart. 2005. 'Introduction: Ethnographies of Historicity', *History and Anthropology* 16(3): 261–74.

Hirsch, M. 1999. 'Projected Memory: Holocaust Photographs in Personal and Public Fantasy', in M. Bal, J. Crewe and L. Spitzer (eds), *Acts of Memory: Cultural Recall in the Present*. London: University Press of New England, pp. 3–23.

Hirsch, M., and L. Spitzer. 2010. *Ghosts of Home: The Afterlife of Czernowitz in Jewish Memory*. London: University of California Press.

Hodžić, H. 2008. 'Prijetnje Fazlagiću, opet!' *Gacko.net*. Retrieved 12 October 2014 from http://www.gacko.net/vijesti.htm.

Holquist, M. 1981. 'Glossary', in M.M. Bakhtin *The Dialogic Imagination: Four Essays*. Austin: University of Texas Press, pp. 423–34.

Homogeceka. 2011. 'Telefonski imenik Gacka 1992. godine'. Retrieved 3 July 2014 from http://www.gacko.net/biljeg_vremena_2.htm.

Hony, H.C., and I. Fahir. 1957. *A Turkish–English Dictionary*. London: Oxford University Press.

Hörman, K. 1889. 'Kumstvo u Muhamedovaca', *Glasnik Zemaljskog Muzeja* 1: 36–38.

———. 1996. *Narodne Pjesme Bošnjaka 1*, edit. with an introduction by Đenana Buturović. Sarajevo: Preporod.

Hromadžić, A. 2011. 'Bathroom Mixing: Youth Negotiate Democratization in Postconflict Bosnia and Herzegovina', *PoLAR: Political and Legal Anthropology Review* 34(2): 268–89.

———. 2012. 'Once we had a House; Invisible Citizens and Consociational Democracy in Postwar Mostar, Bosnia and Herzegovina', *Social Analysis* 56(3): 30–48.

———. 2015. 'On Not Dating Just Anybody: The Politics and Poetics of Flirting in a Postwar City', *Anthropological Quarterly* 88(4): 881–906.

Human Rights Watch. 2014. 'Iraq: ISIS Kidnaps Shia Turkmen, Destroys Shrines: Pillaging, Threats In Capture of Villages near Mosul'. Retrieved 25 July 2015 from www.hrw.org/news/2014/06/27/iraq-isis-kidnaps-shia-turkmen-destroys-shrines.

Huntington, S. 1996. *The Clash of Civilizations and the Remaking of World Order*. New York: Simon and Schuster.

Hutton, R. 2001. *Stations of the Sun: A History of the Ritual Year in Britain*. Oxford: Oxford University Press.

Hynes, M. 2013. 'Reconceptualizing Resistance: Sociology and the Affective Dimension of Resistance', *The British Journal of Sociology* 64(4): 559–77.

ICTY (IT-08-91). 2010. A. Bašić's testimony in the trial against Stanišić and Župljanin of 2 February 2010. Retrieved 3 May 2015 from http://www.icty.org/x/cases/zupljanin_stanisicm/trans/en/100202IT.htm.

ICTY (IT-96-23 & 23/1) Witness 48's testimony in the trial against Kunarac et al. of 3 May 2000. Retrieved 4 May 2015 from http://www.icty.org/x/cases/kunarac/trans/en/000503ed.htm.

Ingold, T. 1993. 'The Temporality of the Landscape', *World Archaeology* 25(2): 152–74.

———. 1996. 'Introduction', in T. Ingold (ed.), *Key Debates in Anthropology*. London: Routledge, pp. 163–66.

International Committee of the Red Cross (ICRC). 1999. 'Bosnia-Herzegovina: Country Report'. Geneva

Ivakhiv, A. 2009. 'Slavic Religion', in B. Taylor (ed.), *Encyclopedia of Religion and Nature Volume II*. London: Continuum, pp. 1557–59.

Ivančević, P. 1897. 'Srpsko pobratimstvo u narodnim ustima', *Bosansko-hercegovački istočnik* 11(11): 415–18.

Ivanov, V., and V.N. Toporov. 2001. 'Jarila', in S.M. Tolstoj and Lj. Radenković (eds), *Enciklopedija: Mitologijski rečnik*. Beograd: Zepter Book World, pp. 237–38.

Jansen, S. 2009. 'Hope and the State in the Anthropology of Home: Preliminary Notes', *Ethnologia Europaea* 39(1): 54–60.

———. 2015. *Yearnings in the Meantime: 'Normal Lives' and the State in a Sarajevo Apartment Complex*. New York: Berghahn Books.

Jansen, S., and S. Löfving. 2008. 'Introduction: Towards an Anthropology of Violence, Hope and the Movement of People', in S. Jansen and S. Löfving (eds), *Struggles for Home: Violence, Hope and the Movement of People*. New York: Berghahn Books, pp. 1–23.

Jenkins, R. 1999. 'Ethnicity Etcetera: Social Anthropological Points of View', in M. Bulmer and J. Solomos (eds), *Ethnic and Racial Studies Today*. London: Routledge, pp. 85–97.

Joy, C. 2012. *The Politics of Heritage Management in Mali: From UNESCO to Djenn*. Walnut Creek, CA: Left Coast Press.

Judge, R. 1979. *The Jack-in-the-Green: A May Day Custom*. Ipswich: D.S. Brewer.

Juynboll, G.H.A. 2007. *Encyclopedia of Canonical Hadith*. Leiden: Brill.
Kabakova, G.I. 2001. 'Kumstvo', in S.M. Tolstoj and Lj. Radenković (eds), *Enciklopedija: Mitologijski rečnik*. Beograd: Zepter Book World, pp. 317–18.
Karadžić, V.S. 1823. *Narodne srpske pjesme: pjesme junačke najstarije. Volume 2*. Leipzig: Breitkopf & Härtel.
———. 1841. *Srpske narodne pjesme: knjiga prva, u kojoj su različne ženske pjesme*. Vienna: Štamparija jermenskog manastira.
———. 1852. *Srpski rječnik, istumačen njemačkijem i latinskijem riječima*. Vienna: Štamparija jermenskog manastira.
Karamatić, M. 2012. *Izbor tekstova 1*. Retrieved 12 December 2012 from http://www.bosnasrebrena.ba/v2010/spisateljstvo/knjievnost-bosanskih-franjevaca/izbor-tekstova-1.html.
Katičić, R. 1989. 'Hoditi – roditi: Tragom tekstova jednoga praslavenskog obreda plodnosti', *Studia Ethnologica* 1: 45–63.
Kazazić, E. 2006. 'Voda sa bezbroj imena. Priča o rijeci: Mušnica kojoj promijeniše ime'. Retrieved 23 February 2011 from http://www.gacko.net/voda_sa_bezbroj_imena.htm.
Kecmanović, N. 2007. *Nemoguća država: Bosna i Hercegovina*. Belgrade: Filip Višnjić.
Kingsley Garbett, G. 1970. 'The Analysis of Social Situations', *MANNS* 5(2): 214–27.
Knežević, A. 1871. '"Otci" kraljevstva bosanskoga', *Vienac* 3(22): 344–47.
Knight, C.D. 2004. *Decoding Fairy Tales. (An extract from Chris D. Knight's unpublished PhD thesis Menstruation and the Origins of Culture, 1987)*. London: Radical Anthropology Group. Retrieved 22 August 2015 from http://radicalanthropologygroup.org/sites/default/files/pdf/class_text_020.pdf.
Kolind, T. 2008. *Post-War Identification: Everyday Muslim Counterdiscourse in Bosnia Herzegovina*. Aarhus: Aarhus University Press.
Kononenko, N. 2007. *Slavic Folklore: A Handbook*. Westport, CT: Greenwood Press.
Korp, M. 2005. 'Religious Landscapes as Architectonic Sites', in B. Taylor (ed.), *Encyclopedia of Religion and Nature. Volume I*. London: Continuum, pp. 112–13.
Kovačević, K. 1889. 'O Đurđevu-dne', *Bosanska vila* 8: 119.
Kovacs, M.G. 1989. 'Introduction', in M.G. Kovacs (ed.), *The Epic of Gilgamesh*. Stanford: Stanford University Press, pp. xvii–xxxiv.
Kranjc, A. 2004. 'Dinaric Karst', in J. Gunn (ed.), *Encyclopedia of Caves and Karst Science*, London: Fitzroy Dearborn, pp. 591–94.
Krauss, F.S. 1908. *Slaviche Volkforschungen*. Leipzig: Verlag von Willhelm Heims.
Kretzenbacher, L. 1971. *Rituelle Wahlverbrüderung in Südosteuropa. Erlebniswirklichkeit und Erzählmotiv*. Munich: Bayerischen Akademie der Wissenschaften.
Krvavac, H. (director). 1984. *Izgradnja rudnika i termoelektrane Gacko*. Script by M. Jovičić and F. Pudelko. Documentary. Sarajevo: Sutjeska film.
Kulišić, Š. 1979. *Stara slovenska religija u svjetlu novijih istraživanja posebno balkanoloških*. Special issue of *Djela ANUBIH* 56(3).
Kulišić, Š., N. Pantelić and P.Z. Petrović. 1970. *Srpski mitološki rečnik*. Belgrade: Nolit.
Kwon, H. 2008. *Ghosts of War in Vietnam*. Cambridge: Cambridge University Press.
Lakha, S. 2009. 'Waiting to Return Home: Modes of Immigrant Waiting', in G. Hage (ed.), *Waiting*. Melbourne: Melbourne University Press, pp. 121–33.
Latour, B. 2005. *Reassembling the Social: An Introduction to Actor-Network Theory*. Oxford: Oxford University Press.

Law on Displaced Persons, Returnees and Refugees in the Republika Srpska. 2005. *RS Official Gazette*, no. 42/05, 26 April 2005.
Leger, L. 1901. *La Mythologie Slave*. Paris: Ernest Lseroux.
Leicestershire Holy Land Appeal. 2007. 'Palestinian Children's Art: St George Art Competition 2007'. Retrieved 25 July 2015 from http://leicester-holyland.org.uk/George_Downloads.htm.
Levinas, E. 1969. *Totality and Infinity: An Essay on Exteriority*. Pittsburgh: Duquesne University Press.
———. 1989. 'Time and the Other', in E. Levinas and S. Hánd, *The Levinas Reader*. Oxford: Basil Blackwell, pp. 38–58.
———. 1991. *Otherwise than Being or Beyond Essence*. Dordrecht: Kluwer Academic Publishers.
———. 1998. *Entre nous: On Thinking-of-the-Other*. New York: Columbia University Press.
Lévi-Strauss, C. 1963. *Structural Anthropology*. New York: Basic Books.
———. 1969. *The Elementary Structures of Kinship*. Boston: Beacon Press.
Lilek, E. 1893. 'Vadjenje žive vatre u Bosni i Hercegovini', *Glasnik Zemaljskog muzeja u Sarajevu* 5: 35–36.
———. 1894. 'Vjerske starine iz Bosne i Hercegovine', *Glasnik zemaljskog muzeja u Sarajevu* 6: 141–66; 259–81; 365–88; 631–74.
Lockwood, W.G. 1974. 'Bride Theft and Social Maneuverability in Western Bosnia'. *Anthropological Quartertly* 47:3: 253–69.
Loma, A. 2001. 'Jarila', in S.M. Tolstoj and Lj. Radenković (eds), *Enciklopedija: Mitologijski rečnik*. Belgrade: Zepter Book World, pp. 238–39.
Lord, A.B. 1991. *Epic Singers and Oral Tradition*. Ithaca, NY: Cornell University Press.
———. 2000 *The Singer of Tales*. Cambridge MA: Harvard University Press.
Low, D.H. 1922. *The Ballads of Marko Kraljević*. Cambridge: Cambridge University Press.
Lučić, I. 2012a. 'Trebišnjica. Jučer najveća ponornica, danas tvornica struje, sutra...?', *Ekonomska i ekohistorija: časopis za gospodarsku povijest i povijest okoliša* 8(8): 14–28.
———. 2012b. 'Shafts of Life and Shafts of Death in Dinaric Karst, Popovo Polje Case (Bosnia & Herzegovina)', *Acta Carsologica* 36(2): 321–30.
Luján, E.R. 2008. 'Procopius, De bello Gothico III 38.17–23: A Description of Ritual Pagan Slavic Slayings?', *Studia Mythologica Slavica* 11: 105–12.
Mackenzie, G.M., and P.A. Irby. 1877. *Travels in the Slavonic Provinces of Turkey-in-Europe. Volume 1*. London: Daldy, Isbister and Co.
MacLahlan, H. 1990. 'St George', in A.C. Hamilton (ed.), *The Spenser Encyclopedia*. London: University of Toronto Press, pp. 329–30.
Maksimović, D. 2012. *Celokupna dela. Prvi dio*. Belgrade: Zadužbina 'Desanka Maksimović'.
Malcolm, N. 1995. *Povijest Bosne*. Sarajevo: DANI.
Malinowski, B. 2002. *Argonauts of the Western Pacific*. London: Routledge.
Marcus, G.E. 1995. 'Ethnography in/of the World System: The Emergence of Multi-Sited Ethnography', *Annual Review of Anthropology* 24(1): 95–117.
Massey, D. 1994. *Space, Place, and Gender*. Minneapolis: University of Minnesota Press.
Massumi, B. 2002. *Parables for the Virtual: Movement, Affect, Sensation*. London: Duke University Press.
Matzke, J.E. 1902. 'Contributions to the History of the Legend of Saint George, with Special Reference to the Sources of the French, German, and Anglo-Saxon Metrical Versions, Part 1', *PMLA* 17(4): 464–535.

May, J., and N. Thrift (eds). 2001. *Timespace: Geographies of Temporality*. London: Routledge.

Merleau-Ponty, M. 2005. *Phenomenolgy of Perception*. London: Routledge.

Mezzofiore, G. 2015. 'Iraq: Isis Blows Up 10th Century Assyrian Catholic Monastery Near Mosul', *International Business Times*, 10 March. Retrieved 25 July 2015 from www.ibtimes.co.uk/iraq-isis-blows-10th-century-assyrian-catholic-monastery-near-mosul-1491281.

Mijatovich, C. 1917. *The Memoirs of a Balkan Diplomatist*. London: Cassell and Company Ltd.

Mikhailov, N. 2002. *Mythologia slovenica: Poskus rekonstrukcije slovenskega poganskega izročila*. Trst: Mladika.

Milanović, P. 2002. 'The Environmental Impacts of Human Activities and Engineering Constructions in Karst Regions', *Episodes* 25(1): 13–21.

Miljanov, M. 1967. *Život i običaji Arbanasa. Sabrana djela* 2. Titograd: Grafički zavod.

Minkowski, E. 1970. *Lived Time: Phenomenological and Psychopathological Studies*. Evanston, IL: Northwestern University Press.

Mitterauer, M. 2010. *Why Europe?: The Medieval Origins of its Special Path*. London: University of Chicago Press.

Miyazaki, H. 2004. *The Method of Hope: Anthropology, Philosophy and Fijian Knowledge*. Stanford, CA: Stanford University Press.

Mojzes, P. 1986. 'Religious Liberty in Yugoslavia: A Study in Ambiguity'. *Occasional Papers on Religion in Eastern Europe* 6(2): 23–41.

Monroe, W.H. 1970. *A Glossary of Karst Terminology*. Washington, DC: United States Government Printing Office.

Mostarac. 1896. 'Šišano kumstvo', *Zora* 1(4–5): 158–59.

Mueller, L. 1996. *Alive Together: New and Selected Poems*. Baton Rouge, LA: Louisiana State University Press.

Mulaomerović, J. 1997. 'O svetome bosanskome podzemlju', *Naš Krš* 17(30): 43–75.

Musabegović, S. 2008. 'Interview by John Feffer'. *The Balkans Project*. Retrieved 12 March 2013 from http://balkansproject.ips-dc.org/?p=203.

Nametak, A. 1962. 'Neki narodni običaji i lokalne tradicije muslimana u Podgorici (Titogradu)', *Glasnik etnografskog muzeja na Cetinju* 2: 190.

National Assembly of Republika Srpska. 2015. 'Narodni poslanik Miladin Stanić Ministarstvu industrije, energetike i rudarstva'. Retrieved 1 February 2016 from http://narodnaskupstinars.net/.

Navaro-Yashin, Y. 2012. *The Make-Believe Space: Affective Geography in a Postwar Polity*. Durham, NC: Duke University Press.

———. 2009. 'Affective Spaces, Melancholic Objects: Ruination and the Production of Anthropological Knowledge', *Journal of the Royal Anthropological Institute* 15(1): 1–18.

Nettelfield, L.J., and S.E. Wagner. 2014. *Srebrenica in the Aftermath of Genocide*. Cambridge: Cambridge University Press.

Newby, G.D. 2002. *A Concise Encyclopedia of Islam*. Oxford: Oneworld Publications.

Nezavisne Novine. 2011. 'Korićka Jama – 70 godina od stradanja Srba'. Published 4 May 2011. Retrieved 26 May 2013 at http://www.nezavisne.com/novosti/bih/Obiljezeno-70-godina-od-ubistva-130-Srba-kod-Koricke-jame/92336.

Ng, S.F., and K. Hodges. 2010. 'Saint George, Islam, and Regional Audiences in Sir Gawain and the Green Knight', *Studies in the Age of Chaucer* 32: 257–94.

Niškanović, M. 1978. 'Ilindanski dernek kod turbeta Djerzelez Alije u Gerzovu'. *Novopazarski Zbornik* 2: 165.

Nodilo, N. 1981. *Stara vjera Srba i Hrvata*. Reprinted from the following editions of *Rad Jugoslavenske akademije znanosti i umjetnosti*: 77–86, 89, 91–94, 99–102 from 1885 to 1890. Split: Logos.

Nuremberg Military Tribunals. 1949. *Trials of War Criminals before the Nuremberg Military Tribunals under Control Council Law No. 70, Vol 2*. Washington DC: US Government Printing Office.

Nuttall, M. 1992. *Arctic Homeland: Kinship, Community and Development in Northwest Greenland*. Toronto: University of Toronto Press.

Omerika, N. 1999. 'Mostarska pjesnička škola: Pjesnici Mostara koji su stvarali na orijentalnim jezicima u periodu od XV do XX stoljeća', *Most* 119/30. Retrieved 20 June 2014 from http://www.most.ba/030/0461.htm.

Ovsec, D. 1991. *Slovanska mitologija in verovanje*. Ljubljana: Domus.

Papo, E. 2008. 'Klaro del dija: prevod sa ladina'. Retrieved 15 November 2013 from http://www.benevolencija.eu.org/component/option,com_docman/task,doc_view/gid, 153/.

Parkes, P. 2004. 'Milk Kinship in Southeast Europe: Alternative Social Structures and Foster Relations in the Caucasus and the Balkans', *Social Anthropology* 12(3): 341–58.

Parry, M. 1971. *The Making of Homeric Verse: The Collected Papers of Milman Parry*. Oxford: Clarendon Press.

Pavković, N. 1982. 'Etnološka koncepcija nasleđivanja', *Etnološke sveske* 4: 23–39.

Pawlikowski, P. (director). 1992. *Serbian Epics*. London: BBC Documentary

Peleikis, A. 2006. 'The Making and Unmaking of Memories: The Case of a Multi-Confessional Village in Lebanon', in U. Makdisi and P.A. Silverstein (eds), *Memory and Violence in the Middle East and North Africa*. Bloomington, IN: Indiana University Press, pp. 130–50.

Perica, V. 2002. *Balkan Idols: Religion and Nationalism in Yugoslav States*. Oxford: Oxford University Press.

Perlman, D., and L.A. Peplau. 1981. 'Toward a Social Psychology of Loneliness', in S. Duck and R. Gilmour (eds), *Personal Relationships 3: Personal Relationships in Disorder*. London: Academic Press, pp. 31–56.

Pešikan-Ljuštanović, Lj. 2002. 'Zmaj i svadba u usmenom pesništvu Južnih Slovena', *Zbornik Matice srpske za slavistiku* 62: 7–24.

Peust, C. 2011. 'How Old Are the River Names of Europe? A Glottochronological Approach', *Linguistik Online* 70(1). Retrieved 4 June 2016 from https://bop.unibe.ch/linguistik-online/article/view/1749/2969.

Pine, F. 2014. 'Migration as Hope: Space, Time and Imagining the Future', *Current Anthropology* 55(Supplement 9): 95–104.

Plotnikova, A.A. 2001. 'Susret', in S.M. Tolstoj and Lj. Radenković (eds), *Enciklopedija: Mitologijski rečnik*. Belgrade: Zepter Book World, pp. 524–25.

Powell, K. 2010. 'Making Sense of Place: Mapping as a Multisensory Research Method', *Qualitative Inquiry* 16: 539–55.

Qleibo, A. 2011. 'Baal, al-Khader and the Apotheosis of Saint George', *This Week in Palestine* 63: 4–9.

Ramet, S.P., and M. Valenta. 2011. 'Bosnian Migrants: An Introduction', in S.P. Ramet and M. Valenta (eds), *The Bosnian Diaspora: Integration in Transnational Communities*. London: Ashgate, pp. 1–23.

Ransome, P. 2013. *Ethics and Values in Social Research*. Basingstoke: Palgrave Macmillan.
Republican Bureau of Statistics of Bosnia and Herzegovina. 1991. 'Popis stanovništva, domaćinstava, stanova i poljoprivrednih gazdinstava 1991: Prvi rezultati za stočni fond po naseljenim mjestima'. Socijalistička Republika Bosna i Hercegovina. *Statistički bilten* 221. Retrieved 20 March 2016 from http://fzs.ba/wp-content/up loads/2016/06/STOCNI-FOND-PRVI-REZ-1991.pdf.
Republika Srpska Institute of Statistics. 2017. 'Popis stanovništva, domaćinstava i stanova u Republici Srpskoj 2013. godine'. Retrieved 3 August 2017 from http://www2.rzs .rs.ba/static/uploads/bilteni/popis/gradovi_opstine_naseljena_mjesta/Rezultati_ Popisa_2013_Gradovi_Opstine_Naseljena_Mjesta_WEB.pdf.
Rihtman-Auguštin, D. 1990. 'Metamorforza socijalističkih praznika', *Narodna Umjetnost* 27: 21–32.
RiTE Gacko. 2014. 'Predsednik Republike Srpske Milorad Dodik boravio u radnoj posjeti RiTE Gacko'. Retrieved 5 July 2015 from http://www.ritegacko-rs.ba/wp-content/ uploads/2014/07/Председник-Републике-Српске-Милорад-Додик-боравио-у-радној-посјети-РиТЕ-Гацко.pdf.
Rodham Clinton, H. 2010. '15th Anniversary of Dayton Peace Accords: Press Statement'. Retrieved 4 September 2013 from https://2009-2017.state.gov/secretary/ 20092013clinton/rm/2010/11/151619.htm.
Rosaldo, R. 1989. 'Grief and a Headhunter's Rage', in R. Rosaldo (ed.), *Culture and Truth: The Remaking of Social Analysis*. Boston, MA: Beacon Press, pp. 1–21.
Rushdie, S. 1992. *Imaginary Homelands: Essays and Criticism 1981–1991*. New York: Penguin Books.
———. 2006. *Midnight's Children*. London: Vintage Books.
Sack, R.D. 1983. 'Human Territoriality: A Theory', *Annals of the Association of American Geographers* 73(1): 55–74.
———. 1986. *Human Territoriality: Its Theory and History*. Cambridge: Cambridge University Press.
Sahibzada, M. 2009. 'Khadir', in J.E. Campo (ed.), *Encyclopedia of Islam*. New York: Facts on File, pp. 428–30.
Salapura, N. 2015. 'TE Gacko 2 će biti u vlasništvu RS', 1 June. Retrieved 6 August 2015 from http://www.nezavisne.com/posao/privreda/TE-Gacko-2-ce-biti-u-vlas nistvu-RS/308054.
Sands, K.Z. 2006. *Sufi Commentaries on the Qur'an in Classical Islam*. London: Routledge.
Sarač-Rujanac, Dž. 2013. 'Ajvatovica: A Bridge between Tradition, National and Religious Identity', *History and Anthropology* 24(1): 117–36.
———. 2014. '"European Mecca" or Ajvatovica as a Sacred Place and a Tourist Destination in a Bosnia and Herzegovina', in M. Katić, T. Klarin and M. McDonald (eds), *Pilgrimage and Sacred Places in Southeast Europe: History, Religious Tourism and Contemporary Trends*. Berlin: Lit Verlag, pp. 115–29.
Scarry, E. 1985. *The Body in Pain: The Making and Unmaking of the World*. New York: Oxford University Press.
Schäuble, M. 2011. 'How History Takes Place: Sacralized Landscapes in the Croatian-Bosnian Border Region', *History & Memory* 23(1): 23–61.
Scheper-Hughes, N. 1995. 'The Primacy of the Ethical: Propositions for a Militant Anthropology', *Current Anthropology* 3: 409–40.
Schweizer, H. 2008. *On Waiting*. London: Routledge.

Scott, J. 1985. *Weapons of the Weak: Everyday Forms of Peasant Resistance*. New Haven, CT: Yale University Press.
———. 1990. *Domination and the Art of Resistance: Hidden Transcripts*. London: Yale University Press.
Segal, S.M. 1935. *Elijah: A Study in Jewish Folklore*. New York: Behrmans Jewish Book House.
Selimović, M. 1966. *Derviš i smrt*. Sarajevo: Svjetlost.
Sharon, M. 1983. 'Ludd', in C.E. Bosworth, et al. (eds), *Encyclopaedia of Islam: New Edition*. Leiden: Brill, pp. 798–803.
Shaw, R., and C. Stewart. 1994. 'Introduction: Problematizing Syncretism', in C. Stewart and R. Shaw (eds), *Syncretism/Anti-syncretism: The Politics of Religious Synthesis*. London: Routledge, pp. 1–26.
Sidaway, J.D. 2007. 'The Poetry of Boundaries', in K. Rajaram and C. Grundig-Warr (eds), *Borderscapes: Hidden Geographies and Politics at Territory's Edge*. Minneapolis, MN: University of Minnesota Press, pp. 161–82.
Sidran, A. 2011. 'Interview by Maja Hrgović: Abdulah Sidran: Suživot je atentat na život'. Retrieved 7 May 2013 from http://www.novilist.hr/Kultura/Knjizevnost/Abdulah-Sidran-Suzivot-je-atentat-na-zivot.
Šijanec, F. 1917. 'Nastrižno kumstvo', *Dom in svet* 30(9/10): 301.
Sivrić, I. 1982. *The Peasant Culture of Bosnia and Herzegovina*. Chicago, IL: Franciscan Herald Press.
Skok, P. 1971. *Etimologijski rječnik hrvatskoga ili srpskoga jezika. Volume 1: A-J*. Zagreb: Jugoslavenska akademija znanosti i umjetnosti.
———. 1972. *Etimologijski rječnik hrvatskoga ili srpskoga jezika. Volume 2: K – poni'*. Zagreb: Jugoslavenska akademija znanosti i umjetnosti.
Smith, A. 1999. *Myths and Memories of the Nation*. Oxford: Oxford University Press.
Smith, G.A. 1901. *The Historical Geography of the Holy Land: Especially in Relation to the History of Israel and of the Early Church*. London: Hodder and Stoughton.
Smith, W. (ed.). 1844. *Dictionary of Greek and Roman Biography and Mythology. Volume 1*. London: Taylor and Walton.
———. 1884. *Smith's Bible Dictionary*. Grand Rapids, MI: Christian Classics Ethereal Library. Retrieved 25 June 2013 from http://www.ccel.org/ccel/smith_w/bibledict.html.
Softić, A. 2005. *Zbornik bošnjačkih usmenih predaja*. Sarajevo: Sarajevo Publishing.
Soloviev, A. 1949. 'Saint Gregoire, patron de Bosnie', *Byzantion* 19: 263–79.
Sorabji, C. 1989. 'Muslim Identity and Islamic Faith in Sarajevo', Ph.D. dissertation. United Kingdom: University of Cambridge.
———. 2008. 'Bosnian Neighbourhoods Revisited: Tolerance, Commitment and Komšiluk in Sarajevo', in F. Pine and J. de Pina-Cabral (eds), *On the Margins of Religion*. New York: Berghahn Books, pp. 97–112.
Stewart C. 1999. 'Syncretism and Its Synonyms: Reflections on Cultural Mixture', *Diacritics* 29(3): 40–62.
———. 2008. 'Preface to the Greek Translation of Demons and the Devil'. Retrieved 15 July 2015 from http://www.ucl.ac.uk/anthropology/people/academic-teaching-staff/charles-stewart/Preface_to_translation.pdf.
———. 2011. 'Hybridity, Syncretism, Mixture', *Portuguese Studies* 27(1): 48–55.
———. 2012. *Dreaming and Historical Consciousness in the Island Greece*. London: Harvard University Press.

Stewart, K. 2007. *Ordinary Affects*. London: Duke University Press.
Strathern, M. 2004. *Partial Connections*. Oxford: Altamira Press.
Swayd, S. 2006. *A to Z of the Druzes*. Plymouth: Scarecrow Press.
Szalc, A. 2012. 'In Search of Water of Life: The Alexander Romance and Indian Mythology', in R. Stoneman, K. Erickson and I.R. Netton (eds), *The Alexander Romance in Persia and the East*. Groningen: Barkhuis Publishing, pp. 327–38.
Tahirović Sijerčić, H. 2011. *Romani Dictionary: Gurbeti – English / English – Gurbeti*. Toronto: Magoria Books.
Tigay, J.H. 2002. *The Evolution of the Gilgamesh Epic*. Wauconda, Illinois: Bolchazy-Carducci Publishers.
Titon, J.T. 1980. 'The Life Story', *Journal of American Folklore* 93: 276–92.
Todorova, M. 1997. *Imagining the Balkans*. Oxford: Oxford University Press.
Tomašić, D. 1948. *Personality and Culture in Eastern European Politics*. New York: George W. Stewart Inc.
———. 1993. 'Plemenska kultura i njeni današnji ostaci'. *Društvena istraživanja* 8(6): 889–906.
Trevor, R. 1911. *My Balkan Tour: An Account of Some Journeyings and Adventures in the Near East Together with a Descriptive and Historical Account of Bosnia & Herzegovina, Dalmatia, Croatia & the Kingdom of Montenegro*. London: John Lane the Bodley Head.
Trifunovski, J.F. 1957. 'Etnografske beleške iz Vranjske', *Glasnik etnografskog muzeja u Beogradu* 20: 158–73.
Trojanović, S. 1930. *Vatra u običajima i životu srpskog naroda*. Beograd: Srpska Kraljevska Akademija.
Truhelka, Ć. 1894. 'Tetoviranje katolika u Bosni i Hercegovini', *Glasnik Zemaljskog muzeja u Bosni i Hercegovini*. 6(2): 81–88.
———. 1911. 'Testament gosta Radina: Prinos paterenskom pitanju', *Glasnik Zemaljskog muzeja u Bosni i Hercegovini* 23(3): 354–375.
———. 1941. *Studije o podrijetlu: etnološka razmatranja iz Bosne i Hercegovine*. Zagreb: Izdanje Matice Hrvatske.
Tsing, A.L. 2004. *Friction: An Ethnography of Global Connection*. Princeton, NJ: Princeton University Press.
Tuan, Y. 2011. *Space and Place: The Perspective of Experience*. London: University of Minnesota Press.
Turner, V. 2008. *The Ritual Process: Structure and Anti-structure*. New Brunswick, NJ: Aldine Transaction.
Tweed, T. 2006. *Crossing and Dwelling: A Theory of Religion*. London: Harvard University Press.
UNESCO. 2014. 'Spring Celebration: Hıdrellez or Saint George's Day: For Inscription on the Representative List of the Intangible Cultural Heritage of Humanity in 2014' (Nomination File No. 01006). Paris: UNESCO. Retrieved 12 June 2015 from www.unesco.org/culture/ich/doc/download.php?versionID=30321.
V.N. 2012. 'Patrijarh Irinej: Kosovo je srpski Jerusalim'. Retrieved 29 June 2013 from http://www.novosti.rs/vesti/naslovna/reportaze/aktuelno.293.html:386102-Patrijarh-Irinej-Kosovo-je-srpski-Jerusalim.
Van Seters, J. 2005. 'Elijah', in L. Jones (ed.), *Encyclopedia of Religion. Volume 4*. London: Thomson Gale.
Vasiljev, S. 1996. *Slovenska mitologija*. Beograd: Velvet.

Verdery, K. 1999. *The Political Lives of Dead Bodies*. New York: Columbia University Press.
Vernon, M.D. 1971. *The Psychology of Perception*. Middlesex: Penguin/Pelican.
Vidan, A. 2003a. *Embroidered With Gold, Strung With Pearls: The Traditional Ballads of Bosnian Women*. Cambridge, MA: The Milman Parry Collection of Oral Literature.
———. 2003b. *Zlatom veze, a biserje niže: Tradicionalne pjesme bosanskih žena: excerpts*. Retrieved 21 June 2014 from http://www.gacko.net/dr__aida_vidan_9.htm.
Virgil. 2006. *Georgics*, trans. P. Fallon. Oxford: Oxford University Press.
Virilio, P. 2007. *Negative Horizon: An Essay in Dromoscopy*, trans. M. Degener. London: Continuum.
Vucinich, W. 1976. 'A Zadruga in Bileća Rudine', in R.F. Byrnes (ed.), *Communal Families in the Balkans: The Zadruga. Essays by Philip E. Mosely and Essays in His Honor*. London: University of Notre Dame Press, pp. 162–86.
Vukanović, N. 2012. 'Partijskom knjižicom SNSD-a do posla u RiTE Gacko', 4 June. Retrieved 24 February 2016 from http://www.6yka.com/novost/24463/partijskom-knjizicom-snsd-a-do-posla-u-rite-gacko.
Wagner, R. 1986. *Symbols that Stand for Themselves*. London: University of Chicago Press.
Wagner, S. 2008. *To Know Where He Lies: DNA Technology and the Search for Srebrenica's Missing*. Berkeley, CA: University of California Press.
Walker, W.S. and A.E. Uysal. 1973. 'An Ancient God in Modern Turkey: Some Aspects of the Cult of Hizir', *The Journal of American Folklore* 86(341): 286–89.
Washburn Hopkins, E. 1905. 'The Fountain of Youth', *Journal of the American Oriental Society* 26: 1–67.
Wastell, S. 2001. 'Presuming Scale, Making Diversity: On the Mischiefs of Measurement and the Global: Local Metonym in Theories of Law and Culture', *Critique of Anthropology* 21(2): 185–210.
Wehr, H. 1976. *A Dictionary of Modern Written Arabic*, ed. J Milton Cowan. Ithaca, NY: Spoken Language Services, Inc.
Wenzel, M. 1965. *Ornamental Motifs on Tombstones from Medieval Bosnia and Surrounding Regions / Ukrasni motivi na stećima*. Sarajevo: Veselin Masleša.
West, R. 2006. *Black Lamb and Grey Falcon: A Journey through Yugoslavia*. Edinburgh: Canongate.
Wheeler, B.M. 2002. *Moses in the Qur'an and Islamic Exegesis*. London: RoutledgeCurzon.
Williams, P.W. 2004. 'Karst Evolution', in J. Gunn (ed.), *Encyclopedia of Caves and Karst Science*. London: Fitzroy Dearborn, pp. 1020–26.
Witness B-1122. 2003. Transcript from the trial of Slobodan Milošević (IT-02-54) 'Kosovo, Croatia and Bosnia' from Tuesday 21 October 2003. Retrieved 3 May 2015 from http://www.icty.org/x/cases/slobodan_milosevic/trans/en/031021ED.htm.
Wittgenstein, L. 1997. *Philosophical Investigations*, trans. G.E.M. Anscombe. Oxford: Blackwell Publishers.
Zaliznjak, A.A. and A.D. Shmelev. 2007. 'Sociativity, Conjoining and the Latin Prefix com-', in V.P. Nedjalkov (ed.), *Reciprocal Constructions*. Amsterdam: John Benjamins Publishing Company, pp. 209–30.
Zaroff, R. 2002. 'The Origins of Svantevit of Rügen', *Studia Mythologica Slavica* 5: 9–18.
Zeitlyn, D. 2008. 'Life-History Writing and the Anthropological Silhouette', *Social Anthropology/Anthropologie Sociale* 16(2): 154–71.

Živković, M. 2011. *Serbian Dreambook: National Imaginary in the Time of Milošević*. Bloomington, IN: Indiana University Press.
Z.Z. and Homogeceka. 2010. 'Konjske trke na austrijskoj granici u Hercegovini'. Retrieved 12 March 2016 from http://www.gacko.net/zaboravljeno_gacko.htm.

Index

abyss, 69, 73–76, 77, 103, 109, 114, 136; 162, 175, 196; epistemological, 54n18; between discourses of communal life, 154; of ideological projects, 115; watery, 196. *See also* Jama Dizdaruša; Korićka Jama; mass grave; *ponor*
act, 23, 36, 94–96, 98–99, 110, 130–31, 134, 141, 176–79, 206, 248; avoidance of, 62, 181, 205. *See also* post-act
actant, xiiin4, 94, 112n10, 134
Ae'gipan, 202
affect: and encounters, 1–3, 6, 15, 17, 23, 50, 90, 114–18, 121, 125–26, 130, 135–36, 139, 143, 149, 153–55, 176, 238, 240, 245; and remnants, 5, 6, 13, 23–26, 48, 82, 88, 90, 94–95, 98, 111, 114, 117–18, 121, 125, 127, 153–55, 159–63, 165, 175, 195, 200, 204, 235–36; and *kumstvo*, 20, 130, 135–36, 139, 143, 148–49; and home, 82, 85, 90, 94–95, 98, 111, 125, 127, 155, 246; and understanding, 22–23, 25–26, 48, 50, 57, 85, 96, 121, 127, 141, 153, 163, 169, 195, 204, 235–36, 238, 240, 246; and language, 23, 96, 111, 117, 153–55, 159–63, 175, 195, 236; and silence, 96, 111, 236; and post-act, 176, 195; and resistance, 98, 111, 112n11, 116, 118, 148–49, 153, 155, 160–63, 165, 169, 175, 236; and landscape, 48, 88, 90, 95, 98, 111, 114, 117–18, 121, 127, 139, 153–54, 159–63, 165, 169, 195, 204, 235–36, 246; and chronotope, 57, 70, 82, 95, 98, 111, 114, 118, 163, 236; and food, 125–27; and time, 120, 135, 148–49; and emotion, 135, 154; and violence, 4, 90, 95, 98, 116, 236; and nationalism, 70, 153–65, 200, 235; ordinary, 90, 163, 165; turn toward, 3, 5, 235–38, 240, 245
Agapkina, Tatyana A., 204, 230
agency, xiiin4, 10, 12, 29, 31, 41, 45, 47, 52, 89, 129, 153, 161, 191, 201, 206, 212, 221, 232n10
Ahmed, Sara, 119, 127
Ajvatovica, 42, 44, 48, 54n20, 151n6, 230
Ajvaz Dedo, 48, 221
al-Khader, the town of, 219–20. *See also* Khidr
al-Majlisi, Mohammad Baqer, 190, 209, 220, 232nn20–21, 233nn28–32
Al-Salt, 219
Alawites, 205
Albania, 20, 144, 157, 239
Albera, Dionigi, 12
Alevis, 205
Alexander the Great, 189, 207–9, 232n21
Ali ibn Abu Talib, 63
Aliđun, 3, 4, 11, 43, 44, 53n2, 63, 65, 66, 83, 107, 137, 177, 180, 223–24. *See also* Elijah's Day
Alija, 1–3, 25, 53n1, 59, 63, 65, 67, 76, 77, 78n6, 78n7, 137, 218, 223, 235, 237–38. *See also* Đerzelez, Alija; Ilija
altar, 193, 201, 214
amulet, 48, 184, 221, 230, 246
anchor, x, 29, 82, 83, 88, 116, 118, 127, 128, 150, 191, 145
Anderson, Benedict, 76
animals, 3, 175, 202; birds, 80, 171, 207; bull, 162, 208, 221, 230; cattle, 4, 30, 34–35, 49, 60–63, 80, 89, 101, 108–109, 113, 119, 126, 128, 140, 172, 180,

183–86, 190–91, 198, 202, 216, 220–23; chicken, 85, 101, 125; domestic, 61, 126, 185, 190, 201, 204, 206, 227; goats, 179, 185, 200–3, 221; horse, 34–35, 43, 65–66, 134, 167, 184, 189, 191, 194, 197–98, 200, 202, 217, 219, 221, 223, 225–27, 232n7; human fish, 171–72; nondomestic, 67, 122, 133, 134, 172, 214, 237; pigs, 101; rams, 48, 230; roosters, xii, 79–80, 124, 199; shed, 62, 117, 141, 183, 185, 191, 220, 224; sheep, 34–35, 61, 107, 136, 185, 191, 219, 223; wolves, 34, 61, 113–14, 124, 133–34, 202, 246. *See also* snake
annual cycle, 1–6, 8–9, 15, 17, 30, 44, 49, 54n16, 59–67, 150, 193, 198, 228, 235
Annunciation, the, 4, 9, 44, 61, 78n3, 78n4, 182, 202
antagonistic tolerance, 115
anti-syncretism, 4, 11–14, 17, 62, 148, 155, 191, 196, 206, 214, 220, 234–35, 241, 248–49
antichrist, 216, 232n24. *See also* Dajjal
Apollo, 190, 196–97
Appadurai, Arjun, 37, 68
apparitions, 77, 81, 95, 102, 245; of the Holy Virgin, 42, 43. *See also* ghosts; spirits
archetype, 47, 197, 232n18
architecture, 24, 47–48, 69, 74, 86, 88, 154, 157, 191, 199, 204, 213–14, 248–49, 250n2
archive, 13, 31, 48–50, 52, 126
Arnautovići, 220
aspen. *See under* trees
Assumption, the, 19
Athena, 197
August, the month of, 1, 9, 27, 37, 44, 63, 65, 71, 76, 80, 220, 223, 240. *See also* Elijah's Day
Austria-Hungary, 41, 141, 151n16
authenticity, 13, 27, 70, 159–60, 175
autumn, 101, 102, 110, 161 180, 210, 219

Baal, 196, 203, 213, 221
Baba Mountain, 80, 101
Babylonia, 203
Bahori, the village of, xv, 85, 119, 140, 186

Bakhtin, Mikhail, xiv, 6, 13, 23, 58, 79, 114–15, 118, 155, 175–76, 241
balije, 157
Balkan Peninsula, 7, 16, 18–19, 22, 38–39, 46–47, 77, 89, 98, 121, 133–34, 141, 151n12, 151n15, 152n18, 156–57, 168, 177, 187, 192, 197, 200–1, 204, 211–12, 220, 238, 240
Banks, Marcus, 38
Baskar, Bojan, 14, 149
Basso, Keith, 95–96
battle, 7, 19, 32, 34, 71, 92, 198, 206, 243, 249–50; of al-Ludd, 216–17; of Kosovo, 12, 70; of Sutjeska, 51
bećarac, xi, 16, 81, 171, 227
Belaj, Marijana, 42
Belaj, Vitomir, 54n12, 193, 202–3, 212, 217–18, 232n13, 233n31
Belgrade, 100
Bellerophon, 197
ben Levi, Joshua, 218
Berber, Neval, 18
Bergson, Henri, 40, 103
Bethlehem, 216
Bileća, the town of, 80, 131, 136, 192, 224–25
birds. *See under* animals
Bjelasnica Mountain, 74, 201
Bjelica, Milija, 74
Blagaj, the town of, 205
Blagovijest. See Annunciation, the
Bleiburg, 42
Bloch, Ernst, 86
Bloch, Maurice, 142
Bogdanović, Bogdan, 47
Bogišić, Valtazar, 131, 143, 151n11, 151n15
bonfire, 16, 19, 44, 50, 61, 117, 176, 182, 185–86, 198, 202, 211. *See also* fire
border, 21, 30, 59, 69, 75, 77, 134, 141, 144, 150; as frontier, 141. *See also* boundary
Bosniaks, 24, 33, 38–40, 42, 47, 54n19, 71, 91, 99, 122, 126, 138, 146, 239, 242
Bosnian Church, 187–188
Bosnian Kingdom, 188, 220
Bougarel, Xavier, 21, 46–47, 146, 156
boundary, 11, 13, 15, 21, 31, 37–40, 44, 52, 60, 63, 66, 106, 118, 142, 175, 177,

193, 199, 209, 213–14, 230, 234, 239, 248–49. *See also* border
Bourdieu, Pierre, 40, 52, 113
Bowman, Glenn, 15, 21, 54n11, 154
Bracewell, Wendy, xiv, 141–42, 148, 156–57, 165n3
Branilovići, the village of, xv, 54n17, 73, 91, 158, 183
Braudel, Fernand, 29
Brčko, the town of, 119, 144
breastfeeding, 101, 134, 191
Brestovac, the spring of, 171
bride. *See under* marriage
bridle, 197, 219
Bringa, Tone, 43–46, 99, 112n2, 146, 151n12
Bryant, Rebecca, 13, 41, 126, 146
bula, 159–60
Bulgaria, 149, 199
Byzantine: Empire, 12–13; 207, 218; Alexander Romance, 207–8; church, 213

Čajkanović, Veselin, 54n12, 130, 133, 151n12, 152n24, 152n26, 152n31, 203
Cantacuzenus, Emperor, 218
Caplan, Pat, 27
Carica, the spring of, 152n27, 210–11
Carpo, 210
Carter, Paul, 29
Catholic Christians, 16, 18, 19, 24, 38–39, 41–42, 132, 144, 148, 188–89, 220
cattle. *See under* animals
cave, xv, 3, 27, 50, 68, 73, 80, 101, 103, 116, 162, 171, 173, 193–94, 196–99, 230, 232n6, 239; Qur'anic surah, 206; and exile, 68, 80, 101, 103, 171; and fairies, 73, 162, 193. *See also* Maiden's Cave, the; Hrustovo Cave; Fairy's Cave
Cedar Forest, 208
Çelebi, Evliya, 172
Čemerno Mountain, 60, 161, 168
census, 16; in Gacko and wider Bosnia, 28–29, 31–34, 35–36
Cerberus, 209
čerge, 117, 122 (see also Gurbeti)
Cernica, the village of, 32, 68, 86,

Četnik, 42, 47, 60, 140, 152n29, 156–158, 165n4
Charites, 209
Charon, 209
children: and displacement, 68, 85, 102–4, 110, 245; and home, 110–11; and Khidr, 206–7; and *kumstvo*, 129–33, 136–37, 140–41, 143, 152n19, 186; as inheritors, 92, 97, 103, 124–25, 132, 245; caring for, 109, 184, 185, 216, 230, 245; childbirth, 15, 123; childlessness, 184, 199, 216, 246; on Annunciation, 61; on George's Day, 16, 62, 111, 117, 119, 137, 181–82, 185–86, 191–92, 195, 202, 211, 216; on John's Day, 19, 50; christening of, 43, 129; decorated with flowers, 184–85; drawings of, 249; in winter, 61, 113; killed, 74, 141; male, 108; many, 34, 223; on Elijah's Day, 65, 137–38, 222–24; on Peter's Day, 198; on swings, 16, 62, 111, 117, 181–82, 194, 204, 250; on wedding day, 108; only child, 34, 84, 111; sayings about, 172, 223; sonogram, 194; *The Child Bride*, 105. *See also kumstvo*; pregnancy; fertility; breastfeeding
Chimera, 198
Christmas, 11, 137, 188, 201, 231n4
chronography, 53, 127
chronotope, 5–6, 8, 17, 57–59, 63, 66, 68–70, 74–77, 90, 95–97, 99–100, 118–20, 124–25, 127–28, 137–39, 142, 148, 154–55, 163, 230, 234, 236, 240–41, 243, 247, 249. *See also* schizochronotopia; ethnoscape; sacroscape
chthonic beings, 7, 73, 193–95, 198–99, 202, 208–9, 221, 232n19. *See also* underworld
church, 43, 66, 69, 219, 238, 248; in the town of Gacko, 69, 70, 72, 199–200, 247; in Kazanci 13; in Jajce, 19; Catholic, 42, 148, 188, 189, 220; of St Elijah in Nadanići, 44–45, 65; 74, 76, 113, 137, 224–25, 227–29, 230; in al-Ludd, 213–16; prohibitions of *kumstvo*, 133, 148. *See also* Bosnian Church; Serbian Orthodox Church

cigarettes, 23, 81, 106
circumcision, 43, 81, 206; *kumstvo*, 129–31, 133
clergy, 39–40, 44–45, 70, 199; Archbishop of Genoa, 191; Catholic priest, 148; Hittite priest, 196; *hodža*, 10, 45, 106, 159–60, 197; imam, 99, 199, 205; Jewish priest, 192; Orthodox bishop, 36, 74, 200, 202; Orthodox priest, 44, 99, 144, 148, 181, 200; patriarch, 70; *Reis-ul-ulema*, 42, 45. *See also* church; Islamic Community; Serbian Orthodox Church
clock, 57, 79, 124, 194
clothes, 19, 62, 70, 78n5, 81, 85, 108, 118, 131, 136, 159–60, 163, 182, 188, 202, 211, 214, 222–23, 225, 228
coexistence, 12, 17, 37, 71, 89, 242
coffee, 15, 23, 51, 79, 81, 87, 89, 99, 108–9, 116, 119, 126, 127, 134, 200, 223
cognitive map, 28, 50–53, 123, 124, 195, 243
Cohen, Anthony, 2, 110
collaborators: religious institutions as, 99; Nazi 152n29, 156, 157
commemoration, 42, 74, 75, 77, 94. *See also* monument
communism, 23, 65, 238. *See also* socialism
competition, 4, 14, 16–17, 43, 61, 185, 198, 226–27
competitive sharing, 16–17, 115
confluence of two rivers (or seas), 206–9, 216–17. *See also* Khidr; Dajjal
Connerton, Paul, 94, 110, 176, 241
consciousness, 19, 26, 98, 111, 116, 119–20, 153–55, 165n3, 178; double, 75. *See also* nonconscious, the
contract, 129, 130, 132, 133, 136, 138, 139, 147, 148
Coomaraswamy, Ananda Kentish, 205, 208, 214
cosmogony, 249
cosmology, 17, 176, 178, 209; Bosnian, 3, 20, 44, 133, 174n5, 199, 231; of the Field of Gacko, 7, 10, 14, 21, 44, 76, 83, 129, 154, 163, 176, 228, 231, 237, 240, 243; Slavic, 18–19, 73, 169, 240

Couroucli, Maria, 12
Crapanzano, Vincent, 10, 89–90, 239
creativity: of waiting, 10, of political resistance, 76, 133, 249
Croatia, 22, 38, 39, 42, 46, 54n6, 73–75, 83, 86, 152, 157, 187, 212, 239
Croats, 19, 24, 29, 33, 38, 39, 41, 42, 54n12, 70, 132, 146
crops, xi, 4, 9, 24, 30, 35, 48–49, 58, 62, 102, 116, 127–28, 154, 172, 195, 202, 205–6, 220, 222, 250. *See also* harvest
crossroads, 69, 211, 250; and *kumstvo*, 133
Cruikshank, Julie, 101
Crusades, the, 187, 188, 213
Cvijić, Jovan, 46
Czernowitz, 28, 97

Dagon, 213–14, 232n24, 233n27
Dajjal, 216–17, 232n24, 233nn26–27
dance, xii, 9, 18, 43, 66, 106, 119, 123, 124, 186–87, 188, 189, 212, 220, 226; *kolo*, 4, 19, 45, 50, 106, 123, 137, 179, 186, 188, 198, 205, 212, 223, 224, 227
Danube, 182, 194–95
Dayton Peace Agreement, 15, 22, 39, 51, 52, 78n2, 246
de Certeau, Michel, 50, 52
de Genova, Nicholas, 83
death, 3, 7, 10, 23–24, 35, 42, 58, 71, 73–75, 77, 81, 86, 88, 90, 111, 113–14, 116, 119, 123, 129, 135, 137–39, 189, 190, 194, 199, 203–4, 206–7, 209, 217, 219, 242
Demeter, 210
Demetrius, 210, 218–19
Demetrius' Day (*Mitrovdan/Kasum*), 4, 11, 80, 86, 156, 161, 186, 210, 218–19, 243
đerdek. *See under* marriage
Đerzelez, Alija, 63, 134–35, 152n20, 152n23, 152n25, 197, 198, 218, 232n8, 233n29
Devon Karst Research Society, 27, 172
Dhu'l Qarnayn, 232n21. *See also* Alexander the Great
dialogue, xiv, 8, 13, 26, 49, 94, 114, 175, 178, 230

diaspora, 32, 34, 42, 49, 69, 83–84, 104, 138, 140, 247; and Elijah's Day, 4, 9, 44, 83–84, 91, 111, 228
dimije, 159–60, 163, 182, 223. *See also* clothes
Dinaric: mountains, 4, 46–48, 73, 77, 157, 168, 173, 231, 239; type, 46–48
Diocletian, 189–90
Dionysus, 203, 232n14
disorientation, 120, 127, 235, 237. *See also* orientation
displaced persons, 24, 28, 30, 67, 82, 83–84, 88, 100, 102, 112n7, 126. *See also* refugees
displacement, 30, 35, 103, 104, 110, 112n3, 246
Dizdar, Mak, 151n8, 250
Dizdarević, Đula, 14, 66, 80
Djevojačka Pećina. *See* Maiden's Cave, the
Dobri. See Good, the
Dobrinja, the suburb of, 59
Dodik, Milorad, 11, 51, 54n9, 247
Douglas, Mary, 136, 241, 248
dova. See under prayer
dragon, 73, 111, 134, 182, 191, 193–98, 200, 202, 203, 210, 217, 221, 232n19, 248–49; Order of, 187, 188
dreams, 8; and agency, 26, 48, 94–96, 144; of Ajvaz Dedo, 48; lucid dreams and home, 94–96, 238; daydreams and dreamlike states, xii, 26, 85, 96, 226; socialist, 35; nationalist, 48; and affect, 90; in epics, 134, 198; and *pobratimstvo,* 144
drinks, 4, 43, 66, 81, 109, 122–23, 125, 132, 134, 194, 198, 207–8, 223, 225
Dubois, W. E. B., 75
Duijzings, Gerlachlus, 20–21, 38, 39, 42
dwelling: organization of, 20, 145; of Gurbeti, 27, 97, census and, 32, 33; and landscape, 53, 120, 127, 177, 245; of mythological creatures, 73, 161, 196; room, 85; transformation of, 145; that continued to dwell, 236. *See also* home; seasonal residence

East Sarajevo, 37, 51
Easter (*Uskrs/Vaskrs*), 137, 231n4

economy, 1, 4, 15, 17, 32, 34, 35, 51, 62–63, 75, 81, 84, 96, 99, 122, 125–26, 135, 150, 154, 171, 172, 234, 237, 243
Ederlez, 205, 210–12, 217–18, 234. *See also* George's Day
Eid (*Bajram*), 11, 137, 222
El, 214, 232n24
elderly, the: returnees to the Field, 6, 34, 60, 65, 73, 75, 84, 89, 96, 100, 104, 105, 122, 124, 162, 247; and respect, 108; on Elijah's Day, 66; on George's Day, 211; and nationalism, 68; 89, 219
Eliade, Mircea, 197, 249
Elijah: narratives of, 175–78, 217–18, 220–21; and George, 178, 180, 187–89, 205–6, 211, 213, 217–18, 220–21; and Khidr, 178, 205, 210–11, 213, 217–18, 220–21; two faces of, 1, 7, 14, 53nn1–2, 76, 137, 174, 235, 237; Thunderer, 9, 62, 127, 152n33, 220, 231, 245; and oaks, 37, 184, 221, 231; as rain-giver, 53n5, 151n8, 180, 196, 217–18, 220; and Passover Seder, xii, 205; church of St, 65, 113, 230; chair of, xii, 24, 84; Fiery, 220; anti-syncretic, 191, 196; and Perun, 63, 197, 220–21; and Ajvaz Dedo, 221; and immortality, 216–17, 220; and Baal, 196, 213, 221; protector of Nadanići, 222. *See also* Elijah's Day; Ilija; Alija
Elijah's Day, xi, 1–5, 7–11, 14–16, 25, 27, 30, 32–33, 35, 39, 43–44, 53n5, 59, 63, 66, 76–77, 80, 83–84, 91–92, 99–100, 102, 107, 110–11, 113, 128, 137–38, 151n6, 171, 175, 177–78, 180, 188, 193, 203, 205, 220–29, 231n4, 238–40, 242, 245–46, 248–50. *See also* Jasike; Nadanići; Kula
encounter, x–xi, xiiin5, 1–3, 5–8, 12, 14, 16–17, 23–24, 26, 49, 60, 77, 90, 114–16, 118, 124, 135, 141, 143, 149, 153–55, 163, 169, 171–72, 175, 192, 231, 234–38, 241, 245, 249
England, 186–87, 189, 191, 192
Enkidu, 208
environmental degradation, 27, 169, 171–72, 244, 246–48
epics, 6, 14, 23, 46–47, 49, 63, 80, 82, 86, 98, 114, 134–35, 147, 152n24, 153–65,

194, 197–98, 200, 204, 208, 218, 238, 240, 246, 250. *See also* gusle
epoch, 57–58, 155, 231
Errante, Antoinette, 49
ethnic antagonism, 37, 39, 47, 68–69, 116, 141
ethnic cleansing, xiii, 13, 36–37, 91, 99, 154, 157, 158, 160, 163, 165, 248. *See also* purification
ethnic conflict, 37, 68
ethnicity: and ethnonyms, 33, 39–42, 121, 121–22, 127, 132, 146, 188, 235, 239; and ethnie, x, 37, 158; and ethnic engineering/mapping, 2, 5, 11, 16, 33–36, 39–42, 47, 54n6, 67–75, 76, 91, 100, 104, 145, 147, 154, 157, 187, 234–35, 246; challenges to, 15–16, 21, 25, 29, 34, 36–41, 48, 60, 67–69, 73–77, 99, 114, 123, 131, 137, 141–42, 146, 150, 154, 160, 162–63, 165, 187, 189, 230, 235–36, 238–39, 249; discourse of, 7, 16, 37–40, 42, 46–47, 68, 133, 141, 146–47; and saints, 41. *See also* ethnoscape; ethnic cleansing; ethnic antagonism; homogenization; nationalism
ethnography, 5, 22, 28, 40, 78n7, 99, 112n9, 133, 152n18, 161, 165n1, 175, 201, 204, 231n5, 238, 240; problems with, x, xiiin3, 26, 36–38, 50, 53, 169
ethnology, 19, 46, 175, 204, 212
ethnoscape, 58, 67–76, 99, 100, 240, 249; Appadurai's concept of, 37, 68; Smith's concept of, 68–69. *See also* sacroscape; chronotope
etymology, 23, 53, 67, 73, 115, 121, 127, 130, 150n1, 151n6, 168, 177, 193, 201–4, 210, 232n24, 240
Europe, 7, 13, 18, 39, 47, 48, 61, 83, 160, 168, 173, 190, 204, 221
European Union, 22, 100
Evans-Pritchard, Edward Evan, 50, 61–62
Evans, Arthur, 18–19
everyday, the, 13, 15, 24, 28, 50, 52, 77, 86, 98, 109–10, 116, 120, 124, 140, 146, 147, 150, 154, 165, 206, 212; absence of, 77, 98, 109–10, 212

Ewing, Katherine, 54n18
exile, xiiin7, 22, 58, 68, 74, 80–81, 84, 88, 90, 91, 101, 104, 116, 119, 121, 122, 126, 153, 154, 171, 238
exogamy, 15, 67, 105–107, 117–18, 130, 139, 144, 146–47, 197
ezan. *See under* prayer

Fabian, Johannes, 128
fairies, 3, 50, 73, 81, 95, 105, 133–34, 159–63, 193–94; absence of, 95, 105, 163; dwellings of, 73, 134, 159–63, 193–94, 237, 246; sighting of, 162–63; kinship with, 133–34, 237, 246
Fairy's Cave (*Vilina Pećina*), 162, 193. *See also* fairies; caves
family resemblances, 61, 176, 178, 207
Fazlagića Kula. *See* Kula
Federation of Bosnia and Herzegovina, 100, 246
fertility, 4, 7, 19, 30, 48, 62, 63, 80, 83, 111, 132, 178, 184, 187, 190–92, 194–99, 201–4, 208, 210, 211, 214, 216, 218–21, 233n27, 243
fez hat, 74, 159, 160–61
Field of Gacko, the, x–xii, xv–xvi, 1–17, 19–27, 30–35, 37, 39, 41, 45–47, 49–50, 52–54, 57–63, 65–71, 73, 75–77, 79–86, 88, 90–92, 94–100, 102–6, 109–11, 113–35, 137–42, 145–50, 153–57, 159–63, 165, 168, 171–78, 180, 185–86, 193, 196, 206, 210–11, 219–22, 225, 228, 230–31, 234–50. *See also* Gacko, the town of
Filan, Kerima, 63, 190
Filipović, Milenko S., 132, 133, 139, 144, 145, 148, 152n31, 220
Finci, Jakob, 39
fire, xv, 9, 16, 19, 61, 109, 117, 141, 179, 181, 185–86, 198–99, 205, 211, 216–17, 220. *See also* bonfire
fistfight, 43, 66, 226–227
flowers. *See under* plants
Foča, the town of, 53n4, 225
Foley, John, 152n32, 159, 162,
Fontein, Joost, xiv, 17, 235–36
food, 4, 9, 15, 34, 49, 60–61, 63, 66, 85, 101, 102, 122, 123, 125, 139, 149, 178,

206, 223; apple, 85, 102, 107; baklava, 225; bread, 44, 61, 107, 109, 181, 183, 225; breastmilk, 101, 129–30, 134, 134n12, 152n18, 194; cheese, 101–2, 112n17, 125–26, 225, 228; fish, 172; grain, 10, 107, 151n8, 201, 232n11, 224; *gurabije*, 225; *halva*, 124, 151n7; *kajmak*, 101–2, 125–27, 228; meat, 34, 102, 109, 112n17, 118, 152n29, 183, 185, 225; milk, 85, 101, 108, 126, 190, 198, 223; offering to Khidr and Elijah, 205; *pirjan*, 102; *pita* (pie), 109, 112n17, 225; *pogača*, 61, 107, 225; potato, 112n17, 183; *rahat lokum*, 225; *slatko*, 15, 125, 127, 250; smoked meat, xi, 101–2, 181, spit-roast meat, 118, 225, 228; stew, 183; sweets, 16, 200

forest, xv, 48, 61, 86, 156, 186, 202, 208, 221, 245. *See also* trees

formulae of rapport, 129

Foucault, Michel, 248–49

fragility, 9, 25, 112n12, 146, 173, 207

Fraser, Julius Thomas, 127

Frazer, James George, 7, 199, 203, 216, 232n14

Freud, Sigmund, 153, 155

friction, 5, 17, 37, 114, 137, 241

Gacko, the town of, xvi, 3–4, 22, 28, 30, 32, 49, 67, 70–72, 80, 85, 91, 99–100, 119, 132, 138, 154, 199–200, 238, 242, 246–47; official internet presentation, 28–29, 242; diasporic internet presentation, 28–30, 91. *See also* Field of Gacko, the; power plant Gacko

Gaia, 197

Gajret, 42–43

ganga, xi, 16, 227

gastarbajter, 84, 122

Gatačko Polje. *See* Field of Gacko, the

Geertz, Clifford, 37

Gelasius I, Pope, 189

Gell, Alfred, 52, 62

Gellner, David, 12

genocide, 157–59, 165n5, 200

George, St, 2, 25, 53n2, 63, 83, 100, 111, 175–78, 186–221. *See also* maiden, the; Khidr; dragon; Demetrius; Jarilo

George's Day (*Đurđevdan/Jurjevo*), xi, 2, 4–5, 7, 11, 16, 18–19, 30, 44–45, 52–53n2, 54n16, 63, 86, 101–2, 120–22, 124, 128, 137, 138, 147, 151n6, 152n27, 153, 156, 161, 171, 175, 177, 179–86, 188, 192–94, 196–99, 202–5, 208, 210–12, 216–19, 222, 231, 237–39, 243, 246, 250. *See also* swing; nettle; bonfires; *omaha*

Georgics, the, 7–8, 12, 31, 54n16, 63, 117, 133–34, 152n23, 161, 175, 177–80, 181, 187, 189–94, 196–99, 202, 204–10, 212–18, 219–23, 228, 230–31, 232n18, 233n29, 237, 239, 246–48, 250n2

Georgieva, Cvetana, 149

Gerzovo, the village of, 14, 63, 218

ghosts, 3, 77, 81, 95, 102, 105, 112n4, 192, 200, 246, 250. *See also* apparitions; ghosts

gift, 99, 108, 125, 131, 136, 142–44, 149–50, 151n16, 216

Gilgamesh, 208–209

girdle, 191–92, 199

goat. *See under* animals

godparenthood. *See kumstvo*

Golden Legend, the, 186, 191

gomile, 102, 123

Good, the, xi, 77, 89, 112n8, 217, 250

Gornje Čelo, 16

Gračanica Monastery, 69, 78n11

Gračanica, the river of, 168, 172

Gradačac, the town of, 22

gradina, 245

graffiti, 51, 60, 70–73, 242

grammar: affective/of the body, 6, 26, 162, 163, 250; of poetry, 159, 162; grammatical mood, 89; grammatical tense, 91, 100, 109

Grandits, Hannes, 143

grandmother, xii, 65, 80, 87–89, 101–2, 105, 125, 127, 163, 180–81, 225, 243, 245

grave, xi, 3, 18, 69, 71, 77, 86, 88–89, 91, 95, 102, 124, 141, 194, 213–16. *See also stećci*; mass grave

Grujić, Marija, xiv, 92, 112n5

Gurbeti, xi, 2, 4, 6, 14, 17, 27, 30, 40, 52, 60, 64, 79, 88, 97, 104–5, 114, 116–28,

132, 149, 150n2, 151n5, 154, 181, 186, 210, 237–39, 250. *See also* Roma; Gypsies
Gurbetišta (Gurbeti places), 63, 97, 105, 117–18, 120–24, 126, 132, 151n5, 186, 210, 238
gusle, 6, 47, 98, 153, 155–65, 200–1, 227, 228
Gypsies, 2, 63, 116–17, 121, 123, 126, 133, 180, 186, 189. *See also* Gurbeti; Roma

habit-memory, 40
habitual strangeness, 117–19, 127–28, 237
habitual, the, 6, 40, 102, 112n11, 115, 117–20, 127–29, 159, 160, 176–78, 236–37, 239
habitus, 40, 154
Hadaad. *See* Baal
Haddad, Hassan S., 54n16, 63, 178, 205, 221
Hades, 203, 209–10. *See also* underworld
hadith, 207, 216–17, 232n17, 232n25, 233n26
Hadži Vasiljević, Jovan, 144
Hadžijahić, Muhamed, 20, 48, 54n13, 151n8, 187
hair: cutting on George's Day, 117, 181, 186, 191; cutting and *kumstvo,* 129–33, 142–45, 148; cutting before Elijah's Day, 223; tearing of, 19; fairy's, 163; Elijah's, 220
hajduk, 46–47, 86, 102, 156, 165nn2–3. *See also* outlaws
Halbwachs, Maurice, 94, 96
Halilovich, Hariz, 39, 67, 82, 88, 112n3, 145
Hammel, Eugene, 132–33, 135, 143, 151n10
Hamzić, Vanja, 15, 55, 112n11, 167
Hangi, Antun, 129, 131, 133, 148, 152n19
Hanuš, Ignác Jan, 19
harmony: of life, 17, 95, 97, 237; of song, 227, 237
harvest, 1, 6, 8, 9, 30, 58, 63, 79, 102, 139, 206, 219, 235
Hayden, Robert, 15–17, 54n11, 115, 146
heaven, 74, 148, 208, 220, 226
Helios, 210

Henig, David, xiv, 4, 41–44, 53n5, 54n15, 54n20, 133, 146–47, 151n10
Heracles, 209
herbs. *See under* plants
heritage, 7, 12, 18, 24, 26, 27, 46, 75, 80, 100, 102, 111, 123, 124, 130, 132, 136, 144, 149–50, 159–60, 171, 195–97, 211, 221, 228, 247–50
hero, 3, 46–47, 51, 63, 70, 72–73, 86, 114, 134–35, 153, 156–59, 162, 165n1, 168n8, 189, 197–98, 201, 204, 207–9, 218, 232n18, 237, 242, 246, 250
Herzegovina, the region of, 28, 67, 131–32, 142
hidden transcript, 174
hiding, xi, 17, 62, 68, 80–81, 83, 101, 130, 156, 163, 168–69, 171, 173–74, 205, 207, 209, 213, 219, 245
hilltop, 16, 18, 44, 61, 102–3, 176, 179, 186, 202, 211, 245
Hirsch, Eric, 25, 67
Hirsch, Marianne, 28, 97, 103
historicity, 24–26, 111, 141
history: as Big History, 24, 26, 28–30; different sides of, 11; historical change, 6–8, 20, 149, 230, 241; as historiography, x, 22, 24–26, 28–30, 46, 118, 127, 141, 165n3, 175, 245; *l'histoire événementielle,* 29; life-hi/story, xiin2, 49–50; and the *longue durée,* 48; and nationalism, 17, 28–29, 35, 40, 73–74, 157, 160, 200, 242; oral, 82, 98; and the body, 1, 5, 6, 23–26, 29–30, 40, 58, 92, 97, 118, 122, 124, 143, 148, 230, 236, 238, 245; and waiting, 8–9, 25
Hodinići, the village of, 15, 54n17, 102, 122, 162, 245
holiday, xiiin8, 14, 34, 44, 76, 91, 136, 138, 181, 199–200, 222
home: landscape as, 2, 63–64, 67, 81, 86, 89–90, 96, 235; decoration of, 62, 192, 216, 219; the homely, 77, 81, 85, 88–90, 92, 98, 110–11, 119, 125–26, 146, 155, 234, 236, 243, 245, 248; and encounters, 9, 15, 66, 86, 89–90, 104–5, 122, 125–26, 137, 139, 146; temporal structures of, 1, 3, 5–6, 10,

28, 60, 63, 67, 77, 79–86, 89–92, 94, 96, 100, 111, 119, 121, 149, 236, 242. *See also* unhomely, the
homeland, 3, 82, 243, 246–48
homogenization, xi, 3, 11, 15–16, 18, 35, 37–39, 41, 48, 51, 53n3, 62, 67–69, 98, 108, 154, 230, 246
hope: method of, 82, 249; as negotiation, 6, 9, 83–86, 88–92, 97, 103–4, 111, 128, 199–200, 206; pronounced, 86, 92, 187; and proximity, xii, 5, 141–142, 149, 212; and restoration of landscape, xii, 2, 5, 15, 83–86, 90–92, 97, 103–4, 111, 171, 177, 199–200, 206, 242
Horae, 210
Hörman, Kosta, 129, 131, 134, 136, 151n16, 152n31
horse. *See under* animals
house: and *kumstvo*, 129–31, 133, 135–37, 139–40, 142, 145; meetings, 67, 114, 131, 135–37, 186, 223, 225–27; and neighbourhood, 20, 66, 74, 89, 122, 182, 237; and return, 34, 84, 88–92, 104–5, 109–10, 245, 247; and ritual, 44, 62, 106–108, 117, 123, 133, 174n3, 181–82, 184, 186, 188, 191–92, 198, 205, 216, 220; and romance, 62, 117, 184, 192; and ruination, 24, 60, 70, 74, 80, 88–90, 92, 94, 101–2, 126, 139, 157–58; separation of, 79, 112n2; and war, 80, 94, 101, 245, 247; and winter, 60, 86, 220; and women, 65, 104–110, 181, 223, 226
Hromadžić, Azra, 15, 39, 54n10
Hrustovo Cave, 194
human condition, x, 103, 149–50, 234
hybridity, 12, 15, 111, 115, 234–35; linguistic, 155, 238; architectural, 213–15. *See also* syncretism
hydronym, 168–170, 174n2, 211. *See also* river
Hynes, Maria, 98
hyssop (*miloduh*), 62, 185, 192–93. *See also* plants

icon, 188, 214, 216–17, 219
ideology, 10, 23–25, 27, 39–40, 48, 69, 99, 115, 147, 157, 160, 165n3, 187

Ilija, 1–4, 25, 53n1, 59, 63, 65, 67, 76–77, 78n7, 137, 152n33, 220, 223, 235, 237, 238. *See also* Elijah; Alija
Ilindan, 4, 43, 53, 63, 66, 76, 137, 177, 224. *See also* Elijah's Day
Illuyanka, 196
Illyrians, 102, 123, 238, 245
immortality, 83, 209, 216–17, 220, 232n7
In-Other, 5, 6, 13–14, 25, 60–61, 113–34, 143, 147, 149–50, 154, 160, 165, 168–69, 219, 230, 235–37, 246, 248, 250. *See also* encounter
Inara, 196
incantation, 143, 189, 211. *See also* prayer
incest, 198, 202–3
India, 105–6, 109, 204–5, 208
Indo-European: beliefs, 7, 18, 73, 177, 195, 203, 204, 212, 228, 236; language, 115, 150n1, 202
infertility, 178, 195, 197, 204, 216, 219. *See also* fertility; pregnancy
Ingold, Timothy, 50, 53, 79, 177
instrument, 6, 98, 122, 124, 155, 157–60, 162, 200, 227, 232n10. *See also* gusle
International Criminal Tribunal for the Former Yugoslavia (ICTY), 69–70, 76, 138, 141, 158, 200
International Workers' Day, 44. *See also* May Day
Iraq, 248, 250n2
Irby, Adelina Paulina, 18
Ishtar, 192, 203, 208
Isis, 203
Islamic Community in Bosnia and Herzegovina (organization), 42–43, 45, 99, 247
Islamic State, 248, 250n2
Israel, 14, 31, 53n4, 213–14, 220, 239, 249. *See also* Palestine
Ivančević, Petar, 143–44
izijes, 184, 246. *See also* trees: oak

Jack-in-the-Green, 204
Jacob of Seroug, 207
Jagoda, Flory, xii
Jajce, the town of, 19
jama. *See* abyss

Jama Dizdaruša, 73–74. *See also* abyss; Korićka Jama
Jansen, Stef, 59, 78n2, 81–83, 90, 110, 171
Jarilo, 63, 198–99, 201–3, 208, 210
Jasike, 14, 35, 43, 65–66, 225, 230, 238, 240
Jesus, 151n8, 191, 216–17, 232n24, 233n26
Jews, xii, xiiin6, 28, 39, 42, 97, 189, 192, 213, 218, 231n5
Jirjis (Đirđis), 190, 209, 218, 250n2. *See also* George, St; Khidr
John, St, 143, 151n8, 152n24
John's Day (*Ivanjdan*), 11, 16, 18, 19, 50, 198, 239
Jordan, 218
joy (*rahatluk*), 95, 182
Joy, Charlotte, 27
Jugovići, the village of, 84
Jupiter, 220–21
Jurjevo, 4, 53, 62, 177, 180. *See also* George's Day

kajmak. *See under* food
kalajisanje (tinning), 63, 122, 124–26, 186
Kalē, 207
Kalinovik, the town of, 224
Karadžić, Radovan, 158, 200
Karadžić, Vuk, 135–36, 152n33, 158, 194–95, 200–1
karst, 1, 4, 27, 32, 59–60, 73, 75, 77, 123, 168–69, 171–73, 203, 237
Kasum, 4, 218–19. *See also* Demetrius Day
Kazanci, the village of, 13, 219
Khidr, 63, 178, 203–210, 212–21, 232nn20–22, 237, 248, 250n2. *See also* George, St; Elijah, St; Ederlez
Khidrellez (see Ederlez)
kijamet, 80
kitchen, 49, 85. *See also* home
Ključ, the fort of, 32, 80, 162, 201
Knežević, Antun, 187, 231n2
knight, 178, 187, 188–89, 191, 197, 214
Knight, Chris D., 194
Kolind, Torsten, 15, 47–48, 78n2, 86, 97, 119, 150
kolo. *See under* dance
komšiluk, 20, 54n15, 145–47. *See also* neighbourhood

Komušina, 19
Kononenko, Natalie, 19, 54n12
Korićka Jama, 73–75, 242. *See also* abyss; Jama Dizdaruša
Korita, the village of, 73–74, 157, 242
Korp, Maureen, 228
Kosovo, 12, 20, 41–42, 46, 54n6, 69–70, 219, 239, 242. *See also* battle: of Kosovo
Kovačević, Kosta, 196, 198
Kovačević, Stojan, 69
kraj, 67, 78n8
Krauss, Friedrich Salomon, 161, 165n1
Kreševo, the town of, xv, 16, 19, 31, 50, 53n4, 198, 239
Križ, the hill of, xv, 179, 211
Krvavac, Hajrudin, 34
Kula, the village of, xv, 3, 24, 26, 33, 34–35, 45, 50, 54n17, 65, 67, 71, 83, 84, 85, 89, 99, 140, 151n5, 157, 159–60, 162, 165n7, 171, 183, 199, 223–26, 228, 229, 242
kumstvo, 6, 16, 20, 67–68, 99, 116, 127–52, 186, 237
Kunovo inscription, 151n8
Kwon, Heonik, 97

l'histoire événementielle, 29
La Benevolencija, 42,
Ladino language, xii, xiiin7
Lakha, Salim, 10
landscapes of seasonal order, 4, 228, 243
language: and affect, 23, 153–55, 175; and landscape, 159–62, 175; and the un-narratable, 94–96, 112n3, 126, 153, 236; post-, 95; pre-, 95; political, 10, 37–38, 41, 51, 70, 71; and story, 10, 50, 101, 126; of encounters, x–xi, 15, 23–24, 50, 114, 153–55, 213
Latour, Bruno, xiiin3, xiiin4, 112n10
Leger, Louis, 19
Levant, 63, 196, 213
Lévi-Strauss, Claude, 38, 203
Levinas, Emmanuel, 79, 113–16
Libya, 191–192
life-hi/story, xii, 49–50, 71, 81, 88, 206
lightning, xi, 7, 9, 62, 72, 129, 181, 220–21, 231, 245–46

lile torches, 198
Lockwood, William, G., 139, 151n10, 152n28
Löfving, Staffan, 81, 82, 110–11
London, 31, 37, 48, 85, 118, 122
loneliness, xv, 104–6, 109–111, 112n12, 116
longue durée, 48
Lord, Albert, 134, 154, 157–60, 165n6, 240
Lotan, 196
Lučić, Ivo, 73, 168–69, 171, 173, 174n1, 231
Lydda (Lod/al-Ludd), 189, 213–220, 232n24, 233nn26–27, 233n30

Macedonia, 19, 20
Mackenzie, Georgina Muir, 18
magic light, xi, 50, 77, 89, 95, 141
magic, xi, 62, 77, 95, 131, 141, 149, 151n8, 156, 162–63, 192, 196, 199, 207, 230
Mahdi, 205
Maiden, the, 111, 191–99, 203–04, 208, 210, 230–31, 232n6, 237, 239. *See also* Maiden's Cave, the; George's Day
Maiden's Cave, the, 193–94, 196, 230, 232n6, 239. *See also* cave
majka Kana, 193
majka Nura, 104,
Maksimović, Desanka, 79, 111n1
map, 5, 15, 21–22, 24, 32, 36, 45, 50–53, 67, 111, 118, 123, 124, 127, 153, 169–70, 174n4, 195, 240, 243, 244. *See also* cognitive map
Margitić Jajčanin, Stipan, 188, 220
Marko, Prince, 134–35, 152n23, 161, 197
marriage: 'inter-religious'/mixed, 13, 15–16, 106, 118, 130, 146–47; and Elijah's Day, 65, 224, 225–26; and house, 79, 105–8; and *kumstvo,* 129–30, 135–37, 138–39, 146; and running into wheat, 224; and song, 182, 184, 226; and *boščaluk* (gift), 108; and *nakonče,* 108; and đerdek, 106; bride, 104–110, 117, 182, 192, 195, 225; exogamy, 106, 144; husband, 105, 108, 245; Khidr's, 232n21; prohibition of, 144, 146–47; proposal prediction, 44, 117, 183, 202; proposals, 16, 106, 226; stealing of bride, 106; to dragon/monster,

195–97; wedding, 15, 28, 106–7, 123, 129–30, 136–37, 191, 192, 224; wife, 85, 91, 107, 144, 199, 203, 226
mass grave, 6, 67, 73, 77, 237, 242
Massey, Doreen, 70
Massumi, Brian, 153–54
Maurer, Desmond, xiv, 151n16, 232n18
May Day, 11, 44, 204
Mediterranean, the, 13, 63, 195, 210, 218
Međugorje, 42, 54n4
memorial. *See* monument
memory, 5, 6, 10, 24, 28–29, 40–41, 53, 71, 77, 79, 80, 82, 90, 94, 96, 100–1, 103, 110–11, 116, 123, 128, 153–54, 160, 176, 194, 197, 200, 210–11, 240–42, 249
memoryscape, 28–29, 123
Merleau-Ponty, Maurice, 96–97, 109
Mesopotamia, 208–9, 213, 233
Metohija: as Gacko, 3; Kosovo and, 70; hotel, 199
Michael, St, 231; Day of, 147
migration, xi, 7, 28, 34, 83–84, 104, 122, 145, 206. *See also* displaced persons; refugees; return; *Gastarbaiter*
Mihailović, Draža, 60, 157–58, 242
Milanović, Petar, 169, 171, 172
Miljanov, Marko, 144
milk. *See under* food
milk kinship, 129–30, 134, 151n12, 152n12. *See also* sworn kinship
millet, 41
miloduh. See hyssop
Milošević, Slobodan, 76–77
minaret, 13, 160–161, 219
Mitrovdan. See Demetrius' Day
Miyazaki, Hirokazu, 82, 249
Mladić, Ratko, 70, 72, 242
moba, 66, 139
Mokro, the village of, xv, 53n4, 198, 239
monster, 196–97, 208, 209
Montenegro, 67, 144, 157, 224, 239
monument, 40, 51, 71, 74, 199, 213, 241, 242
moon, the, 133, 189, 194, 211, 212; moonlight, 74, 223
Moses, 206–9, 217–18
mosque, 13, 45, 65–66, 69, 80, 85, 91–93, 101, 137, 157, 189, 199, 213–14, 219,

224–27, 229, 232n23, 238, 247, 248, 250n2
Mostar, the city of, 9, 28, 66–67, 83, 85, 91, 100–1, 126, 140, 142–43, 151n8, 227
mother, 22, 61, 79, 101, 106, 117, 133, 134–35, 137, 181, 184, 185–86, 190, 194, 219, 222; in-law, 107–9; co–, 130, 151n12; earth, 194, 197, 210. *See also* grandmother
mountain, xv, 3–4, 19, 32, 46–48, 51, 60, 68, 74, 80, 86, 101, 105, 114, 116, 124, 134, 141, 146, 154, 156, 159, 161–62, 168–69, 173, 197, 201, 221
Mueller, Lisel, 92
Muhamedans, 131, 143, 144, 216
Muhammad, the prophet, 63, 216, 220, 232n17
music, xii, 7, 9, 51, 119, 122–23, 223. *See also* song; instrument

Nadanići, the village of, xv, 4, 33, 43, 50, 65, 70, 76–77, 101, 113, 137, 222–24, 229
nakonče. See under marriage
namuša, 16, 106, 226
Napredak, 42
nationalism, xi, 3–4, 6, 11, 14, 17, 19, 24, 27, 35, 38, 41–42, 46–48, 51, 54n6, 54n9, 60, 66–71, 73–77, 83–84, 98, 100, 116, 118–19, 123, 128, 131, 154–65, 172, 174, 177, 187, 206, 213, 230, 235, 241–42, 246, 240, 250
Navaro-Yashin, Yael, 13, 23, 26, 112n9, 154, 160, 163, 236
Naxos, island of, 25–26
Nazis, 29, 42, 73–74, 97, 152n29, 156–57
neighbourhood, 16, 18, 20, 40, 46, 49, 66, 68, 74, 80, 85, 89, 104, 107–8, 110, 115, 126, 131, 138, 145–47, 149, 158, 162–63, 171, 182, 206, 224, 226, 237, 246
Nereids, 210
Nettelfield, Lara, 71, 82, 88, 112n6
nettle (*žara*), xi, 16, 44, 62, 92, 102, 117, 181–83, 185, 195, 201–2, 211, 246, 250
Nevesinje, the town of, 71, 131, 136, 139, 224–25
New Orleans, 92
Niškanović, Miroslav, 63

nomads, xi, 4, 6, 27, 52, 63, 88, 116, 121, 126, 150, 206, 237–38
non-Serbs, 28–29, 70, 157, 247
nonconscious, the, 25–26, 37, 98, 111, 153–54, 159, 235
nonhumans, xiiin4, 3, 13, 27, 40, 48, 60, 62–63, 75, 81, 96, 116, 119–20, 124, 127, 129, 168, 174, 228, 234, 241, 246
Nuer, the, 61–62
nur. See magic light
nymphs, 114, 133, 189, 199. *See also* fairies

omaha, 44, 62, 192–93, 197, 208. *See also* water; George's Day
ontology, 54n18, 61, 85, 114, 116, 118, 120, 177, 213, 250
Oral-Formulaic Theory, 154, 159, 162, 194–95, 200
orientation, 2, 6, 9–10, 13, 45, 48, 82, 86, 100, 114, 119–21, 123, 127, 128, 151n8, 212, 235–37, 240, 247–49. *See also* disorientation
Orthodox Christians, 2, 41, 65, 122, 131–33, 137, 144, 147–48, 157, 178, 188, 203, 219
Osberg, Richard, 191, 192
Osiris, 203
Osman Pasha, 13
Ottoman Empire, 13, 29, 41, 46, 70, 141, 156, 172, 188, 196, 250n1
outlaws, 46, 47, 69, 86, 102, 134, 155–56, 161, 165n4, 186, 204

Palestine, 7, 14, 30–31, 53n4, 175–76, 186, 189, 190, 212–19, 232n22, 239, 249
Parkes, Peter, 151n12, 152n18
Parry, Milman, 154, 159–60, 200–1, 240
Partisans, the, 34, 42, 152n29, 224
Passover Seder, xii, 205
past, xii, 2–3, 5, 8–10, 12, 17, 23, 25–27, 29, 40, 45, 49, 53, 58, 70, 77, 79, 81–83, 88–92, 94, 96–101, 105, 109–111, 125, 128, 149, 153–54, 157, 160, 175, 197, 212, 234, 236–38, 241, 243, 245, 250
paths: of knowledge, x, 14, 22, 49, 52, 81, 111, 169, 201, 205, 219, 221, 228, 235, 245; in landscape, 49, 51–52, 76, 90, 92, 102, 105, 111, 126, 165, 169, 221, 225,

235, 230; of bodies on the move, 63, 83–84, 90, 126, 238; of nationalism, 51, 73, 76, 165; chronotopic, x, xii, 57, 76, 81, 90, 96, 105, 110, 111, 126, 245
Patron saint day (*slava*), 18, 137, 186–88
patron saint, 18, 137, 186–88, 205, 216
Pavković, Nikola, 144
Pawlikowski, Pawel, 158
Pečuriš, the valley of, 122–23, 151n5
Pegasus, 197
Peleikis, Anja, 150
Perica, Vjekoslav, 41–42, 45
Persephone, 210
Perseus, 196
Persia, 190, 209
Perućica, the forest of, 221
Perun, 63, 197, 202–3, 210, 220–21, 230–31
Pešikan-Ljuštanović, Ljiljana, 198
Pešter, the plateau of, 203
Peter, St, 11, 18, 231n4
Peter's Day (*Petrovdan*), 11, 16, 198, 231n4, 239
phantom limb, 6, 94, 96, 111,
Pharaoh, 196
Piedmont, 70
pilgrimage, 19, 23, 27, 30, 42, 48, 53n5, 151n6, 162, 193, 205, 214, 218, 230, 239. *See also* Ajvatovica; Maiden's Cave, the
Pine, Frances, xiv, 86
pit. *See* abyss
pita (pie). *See under* food
pitcher (*ibrik*), 108, 193–94
plants: education into, 101–3, 243, 245; flowers, 62, 85, 89–90, 98, 102, 185, 192–93, 223, 243–45; grass, xi, 80, 123, 180, 209, 224; herbs, 7, 30, 60, 62, 81, 89, 101–2, 183–85, 192–93, 206, 208, 243; and home, 89, 185, 243–46; and rejuvenation, 62, 190, 201–4, 209, 218; and sexuality/fertility, 62, 117, 182–85, 210–11, 216, 243, 246; shrubs, 89, 102, 105, 192, 211, 243; and spirits, 62, 192–93; in springtime, 62, 102, 117, 119, 125, 180–86, 192–95, 202, 208, 211, 216. *See also* trees; hyssop; nettle; amulet
Ponor (toponym), 183, 185, 193

ponor, 168, 183, 196, 209. *See also* abyss; sinking river
Popovo Field, 71
post-act, 176–77, 180, 222
post-encounter, 24
postmemory, 103
power plant (Gacko), 4, 9, 27, 34–36, 64–67, 91, 99, 137, 169, 172, 224–25, 230, 237, 243–44, 246–48
prayer: against devil, 151n8; against dragon, 197; *dova*, 44, 53n5, 106, 193, 197, 232n6, 239; *ezan*, 141, 160–61; for fertility, 106, 190, 193–94, 205, 214–16, 218; of George, 190–91; of Khidr and Elijah, 218; of Khidr, 205; *mevlud*, 45, 222; in the morning of Elijah's Day, 65, 137, 225; *namaz*, 48, 80; at noon on Elijah's Day, 65, 137, 225; prayer-like utterance/action, 90, 111; for rain, 44, 53n5, 151n8, 193, 218; for resurrection, 190; rhythm of, 79, 116; to sun for loved one's return, 196, 198; for water, 48, 54n5; for wheat and wine, 151n8
pregnancy, 62, 107, 211, 216. *See also* children
Prenj, the mountain range of, 221
Prizren, 144
Procopius of Caesarea, 193, 221
Procopius' Day, 9, 11, 62, 181,
Prosvjeta, 42–43
protection: through avoidance of action, 205; deities and, 202; Elijah as protector, 222; environmental and heritage, 27, 171; from evil, 216, 230; George/Khidr as protector, 187, 188, 190, 216; and *kumstvo*, 129, 134–36, 138–42, 148; of land, 196; from verdigris, 125; of virginity, 192. *See also* amulet
proverb, 1, 10–11, 14, 23, 49, 54n7, 57–58, 61, 63, 65, 67, 78n3, 78n4, 78nn6–7, 78n9, 86, 91, 110–11, 112n16, 128, 136, 147, 151n9, 152n26, 152n34, 156, 172, 174n6, 180, 184, 186, 219, 223, 232n11–12, 236
proximity turn, xi, 17, 235–38, 240
proximity, xi, xiiin5, 1, 3, 5, 11–14, 16–17, 20, 23–25, 37, 39–40, 48, 60, 62, 66,

68, 71, 75, 113–16, 118, 120, 124, 126, 130, 135, 139, 145–47, 155, 235–238, 240, 243
Prozor, the town of, 107
purification: ethno-religious, 3, 13, 53, 54n6, 71, 91, 98, 248–49; rituals, 66, 168–69, 193. *See also* ethnic cleansing
Python, 196–97

Qleibo, Ali, 203, 213, 217–19, 232n24
Qur'an, the, 66, 99, 107, 206, 207, 217–18, 232n17

Ramadan, 11, 124, 151n7
Ratiš, 53n4, 239
refugees, 9, 49, 66, 82–85, 90, 122, 126, 145, 17. *See also* displaced persons; return
remnants, xi, 5–6, 12–13, 17, 23, 26, 53n3, 83, 92, 96, 102, 111, 120, 130, 153–55, 160–63, 173, 176, 193, 199–201, 204, 213, 236
Republika Srpska, 32–33, 36, 51, 71, 112n7, 246
resistance, 6, 10, 14, 25, 28, 44, 76–77, 88, 98, 100, 119, 156, 174, 189, 198, 213, 236, 248–49
restoration, 40, 42, 45, 80, 84–86, 91–92, 98, 111, 126, 147, 171, 195, 200, 249
resurrection, 190, 196, 201–4, 207, 209, 212, 214, 217
return: and returnees (*povratnici*), xi–xii, 3, 6, 9–10, 26, 29–30, 32–34, 36, 39, 44, 47, 60, 65, 67–68, 73, 80–86, 88–92, 94, 96, 100, 103, 104, 110, 111, 112n4, 112n6, 116, 119, 122, 126, 140, 148, 157–58, 171–72, 199, 210, 228, 242–43, 245, 247; Elijah's return, xii, 2, 8, 30, 91, 110, 175, 221, 227–28, 242, 245; eternal return, 9, 169, 249; Gurbeti vernal, 116, 118–19, 121–23, 132; of birds, 171; of Georgic characters, 156, 186, 202–03, 210; of landscape, 9, 95, 118, 245; of time, 9–10, 79, 82, 95, 109, 242, 249; of war, 22, 116; process of, 83, 91–92, 140, 148; return to return, 2, 121; returning dead, 88; safety, 22, 68, 74, 81, 84, 103; struggle to, 84, 88, 92, 171; sustainable, 84–85, 90; to society, 156, 186. *See also* seasonal residence; refugees; displaced persons; home
Rihtman-Auguštin, Dunja, 44
ritual, x, xv, 2–4, 6–7, 11, 14, 16–19, 19, 21, 23–24, 30, 35, 41, 43–44, 48–50, 52, 61–62, 66, 70, 74, 78n5, 88, 94, 115–16, 118, 120, 123, 127, 129, 131–33, 136, 141–43, 145, 147, 149, 150, 156, 168, 176, 187, 189, 191–95, 197–99, 201–5, 208–9, 211, 213–14, 217, 221, 225, 230–31, 232n14, 235, 237, 239, 242, 245; circumnavigation, 199, 205
river, 3, 7, 22, 73, 134, 151, 168–69, 171–75, 178, 183, 193, 196–97, 199, 204–6, 208–9, 216–17, 231; *ponornica* (sinking river), 7, 73, 168–69, 171–75, 178, 193, 196, 231. *See also omaha*; confluence of two rivers; water
Robin Hood, 156, 204
Roma, 2, 18, 29, 33, 39, 40, 52, 63, 88, 116, 121, 126, 132, 152n27, 178, 189, 205, 210–12, 217, 238–39. *See also* Gurbeti, Gyspsies
Romania, 97
roosters. *See under* animals
Rosaldo, Renato, 23, 27
ruination, xi, 3, 7, 60, 69, 89–90, 120, 152, 161, 163, 173, 196, 201, 230, 236, 238, 241
ruptures, 5, 9, 49, 78n2, 81, 109, 117, 165, 204, 241
Rushdie, Salman, 82, 125
Russia, 22, 187, 221

Sack, Robert, 69
sacrifice: to the dragon, 191, 194–96, 199; to magical beings, 193; to Dionysus, 203; to Perun, 221; on George's Day, 19, 203, 219; against, 191; and water, 168–69, 193, 196, 203; on Elijah's Day, 203; blood, 194, 214, 219; national, 75; and renewal of time, 194. *See also* ritual
sacroscape, 58–63, 66, 68, 75–76, 99, 100, 240, 243, 246. *See also* ethnoscape; chronotope
Sarajevo, xii, xiiin6, 21–22, 31, 51–52, 53n4, 83, 100, 103, 145, 147, 174n2, 205, 231n5

saying. *See* proverb
scales, 32, 36–38, 60, 68, 81, 98, 99, 105, 126, 137
Scarry, Elaine, 95
Schäuble, Michaela, 75, 77
Scheper-Hughes, Nancy, 26
schizochronotopia, 5, 57–58, 68–69, 71, 76, 77n2, 241. *See also* chronotope
Schweizer, Harold, 8, 234
Scott, James, 98, 174
SDS (Serb Democratic Party), 9, 76
sea, 182, 193, 194–96, 202, 204, 206–9. *See also* water
seasonal residence, 32–33, 67–68, 100, 120–21, 123, 132, 156
Sedlo, the passage of, 32
šehid, 71
Sejdić, Dervo, 39
Selimović, Meša, 192
Serbia, 11, 22, 38, 41–42, 46, 54n6, 69, 70, 100, 121, 134, 138, 144, 147, 156–58, 165n4, 175–76, 198, 200, 203, 239
Serbian Orthodox Church, 41–43, 45, 70, 76, 99, 200
Serbian Orthodox Church, 41–43, 45, 70, 99, 148, 189
Šešelj, Vojislav, 69–71, 73, 242
sexuality, 62, 130, 191–93, 197–98, 204, 243. *See also* plants: sexuality/fertility
sheep. *See under* animals
shelter, 86, 101, 103, 123, 126, 139–40, 230
shrubbery, 89, 102, 105, 192, 221, 243. *See also* home; unhomely, the
Sidran, Abdulah, 71
sigh, 81, 85, 112n3
sijelo, 9, 43, 66, 155, 158–59, 192, 193. *See also* encounter
Silena, the city of, 191
silence, 6, 8, 10, 23, 24, 51, 73, 75, 77, 81, 85, 95–96, 99, 105, 110, 112n3, 133, 200, 234, 236, 249
silhouette, x, xiin2, 1, 113, 149
Silvanus, 202
sinking river. *See under* river
Široki Brijeg, the town of, 74
skin, 119, 127, 130, 202
sky, xi, 60, 79, 147, 130, 203, 220
slatko. *See under* food

Slavic: cosmology, 7, 18, 19–20, 53, 73, 149, 168–69, 179, 193, 201–3, 208, 212, 230–31, 236, 238, 240; pantheon, 7, 19, 53, 62–63, 74, 160, 193–94, 197, 201–3, 210, 212, 221, 230, 238
Smith, Anthony, 65, 68, 70
snake, 73, 133, 196–199, 209, 221, 232n19. *See also* dragon
snow, 9, 60–61, 67, 91, 102, 108, 113, 147, 185, 204, 222–23, 237
SNSD (Alliance of Independent Social Democrats), 36, 51
soap opera, 49, 105–6, 109–110
socialism, 35, 39, 41, 42–44, 46, 139, 156, 189; Socialist Federative Republic of Yugoslavia, 22, 160; and the postsocialist period, 44, 88, 189. *See also* communism
solitude, 104–6, 110, 116. *See also* loneliness
song, xi–xii, 4, 9, 24, 45–47, 49, 71, 79, 98, 106, 111, 122–23, 133–35, 152n25, 152n33, 154–65, 171, 175, 182, 184, 187, 194, 195, 197, 201–2, 205, 211, 218, 226–28, 231n3, 232n8, 240
Sorabji, Cornelia, 41, 43, 54n15, 145–47
spells, 181, 184, 296, 198, 230
spindle, 193–94
spirits, 19, 62, 133, 141, 192–93, 198, 217. *See also* ghosts; apparitions; hyssop
Spitzer, Leo, 28, 97
springtime, xi, 6, 9, 44, 62–63, 66, 85–86, 91, 102, 105, 107, 116–17, 121–25, 132, 137, 156, 161, 171, 176, 180, 183, 185–89, 196, 198, 201–4, 208–210, 217, 219, 228, 237, 249
Srebrenica, the town of, 33, 71, 82, 86, 91, 103, 112n6
stećci mediaeval tombstones, 50, 102, 105, 123, 197–98, 201. *See also* grave
Stewart, Charles, 11–12, 17, 25–26
Stewart, Kathleen, 90, 165
Stolac, the town of, 22, 39, 47, 53n4, 66, 78n2, 86, 97, 119, 152n27, 220, 239
Stolac, the village of, 54n17
storm god, 196
stranger, the, 100, 127, 133, 150, 250
Studenac, the spring of, 182, 225

Sufism, 205, 232n15
summertime, xvi, 4, 6, 9, 60, 63, 66, 86, 90, 101, 109, 113, 122–23, 127, 172, 178, 180–81, 184, 197, 201–2, 217, 219–22, 236–37, 244, 249–50
sun, xii, 1, 18, 59, 65, 76, 79–80, 101, 122, 129, 151n4, 181, 183–84, 186, 189, 194, 196, 198, 210, 211, 226, 237, 250
Sutjeska, 51
sweets, 16, 200. *See also slatko*
swing, 16, 62, 111, 117, 181–82, 194, 204, 250. *See also* George's Day
sworn brotherhood/sisterhood (*pobratimstvo/posestrimstvo*), 134–135, 141–44, 148, 151n12, 161. *See also kumstvo*
sworn kinship. *See kumstvo*
synagogue, xii, 214
syncretism, 5–7, 11–14, 17–20, 44, 62, 71, 85, 148, 154–55, 163, 186–87, 191, 196, 206, 212–15, 220, 231, 234–36, 238–39, 241, 248–49. *See also* anti-syncretism
Syria, 190, 205, 207, 216, 248–49

Taaliyaa, 209
Tammuz, 203
teferič, 4, 42–45, 122–23, 137, 151n6, 182, 186, 220, 223, 237
Tenis, 200
tepsija, 125
territory, 13, 16, 29, 32, 34, 37–39, 41, 54n6, 68–70, 74–75, 81, 88, 114, 153, 155, 250
Texas, 86
Thallo, 210
Thor, 221
thorns (*trnje*), 102, 105, 112n9. *See also* unhomely, the
thunder, 9, 63, 181, 203, 220–21, 231
Tikhon of Zadonsk, St, 202
Tilley, Christopher, 53
time: and cockcrow, xii, 79, 80; and home, 79–112; and In-Other, 113–52; and *kijamet*, 80; and modernization, 34–35; time and solitude, 104–111; time and remnants, 153–65; appropriate, 62, 79–81, 177; control of, 191–94; distimement, 84, 104, 11;

epoch, 57–58, 155, 231; impersonal, 109; joyful, 2, 15, 66, 95, 131, 136, 150, 182, 220, 224, 250; Last Hour, 216–17, 233n26; oecological, 61, 66; stoppage of (slumber), 194–95; structural, 61, 66; telling, 79–80, 124, 223–24, 238; temporal transposition, 8, 81, 96, 243; time-reckoning, 3, 26, 53, 61, 66, 81, 121, 127, 234; *vakat*, 57–58, 67, 231; *vrijeme*, 57–58, 127. *See also*, encounter; waiting; loneliness; chronotope
Tito, Josip Broz, 22, 42, 51, 65
Titton, Jeff, 50
Tjentište, 51
tolerance, 47, 71, 141. *See also* antagonistic tolerance
Tomašić, Dinko, 46–47, 152n31
toponyms, 24, 32, 34, 52–53, 63, 124, 168–69, 174n2, 174n4, 193, 209, 214, 221, 233n27, 240, 242
touch, 90, 114, 127, 143, 221. *See also* encounter
treba, 168–80, 174n3–4
Trebinje, the town of, 168, 170, 174n4
trees, xi, 27, 243, 250; abandoned, 92; and lightning, 221; and Perun's name, 221; aspen (*jasika*), 65, 224–25, 230, 240; birch tree (*breza*), 182; branches for bonfire, 49–50; cornel (*drijen*), 183–85, 194, 211, 216; fruitful, 190, 210; hollow 151n8, 199; hornbeam (*grabovina*), 184; large, 62, 65; maple (*javor*), 185, 200; Mila's, 89–90, 93; mulberry tree (*murva*), 102, 182; oak (*hrast, dub*), 37, 182–84, 221, 231, 246; old, 117; olive, 228; pine, 151n8; produced by George/Jirjis/Khidr, 190; refusal to cut, 245; stumps of, 117, 182, 228; walnut (*orah*), 102, 182, 200; wild plum (*džanarike*), 102; willow (*vrba*), 62, 181–82, 184, 211, 216, 246; yew (*tisovina*), 184, 221, 230; young, 45. *See also* plants
Trevor, Roy, 19
Triglav, 74
Trinity Day (*Trojčindan*), 70, 78n10
Troglav Mountain, 74

Truhelka, Ćiro, 54n14, 188, 231n4
Tryphon Day (*Tripundan*), 60
Tuan, Yi-Fu, 120, 127
Turk, the, 131, 143, 144, 151n15, 159, 188, 220
Turkey, 18, 63, 106, 121, 122, 126, 151n3, 151n6, 154, 156, 205, 218
Turner, Victor, 156
Tuzla, the town of, 31, 52, 53n4

Umoljani, the village of, 197
underworld, the, 3, 74, 173, 192–93, 197, 199, 202–4, 208–210, 219, 237
unhomely, the, 81, 85–86, 88, 92, 105, 110–11, 119, 121, 150, 155, 171, 234, 236
United States of America, 22, 28, 35, 75, 78n10, 85
Uruk, 208
Ustaše, 73–74, 139, 152n29. *See also* Nazis
Utanapishtim, 209
utvare. *See* apparitions

vakat, 57–58, 67, 231. *See also* time
Valeria of Tusculum, 202
Valerius, 202
vegetation. *See* plants; trees
veil, 18, 78n5, 157, 159–61. *See also bula*
Veles, 202, 203, 221
Venetian Republic, 141
Verdery, Katherine, 88
Vidan, Aida, 14, 66, 80, 162, 165n8, 240
Vienna Manuscript (Palimpsest), 190
vile. *See* fairies
Virgil, 175, 177, 220, 228
Virgin Mary, 152, 231n4
virginity, 62, 192, 196, 204, 232n21
Visoki, fort of, 220
Visoko, the town of, 4, 52, 53n4, 121, 152n27, 179, 198, 210–12, 216, 238–39
Vitus Day (*Vidovdan*), 11, 19, 54n9
Vladislavić, Sava, 69
Volujak Mountain, 159–62, 164
Voronezh, 202
Vuk Jajčanin, 134, 152n20, 232n8

Wagner, Roy, 57–58
Wagner, Sarah, 33, 71, 82, 86, 88, 91, 103, 112n6

waiting, x–xii, 2, 5, 7–11, 25, 59, 79, 80, 82, 86, 88, 92, 105, 106, 109–110, 117, 124, 205, 211, 218, 223, 234–35, 242, 249, 250. *See also* time
war: 1990s, in Bosnia, xi–xii, 1–2, 4–11, 13, 22, 24, 27, 28, 30, 33, 34, 38–39, 46–49, 51–52, 54n6, 59–61, 63, 67–70, 73–75, 81–86, 88, 97, 101, 110–11, 118–28, 131–32, 136, 138, 140–41, 145–49, 154, 156–58, 171–72, 182, 189, 199–200, 206, 210, 224, 227–28, 234–35, 237–38, 242–43, 246, 249; World War I, 9, 73, 80, 148, 156; World War II, 42, 51, 60, 73–74, 77, 77–78n2, 132, 139, 148, 156–58, 165n4, 242; Balkan Wars, 18, 156; crimes, 155–58, 242; cyclical quality of, 22, 116; *Gothic War*, 193; and sharing, 16; all Serb wars, 75; and Halbwachs, 96; and the village, 101; and Virgil, 177; and George, 187; and Perun, 221. *See also* hiding; shelter
Wastell, Sari, xiv, 36
water, 10, 27, 125, 165, 168–69, 171–174n1, 195, 201, 246, 250; rituals, 44, 48, 62, 107, 131, 152n27, 182–85, 192–94, 196–98, 202, 205, 208, 211, 225, 240; spring of, 66, 79, 101, 123, 152n27, 162, 171–72, 182–83, 190, 193, 195–96, 229, 201, 207, 210–11, 225, 229, 240; mill, 10, 44, 62, 183–84, 192–93, 208; well, 193–94, 196, 198, 204–5, 207; and knowledge, 207, 209, 216; of Death, 194, 198, 203, 209, 217; of Life, 190, 196, 204, 205, 207–9, 214, 217–18. *See also* dragons, fairies, rivers, sea
weather, 57, 80, 101, 114, 116, 127, 151n8, 180–81, 195, 204, 220, 223. *See also* time
wedding, 15, 28, 106, 123, 129–30, 136–37, 191–92. *See also* marriage
weeds (*korov*), 92, 105. *See also* unhomely, the
werewolf, 133
West, Rebecca, 19
willow (*vrba*). *See under* trees
wind, 92, 113, 123, 220, 232n7, 250
witches, 73, 181, 198

witness: to violence, 22, 76; Elijah as, xii, 24, 138, 141, 142; George/Khidr as, 209; of festival, 19, 44, 66, 102, 198, 239; and *kumstvo,* 129, 142
Wittgenstein, Ludwig, 176
wolves. *See under* animals

Yam, 196
Yama, 73
yar root, 179, 201–3. *See also* Jarilo
yew (*tisovina*). *See under* trees
Yezidis, 205, 218, 248
Yugoslavia: second, xi, 9, 13, 22–23, 29, 33–34, 39, 41–45, 47, 51–52, 54n6, 63, 69, 79, 84, 132, 145, 156, 160, 169, 189; first, 41, 43, 139, 157, 160

Zalom, the village of, 139
zavičaj, 67, 82
zdravac (rock cranesbill), 117, 185–86. *See also* flowers
Zeitlyn, David, xiin2
Zenica, the city of, 238–39
Zephyrus, 232n7
Zeus, 197, 202–203, 209–210, 221
zmaj. See dragon
zmija, See snake
Zulfikarpašić, Adil, 43, 47

www.ingramcontent.com/pod-product-compliance
Lightning Source LLC
Chambersburg PA
CBHW070911030426
42336CB00014BA/2364